BARACK OBAMA SR.

BARACK OBAMA SR.
THE RISE AND LIFE OF A TRUE AFRICAN SCHOLAR

ABON'GO MALIK OBAMA & FRANK KOYOO

Copyright © 2012 by Abon'go Malik Obama & Frank Koyoo.

Library of Congress Control Number:		2012904824
ISBN:	Hardcover	978-1-4691-8462-3
	Softcover	978-1-4691-8461-6
	Ebook	978-1-4691-8463-0

All rights reserved. No part of this book may be reproduced or transmitted in any form or by any means, electronic or mechanical, including photocopying, recording, or by any information storage and retrieval system, without permission in writing from the copyright owner.

This book was printed in the United States of America.

To order additional copies of this book, contact:
Xlibris Corporation
0-800-644-6988
www.xlibrispublishing.co.uk
Orders@xlibrispublishing.co.uk

CONTENTS

Dedication 7
Book Description 9
In My Roots 11
Acknowledgements 13
Introduction 17
Foreword 25
Preface 29
Authors' Notes 31

Chapter 1: In 1920s, Karachuonyo 35
Chapter 2: In early 1930s 45
Chapter 3: In Late 1930s 64
Chapter 4: In the Late 1930s Continued 67
Chapter 5: In 1946, Alego, Nyang'oma 83
Chapter 6: Life in Ng'iya in 1947 108
Chapter 7: In 1950s 120
Chapter 8: In the Year 1952 136
Chapter 9: The Steps of the Determined Person 152
Chapter 10: In 1954 and 1955, late 50s, Nairobi 158
Chapter 11: Barack in Paris, France, August 1959 181
Chapter 12: In 1959 and 1960s; Hawaii, United States of America 196
Chapter 13: The Airlifts 198
Chapter 14: 1963, Independence Day; 1964, Barack's return
    to Kenya; 1969, Assassination of Tom Mboya 212
Chapter 15: The grisly road Accident—1971; 1972, Divorce
    Ruth; 1975, Death of Onyango Hussein Obama 262
Chapter 16: Nairobi life 283
Chapter 17: 1982 – Accident Coverage, Death of Barack
    Hussein Obama; Coup attempt 285
Chapter 18: Epilogue 303

Notes 333
Bibliography 338
List of Plates (Picture Gallery) 340

DEDICATION

Dedicated to our father Barack Hussein Obama, David Opiyo Obama, Onyango Hussein Obama, Habiba Akumu Njoga, Billy Obama Were, and George Safan Were. My mother, Grace Kezia Aoko Obama, wife Fauziah, Yasmin, and Halima. My children Kweku, Rashidah, Khadijah, Safiyah, Baraka, Muhammed, Barack, Dawud, Abubakar and Habibah, and all those men and women who have dedicated their lives to their families and to making this world a better place. Muamar Al-Ghadafi, General Mahamat Nour of Chad, and King Abdullah of Saudi Arabia.

Book Description

I have tried to tell the story of my father, our father, as best as I can with the distinguished assistance of my coauthor, Frank Koyoo. Frank came to me with this idea and revealed that he had begun to do a story about my father Barack Hussein Obama. He wanted to write this book, but he did not feel that he was the right person to do it. He knew that his story's subjects were alive, and he proceeded to seek out the one who would have the best and most knowledgeable information about the man. He came to me, and although I, at first, was hesitant and uncertain about his intentions and the project in general, I realized that this was a real opportunity to tell our father's story, an authentic account from an authentic source. We have tried to do our best in telling the story of a man who started out from the heart of the African bushland, traveled to heart of the great American continent, and achieved the highest in intellectual accomplishments, returning to his native Africa, of which he had the highest esteem. His dream was to restore Africa to its historical greatness, to establish and build a new and better place for his people. His goal was for a place where his children and the children of his people lived in a land of plenty in peace, love, and harmony. His passion was education, honesty, and perfection. He had lofty ideals and was generous and kind. He had his shortcomings as is natural for all of us. This is his story; some of it is factual, some of it as close to factual as could be, and others made to most closely fit into the general picture of Luoland, Kenya, and Luo culture. Things did not turn out as he had planned, and life was great at one time and at the lowest at others, but he kept on until he met his death at the young age of forty-six on 26 November 1982. His life was cut short when he was getting back on his feet. There was talk about the circumstances of my father's death. It was difficult to accept that he had died. There was talk that he had been in the company of friends, the identity of whom is still a mystery, and had received some large sums of cash, the whereabouts of which no one has ever been able to determine, a classic conspiracy theory that may have some truth to it because my father was pulling himself together and was getting back on his feet. Somebody somewhere was bound to be threatened and could have had a hand in his death. *Barack Hussein Obama; son of Akumu Nyanjoga (daughter of Njoga).* Years have turned over, and memories have dimmed in some places, but all in all, we have done our best and hope that justice has been done and that you, our readers, find this material excellent to read and to your approval. We hope that wherever he is, he can look back and through us feel vindicated. He did his bit, and now he can look at us and heave a sigh of relief, knowing that we are doing well. Rest in peace, Dad; we love you.

Abon'go Malik Obama

In My Roots

True belonging is the ultimate freedom. A man is in constant search for himself, to feel the comfort of his existence, a world which is truly one's own, where one can live and die with the clear knowledge that all was well. All was well with himself and others. So we look for the essence of existence and for those things that have meaning, substance, and weight. As we move from one place to another, we hold on to all that keeps us focused on who we are. This is our world—east, west, north, or south. And so everyone is wearing Kente cloth bands, African bubu outfits and other signs of expression that seemingly tell the story of their roots. We have come a long way by any measure, and therefore, it is reasonable to rest on our laurels in the midst of surveying our progress. Whether we pat ourselves on the back or feed our appetite for more action is a matter of opinion, opinion of which everybody is entitled to.

What we need to do is examine the issue of culture, that inseparable phenomenon that determines our very existence. Culture embodies environmental and physical conditions with which we can identify and from which we draw strength. There is an outer and inner layer of culture, both of which must be in order and substance. There is genuine and copyright culture, the goal and true objective being to identify that culture that is native to us.

This is the age of synthetic materials, the age of synthetic concepts, and the age of synthetic everything. It is the general belief that man is capable of manufacturing almost anything today. We must insist on what is real. We must avoid at all cost what I term imitation or copyright culture. Genuine culture is an inside job, and we must continue to watch for surface culture, a passing, fleeting affair designed to suck and sap the very existence of real culture. To identify with Africa is the first step while to be African involves going beyond that. I am African and even those of us born in Africa cannot claim an outright affinity with the continent unless the innate cultural heritage is awakened and exposed. So we search for ourselves, sharing our experience, strength, and hopes—seeking solace in our roots. I too seek solace in my roots. In this do—we must do, so that we can truly celebrate our differences and make this world truly our world.

Abon'go Malik Obama

ACKNOWLEDGEMENTS

This is the longest acknowledgement I have ever come across.

Mr Abon'go Malik Obama is one amazing friend. I approached him with this idea, and he accepted. This book has taken us the most precious time that I would have otherwise spent with my friends. However, I decided to take that time to ink something. I'd love to meet the scholar. I believe he had some drop of greatness. What do I mean? In his struggle, I see confidence; in his education, I see determination; and in his family, I see success.

My schedule has been crowded lately. However, I still wanted to read a book, but that particular book was lacking in all bookstores that I regularly visit around town. The search gave way to an idea—a voyage that took me to Kogelo, Alego. A place I naturally call home, my rural home. This is where I met a remarkable man—Abon'go Malik Obama. He didn't disappoint. Compiling the information relayed here has taken us a great journey from nineteenth century, tracing the history that took an immense recollection, from the life of Opiyo, Onyango Hussein, to the generation of Abon'go Malik and George Obama, to that tender generation of Kweku and those yet to be born. Along the dusty path to Ndori from Ng'iya (while clinging onto the backjacket of a speeding motorbike rider), I met Malik on his way, driving to Siaya. He directed me to his grandmother and told me to hang around till he'll be back. But he was fast to promise me that he won't take long. I obliged. I met Mama Sara Onyango face-to-face. I'd known her only through the media. She didn't disappoint too. I sat next to her, peeling off beans from the pods. And her story-telling skill came layer by layer. I asked her several questions—some of the answers I got with little difficulties while others came with real recollection of past events that she could hardly recall; some happenings are almost fading from her own memory. 'This homestead is buzzing with visitors from all over the world, my son,' she said, after we were interrupted by her helper—*Nyar* Gem.

This wasn't the unlikely source of my information but the *answer* to my worry. The book started writing by itself. We would like to thank Mama Sara for the story she gave wholeheartedly. Since it came through her own tongue, the accuracy of the story isn't compromised. And if there is any aberration, then maybe her advanced age would be held accountable. I recall with fondness, the early rising, and the night trips to Kogelo. Sometimes I would alight from a bus to meet a sleepy village at 4 a.m. when there is no trace of life except the low tin-shackle at Ng'iya written in vernacular: *Cham gi wadu* Hotel (share with your colleague hotel). Here two drunkards crawl with their bellies from deep stupor to head home. They don't even know that a night has gone by. They mumbled, 'You can take over. That place is pretty warm.' I want to thank them for their warm heart. I don't think that the doorless structure was warm anyway, but their heart was.

I didn't have anything else to do but to wait for sunrise. A woman's shadow dangled loosely against the moonlight toward me. She is the owner of the 'hotel'. She greeted me with respect and settled to prepare her schedule in a short while; she was joined by her son about fourteen, I guess. The boy began by splitting the firewood using something that resembled a blunt axe. He's still entangled in the syntax maze of mother tongue. Within minutes, the smoke billowed from the tin-shackle. She told me of her clients who prefer taking breakfast so early before heading to Kisumu. 'So the porridge must be ready early enough,' she said. Another gentle lady, sad-faced, with a dark complexion, maybe in her early thirties, bent next to her to wash plastic plates and chipped cups. She told me that's her sister, and she was a widow, with three children. If I was willing, I could take her with me so that I could marry her 'even for free, without dowry'. She emphasized in a light note, while inviting her robust body onto a rickety chair. I told her that I'd look into that. I took it as a joke anyway, but I sadly learnt that both of them were widowed. I urged them to be strong and felt sorry for the loss. She told me that she had seven children that she fed them by herself. I'm grateful to them. They offered hot porridge that I took with glee from the gourd; they treated me with a warm heart. I didn't complain of the dusty table top or the chipped cup in which they poured the brown sugar. The pleasant-mannered (pleasant manner here means 'easy and engaging manner') widow looked jovial, able to reconcile the irreconcilable; or when they refused to collect for payment my hundred shillings bill. To put this experience to rest, they were just amazing. They have finally found their faces on the map of my acknowledgement.

A man whose prevailing image only formed by eager journalists' impression and so thoroughly accepted by the enthusiastic readers. This is a scarcely portrayed image. Malik would rather stop writing than shrug, shelve, or forget his father's love, because his father was full of dreams and visions—the basis of this book. It entails Hawa's personal contacts with her brother. The awful agony she suffered. She remembers a series of dreams that held her mind captive. During the teething stages of this book, a lot poured out from graceful hearts. And I can stand to refute disappointment—if there is aspect that is not tackled, then that's an act of God. Where brakes were needed, we applied in time. We worked against the hailstones, around unavoidable spins, and trudged hills and valleys. Our hands were free and loose with facts, and in an ageless speed, every word went into the record book. Communication flowed freely. And I felt like one of them. Hawa actually repeatedly called me 'my son'. I did my best. But this best was not enough. I still needed Razik, Amir, Mama Kezia, and Said. I was digging deep enough, pressing, and not giving up rescheduling an interview with Obeid due to unavoidable circumstances. I thank you all for volunteering the information with enthusiasm and good heart. You become the pillars of this story.

Razik, particularly, quoted his favourite inspirational piece: 'Every setback is a setup for a greater comeback.'

Also many thanks to Boaz Bolo (my friend and former biology teacher—you formed an important beacon of this production). My brothers, Joab, Isack, and Geoffrey—you are my torch of life. The smile on my face comes through your jokes and love. My mentor, Reverend Julius Kithinji, wife, Meg, and my Nigerian friend, Ibiene Oguntoyinbo, must surely be recognized. You advised me to stop doubting and have a steadfast attitude and forced in me readmittance to action. Ibiene is completely up-to-date in entirely everything—hope you enjoyed your masters at Kings' College, UK and live life to the fullest. I would put cherry on the cake any time for Laz Aswani and Victor Agumbi.

We believe this country would have had a better history if Barack would not have died so early or if TJ wouldn't have been murdered or when his friend Dr Robert Ouko wouldn't have been murdered too and his acid-charred body dumped at *Got Alila*—his death hasn't been resolved. Barack deserves a biography—in his centenary years—the cause of his life was more twisted than more notable scholars other than TJ.

To put things straight, in this book, everything looked general; chief among them was maybe his weakness. Although, at work, if there was a serious man to run that Ministry of Planning and Economic Development after Mboya, it was this same Barack.

He was no psychotic swindler, no chatterbox, not disgraced, but honored—a phenomenal Barack, a go-getter Barack, an economist Barack, a family man, and a charming Barack: everybody's first choice and fairly comfortable man.

I thank John Kang'ethe, Ken Kiunga—you welcomed me any time and made frantic phone calls. May God bless you abundantly!

We are grateful to Jennifer Jagire for her assistance in publishing this book.

Finally, our thanks and appreciation to Mama Kezia Aoko Obama for allowing us to write about her husband and supporting us on this project.

Malik and I mustn't forget ourselves for a job well done.

More importantly to the editorial team.

Frank Koyoo

Introduction

> For a home without daughters is like a spring without a source.
> (Margaret Ogolla)

Those bundled around radios in the forgotten corners of this part of the dark continent, at least for once, wielded hope right in their feeble hands. If there are those who still doubt that Kogelo is the place where mighty men come from, the answer is here at last, Sarah Ogwel Onyango—weather-beaten or maybe bruised by the rigors of life—sat on the third row of the otherwise packed dais with Who's Who in the corridors of power of US politics. Sitting alongside was Malik Obama, his wife, children Kweku and Rashidah, and Mother, Kezia Aoko Obama. From Wall Street to the Main Street, from Honolulu, Hawaii, to the Alaskan Coast line. And those viewing from Palestinian territory to those sitting at the America mid-west shoreline.

The seemingly discomfort of the perfumed-scented class who flinched at being seated on the dais next to some rustic villagers, maybe, could have been felt or . . .

To many it was just a melody; to others it was an anthem that brought tears to the eye. A mix of culture and heritage united in deeper matters of sadness and joy, life and death, peace and war, laughter and fears . . .

They came to witness the endorsement or this inauguration of 'one of their own'.

And they listened to him pretty well—with brick wall attention.

Obama Is Sworn in as the 44th President of the United States of America (21 January 2009), Speech

Thank you. Thank you.

My fellow citizens: I stand here today humbled by the task before us, grateful for the trust you have bestowed, mindful of the sacrifices borne by our ancestors.

I thank President Bush for his service to our nation as well as the generosity and cooperation he has shown throughout this transition.

Forty-four Americans have now taken the presidential oath.

The words have been spoken during rising tides of prosperity and the still waters of peace. Yet, every so often the oath is taken amidst gathering clouds and raging storms. At these moments, America has carried on not simply because of the skill or vision of those in high office, but because We the People have remained faithful to the ideals of our forebears, and true to our founding documents.

So it has been. So it must be with this generation of Americans.

That we are in the midst of crisis is now well understood. Our nation is at war against a far-reaching network of violence and hatred. Our economy is badly weakened, a consequence of greed and irresponsibility on the part of some but also our collective failure to make hard choices and prepare the nation for a new age.

Homes have been lost, jobs shed, businesses shuttered. Our health care is too costly, our schools fail too many, and each day brings further evidence that the ways we use energy strengthen our adversaries and threaten our planet.

These are the indicators of crisis, subject to data and statistics. Less measurable, but no less profound, is a sapping of confidence across our land; a nagging fear that America's decline is inevitable, that the next generation must lower its sights.

Today I say to you that the challenges we face are real, they are serious and they are many. They will not be met easily or in a short span of time. But know this America: They will be met.

On this day, we gather because we have chosen hope over fear, unity of purpose over conflict and discord.

On this day, we come to proclaim an end to the petty grievances and false promises, the recriminations and worn-out dogmas that for far too long have strangled our politics.

We remain a young nation, but in the words of Scripture, the time has come to set aside childish things. The time has come to reaffirm our enduring spirit; to choose our better history; to carry forward that precious gift, that noble idea, passed on from generation to generation: the God-given promise that all are equal, all are free, and all deserve a chance to pursue their full measure of happiness.

In reaffirming the greatness of our nation, we understand that greatness is never a given. It must be earned. Our journey has never been one of shortcuts or settling for less.

It has not been the path for the faint-hearted, for those who prefer leisure over work, or seek only the pleasures of riches and fame.

Rather, it has been the risk-takers, the doers, the makers of things—some celebrated, but more often men and women obscure in their labor—who have carried us up the long, rugged path towards prosperity and freedom.

For us, they packed up their few worldly possessions and traveled across oceans in search of a new life. For us, they toiled in sweatshops and settled the West, endured the lash of the whip and plowed the hard earth.

For us, they fought and died in places Concord and Gettysburg; Normandy and Khe Sanh.

Time and again these men and women struggled and sacrificed and worked till their hands were raw so that we might live a better life. They saw America as bigger than the sum of our individual ambitions; greater than all the differences of birth or wealth or faction.

This is the journey we continue today. We remain the most prosperous, powerful nation on Earth. Our workers are no less productive than when this crisis began. Our minds are no less inventive, our goods and services no less needed than they were last week or last month or last year. Our capacity remains undiminished. But our time of standing pat, of protecting narrow interests and putting off unpleasant decisions—that time has surely passed.

Starting today, we must pick ourselves up, dust ourselves off, and begin again the work of remaking America.

For everywhere we look, there is work to be done.

The state of our economy calls for action: bold and swift. And we will act not only to create new jobs but to lay a new foundation for growth.

We will build the roads and bridges, the electric grids and digital lines that feed our commerce and bind us together. We will restore science to its rightful place and wield technology's wonders to raise health care's quality and lower its costs.

We will harness the sun and the winds and the soil to fuel our cars and run our factories. And we will transform our schools and colleges and universities to meet the demands of a new age.

All this we can do. All this we will do

Now, there are some who question the scale of our ambitions, who suggest that our system cannot tolerate too many big plans. Their memories are short, for they have forgotten what this country has already done, what free men and women can achieve when imagination is joined to common purpose and necessity to courage.

What the cynics fail to understand is that the ground has shifted beneath them, that the stale political arguments that have consumed us for so long, no longer apply.

The question we ask today is not whether our government is too big or too small, but whether it works, whether it helps families find jobs at a decent wage, care they can afford, a retirement that is dignified.

Where the answer is yes, we intend to move forward. Where the answer is no, programs will end.

And those of us who manage the public's dollars will be held to account, to spend wisely, reform bad habits, and do our business in the light of day, because only then can we restore the vital trust between a people and their government.

Nor is the question before us whether the market is a force for good or ill. Its power to generate wealth and expand freedom is unmatched.

But this crisis has reminded us that without a watchful eye, the market can spin out of control. The nation cannot prosper long when it favors only the prosperous.

The success of our economy has always depended not just on the size of our gross domestic product, but on the reach of our prosperity; on the ability to extend opportunity to every willing heart—not out of charity, but because it is the surest route to our common good.

As for our common defense, we reject as false the choice between our safety and our ideals.

Our founding fathers faced with perils that we can scarcely imagine, drafted a charter to assure the rule of law and the rights of man, a charter expanded by the blood of generations.

Those ideals still light the world, and we will not give them up for expedience's sake.

And so, to all other peoples and governments who are watching today, from the grandest capitals to the small village where my father was born: know that America is a friend of each nation and every man, woman and child who seeks a future of peace and dignity, and we are ready to lead once more.

Recall that earlier generations faced down fascism and communism not just with missiles and tanks, but also with the sturdy alliances and enduring convictions.

They understood that our power alone cannot protect us, nor does it entitle us to do as we please. Instead, they knew that our power grows through its prudent use. Our security emanates from the justness of our cause; the force of our example; the tempering qualities of humility and restraint.

We are the keepers of this legacy, guided by these principles once more, we can meet those new threats that demand even greater effort, even greater cooperation and understanding between nations. We'll begin to responsibly leave Iraq to its people and forge a hard—earned peace in Afghanistan.

With old friends and former foes, we'll work tirelessly to lessen the nuclear threat and roll back the specter of a warming planet.

We will not apologize for our way of life nor will we waver in its defense.

And for those who seek to advance their aims by inducing terror and slaughtering innocents, we say to you now that, 'Our spirit is stronger and cannot be broken. You cannot outlast us, and we will defeat you.'

For we know that our patchwork heritage is strength, not a weakness.

We are a nation of Christians and Muslims, Jews and Hindus, and nonbelievers. We are shaped by every language and culture, drawn from every end of this Earth.

And because we have tasted the bitter swill of civil war and segregation and emerged from that dark chapter stronger and more united, we cannot help but believe that the old hatreds shall someday pass; that the lines of tribe shall soon dissolve; that as the world grows smaller, our common humanity shall reveal itself; and that America must play its role in ushering in a new era of peace.

To the Muslim world, we seek a new way forward, based on mutual interest and mutual respect.

To those leaders around the globe who seek to sow conflict or blame their society's ills on the West, know that your people will judge you on what you can build, not what you destroy.

To those who cling to power through corruption and deceit and the silencing of dissent, know that you are on the wrong side of history, but that we will extend a hand if you are willing to unclench your fist.

To the people of poor nations, we pledge to work alongside you to make your farms flourish and let clean waters flow; to nourish starved bodies and feed hungry minds.

And to those nations like ours that enjoy relative plenty, we say we can no longer afford indifference to the suffering outside our borders, nor can we consume the world's resources without regard to effect. For the world has changed, and we must change with it.

As we consider the road that unfolds before us, we remember with humble gratitude those brave Americans who, at this very hour, patrol far-off deserts and distant mountains. They have something to tell us, just as the fallen heroes who lie in Arlington whisper through the ages.

We honor them not only because they are guardians of our liberty, but because they embody the spirit of service: a willingness to find meaning in something greater than themselves.

And yet, at this moment, a moment that will define a generation, it is precisely this spirit that must inhabit us all.

For as much as government can do and must do, it is ultimately the faith and determination of the American people upon which this nation relies.

It is the kindness to take in a stranger when the levees break; the selflessness of workers who would rather cut their hours than see a friend lose their job which sees us through our darkest hours.

It is the firefighter's courage to storm a stairway filled with smoke, but also a parent's willingness to nurture a child, that finally decides our fate.

Our challenges may be new, the instruments with which we meet them may be new, but those values upon which our success depends, honesty and hard work, courage and fair play, tolerance and curiosity, loyalty and patriotism—these things are old.

These things are true. They have been the quiet force of progress throughout our history.

What is demanded then is a return to these truths. What is required of us now is a new era of responsibility—a recognition, on the part of every American, that we have duties to ourselves, our nation and the world, duties that we do not grudgingly accept but rather seize gladly, firm in the knowledge that there is nothing so satisfying to the spirit, so defining of our character than giving our all to a difficult task.

This is the price and the promise of citizenship.

This is the source of our confidence: the knowledge that God calls on us to shape an uncertain destiny.

This is the meaning of our liberty and our creed, why men and women and children of every race and every faith can join in celebration across this magnificent mall. And why a man whose father less than 60 years ago might not have been served at a local restaurant can now stand before you to take a most sacred oath.

So let us mark this day in remembrance of who we are and how far we have traveled.

In the year of America's birth, in the coldest of months, a small band of patriots huddled by dying campfires on the shores of an icy river.

The capital was abandoned. The enemy was advancing. The snow was stained with blood.

At a moment when the outcome of our revolution was most in doubt, the father of our nation ordered these words be read to the people:

'Let it be told to the future world that in the depth of winter, when nothing but hope and virtue could survive, that the city and the country, alarmed at one common danger, came forth to meet it.'

America, in the face of our common dangers, in this winter of our hardship, let us remember these timeless words; with hope and virtue, let us brave once more the icy currents, and endure what storms may come; let it be said by our children's children that when we were tested we refused to let this journey end, that we did not turn back nor did we falter; and with eyes fixed on the horizon and God's grace upon us, we carried forth that great gift of freedom and delivered it safely to future generations.

Thank you. God bless you.

And God bless the United States of America.

By Barack Obama—44th President of the United States of America[1]

Foreword

A man is trying to either live up to his father's expectations or make up for his father's mistakes. I suppose Barack was not part of this fumbling. He lived his own dream, and his life manifested this. And that's why even though he died at a tender age of forty-six, he is still a hero. Some people die at birth, others at teenage age. We should thank God that he made us to be what we are today. And bearing in mind where we came from, a home in shrubbery and still making it to America is no simple feat.

A thick cloud of deceit never shrouded our lives. We were happily married, but in Africa, things are different. There is no particular formula to marriage life. People are still living lives bogged down by the cultural conflicts.

My husband was a young African in a strange land outshining everyone. We forget the times 1959-64 when Malcolm X and Martin Luther King were advocating for human and civil rights, the era of lynchings, Klu Klux Klan, and the like. A black man and a white woman! His boldness and achievement defied the time and all odds. And today he has produced the first black president of the United States of America.

The president of the United States would find this book compelling and shall answer various questions on who his father was. His simultaneous marriages were not his choice but the traditional upbringing and the revelations of his African heritage, the inheritance behind the dark skin. And casually, Barack always had a dream and a focus, a soaring dream an upstage dream that never grew out of pain and hurt but on the tenet of a better society built on mutual agreement. He discredited a society scratched by racism and tribalism, a society flying off its dream and destiny and a society biased against economic growth and progress. One thing I liked about him is the fact that he never forgot his family, especially his children even when he had separated from the wife. He said, 'See, I have another son in United States He is one of you. My pride.' He continually talked of the now president. I particularly remember in 1971, when he took part of his savings and flew to America to see Barack, his son. It was toward Christmas holidays. I think that may not be enough to support his care but is relatively touching to a child who had been waiting to meet his father, his long-lost father. The father he did not even know but relied on what he heard from the people around him. Seeing is believing!

Furthermore, my husband was not involved in politics. But perhaps politics consumed his life. He worked with politicians, and he turned out to be just one of them. In the process, the hard and vigorous politics eventually broke him down. He was mentioned to have participated in the 1982 Coup Attempt. From 1 August to 24 November 1982 Barack was restless; he could not reason properly, as if he had sensed danger. Maybe he thought he had to face the martial courts to answer charges of coup attempt—just like the hell he underwent during 1969 TJ murder trial. One thing I know about Barack is that finance was the least of his worries; he was a strict person at work. And all these attracted private clients in his entire consultancy, and he made good money. What I know is that the government actually caused his downfall. What of the racist climate he was up against during his time in America.

In a straight talk, the authors are bringing a stepwise life history of a man whose intelligence was superior.

During my stint from dating to marriage—subsequent separation and a reunion, he was always very sharp, very sure, and had the least flaws in his life. I know people are now tired with divisive rhetoric as an abusive bigamist or those who explain that he was an egomaniac. His life was never ruined by anything of the sort. I believe all these are mere myths.

After his return from United States, we still lived as a wife and a husband, but in polygamy, you'd take time before you'd see him again. And that's how life turned out to be a complicated affair.

Whatever people write about Barack or his son Barack Jr, all are documented in encyclopedia and other references, and all put the subject of family life into sharp focus or in context. In various biographies or memoirs, all put Barack's life in attenuated chronology.

Whether in style or persuasive arc, all find the comprehensive way to tell the story either in abstraction or complexities—well, you may as well rely on your research or on your ears. But the assurance that comes into play is that this book tries to convey the message in a simple yet interactive focus. Barack was not better than anyone else, but he tried to be a better person. His life has been put on the pedestal of greater historical context. The various crop of writers talk fondly about him negatively and positively. But all is about the voice. The sonorous voice to come to terms with history.

African history started a long time ago—from riding donkeys in roadless country to cars in superways, we'd the least idea that we'd get to where we are today. There were Indians at the railway constructions, mainly the turbaned Sikhs and Maasai, with their ears punctured, in the jungle facing off a marauding lion. During the face-off (tussle), the strange sparkling carvings hanging from their ears depicted their determination. It showed the big figure of troubles they faced in the jungles. There was Africa, and her people had only one hand in their colonies, while the rulers had plenty of parties in typical colonial fashion. He needed to look at Africa in a more skeptical manner; there is the staggering knowledge that we can tap by studying the simple life history of an African family. But first it educates for clear mind. This book is written intelligently and broadly for the mass population that says achievement, from the way you look at it, is contradictory. This book portrays an overly well-crafted analogy to the style of writing. It is both lyrical and descriptive.

Barack had a strong influence, an embracing that hit me well before I hit twenty. And with little effort, he took me over.

People have talked about my late husband's behavior. That he moved from bars and restaurants—from all places they considered too harmful for him. Even though he was a great economist, it is no-brainer that controversy surrounded his married life—all sorts of descriptions: carefree towards alcoholism to wife battering Luo tribesman. See, my husband didn't show any trace of perverted dreams. Pundits describe him as a man who bounced around on two iron legs after his real legs had been amputated. I'm the wife, and I know the man more than any sane figure on the street.

That his drunkenness caused him death—that in 1982, the forty-six-year-old husband rammed into a tree, killing himself: that's another wild allegation. I never saw anyone like my husband hit a pedestrian. But I had a husband who complained of a suicidal felon pouncing on to his car. This book tries to expound on the life of a man who'd lived a normal life. If there is someone out there thinking that he was superman, then he needs to think again. There are women who'll confess of their men living away from reality, men who must visit the pub to have one for the road as they draw policies of the nation. Does that make someone irresponsible? This book talks of a man I knew best—who had big dreams but was taken away by the sudden tragic death.

And now who has a 'perverted dream' that can con millions of people in 'a split of a second'. And I fully agree with what my stepson said about his father—The President of United States of America wrote:

'The brilliant scholar, the generous friend, the upstanding leader—my father had been all those things.'[2]

—Kezia Aoko Obama

Preface

In the name of Allah, Most Gracious, Most Merciful.
Praise be to Allah, The Cherisher and Sustainer of the Worlds:
Most Gracious, Most Merciful;
Master of the Day of Judgement.
Thee do we worship, and Thine aid we seek.
Show us the straight way,
The way of those on whom Thow has bestowed Thy Grace,
Those whose (portion) Is not wrath.
And who go not astray. (The Holy Quran, Surat Al-Fatiha, 1: 1-7)

"Our Lord!
Condemn us not
If we forget or fall
Into error; Our Lord!
Lay not on us a burden
Like that which Thou
Didst lay on those before us;
Our Lord! Lay not on us
A burden greater than we
Have strength to bear.
Blot out our sins,
And grant us forgiveness.
Have mercy on us.
Thou art our Protector;
Help us against those
Who would stand against faith." (The Holy Quran, Surat Al-Baqarah, 2: 286)

"O my Lord! Make me
One who establishes regular Prayer,
And also (raise such)
Among my offspring
O our Lord!
And accept Thou my Prayer.
"O our Lord! cover (us)
With Thy Forgiveness—me,
My parents, and (all) Believers,
On the Day that the Reckoning
Will be established!" [3]
(The Holy Quran, Surat Ibrahim, 14: 40-41)

Authors' Notes

I have tried to tell the story of my father, our father, as best as I can with the distinguished assistance of my coauthor, Frank Koyoo. Frank came to me with this idea and revealed that he had begun to do a story about my father Barack Hussein Obama. He wanted to write this book, but he did not feel that he was the right person to do it. He knew that the subject of his story's children were alive, and he proceeded to seek out the one who would have the best and most knowledgeable information about the man. He came to me, and although I, at first, was hesitant and uncertain about his intentions and the project in general, I realized that this was a real opportunity to tell our father's story, an authentic account from an authentic source. We have tried to do our best in telling the story of a man who started out from the heart of the African bushland, traveled to the heart of the great American continent, and achieved the highest in intellectual accomplishments, returning to his native Africa, of which he had the highest esteem. His dream was to restore Africa to its historical greatness, to establish and build a new and better place for his people. His goal was for a place where his children and the children of his people lived in a land of plenty in peace, love, and harmony. His passion was education, honesty, and perfection. He had lofty ideals and was generous and kind. He had his shortcomings as is natural for all of us. This is his story; some of it factual, some of it as close to factual as could be, and others made to most closely fit into the general picture of Luoland, Kenya, and Luo culture. Things did not turn out as he had planned, and life was great at one time and at the lowest at others, but he kept on until he met his death at the young age of forty-six on 26 November 1982. His life was cut short when he was getting back on his feet. There was talk about the circumstances of my father's death. It was difficult to accept that he had died. There was talk that he had been in the company of friends, the identity of whom is still a mystery, and had received some large sums of cash, the whereabouts of which no one has ever been able to determine, a classic conspiracy theory that may have some truth to it because my father was pulling himself together, and he was getting back on his feet. Somebody somewhere was bound to be threatened and could have had a hand in his death. *Barack Hussein Obama; son of Akumu Nyanjoga (daughter of Njoga).* Years have turned over and memories have dimmed in some places, but all in all, we have done our best and hope that justice has been done and you, our readers, find this material excellent reading and to your approval. We hope that wherever he is, he can look back and through us feel vindicated. He did his bit, and now he can look at us and heave a sigh of relief, knowing that we are doing well. Rest in peace, Dad, we love you.

Abon'go Malik Obama

'This is the story about my father . . .
The man you'd all like . . .
I, not only knew him as a father, but also . . .
. . . As an excellent economist . . .
. . . a brilliant scholar . . .
Kenya has ever produced . . .

He is the father of the forty-fourth president of United States of America, and he is the father of sons and daughters in various spheres of influence . . . he is my father.

—Malik

CHAPTER 1

A Child Is Born Pure and Blameless

In 1920s, Karachuonyo

Her prowess had been a subject of speculation.

And her birth was debatable.

One day, in the year 1922, as the sun reached overhead, in the dry land of West Karachuonyo in Wagwe Village, amidst the billowing smoke from Nyajwala's wobbly grass-thatched mud hut, the fourth wife of Ogwel, a young baby, Sara, gulped the air, an indication that a new life had come into the rather big family. The year was 1922 in the third moon. (She can't remember the actual date when she was born, but she's certain of a particular birth.) The villages around Wagwe, Kanjira, Kamser, and Ngeta Island in South Nyanza, were warming for a daughter. West Karachuonyo is 400 miles from the capital, Nairobi, and lies adjacent to the shores overlooking Uganda and Tanzania borders and part of Nyando District. It borders the blue waters of Lake Victoria. River Sondu meanders its way into the lake at Kobala, forming something close to an ox-bow lake. The countryside land is known to have the 'Seventieth Wonder of the World'—*Simbi Nyaima*—a saline lake with a traditional significance. It is believed to have sunk in and consumed about five thousand people in the middle of the night and no single head or finger was retrieved! When the depression was filled with water, a lake formed—Lake *Simbi Nyaima*, where traditional healers come to fetch the magical water. Karachuonyo was, then, a beautiful nation resting on an expansive savannah land, with rolling hills, swooping fertile Lambwe Valley (except for the killer tsetse flies that injected the deadly protozoa into the helpless inhabitants' bloodstream resulting in sleeping sickness and fatalistic death rate) and inhabited by almost a half a million people—mainly minority Alego Kamser, Abakuria, Arab nations, and the larger Luo—known simply as *Jokarachuonyo* (natives of Karachuonyo). The famous bays—the Kendu Bay and Homa Bay—jut into the lake. Of course, upon mentioning Homa Bay, the rugged Homa hills come to mind, a home to hundreds of chimpanzees, *sitatuga* gazelle, and the noisy hyenas. And the agricultural hub of the Luos, known to be just fishermen.

The animals dotting the semi-tropical landscape are the dark-haired goats, with dull chink of the bells tied around their necks, the heavily bushy eyed sheep, and long-horned cattle.

The tribe living here reaches back for ten generations to Luo subgroups—*Joka Owiny, Joka Omollo, Joka-Jok, and Jo-Padhola*. Individuals from the Alego Kamser Clan would trace their descent back to a specific forefather, *Joka Owiny*. This genealogy would later expose unbelievable tales: fables so mystical and mythical.

This is the same year the prophecy of Nandi Orkoiyot—of a big snaking 920 km of 'parallel iron bars' train, far from modern, that would pass through Nandi land in the Rift Valley 'breathing fire' going to quench its thirst in Lake Victoria at Port Florence, the current Kisumu Town (about fifty miles from Karachuonyo)—had come true. Its construction had started way back in 1901 at the coastal town of Mombasa. The train was therefore dubbed 'Lunatic Express' under construction Chief Engineer George Whitehouse, and Captain MacDonald of Royal Engineers Company who'd carried out the survey work.

The baby yelled soundly, emitting full life and health. Ogwel sired sons, fifteen in total. He continually believed that '*a home without daughters is like a spring without a source*'. In this case, he made it. How?

This particular homestead had been starving from lack of a girl child. And the birth of one was met with joy and jubilation. It meant that the ancestors had let go the curse of ill-fortune and failure in life—meaning the ancestors had received the libations and honor and that they'd participated in the atonement of a given lapse or dishonor. Names were traded on like fish in the market; it took a large percentage of the birth ceremony. This is when young people would learn that '. . . a man shouldn't enter a hut where a woman is giving birth or has recently given birth. It was a taboo.' Trading names was regarded as a noble event, a critical event with an elaborate ceremony of which a crucial decision wasn't solely relied upon. Ogwel was settled for, after dreams that were waited upon never bore any fruit, to the surprise of the people. She was indeed named Ogwel, after Ogwel, her father. Since she was born during the day, her name then was Anyango.

'This is my daughter, and I must name her after myself,' the old man said shyly.

One aspect that actually caused confusion here was the sharing of a name—Ogwel. When one called the young girl, the old man would respond and vice versa. They never took offence anyway. They'd chosen it that way. But the name Anyango would solve the dispute.

Nyajwala's household rolled down with great-elated motivation having borne a girl after a long wait of pouring libation to *Were, god* of the morning star and *Rahuma, god* of deepest and farthest star. She never gave up. And it paid off. Sara talks fondly of her mother; she would shy wisely, 'If one advances confidentially towards the desires of the heart, she'll bombard success unexpectedly.' Sometimes she'd encouraged me to be humble, 'for silence is wisdom.' She gloomed, 'Nothing can replace persistence.' This was meant to prove her detractors wrong. After all, who'd believed that she could bring forth a daughter? Nobody. She reigned in a man's world with great austerity. And she believed bearing another son was as good as not siring at all. An ordeal she'd loved to forget about fast, but she was forced to stay longer.

If one advances confidentially towards the desires of the heart, she'll bombard success unexpectedly, for silence is wisdom . . . nothing can replace persistence.

Ogwel started growing up. The name suggested that her powerful pair of legs could take her to great heights. She simply had 'fast feet'. The father knew that if she doesn't yield to guidance, she might be spoilt indefinitely. This made him look over her more closely, like a hovering hawk. It was unheard of, for a girl to be named after a man and a boy after a woman. Again, exuding confidence, Ogwel's maturity was exaggerated, outclassing some of her peers; with a little structure, she grew fast, but her lack of height was evident. That she made up for with her articulateness and shrewdness. In amazement, at five months, she started tumbling and crawling without any aid. Ogwel ran away on her two feet at the eighth month—with strong character and dignity. Empty and ordinary lullabies couldn't stop her either. At the tenth month, she surprisingly left everybody in awe. She could speak three words, exploiting this new language, *Luo*, with skill and sharpness.

One sunny morning, Sara says that 'the old man was devastated. I was just a young girl who'd fallen sick.' Sitting calmly on a wooden stool, rotating his body slowly atop the low seat, laced with leopard skin like a turtle basking on a log.

He sat outside his mud hut—locally known as *abila*; the aging old man Ogwel scratched his fast balding head, his blinding tiring eyes gazing and quivering. Tears of pain welled up in his eyes and streamed down his cheeks. He stared into the distant land of Kanyada that sloped into the expansive Wagwe; the hilly part of the mid-west Ngeta shoreline looked a little snowy. Sickness had gripped his family, and his only daughter was the victim. The knives of illness were out to haunt his daughter—something he didn't take—lying down. He felt unlucky and misfitted. The daughter for once was paralyzed.

And with a faint, faltering voice, he spoke to the neighbors who'd paid him a visit, one after the other, that chilly morning, squatting on the ground; his knees leaned to the muddy grass, ripping-off the red earth from the soles of his feet. Nothing to cover the poor feet! Shoeless. The lush grass and the millet on the fields took great pleasure from the fast blowing wind while the trees swayed their woes away in the midst of soothing sounds of singing weaverbirds lying peacefully in their nests, not worried about the preying eagle. The old man paused and then snuffed tobacco before placing both hands on his head. He'd looked away—as if he wanted to think of something else. Ogwel was above seventy and aging remarkably well. He spat thick black saliva and his teeth and lips remained black due to the juice of the tobacco. He'd an infectious smile—a smile always in place or just beneath the surface. That easy smile had diminished. Now that smile was nowhere to be seen. Maybe he was deeply troubled and still worried about the little girl, who was cackling and showing serious illness despite her earlier indication of a new lease of health. The little girl had developed fever the previous night.

Sara says, 'Those were some of the low feelings that engulfed the old man though he was a lively father. My body temperature rose steadily. Herbs and other concoctions had been sought from experienced medicine men—and herbalists. Of course, then there were no structures like hospitals. But even today, the hospitals that dot this region are nothing other than trouble.'

As the worried old man looked up—with a dark face glittering from the effects of the sun, crumpled with agony, grave with expectation, listening keenly—the unearthly sounds fused with the commotion from inside the hut, where the treatment of the innocent angel was taking place, distracted his conscience.

Expectations were ripe from the outside. Inside the hut, exhaustion at par! At that moment, peace deserted his heart—the homestead included, windless, almost motionless, only for a few scavenging birds scrambling for tiny insects on the muddy clay ground. Otherwise, the whole neighborhood seemed to stagnate, seemed to be eternal, the day, in a dead slumber. Worried. Sara says that at this moment she'd recall, 'Worry never robs tomorrow of its sorrow or grief; it only robs today of its joy.' Worried in the sense that the old man didn't bet on losing his only daughter. Maybe later he thought whether he'd acted prematurely. No, he had a stock of pain on his mind.

Maybe he'd taken the worry higher as he wanted it.

In those days, an elderly was expected not to show any shadow of worry but to maintain a latent, flamboyant streak. Something he couldn't sustain. His only daughter being sick, clutching at the straw of life! He stared fixedly, tears crawling down his wrinkled cheek. This wasn't a simple matter by all merit, though! He stood on his three feet, the third foot being the walking stick, and stomped around, praying.

He prayed feebly, 'Oh, *God* of the great lake! I remember everything you've guided me through: great miracles, signs, and trials. I believe I've been reverential. Signs and wonders of your works notwithstanding, *Rahuma*, *Gods* of the wise people of *Ramogi*, open my heart again to honor you, send mementos of your great triumph and horror!'

He repeated the same prayer several times as if the gods were asleep.

He wasn't one of the parents who'd spend a dismal boring day with his sons and daughters. He was practically a loving father. And prayer (full of traditional connotations) was his secret weapon.

He had an aging look, wondering, and was pensively moody; *God* heard him. A man who'd seen a lot of unravels right on his face. An eerie silence hung over, yet he exuded confidence amidst a horrendous moment that prevailed and replaced that with confidence. Life wasn't hard anyway, but the tribe's stamina had been greatly affected due to the fact that people were divided on the protection of their loved ones and the love for the same.

Hanging in the air, too deep in his mind, was the notion of exhuming human body parts to end a curse of sickness in the household, or the old tradition of disturbing the dead to appease the living or strange saddening stories of vampires. Shaken and not shattered, these old beliefs lingered largely in his mind. Discipline lay at the center of duty and revelations, and that discipline was seriously needed at the top of the hour.

Discipline lies at the center of duty and revelations.

After an hour-long spell of prayer and persistent belief, Ogwel showed some recovery. She was taking a new paradigm of life. Healing was imminent. The women had worked tirelessly to embrace and blend prayer with love, pouring libations to *Were* in a healing process. Overreliance on traditional medicine was one notable aspect. Of course, there wasn't an alternative. The only sure way, for healing purposes, was herb usage. And that was what was relied upon day and night.

The baby threw some jabbers, burped, gazed around, and asked for *Mama*. With a radiating smile on her face, piercing a warm, savvy look, she uttered, '*Mama ere . . . ere baba?*' By that, she meant 'Where's Mama . . . where's Papa?'[4,5]

Sara grew fast in this small corner of paradise. Many people wondered where the years had gone. She was the firstborn daughter and maybe the only one, for the years had caught up with her mother that she couldn't give birth again. The ailing old man, Ogwel, proudly concluded an initiation rite of passage for his only daughter in a ceremony that saw five bulls and countless cockerels slaughtered. This initiation involved the removal of six lower teeth. She was therefore introduced into a full rigor of life, ready to receive proposals from aspiring sons of *Ramogi*. Men suitors, half prepared—unable to raise the required head of cattle to win her—wouldn't even have a glimpse of her beauty. The ever-serious old man, Ogwel, would take none of it—especially those who were known to practice black magic, laziness, and habitual immorality, or living in dry areas, with no food.

'My daughter, whom I dearly love and share a name with, huh, won't be kept to starve,' old man convincingly said to his friends.

And he'd assured himself never to take a huge gamble with her. In fact, that stance equalized him as a man of modest opinion, albeit doubtlessly as a man who'd fought teeth and nail to raise a daughter. And a man whose wings had been clipped when he could only manage boys (and no single girl—for quite a long time), he'd graduated for the notion 'that a one man harpist had to learn to play with others.' He was indeed no longer a one-sided parent.

He would protect her even if it means to do it with his own life. Coming of age, in this stringent situation, his daughter, Sara, blatantly missed the right man for a hand in marriage. She wasn't cheap after all! Yet it was high time to leave the father's homestead and care, to start a new life, a life of her own, in her own home, and bring forth a family. Time wasn't on her side, age catching up with her, weeping over once more life's endless loneliness. In this case, the old man's remarks and judgment as the head of the household was resolute and anecdotal, however, still waiting for a suitable suitor in silence.

And where did this name Sarah (or Sara) come from?

Ogwel's family was a Christian family. In the year 1927, Christianity and Western civilization had gripped this part of the world like a tsunami, some sort of tornado, a violent storm indeed. Ogwel, the old man (one of the converts), was caught in the middle and center of this hailstorm and isolation. He grabbed these drastic new developments as a head start to his unknown destiny. He plunged himself into Christianity. Without these two, he would have been a lunatic long ago. He couldn't let it go. In most parts, *council of Jodongo* (elders) had resorted to clanism, ethnicity, and tribal politics to protect their territorial advantage. In some, they followed Christianity to sort out their spiritual Waterloo, a retrogressive ideology—a scheme to get out of the woods or to remain steadfast against political caucuses, a path to redemption. Something the whiteman read as a blunder of the indigenous, and therefore a secret weapon toward their scramble for Africa.

Or most notably, in those years, was the resistance of Orkoiyot Samoeia Arap Koitalel against the British colonial occupation under Colonel Meinertzhagen. In an organized *pororiet*—war group—the Nandi warriors caused mayhem to the *jorochere* (white men) Kipture treaty notwithstanding.

Or the succession battle dispute of two brothers—alarmed Lenana and the composed Sendeiyo—the sons of Laibon Mbatian; the Maasai Oloibon.

Or the crushing of the first political party in Kenya—the Young Kikuyu Association (KCA) under the firebrand politician, Harry Thuku. And the man was brave enough to set the political realignment straight in the midst of colonial labyrinth. The colonial powers would describe him thus:

'A low ambition masquerading as a high persona.'

But he stood to his ground and later became a prominent political kingpin.

Or the exodus of young men moving into the white farms as casual laborers, to seek ways of settling poll and hut taxes imposed by the same white government. Their hopes dashed by the unpaid dues as hunger continued to bite some parts of the country.

Or the outbreak of the blinding disease spread by tsetse flies in the dreaded neighboring Lambwe valley.

This part of the 'Dark Continent' was facing the most displayed darkest moment of the century. One time an explorer, Sir Henry Morton Stanley, would set foot inland of Africa and fastened the label 'Dark Continent'. He visited the Buganda Kingdom and won the mind of the King Kabaka Mutesa I. Historians revealed that 'he was a man whose explorations were conducted like military operations.'

Ogwel and his daughter knew this very well. In tabloid garment, tailored silk and cotton clothes, *change* had come to Karachuonyo in general and Wagwe in particular. They moved from public denial to private consciousness 'not everything in private is sacred' people say. And change to believe in—hanging and hovering drunkenly in all corners of their heart like a loose pendulum.

Military arsenal and hardware were being sold, tailored garments in plenty. Life had climbed a notch higher, to the rooftop. Hut top. Christianity and traditional belief became the doldrums of more confusion. Ogwel believed that one is required to guard the ways of the old, the culture, while not forgetting the church. That was absolutely a new thing. *Christianity was now the center of growth, while accepting it was the fulcrum of that center.*

While Ogwel took the whole idea with insatiable appetite for a political discourse, his life oscillated between his many wives, politics, and Western civilization. His daughter was very keen on the ideologies and doctrine of the new religion. Behind that façade, she was absolutely lonely. Why? The latter lacked that loophole for abolition in his strength, patterns of structure, hitherto in gracing the best chagrin, that which involved joyous memories. For the former, by and large, politics had no element of consensus, something that Ogwel never preferred. It was an expression of dismay, rigidifying the pros of capital accumulation, making qualitative change more unlikely, ranking in suspicion, characterized by flip-flopping and change of position. Ogwel introduced his family into Christianity; his daughter was baptized Sara, 'after the great woman, Sarah, the wife of Abraham in the holy book of Genesis—the father of faith.' The preacher expounded.

'Sarah had a servant called Hagar, an Egyptian; she allowed Abraham to have a child with her, and Esau was born,' the anonymous lay preacher clarified. Introducing Sarah into Christianity was the father's last mission in this world. She started catechism classes, learned about Jesus Christ, Mary, Mother of God, Abraham . . . and the teachings were pretty interesting! And there was a full name:

Sara Anyango Ogwel.

Naming was just a ritual on its own. Turbulent history started gathering mass, sad news engulfed the Wagwe Village, and bad omen befell the family of Ogwel. In the year around 1934, in the wee hours of the morning on the fifth moon—maybe in May—the old man, Ogwel, died. Wailing rented the air, Nyajwala mourned, and the cowives followed suit, weeping loud enough.

'What might be wrong? What has gone wrong at Ogwel's homestead?' a neighbor asked aloud.

The deceased's daughter was traumatized, for days, during the entire mourning season, while his sons wailed openly, right in front of their wives. *Ramogi* people trooped in, with a clatter of hoofs, the procession passed by, turned into a dusty path leading to the homestead to the wailing and mourning of women who'd been regrouping in small assemblies. Others remained primly silent, holding their cheekbones pensively, and pondering whatever would follow. Relatives and friends came in sizeable quorum from Seme to Kobura in Kisumu. Relatives from Migori and those from Kanyada arrived to witness his last resting place. And they couldn't contain themselves. Sara cried. She refused to be comforted, the grief was bitter. She knew, for sure, she wouldn't see him again. For she'd been taught in the catechist classes that there is resurrection of the dead. As she stood by the motionless body, as if waiting, tears rolled freely. The body, draped, wrapped in hides and a yellow-and-blue-stripped blanket, was lying on a mat. The old man's grave was dug hurriedly, for it was a rainy season, and the flooding water would cover the grave much faster before the body was laid. The two needed each other, and the family life was awesome, but they had to separate. Perhaps this was a premonition of her life. She thought that he deserved to live forever. But now it was impossible.

For death is inevitable.

Now that the father was no more, Sara says, 'I was prepared to clear the clatter in my life and start afresh. Though I was still a young girl, I had to start life anew.'

And afresh she started. The stubborn door in her mind—for not accepting the reality—began to creak open.

Later—a few days later—Ogwel was laid to rest. The Wagwe people felt remorseful, young people barricaded paths, causing disquiet for days.... After the burial, the whole family was shaved—as a sign of grief. And during *tero buru* (a traditional ritual after burial), Omar, the first cousin of the old man, Ogwel, inherited the entire homestead according to the *Luo* custom. The *council of elders* sat and agreed unanimously that Omar, being the closest friend of the family, was to inherit the place left by his cousin. It was the trickiest inheritance. Ogwel had many wives, and each wife was going to be assigned a different husband. For Nyajwala, she got Omar. That would be Sara's stepfather. So they built a new hut for a new beginning as the previous one was destroyed.

'Thus . . . ,' Sara says, 'Then everything went into a massive slumber.'

It was the time when the drum fell silent.

And the traditional harpist stopped strumming and had left having camped for days.

And the shakers stopped rattling.

And the mourners, who couldn't look at the dead body beyond the face, had left.

And they appeared taken aback by the 'bizarre' death.

Sara, the only daughter, found herself in a rather precarious position—losing one father to death and accepting a 'new father'—a Muslim, came almost immediately. Her emotions had hit the roof. It was one of the trying times ever. One thing that was evident was the belief: she started a Muslim 'livelihood', meeting Muslim friends and families and going to the mosque. Islamism had gone to the interior Kendu Bay. The Oman Arab merchants, who exchanged goods with the natives in a barter trade system, were spreading it. In real-life situation, Islam spread, by and large, catalyzed by trade across the lake. To date, in all corners of Kendu Bay, Muslim population is more or less equivalent to that of Christians.

Omar was one of the '*Imams of Kendu Bay.*'

Chapter 2

There is no such thing as an omen. Destiny does not send us heralds. She is too wise or too cruel for that.

(Oscar)

In early 1930s

Days went by and destiny turned to moons, moons to seasons, and seasons to years. The word years only came when they discovered the British calendar. Omar's family in general, and the young lass in particular, were pensive; and as the welling roaring waves, like a full-throated song, knocked at one's inner spirit with its swagger, so was the pebbled shoreline of the lake stretched out. Wet and gleaming. With *Kit Mikai* (granite tors) cliffs rising crescent in translucent light, livid, and layered, pocked with tiny caves peaceful and inhabited—with the soft smack of water lapping their flanks, half a dozen large canoes bobbed at anchor in the shoreline. Crying babies slung carelessly on the back of hungry mothers. A distance away was watchful teenagers with catapults ready to shoot at the low flying birds from Lake Victoria. And the setting sun kissed goodbye to the world of humanity—catching the night sentinels, overgrown with loneliness on the lower west. On the Upper Side, Lang'o Tribe were war-like; they shot poisoned arrows that hit young men of Luo *Ramogi* like swords of steel, their blood flowing freely anointing the land of Nyakach, Seme, Ugenya, and the outskirts of Alego. The peaceful agile young fishermen, with untidy beards, squatted mending their nets while the women came to buy slit-smoked fish. The *Lang'o* executed vengeance on these young souls, ostracizing nature like the grip of a gambler. There was much to remember and little to forget, for life waned away in disguise, taking away its treasure and leaving a poor trail of humanity. The current Kendu Bay shoreline was a beehive of activity where people came from all sorts of life—sea of humanity—to purchase

*Mbuta (*Nile perch), and sardines. And barter trade was the in-thing. Areas around Karabondi, Kanyadhiang, Wath bala, Kamser, and *Simbi* indulged in fishing, and fishing paid well. The Oman Arabs yachted into Kendu Bay from Zanzibar through Uganda and Mageta Island. However, they found it almost impossible to sail to the bays—hundreds of heavily armed warriors would rise with dangerous weapons to attack—the frightful, religious Oman traders would sometimes shoot, provoking a dangerous face-off. And Arabs died in numbers. The highest recorded kill rates ever in the dreaded island! Luos living in Mageta showed no tangible evidence of progress and that they lacked moral concomitants. The Mageta warriors consisted of young men drawn from Kendu Bay, Homa Bay; among them, the Alego Kamser, Kanjira, Wagwe.... These men were regarded as vulgar, strange, and completely irrational. To the travelers, they depicted Africa as a dark, alien, and evil society. Trade brought them. And they spread Islamism in the process.

For life waned away in disguise, taking away its treasure, leaving a poor trail of humanity.

In the far east of Karachuonyo, a young man, in his forties, with two wives, Halima Onyango Hussein, an ardent Muslim, and Habiba Akumu Onyango Hussein, known also as *Nyar Njoga*, was in trouble. Onyango Hussein, the son of great chief elder Obama, who in turn was son of Opiyo, had weathered the storm few could and studious in his defense to marry the love of his life, Sara. He was the second born of Obama Kopiyo and Nyaoke in a family of eight boys and girls Dorsila, Obongo, and Rebecca; Onyango was polygamous grandson of Opiyo, son of Okoth, whose son Obama migrated, long time ago, from Kogelo to Karachuonyo at the invitation of his twin sister Jalan'go. Jalan'go was married to the people of Kanyadhiang village.

Ayub Otolo, a resident of Kogelo, gives the flipside of the story:

'The king of Alego, Ruoth, was about to die, having ruled for four decades. The two sons Ogelo (elder) and Owiny (younger) were warming for the seat that would remain vacant after a short stint. Ogelo was soft-spoken, clear-eyed, and a good debater. He was the heir of the kingdom by the Luo custom. He said, 'Well, I think the old man is not that bad, though. He can still have some energy to serve his people. It is not right for us to start grappling with the succession plan. He still remains the king until he goes to rest with our gods.' That was the son of the king talking to the council of elders who were too willing to choose an heir or to install Ogelo or whoever was willing to take up the seat that would fall vacant anytime.

Owiny, on the other hand, was the younger son—an arrogant, demanding, poor debater, unstyled fighter, who always set up traps to bring down Ogelo. He was not a very good leader according to the report from the council. Unlike Ogelo, whose voice was appealing, clear, and resonant—Owiny had a hazy voice, loud and just a package of noise. People had started digging out who'd replace the ailing king. Heads rolled in reflex when Owiny short-changed his elder brother and with a sleek political game plan with no blight, took over. Ogelo bowed down saying, 'My younger brother, Owiny, has taken (from me) the chieftainship—through a proxy means. But I know I will retain my chieftainship in more advanced role at the right time. My great-grandson shall rule the globe through the most powerful nation in the land. Could this be the prophecy of forty-fourth president of United States tracing his dreams from Kogelo? Ogelo had predicted a peaceful rule. Most of the Kogelo clan started to migrate to places they could find land.

Obama's voyage from Kogelo to Kendu Bay was a landmark. And Onyango, his son, had associated himself with the Arab merchants who introduced him to Islamism. In a short stint, he was 'baptized' Hussein. And he found comfort in the name Onyango Hussein Obama. Agreeably, his father, Obama Kopiyo, never stopped him. Onyango was a close friend of Omar, for they shared a lot regarding *Sharia laws* and Islam. Maybe through these engagements, he'd seen the good-looking girl and proposed.

A Karachuonyo girl was suggested, whose beauty had traversed throughout the tiny countryside. Onyango's exemplary craftsmanship partly stemmed from the fact that he didn't shy away from his family status.

In this context, the belief in life *Allahu Akhbar* was not only sedentary but also unshakeable, having the emotional core and psyche of character, of exposure of underneath layers upon layers of descriptive details of the same, achieving piercing elegance with the truth.

Some of his cousins and close friends had married between *five* or *ten* wives, and had countless children and grand children. In fact, as of now, in Kendu Bay, one Asentus Ogwela Akuku 'Danger' has several wives. At twenty-two, the man had five wives and several concubines. At thirty-five, he married the forty-fifth wife. Agreeably, the world's best known polygamist had married

130 times—divorced more than eighty of his wives. As we speak, he has 210 children. (In a recent interview, Akuku confessed that he's not done yet!) But he died lately before pulling another surprise. He was kept in a morgue for at least a month to allow all of his large family to assemble at the burial. Maybe death stopped him. Ooops! That's people of *Ramogi*.

This tells how customs took toll of the people. And whoever isn't mentioned here is not a lucky man.

At this point, he was acting hard to reverse the ravages, the denial of not siring or paying close attention to marrying more women. He'd assumed contentment with his sires. But the community wouldn't accent to that.

Onyango Hussein was a married man—and with three children: two daughters—Sarah Nyaoke and Mwanahawa Auma (or simply Hawa Auma). Besides, there was a son between the two—Barak Obama, named after his father. The three were son and daughters of one Habiba Akumu.

'My people of Alego clan, is it my mistake or a curse? Why judge me!' He'd said, looking rather desperate and jilted.

Sara says he'd told her that he had calmed and prayed to *Were*. Of course, whether he prayed to Allah or *Were*, God was one and nobody could differentiate the two.

Sara says that at one time he'd talked of the trauma he braved . . .

'You chose me in my weakness. I wasn't the best in this . . . but you remained so good, indeed. What should I do?'

He'd done so severally.

'Take away my own life? No! No! Not now!'

Onyango was in his midforties then but walked and spoke like a much older man. He was nicknamed *Chuor silwal*—the husband to a brown one. And the nickname had suited him—it was his true description. Himself, he was 'as black as mass of coal', but a man who'd later fallen in love with white garments.

The question of decorum was underlying in the deeply grooved current challenge. And the man was growing weaker by the day to think; he had to seek *God* for divine advice to strongly refute or rather steer clear of all the utterances and actions that might have been misinterpreted as though it had functional linkages with ethnic bigotry and tribal accustomed jingoism. He acted without demur or shrinking fear, despite the loud will of 'keeping eyes open before marriage, and half shut afterwards.' That was the only option, and the remaining one was to act. Going against such popular stance, in which the council of *Jodongo* (elders) was deeply involved, is not considered a good riddance; it was an unpopular decision anyway! But a small nuclear family was somehow regarded as an element of greed. And that compelled victims to eternal suffering or just mere cowardice.

Onyango Hussein's world collapsed, shifting from obsessions to anticipating reality, replacing emptiness as he took his right foot forward. As per the statement, *keeping your eyes open once before marriage and half shut afterwards,* Onyango, a young man, arrived in the household of Omar with the purpose of betrothing this family and that of his late father: the year 1937 in the eleventh moon.

(Sara can't spot the actual dates, but with the traditional calendar, it can roughly be mentioned as a date in November 1937.) He arrived in great style (*nyadhi*) accompanied by other seven strongly built young men and a wizened aged man.

For custom required him to make a well-deserved break outside the main hut—*duol*—the personal mud hut of Omar—waiting for invitation. Onyango was a dark-skinned, tall, robust, and solidly built man, an ebullient and bombastic man—even without his headdress, made of a white-and-black colobus monkey skin, the towering figure still maintained a well-deserved height, his head and shoulders above all of his peers—a man of high esteem, respect, style, and glamour. Here, he'd maintained a surprisingly sullen and reserved mood. He held a spear and a shield in both hands. His body was splashed with white war paint all over his black-complexioned skin. He was the only one without a ritually tattooed face; maybe the blackness had sucked the ritual marks, but he wore a tiny piece of leopard skin—the rest had their faces contoured—tiny that it never reached his midlap.

'And who'll never listen?' He came in this particular sleepy homestead like a thunderbolt; the troupe from Kamser Alego and Kanyadhiang villages consisted of Ojando Oranga, Ng'iela Aguko, Obonyo Konyuka, Onyango Oyier, Okaka Biro, Ndalo Ayus, his elder brother (first son of Nyaoke), and a wizened old man Owiny Aloka. Ndalo Ayus was Onyango's brother. Their mother Nyaoke was the first wife of Obama Kopiyo. In the same breath, tension grew to epic degree. Serious truth and unexpected secrets came to the fore.

For Onyango Hussein was a married man, a polygamist, with two wives, an intricate eventuality. Akumu *Nyar* Njoga—*Habiba*—had escaped several times to her father's on account of disagreement between her and Onyango. She complained that 'Onyango is always on travels.' Maybe because of this loneliness, she kept moving up and down. She would leave behind her two daughters, Sara Nyaoke, Hawa Auma, and a son, Barak. Akumu, popularly known as *Nyar* Njoga (daughter of Njoga), was an awesome wife. The lady came from Karabondi Village and was born in 1918 to a peasant farmer-cum fisherman—Njoga, and the mother, Oleny Obwogi (*Nyar Toro*—daughter of Toro) from Nyakach. Kadiang'a. Akumu had a close resemblance to her mother, and when she'd grown to teenage years, many people confused her to the mother. Her mother hailed from the mountainous hills of Nyakach, Kadiang'a Clan, overlooking the lake, about two hundred miles from Kendu Bay. The tall, brown intelligent lady, who gave birth to Barak on 18 June 1936, was such an industrious, witty, and talkative woman and had lots of issues.... Her father, Njoga, was one of the elders—a council member who raised his daughter with a good intent—according to the rules of the land. The old man is buried at Bware School, Akwakra, near the 'mysterious' saline lake Simbi Nyaima. Beside his grave is that of Oleny Obwogi *Nyar* Toro—Akumu's mother.

The polygamist Onyango had two women of integrity. Even the elders envied him. But *Nyar* Njoga was one of a kind. She'd brought up the boy in a traditional way, and his upbringing plunged a sense of responsibility—this responsibility was bred in him, the boy, Barak Obama.

For the *first* wife, Halima, issues remained history and mystery; Halima was a lovely, well-behaved, quiet, and cool-tempered woman. 'But *Were, God* of the rising sun, denied her a child. He never saw it prudent enough to shower her with blessings of childbearing—she remained childless and shame took toll of her,' Sara says. She decided then to go back to her brothers—to live with them as *migogo*—a woman who has separated from her legal husband, for whatever reason, and has sought refuge at her own father's homestead.

'She lived a childless life for seasons until she gave up and later took to her heels,' an elder reasserts. 'Cursing and blaming the Mother Nature for not answering to the norm, intricate matters, indeed, for people who didn't know what barrenness is all about. They thought it a curse from the supernatural being. On her arrival at her father's homestead, she was well received by a horde of tribal elders, grass-skirted elders, who took her through a ritual of acceptance. She died in Kadem Village and was buried at her father's homestead. Onyango took a large herd of cattle to her father's, in a ritual ceremony.

For Akumu, life was oscillating between success and failure. She already had a son and daughters, only a few marital woes here and there to iron out. This particular son is who, well, would form the integral part of this story.

The aggressive boy born at the nightfall of unspecified season in 1936 had started asking questions that added nice zing to his life. What would become of an unobtrusive lifestyle?

A painful spasm, maybe, ran down the old man's spine, for him being alone was as suspicious as it was wrong in the measure of *chik* (law) and no sane father, not easily dissuaded, strict Omar, or the now deceased, Ogwel, would have eluded such a man to take his daughter away. Even religion couldn't allow him to be so soft or just being so complacent.

'Warming for a catastrophe? No. My daughter would suffer from the mediocre and a chagrin of shame! And I won't allow that,' Omar said.

That was hypocritical, yet, he found himself relenting to some realities.

In fact, the old man would have raged and yelled and even given a thousand reasons why it'd happen only over his dead body. 'That would be throwing his daughter to the wolves.'

Maybe, he'd put the bride price higher to try his temperament or test his patience and seriousness. Yet, at the end, Onyango had a plan, a passionate appeal. Ugly—yes, it was ugly enough, but one thing dearer to him then was Sara than the wealth of the entire part of the land. He faced this dark vacancy with good rapport and soberness. Marriage was a complicated process as compared to what you see nowadays.

Chik (traditional rules) were adhered to the letter. There was nothing like temporary marriages or marriage of convenience—hurriedly arranged and shaky in its institution. Nonetheless, conversely, it was a relish. For during the days of Sara, so many girls themselves favored polygamy.

A man who couldn't marry several women was considered squalor, and his background was often scrutinized. A girl from a large home, like Sara's, will always compel her husband to marry another wife or many other women, 'sometimes literally helping the husband to find a wife including her own sister,' an elder assured. The wealth clock was closely ticking away. A woman who opts to get more cattle in payment of dowry was highly regarded, talked of, strangely respected, and severely revered. For Sara, it was no exception.

As their arrival time wore on, a messenger, Owiti, a young man from the neighborhood, Kanjira Village, was dispatched to inquire what exactly had brought them. For a homestead, with a 'pure' girl, ready for hand in marriage, was protected as a unit. Owiny Aloka cleared his eyes with his forearm and waved frantically; he cleared his voice, found his tongue, and then spoke thus:

'Young man . . . ,' he paused, 'my name is Owiny Aloka, and these strong men are my nephews . . .'

Strength was a composite of victory and was inevitably mentioned in any 'opening speech.'

'. . . We've come here all the way from Kogelo clan. We are Kamser Alego living in Kanyadhiang Village, East Karachuonyo,' he continued.

He took some calculated, authoritative steps in front of his crew, like a charged captain.

The Kogelo clan had lived in Karachuonyo for quite some time, with three generations to reckon with as the storm over acquisition of land brewed silently and issues of marriages caused another more turbulent dispute. Many regarded the Alego Kamser as savages who were eking out their living by inter-marrying so as to protect and cover up their existence. With all in mind, the Aloka fellow would continue . . .

Said he, '. . . for a hand in marriage to your beautiful daughter, Sara, whose beauty has traversed every corner of the larger Savannah land!'

He paused, enjoying the tension he'd created, looking down, the tip of his spear radiating against the sunrays—almost razor sharp.

'Are we welcomed?' he asked, sarcastically.

The Owiti man was confused; the issue of Sara's marriage had been shrouded in a veil of secrecy. No mentioning without the authority of Omar himself! His face distorted through the stagnant water nearby.

'Of course, you're all welcome, my brothers from Alego clan. We're good people, and that's why you've come all that far. We can't just decide to chase you away. Although, you know the savannah land is polarized due to the recent attacks from cattle rustlers. But that won't stop us from playing your host. Feel welcome, anyway!' the frozen Owiti finally said after a short thoughtful pause. 'And as you know, the Wagwe Clan are free to marry the Alego clan though you live in our midst.'

Sara says Owiti was such a decent man who had the respect to talk in such forum. Only disciplined young men would be allowed to handle such a contingence. Again, the Alego people were known to possess unquestionable hardworking skills; they were the first to exchange goatskins for the khaki shorts, a stock of leopard skins for coins and food, or sheepskins for women's *lessos*. This is the community that Barak was to be raised in.

Onyango knew Omar. They'd been friends. They worshipped together at the mosque. And these connections enabled him to create the marriage about to be solemnized. As the tradition dictated, he'd to come in rather formal way—in respect of the custom.

Owiti continued, '. . . but first, you'll excuse me to inform the old man, Omar, and the elders of your visit and the nature of your mission, for he's the father of the beautiful Sara. He must surely know what has brought you this far!'

'You're free to do so, young man,' Aloka replied.

He turned and raced up, stumbling on a rock lying nearby; the rock left the outside of his right foot bleeding. That never moved him anyway as he climbed—an anthill—back for consultation. Owiti was an upcoming negotiator and warming for a seat in the wise *council of elders*. They were welcomed anyway. Why not? With their 'purse' fully laden? Omar showed confidence when he spotted a well-groomed man with a resounding discipline just from his looks. A man he knew quite well! Instincts guided him to correctly guess. Culture dictated that a wise man, advanced in age, was to form the integral part of the negotiation, ineligible assembly on a fantastic assignment. With evident warmth from the host, they settled on the goatskin laid on the floor; the few three-legged small traditional stools weren't enough for everyone. *Kon'go*, the local brew was brought. It was a sign of wealth. And drinking started at a 'snail speed' before assuming a crescendo. Loud laughter poured out of the tiny 'window', maybe, from the effect of the liquor. Meanwhile, Omar remained adamant and mute, and Onyango did the same, remained quiet and unperturbed. Some disruptive smiles and welcoming *donjis* as council of *jodongo* tumbled in were evident. Omar kept his eyes wide open, grazing raucously above the other men fixed on the 'strangers' as they leisurely devoured the brew using *seke*—firm reed-like straw, long enough to reach the farthest pot.

'And what might have brought you this far?' one elder asked, after a long silence.

'Good question. My friends, we're here for a noble cause,' Aloka answered, taking a sip of the brew from the traditional straw.

'Our son, who is seated here . . . ,'

Pointing at Onyango Hussein as he proceeded,

'. . . is looking for a hand in marriage to your daughter whose beauty has transcended hills and mountains and reached the people of Alego, in Kogelo and Kanyadhiang in Alego Kamser. We're surely glad to be given this chance! You . . .'

A stammering elder shot up:

'In other words yo . . . yo . . . you want to convince us that this man, Onyango, has never . . . married before, that our daughter S . . . Sa . . . Sara is going to be his Mikai, his first wife, huh? He looks advanced in age!'

Turning to the rest of the elders, 'Or my fellow elders, what do you say? D . . . do . . . you see that we're about to be duped, huh?' a stammering elder interrupted.

There was a commotion when consultation started. But it didn't last for long before Aloka resumed.

'Yo—you see my brothers, your questions are all right. And your fears are undisputed. I won't speak much. I'll let our son, Onyango, to answer all your queries . . . I think he is better positioned to be the one answering this kind of questions.'

This wasn't supposed to be; all negotiations were done without the would-be son-in-law's involvement nor was he given a chance to speak, for he was a special guest. It wasn't a good move. Aloka had limited options, but he had to relinquish his chance to allow Onyango speak.

'He's free to do so.'

Onyango stood up; tension filled the hut like a visible cloud of smoke.... His heavily built body tumbled up for an upright posture. The dark complexion was pleasing. *Ramogi* people were just as dark as soot. Then he spoke, 'My fathers, my brothers, and my elders, I'm here not like a thief or a prophet, not like a robber or a naysayer, but like a humble son of Alego to put forth my marriage proposal. I've been married before to two wives. Yes, but . . . ,' he began.

'Two wives? That's ridiculous . . . ,' the eldest yelled aloud.

'Yes, two wives, my father. One, Halima Hussein from Kadem, my beloved, she never got the blessing to have a child. I had loved this woman from the bottom of my heart.'

There was eerie silence.

'. . . And as you know in *Ramogi*, a man is man enough when he sees his children chasing the wind at sunset, girls carrying bundles of firewood from the forest, and boys with hoes from the fields. That's his happiness. Without that, he's no man. That makes him proud and composed. For Halima, and as fate has it, my fathers, there're some things in this vast savannah land that we can't change though they exist. They may be natural or supernatural, ordinary or extraordinary, because we're not *gods*. Halima had decided to quit our home for her father's, maybe due to frustration of not giving birth! She didn't have an option but to allow me to marry and have another life with *Nyar* Njoga (daughter of Njoga) otherwise Habiba Akumu. This is the woman whom I have children with. The West Karachuonyo girl, daughter of Karabondi Village, is lovely and naïve, at the same time. Indeed, our lives, together, have brought better tidings—three children to be proud of, Sara Nyaoke, Baraka—in short Barak, and Hawa Auma. I named Barak after my good friend I met in Zanzibar—Ahmed Baraka, who was later, killed by the Germans in a fierce battle with the British. May you rest in peace, son of Oman! Again, I left a while ago to visit the war-torn land of Zanzibar at the time Barak was born. Akumu wasn't happy with this arrangement despite my persuasion that I'll be back then, maybe in a short while. That's when hell broke loose. She got carried away and abandoned the young Barak and his sisters. The youngest, Hawa, about four moons old or so to seek for me to a land she knew little about—at least, according to the report she left behind. She broke off the hook of the elders and left for her father's in Karabondi Village instead, though she never stayed there. In the meantime, my departure cost me a lot. Or maybe due to other issues, I still have to come to terms with. People of Wagwe, this was a tragedy. I'm here to salvage myself and the lives of the young ones from the agony of it. Elders, just a few seasons ago, I heard that my wife, Habiba Akumu, is actually at her father's homestead and is complaining of being lonely most of the time.

'So you got the guts to tell us that you will take care of three wives, especially if the two come back?' the spokesman asked with a guttural grunt. 'How do we know that you will manage?' he joked.

'Yeah . . . You ought to explain,' the youngest elder emphasized, almost biting his tongue. He was dead earnest.

'No . . . Not that I can't. Akumu finds herself so lonely. And that's the barrier I want to break.'

'All right. You can now sit down.'

'Thank you, my fathers, but before I sit, I would like to appeal to my good father, Omar, to consider my proposal for I can't resist any longer the good attributes of your beloved daughter, Sara.' Everybody roared with laughter.

Sara concurs that these actually caused rapturous laughter. And such were his winning points compared to suitors who had come earlier or those who came after him. His sense of humor was amazing.

'. . . We've all heard your predicament, and we believe it's a genuine case. We must excuse ourselves for further consultation,' Omar's negotiator clarified.

'Yes, we need to excuse ourselves for consultation, hope the visitors will bear with us for a short while,' Omar agreed.

The entire 'host' team trooped out for a word. Sara says that many questions were posed like the following:

> *What can we say about this man?*
> *Can he take good care of our daughter?*
> *Is he abusive that women just walk away from him?*

The people of *Ramogi* would marry as much as they wanted. It only depended on wealth. Whoever couldn't marry many women was only limited by the size of his flock and not morals or restrain.

So many questions came in: hard questions and tricky questions for unpredictable decisions, the decisions that could have gone either way. They unanimously agreed to give him a shot—a chance.

'My people, I think . . . let's not judge him now,' Omar resolved.

'You're right. Judgment isn't good at the moment,' the spokesman concurred.

All this time Sara was very keen, watching from a tiny fissure on the grandmother's hut. All the conversation fell on her ears. Now this gives her the opportunity to pour it on to our ears as well—raw and told instantly firsthand.

As a father, his decision carried the day—had more weight. Again, Omar was a very respected man within his circles of influence due to the seat he held in the *council of elders*. He was adamant but a wise man, though.

Meanwhile, their absence enabled Aloka's team to discuss way forward and any likely eventuality. When they finally settled, negotiation started afresh. On a new platform, that seemed a bit challenging to Aloka.

Negotiations were the most important aspect; spokesmen from both sides were the main instruments here, wrestling one another in a war of words, although, introduction grew interesting as the host played 'cat and mouse' game in their quest to know the uttermost pertinent details of each other.

'And may I ask . . . ,' one spokesperson would begin, before attempting to pin down the vulnerable visitors in judgment. Conversations were cordial, grew comical, and the negotiations were made, agreement reached, a bride price set, 'fat enough to bring the world to an end or shake it and tear it down.'

Twenty heads of cattle, fourteen goats, and a ram, that was Sara's bride price! The actual stock wasn't documented—for Onyango had sent some livestock later 'just as part of appreciation'.

And as Onyango's entourage was given time-off to ponder on the agreement, Aguko, in a drunkenly slurring mood, shot up in advice.

'Twenty heads of.... Of what? Are we nuts or aren't we hoodwinked? That's too much for a third wife, Onyango! And you agreed? No ... No, No way. These people want to exploit us! They're playing some tricks here. And we believe them?' Ng'iela Aguko protested, feeling a bit tipsy from the liquor evidently, and furrows of anguish showed on his face.

'Maybe he was drunk, the profound impression was iniquitous and wasn't a good model for a man of his caliber,' Sara recalls.

'See, *chang'aa* of those days was very sharp. It can tear your heart apart.'

Chang'aa was a brew but locally known as *kal* or *andiwo* or *kong'o*. Recently, it was renamed *senator* after the then Senator Obama's visit in 2006. It's like a mainstay for some people. They drink and spend their nights in the cold. Others were swept away by the torrent floods after a daylong drinking spree, death rate from alcoholism rising steadily in the National Grid.

These sentiments, Onyango didn't take lightly.

'Shut up, Aguko, we're still visitors. You must tame your tongue, and there's no sense of protesting now. Second, I'm the owner of the wealth. I'm not inviting anyone to help me settle it. Third, this is my wife. I'm not marrying her for anybody. And I'm at no one's discretion to influence my decision or my choice. She's going to be my wife! And that will remain until I change it myself.'

The rather calm Onyango reiterated, to counter the shocked Aguko's sentiments.

'Indeed, love was in the air!' Sara says.

It was undisputed. It left people in shock and disbelief.

Sara's mother and grandmother kept silent. And silence accepted them. The bride price was so enormous; they believed that even theirs didn't even get a fraction closer to hers.

Quandary news of such a bride price spread like wild fire, from Seme to Karungu. News reached the people of Kogelo in awe. *Or* (son-in-law) as he'll be called, Onyango, remained calm for the better part of the negotiation in his black flesh, tight-lipped: internally at war with himself, his heart being the battlefield. And the beat remained the only source of sound of commotion.

Chik required of him never to burst into fits of laughter or giggle or be joyous or some sort of wild gaffes, to tame his tongue, never flinch an eyelid or any form of movement—some form of captivity. Sara was truly a Nobel prize contender; indeed this noble prize slowly crept into the family—after decades. But no one would have predicted it, then. This outlook could have been easily summarized by all love verses in the holy book. The Koran, the Bible . . . name them!

'May we introduce our jewel to people of Alego so that they can see whether what we're giving them is worth?' Omar uttered amidst claps.

Sara, irresistible lass, was brought; tension still high and men stiffened in their skin. And she was in the company of her grandmother and mother. Traditionally, that was the arrangement. Young girls spent most of their life with their grandmothers to learn cooking, while the grandsons with their grandfathers. Maybe to learn war tactics, hunting skills, wooing girls . . . among other skills.

In majesty, she walked, eyes fixed on Onyango Hussein, lips ochre, and red hot, and wild beads earrings dangling precariously from her well-shaped ears. Beauty was deep in the skin. A tiny leopard skin hung from a sharp waistline, culturally, known as *onyimbe*, moving left and right. The men would wear '*omete*' to cover their nakedness. Her well-curved cheeks evident, expressing her beauty helplessly. Shekels jingling, rhythm of bidding breasts intact, not sagging—a jewel indeed.

'I could feel my teeth crumbling inside my mouth like tiny grit,' he later told her. As the Luo old saying goes, like lightning, good luck rarely strikes twice at the same place, but it leaves a trail of disaster in a single hit.

Her well-curved cheeks evident, expressing her beauty helplessly . . . He could feel his teeth crumbling inside his mouth like tiny grit.

Onyango reached a point of needing more resilience in response to his larger marital woes. At this point, he trumpeted his ability, securing this lass made him believe that people mustn't undermine themselves. Work hard to secure their fast-slipping opportunities or just chances lest chances and ambitions go up in smoke or burn down in bonfire. In that brief show, maybe interpreted as some sort of modern catwalk in the runaway auditions, Sara left, grandmother on tow behind her, back to the grandmother's hut and the promise that the cattle, goats, and the ram will be driven into Omar's cattle shed by the next moon. Meanwhile, after the conclusion of that ceremony, more laughter and entertainment continued in earnest, men in a dance, some throwing their arms over their head to do a *jig*. *Kon'go* flowed freely, irrigating the lungs of the young men like fountain gushing out its waters in a free fall. This particular brew was taken with dignity, for it was strong lest you fell asleep in the bucket of *Kon'go*. Too bad for *Or* (son-in-law)! Midway, a calabash of *Kong'o* was poured on the floor, 'for ancestors must drink with us,' an elder said. This was purely forgotten, but they did it at last.

Drinking went on and on . . .

'Can you refill the pot?' another elder demanded.

'Yes . . . No. Oh yes, I . . . I mean more drink please,' Omar reaffirmed, between sips of brew. One woman rushed to fill the pot. She was the wife of Omar's spokesperson.

Furthermore, food was brought in plenty; fresh tilapia from the lake, boiled or those fried under deep cow-oil, *aruda* (traditional herbs) taken with *kuon maliet* (millet meal)—served hot. Men ate and continued endlessly with the delicacy . . . Aloka wiped the last soup off the clay bowl with a lump of *ugali*. The suitors finally left, in an extravagant portrayal of victory—common with young men from the lakeside. *As if they're hysteric!*

Up and close—a warm, pompous, and gracious welcome awaited them back home in a show of legendry. The Luo custom reveal thus:

> '*A lone hunter who goes single-handedly to the wilderness kills a rare sitatuga gazelle and brings it back home for a warm feast.*'
>
> Or '*a rebel who turns patriot for the same people who discredited him.*'

He was none of the gossiping flirtation, by-complement type. He had won.

'Onyango won. You made us proud!' a young man in a traditional headgear and a spear shouted, thumping his feet hard on the bare earth. Women wondered what he was up to, and they expressed it in a sarcastic laugh. Hitherto, Onyango believed (and his gaze was most intense) at two very different kinds of moments, as his head tilted back in conversation with the accomplishment, ever so subtly in a proud, commanding angle.

'It's my good appeal that has gotten me this far,' he told the reluctant Owiny Aloka. '. . . I hope my existing trajectory would work because this woman I'm about to marry will meet full-grown Barak, my son, and Mwanahawa, my daughter. To him that wasn't a shallow observation but rather some command button to what might erupt.

'What shall I do if she refuses them?' Owiny Aloka was a wise man. He spoke with integrity.

'You don't have to worry, young man. This woman shall understand. Maybe he'd advised him, as in Luo custom—in marriage, if you can't be a muskie be a bass.'

'Change every time a thing gets thick. Believe me, I've the experience. More so, you've explained everything to your in-laws.'

'But—how . . . ?' Onyango wondered.

As the entourage got close to Kanyadhiang at a confluence of River Ramba and River Awach, they stopped to rest and to quench their thirst. The water was gold-colored, maybe due to the red earth it gathered upstream. It drained freely. The terrain of the banks was ragged, granite-like, *Kit Mikai* stones were hanging precariously, the simmering water from the rocks was fresh for drinking, and the white and gray lichens were glittering from the midday sunrays on the rocky tors. Aloka Owiny, the son of Agumba Bogi, died in his short nap. Trouble arose. His last conversations, as described by one of the surviving friends' son, Okoth Oyier are as follows:

'No matter how gentle a woman may be, no matter how much awareness she has, she's still the wife of a man, though the man must strike a common ground for coexistence. Men who do nothing about this are doomed to fail.' His eyes widened.

'It isn't by the size that you win or you fail. It's by misunderstanding that you fail and through understanding that you win.'

Okoth, the suave tiny-looking man, extremely intelligent, tells of the *big story* in a more understanding preposition although he doesn't seem well. From the look on his long thin fingers, he tends to be suffering from some serious skin ailment—the peeling skin wrapped up his rather little frame and lightweight. Okoth would die soon due to old age. Then he was only sixteen.

'But why should I remain just quiet and do nothing about it? And why?' Onyango asked.

'And why not?' Aloka was in arms.

'Because, it doesn't seem so anyway. I don't think so, Aloka.'

'No, you're a great man, Onyango. Not a vacant. You're so kind, that's why I believe in you than anything else in this world.'

'I see.'

'Yes. I used to be like you, a doubter. But the world changed me. The world was changing. Like it was sweeping some wind to the coastline.'

An eerie silence quickly engulfed the commotion. Aloka bowed down to death.

Sara says, 'The entourage was devastated. And such a distasteful situation really shackled him. Aloka is someone he'd not only believe, but he also liked him. But now they're going to remain apart like some sort of leprous colony. Pondering what would come next.'

'Indeed, great words, wise counsel, a man of valor, a great orator, and negotiator. Rest in peace, son of Alego,' Onyango Obama eulogized, his arms holding tight to the spear and the shield, in solidarity with the sudden loss of a wise man. Onyango turned around, distraught. The other men looked to his direction.

'It's not what happens to us that matters now. It's dawning that we've lost one of our own. A great negotiator, one who has shown determination, battled out equally competent suitors to earn us a wife. It's a great loss. But our response to what has happened is what will hurt the rest, our village.'

He spoke to the entourage, downcast and pensive, up in arms with their weapons. See, the people of Ramogi weren't ruthless!

'Let's remain calm, my brothers,' he said. His eyes filled with torturous tears. They wrapped the body with wild leaves and tiny branches and carried it home for burial. Meanwhile, Sara's heart sunk. She became restless. Issues galore.

Sara concurs that 'she was distressed'. Her heart was distressed, and her body felt cold like some sort of flies drenched in grease and they can't fly off.

'What might be wrong?' she thought. 'Maybe something happened to them in the jungle.'

Chapter 3

All difficult things have their origin in that which is small.
(Anonymous)

In Late 1930s …

The difficult situation of chasing love while living on the edge was finally over or just lonely but avoiding love. Onyango had the skills no woman could resist. And as the first blade of grass shot up from Aloka's grave, in a reverse twist, on the sixth moon of the year 1937, Onyango sent out another strong contingent with the bride price to deliver to the vast land of savannah East of Karachuonyo, the homeland of Omar—the heartland of Kendu Bay. At the wee hours of the morning, at the crack of dawn (for they had traveled all night), the strong young men, fifteen in total, arrived at Omar homestead, drove the cattle in, but then, they were still waiting for the host to come out to receive the herd. A nonstop preying on grassy canopy ensued as they sought for a vantage point of entry. A full-blown insurgency was on the offing like 'a hungry fox waiting to pounce on a wayward chicken'.

The men, accustomed to surviving in the bush for long stretches across Homa Bay and Asembo Bay and of Kanyamwa areas, attacked the receiving side in what is called 'mock fight' locally known as *amen*; it was a question of agility verses power *with no excessive signs of violence*. These men from Alego dressed the opponents in fatigues—characteristic of guerrilla warfare. Sara was quickly and hurriedly hauled away in a rush custom. And the Alego men disappeared with her into the bush, deep into the thicket.

A full-blown insurgency was on the offing like 'a hungry fox waiting to pounce on a wayward chicken'.

Omar then resented and picked strong resolution, conveying deep concern over his departing doting daughter to a foreign land. He walked tall in a climate of abject confusion and terror. 'Part of his heart had left him!' Sara left Wagwe, East Karachuonyo; with her, she left a classic rags-to-riches and grass-to-grace human story. It was indeed easy to feel sorry for her, but she'd change the destiny of her life. Likewise, Omar, rather taken aback by this level of impatience, with a huge chunk of excruciating remorse, knew his role and that was what he was protecting. Sara's departure was a turning point in both ends of the two worlds now connected and bonded through a whining conscience (that whining conscience put into the test). And Nyajwala remained patient and happy. The trek was rough. Yet, the young men continued yelling and singing, wailing ferociously. That ferocity, that sparks, took them to a memorable treble! It's wearily strange enough; some kept giving her a quizzical look, suggestive of her beauty and glamour.

She was awesome, no fault, and beautiful.

On one morning of the sixth moon of 1937, approximately three days by the contemporary calendar, the young men arrived in Kanyadhiang unexpectedly; preparations were at top gear, women engrossed with explored obsession to have a glance at the new bride. Elderly women milled and danced around her in circles, in a matching troupe, to welcome her. Akumu had been brought earlier—back from Karabondi Village—from her father's homestead. Sara's arrival wasn't good news anyway.

Strangely, a hungry and haggard-looking madman (clans have a mad man to suffice the communal equation) kept laughing to the dismay of many and maybe uttering strange things from afar 'like angry man trying to dry his bleeding sword on his thirsty tongue. And hunger won't let him rest.' That shows how the chances of conflict in the communities would certainly be greater were it not that the world wasn't divided, between the sane and the insane. The restless son of a man grew new ethics of life. He couldn't hide showing a hint of shame from his disgraceful and arrogant behavior—in a gratuitous violence with the unseen.

Like angry man trying to dry his bleeding sword on his thirsty tongue. And hunger won't let him rest.

Sara, together with the entire entourage, arrived in Kanyadhiang Village and in a marriage ritual similar to a wedding procession according to Luo tradition. Onyango was ready to receive *miaha* (new bride) and the *council of elders* gathered to 'bless the home'. Drums were beating, and the horns were blowing characteristically in a show of unity and a sense of communality. Sara joined the women and soon found herself in the midst of entertainment—a *dodo* dance. She was versed in this one! The women kept, outside the lane, Sara sandwiched—it was her party anyway—dancing slow, stupid steps and screaming a wild and most inharmonious chant, maybe for the ebb of ancestral piety; they were singing songs of awe and throbbing the rhythm of received music. Sara, at least, was growing in confidence, and the dance was taking a crescendo. One woman, attended upon Onyango Hussein, and the other young men, ran through that crowd with a gourd of calabash full of ashes—wood ashes, a handful of which she showered over their heads powdering them like millers. This by itself was to dispel the bad spirit in dynamism of religion that rather lies in the influence of the spirit world on the daily life and to the importance attached to the use of magic. Such a ceremony was important, an indivisible entity penetrating the understanding of marriage institution. It ended in earnest. Reality dawned on her. She had started a new life, a cowife, Akumu, to reckon with.

Chapter 4

There is a time in every man's education when he arrives at the conviction that envy is ignorance; that imitation is suicide; that he must take himself for better, for worse, as his portion; that though the universe is full of good, no kernel of nourishing corn can come to him but through his toil bestowed on that plot of ground which is given him to till. The power, which resides in him, is new in nature, and none but he knows what that is which he can do, nor does he know until he has tried.

(Emerson)

In the Late 1930s Continued...

Her understanding of family and education issues took a different turn. Having Barak to take care of, even before she gave birth to a child of her own! In fact, her cute and flippant organization skills were far from perfect—not common in those days. Akumu had been on and off, going to Karabondi Village and staying there for days, if not months. Sara's wisdom had all the trappings of today's contemporary independent city girl—she appeared to live a guilt-free life, a life of hard work, which embodied the dreams and aspiration of her generation.

She was indeed part of the solution to Onyango's hardly fought success and pursuit of happiness and largely inherited woes. Many people queried the reason for her being vocal. Her response was equally memorable.

'Success is my habit... not an advice,' Sara said curtly.

'Onyango married a habit, a choice. That's what people want to hear,' she equipped.

Blowing her own trumpet?

No . . . But she was damn right, very right, without mincing her words. Was she supposed to ask someone to blow it if she could blow it herself? The young Barak was growing up, real fast, with all styles in his head, a mechanical herd boy who was curious to know what was 'outside there,' increasingly doubtful: outside Kogelo and Nyang'oma, the native homeland; outside East and West Karachuonyo; and outside the native bartering town of Kisumu; or simply what lay beyond the four corners of his father's hut. He played fast and was loose with the facts. His sister was, however, adamant to think about change. She was always asking the whereabouts of the mother whenever her father made a comeback from his many travels to Zanzibar through Tanganyika or from Nairobi.

'Father, have you met my mother?'

'Is she fine?'

'When is she coming back?'

'Will she come with another child?'

And the questions kept streaming in, one after the other. Surprisingly, there was no tentative answer!

The introduction of *pesa*, the Whiteman's coins, and *Christianity*, the belief of the Whiteman's God, was met with resistance and acceptance in the same magnitude. They brought major confusion as well. *Jawar* was Yesu Kristo (Jesus Christ in Luo), the savior. Sara says Barak wasn't sure of such fast-changing situations. He believed that there was indeed something going wrong somewhere. He would ask her: 'Mama . . . . And who's this *Yesu*? Who is he?'

Maybe he thought that the traditional aberration had caused people to look for some other means of tracking the truth.

'These two "animals" have enveloped people in a lifestyle of greed and extreme materialism,' Sara replied.

'A kind of emotion only depicted in you . . . the youths.' Lots of white travelers arrived in Gendia Mission; it marked the first direct encounter with Whites:

one Doctor Livingstone had recruited many local leaders to spread the gospel. And Gendia Adventist Mission was fast growing as various missionaries kept streaming in and were warmly welcomed by the local pastors. One of them, renowned Pastor Isack Okeyo took them to visit homes as they healed the sick, and they'd come face to face with young people. It is not known whether he met him, but there is likelihood that Barak was indeed part of a large group of young boys whom they'd preached to and was one of the first few boys to join Gendia Adventist Primary School. Others who later became lay preachers and catechists included Oyuma and Ojuok among others.

Traditional life institution headed to the south and window of opportunity was fast closing. Back to the old ways, men took to their heels with interest in the latest fashion masked in inner confusion and obsession. People around Kanyadhiang, within and far away, were both happy and despondent in ushering new ideas, perfect and imperfect in accepting Christianity and Jesus, *Yesu*, a man they were clueless about.

'What became of Obong'o Nyakalaga, *Rahuma*, god of the lake? Was he no longer in control of the community stronghold?' This *Yesu* was confusing. Later many people went ahead from criticizing their belief in *Yesu'* to examining and criticizing themselves and their ancient religion. People of Seka, Kauma, and Oriang, all accepted the new religion. It was a new symbol of another era of spiritual consumption. It took Kanyadhiang and, indeed, the entire Kendu Bay by storm. *It was a new symbol of another era of spiritual consumption.*

'Barak Obama's rating was fast growing, expressing a ripe desire to join the new religion, to follow *Yesu* and *Jeremia Jahulo* (prophet Jeremiah) his favorite,' Sara says.

The missionaries spread the new message of hope. But he was already a Muslim! 'Two religions are equal to no religion,' the Luo saying teaches.

'Now, what's hope for?' Barak, maybe, asked in dismay.

With stored enthusiasm, he found himself mingling with the *Jorochere* (whites), *joneno* (new converts), and *joote* (catechists)—largely Africans. Listening to them, with some of the description of the religion not real good, the storylines are more evocative, you know, a little commentary. The 'mysterious' book surfaced, otherwise, *Muma Maler*, the Holy Bible, and the major handbook for the new religion, shocking adjustment indeed.

Sara recalls the days the old man would criticize the religion . . . not that he was against its teaching or its preachers but due to the fact that he'd already glued his soul in Islamism.

Some of the conversations are still abstract in her mind. She remembers some . . .

'One thing in this new religion is that it's too complicated,' Onyango said, looking a bit upset.

'Why do you say such a thing?' Sara replied, composing herself to sound rational.

'Look . . . oh no! How do you listen to these . . . ?' Onyango wondered. 'If it's war, let it be war. I like war because it's allowed in politics. A politician is a warrior. No compromise,' Onyango said.

He was looking elated. You would easily disbelieve him even before he opened his mouth. 'How do you believe in a colonial British evangelist wielding a gun in one hand and a Bible in the other? That's ridiculous.'

His argument echoed with a heavy Luo accent.

A colonial British evangelist wielding a gun in one hand and a Bible in the other.

Expressing confidence, he had criticized the religion to its bone.

'No. No . . . no . . .' Onyango refuted, so much convinced.

'. . . Their preachers are a con, false prophets. They give a little with one hand and forcefully take a lot with the other. I can't follow blindly things I'm clueless about. It isn't right by all stretches of imagination. These are rare spectacles only conceivable in the fantasy world, that world of *Yesu*. Politics will point this . . . religion and the so-called faith will sweep it down. Am tired of this!' He sobbed in silence.

Giving a little with one hand and forcefully taking a lot with the other.

At this point, Sara felt that politics had penetrated deeply into her husband's head and that no form of healing would make him well. She felt wretched and defeated in this argument. He left an indelible mark in her heart, anyway. She vowed to God in a show of solidarity 'not to be so reticent about traditional frustrations'. This new faith pointed to a new paradigm shift of competition between traditional faith, politics, and the new religion, the gospel of *Yesu*, maybe with stronger determined followers.

'See, every day brings with it yet another potentially earth-shattering event,' Onyango reiterated. 'This new religion has ripped the village in shreds.'

He meant it, not taking his eyes off her.

'I am leaving . . . I am leav . . . ,' Onyango said attracting her attention. 'What did I hear you say . . . ?'

'What have I just heard?' Sara retorted. 'Nothing bad, I hope. I . . .' Sara interjected looking a little furious.

'Politics has blown you away from us. You're now broken down to unproportional level.

'Where do you want to go? To fight the *Jerman*—Germans—in Tanganyika?

'Or what do you want, my . . . to work for the *jorochere*—the whites?'

She continued, 'In those far and distant places? Don't you realize that we need to mend our marriage . . . to bring up your son and daughter? . . . Come on, *wuod* Alego (son of Alego). Where? Why depart? Fine, I'll go with you.'

It took a moment for the words to sink in. He looked up and a broad grin creased his freckled face.

Onyango was resolute and determined to leave, the air around him crackling with dissension.

'Go with me?' he said, perturbed . . . Then to himself, 'Where does she want to go?'

Sara was not finished yet.

'Look . . . ,' she said, her voice curiously flat, '. . . at your son, Barak, and your daughter, Mwanahawa. They too need you. They strongly need your attention and your guidance, Papa.'

She said this leaning on the mud wall.

'Barak is so vulnerable. He's a young boy, you know, more vulnerable to this fast-changing world.'

'Eh ee . . .'

'He needs our joint effort . . . that parental love. It's duty, remember! What's your take?' she asked. Barak was hiding in a closet, pensive. He thought he was unobserved. Sara adds, 'He had an expression on his face hard to define. He had gathered all our conversation.' On being noticed, he ran out, like a spear disappearing into the nearby thicket, to sober up. The tension back then was too much to bear. Breathing heavily in the midst of stinging shrubs and papyrus reeds, penetrating deep into the bush, he found a comfortable patching and then went into a long slumber till daybreak. That humbling night, he never spent in his *simba* (hut). The *simba* remained unoccupied, soot hanging leisurely. The fireplace was dotted with small charred pieces of firewood. Ashes were swept up by the air through the mat-twisted 'door'. The 'door' was made of papyrus reeds.

'You can't decide to stay here forever,' Sara surprised him with a soft voice. Then there was a long silence of hesitation. The morning mood was sombre. A bit cowed, Barak replied, 'I'm already alone.'

'Oh . . . that's interesting. Come out of that thicket, Son. You're doing yourself no good,' Sara said.

'I'm going nowhere . . . I won't come out, *Mama*. I want to be alone.'

'Eh . . . enough, take that bloody idea out of your mind,' Sara said angrily.

'Your father departed . . .'

'What?'

'. . . well, I never won our resolve. *In fact, it's an obstacle that will turn out to be our resolve.*'

'Can you explain? I don't understand!'

'This morning your father's friend, Ojijo Oteko of West Karachuonyo, from Kanjira Village Yimbo, came accompanied by his long-time bosom friend,

Nyambuga Simba, an ally from the neighboring Gem Kaluo Kobare and Gideon Magak Odeka from Kokal.'

Apart from the other army recruits, Onyango worked with Magak Odeka in one campsite and served in the same battalion.[6,7] In the process, they became so close that he married off his daughter, Hawa Auma, to Odeka's son, David Amuna Odeka. Hawa Auma still remembers that Onyango, her father, and Odeka, father-in-law, maintained that cordial relationship for the rest of their lives. During this marriage, Onyango insisted that his daughter must be married by a Muslim . . . David was compelled to resign from Christianity. Even his name was changed to 'Daudi'.

Odeka's work in the war was exemplary, and King George of England, in a populous setting, honored him with a certificate. It reads thus:

> In the Name of His Majesty King George the Sixth,

This certificate is awarded to Gideon Magak of South Kavirondo in recognition of the valuable services performed with devotion to duty.

08 June 1939.[8]

The South Kavirondo consisted of Kisii, Karachuonyo, Homa Bay, Mbita, Mihuru, Migori—these regions had their respective chiefs manning various locations—locally known as *dhoudi*.

Apparently, Onyango made sure that his daughter is married in a 'royal' family. And Auma loved it!

At this time, Nyanza Province, headed by a provincial commissioner, F. H. Fazan, a career civil servant who had previously served as an assistant district commissioner for Central Kavirondo from 1911 to 1927, was divided into four districts: Central Kavirondo, North Kavirondo, South Kavirondo, and Londiani. North Kavirondo comprised Samia, Ugenya, Alego, Lumbwa, and Mt Elgon. Barack's forefathers hailed from North Kavirondo.

This particular certificate hangs on a dusty wall at Odeka's graveyard. His 'royalty' the chief of South Kavirondo died in the year 1962. Beside lies the grave of his wife, Dorsila Magak, who died on 10 August 1998. He'll be remembered for the great work he performed not only for himself but also for the global community, during the world war, as a career serviceman with the King's African Rifles.

There's no tentative record to support whether Onyango was awarded a similar certificate.

Hawa says, 'My father was awarded similar certificate just like the one given to my father-in-law. They'd worked together. You understand? But maybe it got lost.'

She says it might have read this way,

In the Name of His Majesty King George the Sixth,

This certificate is awarded to Onyango Hussein of North Kavirondo in recognition of the valuable services performed with devotion to duty.

8 June 1939

Onyango's records have nothing of the sort, but every serving officer was awarded that certificate. Onyango who traces his ancestry from North Kavirondo lived in two worlds—the South and North Kavirondo.

Upon return, Gideon was elected senior chief while Onyango was again sent to Kampala, Uganda, for a more urgent and yet delicate assignment. During that time Gideon was the likely candidate from his village for the seat that fell vacant when the former chief died. Hawa's father-in-law was a man with great demeanor.

Kanjira Village was a heroic land; the Savannah land in South Kavirondo was a home to decorated WW I and WW II (1939-45) veterans, notably Kendo Yona, Ogembo Mbadi, Ojijo K'Oteko, and Odinge Zedekiah of Yimbo, among others. These are Kenya's celebrated WW II veterans. Much has been said about them. A celebrated author, journalist, and 1959 Tom Mboya Airlift beneficiary, Odinge Odera, writes about his brother in this context:

'... My elder brother Zedekiah did not go far with education.' It's not imagined, and of course, it's the stark truth that many boys were recruited into the war by the colonial powers.

The writer would pen that by 1943, when his brother was in Standard Five, he was already conscripted to the colonial army and sent to Burma, '... along with several boys from the village to fight the invading Japanese on behalf of the British Empire.'

This hints other untold stories . . . , and she wanted to hide the fact that Onyango was already gone, gone to fight in Burma.

The irritated Barack would ask, 'And what plan do they have, Mama, tell me?'

'Come out of that thicket fast, Son!' Sara called out.

'. . . Hurry. Go out to the fields to attend to the goats. This cloudy rain might come down any minute.'

She tried to dodge the truth concerning the departure. 'Remember we're going to listen to that British evangelist at *Gendia*, if it's the will of *Were,* then we'll get some food for thought!' At around this time, various missionaries and mainstream churches had a strong influence on people. They prevailed upon the black subject. Among them, the mainstream missions at that time were African Inland Mission that later came to be known as Africa Inland Church (AIC). It never penetrated part of Kendu Bay, though. Another mainstream mission was Seventh Day Adventist (SDA) that penetrated Yimbo (Kadimo) and Kamagambo region like a colossus trudging all parts of Karachuonyo, converting Africans to the new religion. They set one of the missions at Gendia. Up to this date, Gendia has been a vital center for academic excellence and the chief resource center for those seeking health services. At Gendia Mission Hospital in Kendu Bay, the fast slipping lives were recaptured. And its environed inhabitants have been thankful for such a breakthrough. Gendia Primary School Mission was started around this time. It was Barak's starting point in his quest for education in his formative years. (And Kezia Aoko would be baptized at Gendia Adventist . . . , and she had joined Gendia Primary in later years.) Church Missionary Society was the most powerful and largest consolidated entity under the unshakeable hand of Ludwig Krapf—from the coastal city of Mombasa in the east to the inland town of Malaba in the western part of Kenya—just as far as Zaki and Toluka in Mexico is from Manitoba and Saskatchewan in Canada, respectively. The mightiest Lumbwa Independent mission, the Gospel Missionary Society, Bible Church Mission, Pentecostal Church, the Roman Catholic Church, and Seventh Adventist missions were some other influential centers of worship, the latter being the most influential in Kanyadhiang and of which most villagers were part of—apart from Islamism, of course, not knowing the differences, its strength, and 'teeth' notwithstanding. History of these developments and mankind in the region was a struggle between imperial stardom, barbarism, colonial oppression, and civilization.

That afternoon, that windy day, was the *first turning point* for Sara, the daughter of Ogwel from Karachuonyo, the woman brought up by Omar, who was married with the largest head of cattle—the only unprecedented wealth in her generation. When Onyango left for WW II in 1939, tension grew to insurmountable limits; these are the times Akumu would come back from Karabondi and cause mayhem. She would quarrel with Sara to the point of physical confrontation. 'Our war isn't ending now or here. It will be ceaseless,' she said. News would reach Onyango, who never took it kindly. Although, he knew pretty well that such fights were normal in this continent—issues of women rivalry. He had observed this even where he was working, where women got into each other with frying pans and cooking sticks. Others would stab their colleagues to death in a wealth dispute.

Obama, Sara, and his mother arrived to listen to what the *jorochere* had to say—under that cool *bongu* tree, that huge fig tree. Hawa was still very young and had been left behind with a neighbor to look after her. 'They used to leave me behind at the neighbor's hut. And my father questioned why—whenever he was around.' This particular tree was religiously important, it served as a shrine, and to date, its roots still stand at the outskirt of Gendia Village, the present day Gendia market. By then, Akumu would disappear to Karabondi.

Old men and women, children, and grandchildren arrived in equal share; they came in their loads, a good number that made up an audience to hear the word of the 'Western God', not knowing what will follow—an ultimate change and turn around.

In 1944, Habiba Akumu, daughter of Njoga of Karabondi Village, was drunk with loneliness, and the ghost of loneliness receded and took advantage of her, bundled her, and threw her far away. She sat every evening, roily and disturbed, in her tiny hut, lamenting about her emotions and constant fight with Sara. The toil of everyday life triggered her and couldn't offer her a piece of perseverance. And good news was received in equal measure as well—Sara Anyango gave birth to a baby boy on the third day of 1944 in the sixth moon (that is, June, by the British Calendar). Sara named him Omar, after her stepfather. And they moved to Nairobi. So Akumu's loneliness persisted when Barack joined his father in Nairobi.

But quarrelling continued; it took the intervention of the two children, Sara Nyaoke and Barak; Hawa was still a toddler and couldn't know what was going on. The two were up in arms to quell the hard stance of the two warring women. Akumu would listen keenly to Nyaoke because, as the eldest, she had sense of maturity in her utterances.

Onyango himself wasn't in Karachuonyo; he'd secured an arranged job with the missionaries as a cook after leaving Burma and Zanzibar one year before the end of World War II. These were jobs offered to able Africans who had the exposure of European lifestyle and were the reserve of ex-World War II fighters who had returned home alive. Most of them never came back. They either died or were maimed by deadly explosives. Earlier in 1928, the Authority of the Registration of Domestic Servants Ordinance was put in effect by the colonialist in the East African Protectorate after the simmering troubles and pity that ex-soldiers manifested. Through this initiative, many Africans found themselves being recruited into income-generating jobs such as butlers, cooks, drivers, waiters, and gardeners. Many people have tried to connect the work stint of this old man. Where did he work? Whom did he serve? According to Sara, for many years he had worked for several able families. She recalls that 'her husband who'd work for two Americans.' At one point, it's believed that Onyango worked as a cook. The white belonged to a whiteman working at Shankardas House in the heart of the city. The couple lived at Muthaiga. A few meters away from the current American Ambassador's residence. The man was working at United States Information Service (USIS), while wife was at the Hospital Hill School. But her work at the United Kenya Club was paramount. A Briton, Askwith, established the Club, in 1946. It became operational in 1947. As Sara puts it '. . . Barack would go to see his father at the *Mzungu's* residence where he worked. He'd ask at the gate, 'I've come to see my father.'

No one can tell the authenticity of this truth.

The news of family wrangles alarmed him, and he left Nairobi for Karachuonyo in a huff. At that point, Sara had gone back to till her land for cultivation. His family was tearing apart! That day, as part of his vacation, he decided to take the train to the village—the only train commuting to Western Kenya, passing flat tarred roofs of the downtown shanties, the sound of the colonial train echoing, as if it's almost separating apart, as if it's calling on the ancestors. Hussein could feel the rocking sway of the wheels; the sight didn't quite seem familiar. They crossed the rift valley, into large plantations set on the 'white highlands', the view that proved that the colonial powers was ruling Kenya at the time: left and right. Life got disrupted with disappointments, by surprises, and sad news. He wore his favorite white robe or *khanzu*, relaxed under the passing shadow of railway bridges that rolled over the cranky train; he'd smoked his precious cigar and kept his cool, waiting for peace to come. In three days' time,

Onyango was in the bartering city of Kisuma; the train came to a halt. He pulled and hit the road for an epic journey, on foot, to Nyan'goma. His mission was to set a rapport with the elders and close cousins, uncles, and grandfathers in Kogelo—for he'll set his second home here—to join his ancestors for the first time; he spent a few days, and his mind shrouded with an idea to return 'home'—which actually he shared at length with his uncles. He assessed this land and found that it was good enough. On the fifth or so day, Onyango left Kogelo for Kendu Bay in Karachuonyo . . .

A lot was going on in Kendu Bay, a new Head Chief Akoko Mboya (whose name later changed to Paul Akoko Mboya when he was baptized Paul) was lodging complaints to the colonial government through the district commissioner (DC) about 'outsiders' occupying their land illegally. One of them being Onyango Hussein of Alego Clan—'whose land rights lies in Siaya,' he said. Many people of Kamser Alego found themselves in trouble. The DC, the chief, the *headmen*, and the council made several meetings. The DC would then send them to discuss the matter at the grassroots. And when a group of subchiefs assembled, everything was at the heels of collapse for poor Onyango. There was Okoth *wuon* Owuor, the subchief of Kakwajuok Village (whose son, Owuor, later inherited the chieftainship from him). And there were the headmen: Joel Omer, Ogosa, Amoth Kowira (who later became a senior chief), and Awuor Aroka among others. All these assemblies took place in his absence, but the rumor had told it all. Onyango knew that the DC had no legal power over him and that the land in which his livelihood rested was legally his! Guided by the law of the land and not of the queen of Britain.

(Joel Omer later became a pastor and despite the religious disparity with Onyango, they were indeed great friends—he's the father of the first woman member of parliament in *Luo* Nyanza—the long-serving former Karachuonyo member of parliament, Phoebe Asiyo).

When he arrived in West Karachuonyo, the first thing was to see his three children. Sara Nyaoke and Barak, in that order, enrolled again at Gendia School, for education, apart from Islamic religion, this became the big story. Barak, for a second time, stepped in a classroom—Sub-Standard A, the current Standard One. A class he'd dropped a year ago. The atmosphere wasn't conducive for Akumu. Sara Anyango was cuddling her baby boy. However, to Akumu, the man was too strict to cope with, the Muslim doctrine hard to shoulder, and her first attempt to separate from him was evident. One day, she went to buy smoked slit fish at the shore, and she never showed-up again. She'd gone back to Karabondi, her father's home, partly due to harshness of Hussein and partly due to constant wrangles and land disputes.

He'd smoked his precious cigar and kept his cool, waiting for peace to come.

The following day, Hussein got wind of her whereabouts, and he went off to bring her back. The issue of land brought a wider rift between the natives of Karachuonyo and those they grouped as 'outsiders'. There were so many people living here away from 'home', especially in the larger Kamser Alego. It forced Hussein to extend his leave of duty in order to sort himself out, especially following the growing disquiet of the people that became so apparent and loud enough.

In 1946, his problems grew, by and large; the powerful *council of elders'* leader, Mboya Akoko, particularly singled out Onyango and declared war with him. He called him *jadak*, a foreigner; words of the radical leader, who was anti-Islam and didn't tolerate the belief of Muslims, and the strong backing that it gathered. Second, Hussein was a native of Alego and that's where he belonged. Chief Akoko made several meetings again and again, one after the other, to ouster Hussein. He wasn't going to relent on this particular mission. The determined Akoko onslaught was profound, and the pressure made Onyango quit Kanyadhiang Village for Kogelo Nyan'goma—the land of his forefathers. He'd yielded to the rejection and prepared to go back 'home' telling Akoko that in times to come, his lineage would wither and die while that of Onyango Hussein M'Kobama would be on everybody's lips worldwide.

When he was summoned before the then *Luo* elder representative, Koyo Opien *wuod* Nyamwalo (son of Nyamwalo), life started to change. The Luo elder advised that the matter should be handled amicably. And that Kamser Alego Clan, where Hussein belonged, had lived there for decades. It wasn't right to whisk away an entire clan. For custom was against that kind of undertaking. Though the verdict didn't come immediately, Koyo Opien wanted to investigate further and unearth the reason behind the saga. In that process, Akoko went ahead and convinced him, in privacy, that, indeed, 'Hussein wasn't a good example to the village. That he was too wealthy, and he can't tell where his wealth had come from! That he talks of a religion he can't substantiate its origin! That he is a quisling of the Arabs and a stooge of Islamism! That he continues buying land without *council of elders'* approval!' Maybe Koyo was driven by jealousy.

This case went through various segments—most notable was when the head of the Luo Customary Court, Mbira, came over to preside over the verdict. Present were Koyo Opien, Chief Akoko Mboya (accuser), Chief Okoth *wuon Owuor* (father of Owuor), Omer, Aroka, among others. The last two were part of the elders' committee. The airtight case attracted a large audience. Elders such as Ojiero, Agong', Dulo (they included those opposed to the leadership of Chief Akoko) were so bitter that the meeting went chaotic before calm could prevail. And they made it clear that the reason of Hussein's dismissal was baseless and uncalled for. The disillusioned Akoko was puzzled. By that time, a chief was like a governor with immense powers that they could easily abuse.

Mbira was reliable, wise, and well-accustomed. His fiery stance and earlier verdict caught the accusers or the victims unawares. At one point, in one of his sittings, he claimed to have seen a devil walking in the courtroom. When the accusers wavered and ran out, he launched the case afresh—made the much-awaited judgment, and the defenders (who remained calmly in the court's dock, adamantly waiting for the case to be decided)—won the case. The other party was informed, and they all cursed themselves.

Mbira denounced some of the accusations labeled against the suspect—they were lesser for punishment—but he made it clear that the growing brawl wouldn't end soon, and therefore, in his discretion as a judge, Hussein had to leave. But 'his land shouldn't be sold to anybody,' he commanded. It was he to decide whom to inherit the expansive piece of earth. The verdict caught many unawares.

Akoko was particularly unhappy, angered that the judgment had favored Hussein. He made his accusation sound that the inhabitants were to remain the sole custodians of the land, which he'd wanted to grab.

A long voyage to Siaya

On one morning of third moon (around March) of 1946, Hussein gathered the entire household for a long journey. He brought down the five huts that dotted his homestead and cleared the bushy fence made of euphorbia. 'If you go to Kanyadhiang Village and ask where the huts of Onyango Hussein lay,' you'll be shown the five huts and the traces of his fence are still clearly demarcated. *Chik* required him to demolish the huts because they were no longer inhabitable,' Sara says. However, Barak would kiss each hut, as a way of gratitude 'for the service they honored'.

Hawa Auma, the only surviving Barack's biological sister says thus:

> 'We took off. My father had asked for an army van from a friend. And we squeezed ourselves in that tiny moving creature. The journey to Kogelo took many days. During that time, we ran out of fuel, the roads were bumpy, and sometimes we'd gone just through the bush whenever there wasn't anywhere to pass. In the van were Akumu (my mother), Sara Ogwel Hussein (my stepmother) and her baby, Omar Onyango, Nyaoke (my sister), Barak (my brother), and the driver. I can't remember the name of the driver. The lovely baby was nursed in goatskin while I was wrapped in an old shawl. The two of us were still very young. But he was one gigantic figure on the wheels of the van. My father had accompanied the livestock.'

As they departed, neighbors shed tears; the family they'd lived with peacefully was leaving miserably due to disputes. Barak was emotionally touched. He had to leave the friends, the pond by river Awach, where they caught the poor tiny tadpoles, that swampy pond of stinking water from rotting tiny creatures, that pond that smelled iodine. And a village he loved unconditionally, as his first home—a distance away he could turn and see the demolished huts, the neighbors' simple huts, and the beautiful boys grazing in the fields, chasing one another. Was this a formality or just another episode of a big story? Herd boys seemingly bringing down the flying birds with slingshots. Tears would come out helplessly. The younger boys, half-naked and malnourished, running around as the village women, young and old, converged at one particular water point. He couldn't compare the two worlds . . . the world he was leaving behind and the one he was about to go into. Two separate entities.

Hawa says as follows:

> 'Our livelihood such as cattle was driven to Kogelo by some young men as we enjoyed our trip in the cranky van. My father didn't come with us. He'd accompanied the men. And building materials, furniture, and other properties were tied on donkeys.'

The trek to Kogelo wasn't an easy one; the distance took several days. Through Nyakach, they made it to Kano, meandering around the marshy plains—spending days and nights in the cold—with large herd of cattle, sheep, and goats, the Obama's inheritance. The travel was made longer by the fact that Lake Victoria consumes the largest parcel of land between Kendu Bay and Kisuma. Those days only small, slow canoe boats would traverse the rather quiet expansive Lake Victoria spending days in the middle of the soaring waters before making it to the shore. A few boats were available as a means of transport yet so unreliable since a number of them were meant for fishing only. Today fishing and transport is made impossible due to the fact that the waters have been invaded by water *hyacinth*. The weeds entangles onto the propeller of steam engines of ships and motor engines of speedboats. It's said that it harbors a large quantity of wildlife: African black cobra and other snakes, Nile perch, crocodiles, large amphibians, and dangerous hippos. Sara and Akumu, Hawa, Omar, Nyaoke, and Barak, all braved the torrent rains, the muddy earth of Kisuma, the current Kisumu town; they passed Kisian, Lela, Maseno, through narrow sticky paths of Luanda, Sinaga, and Sawagongo to Ng'iya.

The tiring, breathtaking journey led them to Kogelo.

Hawa recalls instances that the van would be stuck in the sticky mud. And Barak would try to help push the heavy van (whenever it's stuck). 'My sister, Nyaoke, would scoff at the whole thing as my two mothers joined in the push. It was a great experience. Although, I was still young—a girl who could hardly talk.'

Later, Barak would tell Malik thus:

> 'Son, after my father was deprived most of the cattle he owned in Kendu, and some died on the way to Kogelo due to fatigue and diseases . . . because of these strained circumstance, we moved here, a slightly fertile land, larger village where we would get support from our own people, the people of Alego. This is where I belong, where I spent my childhood, and whence I capture my happiest memories.'

Part II

Kogelo

Siaya

Chapter 5

Here was a man take him all in all,
We shall not behold the likes of him again.

(Hamlet)

In 1946, Alego, Nyang'oma

Hurriedly, Onyango built his mud huts. Everything had arrived safely.

Although, a few calves died on the way. Hawa says thus:

> 'Indeed the journey was tiring and wasn't so safe. But what I liked most was that the Kogelo clan received us so well as if our arrival was overdue.'

In traditional setup, if one were to build a new homestead near the former, he'd carry the roof of the previous hut and place it on the new one—like an old wineskin patched on the new wineskin: one for Habiba Akumu *Nyar* Njoga, on the right, according to the *Luo* tradition; the second hut, on the left, for Sara Anyango Ogwel *Nyar Omar*; the third was his *duol* (old man's hut). People lived in huts (large huts and small huts). They were made of mud walls, and a long wooden pole would be erected at the center to hold the peaked elephant grass roof. The floor was made of heap of soil leveled and smeared with fresh cow dung. Sara would, therefore, regularly keep it smooth by smearing it with the dung. The doors were made of straw or papyrus reeds. When construction ended, Onyango made a bonfire to 'warm the homestead,' and each of his wives made porridge to symbolize an entry to a new homestead—the smoke from the three-stoned fireplace escaped through the roof, forming a joint stream and then disappeared into the atmosphere. Life started in a low key. The cold muddy huts, for the first time, proved uninhabitable. Akumu and Sara were cowives, who'd learned where to get firewood and where to fetch water 'using the clay pot'. Food such as traditional pumpkins, sorghum, and milk was in plenty, and people liked the diet; there wasn't any inherent preference to these foods—nothing was there to replace them or to catch that rare sardine for supper! And they made new friends in the neighborhood. Sara, in particular, started to hawk traditional vegetables at Nyan'goma in exchange for milk and sometimes coins. The market started when *Bwana* Orengo, the African Church Missionary, first stopped to address the villagers on his plan to initiate a church and a school project. Women, with babies slung dangerously on their backs, hawked porridge and milk to the colonial workers. The workers' god smirked to see the hardworking and determined women brave the cold weather to bring their sales. Barak and his friends would go out to harvest honey—the dangerous drone bees biting the soft tongues of the determined youngsters. They would relieve the swellings using bitter herbs before they'd get back to the homestead. The rural African boy was one hardy creature. They would go out there to look after the cattle, surviving on edible roots, wild fruits, and play games such as *amen* (wrestling). Don't confuse this with AMEN in reverence of 'so be it'. Barak would break away from an opponent with fast footwork when overwhelmed. Athletics was a way of survival. A good athlete was regarded as a gifted person. To date, Kenyans take pride in having produced the best athletes in the world. Many titles and fame have come its way. The marathon title, the steeplechase title among others, is part of the growing achievement in the field events. Many Kenyan athletes have broken new world records in the races. And that's the pride of the nation. When calm returned, they'd mold bulls out of clay, and when hunger struck (while they're in the field), they would suck milk straight from the udder of a docile cow—just like a calf. Calves were left at the homestead so they wouldn't suck before milking time. Still there was a problem; after these suckings, Onyango would complain that the cows never fed properly, that they are 'dry, that's why there's no milk' . . . Barak would not agree. He'd deny that fact; 'the cattle had enough grazing,' he said. The old man had no clue that the poor boy and his friends had extracted the commodity and had sucked the udder dry. Other hostile cows would kick hard when touched. Their milk wouldn't be tampered with till evening—the official time for milking. They'd disciplined the boys.

In early 1946, a fight broke out between Akumu and Onyango, barely three days after she'd given birth to her fourth child—Zeinab Atieno. The root cause isn't known yet, but Hawa points her figures to her stepmother, Sara Onyango, who might have incited the old man's anger against Akumu. 'Maybe she made something up that fuelled everything up,' Hawa says. It should be understood that in the traditional polygamous family, such infighting were commonplace. And there was no limitation to squabbling.

After the disagreement, Onyango thought everything was fine, and that everything was sorted out. But that wasn't going to be a solution. He blessed his daughters and left for work.

In this same year, Akumu escaped moments after Onyango had left for Nairobi—back on his job. Kogelo was left in awe. It was unheard of, for a woman to escape from her homestead, with an infant and leave other older children behind. This time, she went, and never came back, neither did Onyango attempt to look for her nor talk about it. Maybe he thought that 'enough is enough'. As she trudged the rocky terrain to Karachuonyo, Akumu wasn't bothered by the kind of damage that she was about to leave behind. Good or bad, she'd made up her mind. Karabondi Village was her next settlement. The children, Nyaoke, Barack, Omar, and Hawa couldn't understand the reason why!

Hawa says, 'My mother stayed in Karabondi for months. During all that time, my sister Zeinab was growing pretty fast. And my mother had not been married off to Salmin of Kosele, my stepfather. She took quite sometime—before remarrying—maybe waiting for Onyango to apologize . . . or something to that effect.'

(To date, if you go to Kosele and ask where Akumu *Nyar* Njoga was buried, you shall be taken there, at the graveside, and see where the remains of Barack's mother rests.) Maybe a memorial shall be done in her honor. And her life shall be celebrated once again so that she reconciles both with the dead as much as with the living. Although, the husband also died and had left behind two sons, Razik and Amir Otieno. Long live Salmin. Even Zeinab Atieno has since died.

By 1947, a year later, a lot unraveled: Sara was settling down with her school-going Nyaoke and Barak; Akumu was in Karabondi, back in Karachuonyo with her father, Njoga. And Onyango settled again in his job in Nairobi—politics being the balm of his pastime. Politics was his opium. This so-called politics of change cost him.

Hawa says that 'when unknown forces assassinated Tom Mbotela and Ambrose Ofafa, hands were pointed towards *Mau Mau*, which, earlier on, had accused the two of spreading falsehoods about them in churches, meetings, and other gatherings. Ofafa was particularly accused of being part of a church movement that had been at Kaloleni Hall and pitted people against them. This made

Tom Mboya to hold an emergency meeting with the then governor, Sir Evelyn Barring. When this meeting couldn't prompt any action, people went to the streets and protested against the killings. They made guns and explosives. The hand grenades were made from gunpowder, broken glass, stones, and petrol in a can with a wick in it. When the wick was lighted, it would be thrown in the midst of gatherings, exploding and killing white home guards within an area of about forty yards, or anyone it came into contact with.

In fact, in later years, such a protest broke in 1953; a grenade exploded and completely destroyed a room at Ngara Road, killing the occupants.[9]

In 1949, many people suspected to be part of these protests were rounded up and arrested. The fifty-four-year-old cook, Onyango, was a suspect. The old man was picked up in the middle of the night by unknown *afandes* and jailed without trial by the British Colonialist 'due to his involvement in Kenya's Pre-Independence Movement'—the Young Kavirondo Association backers were waylaid and arrested as well. He was the ardent supporter of late Jaramogi Odinga. Onyango was a guest at the colonial prison, the Kamiti Maximum Security Prison around the current tiny township of Thika, and accused under Regulation 6 (1) of the Public Security Act.[10] The old man was subjected to brutal torture that caused him physical disabilities. Some of the protestors were taken to Lukenya Prison even before it became a fully fledged prison unit. But Onyango wasn't afraid of prison. He knew he was fighting for a just cause; that going to this state facility wasn't going to change anything. He later told the authorities, 'If I have to go to the prison, then I have to walk there before you.' Meaning, he'd voluntarily surrender himself for justice to prevail. One prison warden is reported to have called him 'a pathetic cook who'd not let go filthy habits'.

Other people tried to resist these protests—mainly *Mau Mau* sympathizers; they didn't succeed, and they were tried as well and taken to Martial Courts in Mathare Valley at a place called 'Married Quarter'. Here, offenders would be sentenced to death or life imprisonment.

These news of arrest affected Sara a big deal. She felt downcast and overshadowed by the cruel hands of the ruling class—the *Wazungu*. The sad news from the capital wasn't good enough to an ordinary ear. And Sara never took it lightly . . . maybe; she would shed tears to crystallize her frustration and eminent downfall. No, she never gave-up, neither did she exaggerate the news to Barack, nor did she relay this news to Akumu in Kosele. For six months, the old man suffered torture and abuse, sometimes getting overworked in the white farms as part of broader punishment. They'd be taken to as far as the outskirts of Thika Town or in Githigiriri Special Camp or Hola Camp or to join those in various detention camps in manual labor, what they called concentration camps. Here their faces would be covered, frog-jumped, and then they'd be thoroughly beaten so that they disclose the secrets of the movement opposed to the colonial government. In the evening or after a few days, they would be brought back to Kamiti Maximum Security Prison. The movement caused real fear to the government—with every officer being either a 'general' or 'a field marshal'. There was General China, General Stanley, General 'Cargo' among others, and Field Marshal Mwariama, Field Marshal Kimathi etcetera; others were captured in a bungled raid for guns, a routine exercise that actually continued for quite sometime—the government used it as a way of toning down the aggressive Kenyans, those on the forefront to reject the continued oppression.

A number of prison wardens were young men drawn from the British Army; the ruthless boys would hit the older Africans at the knees and at the elbows using a wooden club or would pinch with the dreaded pliers like they did the animals. Victims, the age of their own fathers, would cry for help; that didn't matter to them either, and later, they'd wail for mercy; that also didn't matter anyway . . . but the torture would continue. This is what Onyango went through, and indeed, it was 'un-called-for punishment'. The system had to work, and the British had to rule!

In the meantime, the rest of the victims' families went through similar motions. They'd lost some of their loved ones through brutal death or physical disabilities; others couldn't be traced—those who mysteriously disappeared under unclear circumstances. Nothing unusual, though. No white man would trust the oligarchs around the black leadership. That was absolutely plausible given the contempt with which they treated each other. The first one to grab a *rungu (*a wooden club*)* would corner the other, shouting 'I'll finish you.' And the first to pick a clench fist would blind the other with a surprise massive hit.

Here one would cry until the tears run dry or be reduced to unabashed tears. The two seemed inconsolable and completely out of their emotional depth. The white wardens would laugh uproariously at the helpless victims. The inescapable fact is that the rule was too grave on Africans.

These are memories that Onyango would disclose to Sara, but rather reluctant, to piece the details together, he would weigh his words, careful not to be ambiguous, straight, and clear. He'd not want to inflict on her any communal fear or anxiety, or anything of the sort. And the intrigues never ended there. He was compelled to size up his position as a head of the family. Something that was benign.

A visit by anyone was a welcome relief. Sara would come to visit at the prison facility. The handcuffed Onyango emerged from the closet, wearing a white-and-black-stripped suit. All the culprits on death row wore that kind of clothing. Sara would see him sit down, (the accomplice beside him lit a cigarette) and glance at his crying wife. About hundred or so inmates graced the facility. He thought and strongly believed that the state would gas him. And the state was, maybe, working hard to execute him. And the prison wardens were some of the flunkies or stooges for the same state. She thought that he'd been in a cave for all that time. And there was the reeking foul smell of a combination of different brews; *chang'aa* and cigarettes, *marijuana* . . . the place smelled like something close to an abandoned brewery. Maybe in modern prisons, the smell of sour mash or stale gin or vodka is still evident. Deepening bells, whistles, and shouts was a sign language. He'd felt that time was running slow that days turned too slow to months. Time would move too slowly like some sort of slow glacial movement, like forever. So the 'clean man' dropped spectacular-ness. And commissioning a supply of a toothbrush would take the days he'd been convicted or that he'd spent in prison—*six* months. The six dark months, he suffered the spark and admonishment. The way he was treated at the prison wasn't good. His individuality was bent. It broke his spirit and destroyed his resolve, something that caused a real dent in his life. His reaction to stress and hardship was different. Each convict had his or her own way of overcoming or rather enduring the hardship. In normal circumstances, persons under such conditions would react absolutely differently to stress. One thing that they discovered in prison was to maintain order so that they minimize torture (unnecessary torture and beatings). They became their brother's keeper. The imprisonment brought no good. It became the meeting point for more radical leaders, who'd form alliances and strategize on how to attack the white man and thrash them to a higher level of resistance. They'd taken secret oaths, and everyone seemed ripe to sustain that secret. Here was an innocent soul who'd tried a while ago to strike but failed. He was still a novice in the political radicalism.

The young prison wardens would take away your dignity. And they were ready to do so at the slightest provocation. That made them suited to the job.

Onyango was one man who'd not leave behind 'high spirited effort' whether it came from nurture alone or profound nature; he'd express it to anybody in the surrounding.

Maybe death-row convicts would be gallowed at the Kamitis' open-field gallows center. The procedure, maybe, followed a more discreet method. Or when those facing the same prosecution would be gas treated at the infamous gas chamber, the young prison wardens would wake up in the wee hours of the morning to prepare for the dreaded day. The preparations would involve secret meetings and lobbying. No one would tell who's to dance to the music—face the gallows. Once picked, the prisoner would be forced into a gas cubicle and the doors would be slammed. A thick mixture of acid and water—with an acrid smell of ammonia—would drip from the top onto the victim's naked body: an alkali metal cyanide is forced into the acid mixture that reacts to a cloudy thick gas, striking the victim's breathing system. This forms an oxygen-less vacuum rendering the victim unconscious. The body remains still, the heart stalls, and the lungs collapse. When the valves drain and exhaust, the air valves are opened, and the doors are similarly opened; then the dead prisoner is removed and pronounced dead. This is a system description that is presumed. Although Onyango himself escaped death by a whisker, many people were gassed at the dawn of 1953—the declaration of a State of Emergency, a year before—just a few months after the departure of Elizabeth Alexandra Mary from Masai Mara after her father's death. She was made the Queen Elizabeth II of England. And Onyango remained the only one to narrate the ordeal to his wife Sara and his offspring.

This was the kind of death that some of the victims of Kenya's struggle for independence faced in the able hands of the colonialists.

'Kamitis' idleness and insanity (lack of respect, to be specific) was something that angered Onyango,' says Sara.

Onyango would promise her of freedom. There was an idea that one would gain freedom, that he wasn't fooling her, and that he'd not been convicted of murder. He was one man who'd not burdened Sara with troubles or lament. He treated her with respect far from argument-characterized boiling pot—but close to that man who fought nobody and who'd condemn injustice.

How did Ng'iya come into being? This is a hundred-dollar question . . . but nevertheless, it paved the way for Barack and many other boys to join it!

When Molo Otieno met Albert in 1911 while herding his two cows, *Lando* and *Abika,* nobody knew that a school would be hatched. Albert was an Anglican missionary, who was going places interiorly to expand the relevance of Anglicanism. When he came to Ng'iya, he'd made friends. His trademark flywhisk (given to him by Otieno) earned him a nickname—*Bwana* Orengo ('a man of the flywhisk'). The name 'Albert' was a bit confusing for they weren't an English-speaking community, anyway.

So the locals found it easier to call him '*Bwana* Orengo'.

He had a plan, a grand plan. The Briton, a native of Ireland, found a fertile ground for his plan. Therefore, when he went back to the Diocese of Kisumu—now the Diocese of Kisumu West—where Ng'iya Mixed Primary School falls, he discussed the plan with his superiors and they made a consensus. That year saw *Bwana* Orengo build his tin-house (that he later improved into a block house), with a kitchen, and most notably a bricked-church house—The Ng'iya Anglican Church Mission, so it was named. And St Paul's was its actual filename. Albert started 'preaching the Word' although he found out that people were passive about this; many couldn't read and write. And yet others were too traditional that they couldn't agree with him. Luckily enough, many people were later converted to Christianity. *Bwana* Orengo received the second best friend, apart from Molo Otieno, a Mr Agolla Ong'injo. He was the first convert to be baptized at Ng'iya (by *Bwana* Orengo himself). This signified that Agolla left traditional beliefs for Christianity—something that angered some of the hard-core members of the Luo Council of elders. And the council was a much matured snappy outfit now. And he'd to be summoned several times to drop the religion. He refused. In his defacement of traditional beliefs, he promised the council that he would certainly convince and convert even more people. Evans Agolla Ong'injo worked tirelessly with the provost to start a new alignment of friends. During the baptism of souls, there was Japheth Nandi, father of Professor Tom Odhiambo—the founder of ICIPE at Mbita Point, West Karachuonyo, in Kenya—Manasseh Ogot Nyahaya, Micah Asindi Aloo, Luka Okong'o (the father of Professor Owino), John Aruru Dede, and Eliakim Raten'g Oraa, to name but just a few.

In 1912, the first school, Ng'iya Boys Primary School, was instituted. The pioneer boys to be enrolled were those who had joined the catechist's classes. And their zeal was way too high—to read and write; due to this drive, three grass-thatched ramshackle round houses were constructed for them. They included those mentioned above and those who later joined them: George Robert Obwogo (he became the Bishop of Ng'iya), Ezekiel Apindi (nicknamed

Odondo, the first head teacher of Ng'iya Boys Primary and later ordained a bishop—and a politician came out of him), Eliud Oguna Awindi, Ambrose Ondong', and John Meshack Rambuku. Ambrose became the head teacher when Barack was joining Ng'iya Boys Sector School. He was the one who wrote a recommendation letter to Maseno, urging them to take the boy 'for he is mature and very brilliant'.

The increasing demand for education was insurmountable. When he met young girls craving for education, *Bwana* Orengo invited the visiting British Missionary, Mrs Muller, to Ng'iya. The Briton had a passion for girls, and Ng'iya kept her. Nicknamed 'Abigi'—due to her plump body, the body had a bulging middle, signaling lots of visceral fat—her love for Africans made her the darling of the people. Whoever she came across, or touched in one way or the other, would always talk fondly of her—practically out of love—of her natural physique with a thick yellow fat deep in the abdomen. This is what Luos called Abigi (a synonym of 'big')—Or a slang for 'big bodied figure'. The lady was so friendly that the influx of girls to the mission took center stage and catapulted. How the girls felt comfortable around Mrs Muller and how their lives had been certain was unforgettable—needing to walk the path of success. The number of old women and young girls were damn equal. This made her discuss the matter with her boss. And in the process, two other ladies were brought in order to contain the increasing tally. That was Ms Extand and Esther Lola.

Ms Extand, from Melbourne, Australia, brought great wealth of knowledge from that part of the continent; the villagers nicknamed her *Oiro Andesa*. She was slender, short, with fiery teaching skills. She was known to have a quick footwork. And her chores were hurriedly done, thus the name 'Andesa'. She'd run through a nocturnal schedule. The light of day would just make her start work afresh. She'd made a long list of reforms and leafed full-heartedly through the records. The lady made fundamental reforms. And her association with Lilian Olive Owen—the wife of Walter Owen—brought not only better tidings to the girl and the school but to the entire community. They'd easily put their heads together and made fundamental decisions.

Esther Lola, from the native countryside of London, was a soft-spoken Briton. She would visit homes, criss-cross dangerous streams and rivers, such as Odondo, go to huts doting the Ng'iya Mission Center. Ms Extand and Esther taught adult education and religion to older women in catechism and to those who were preparing to take the seat of deaconess, while the senior Mrs Muller handled girls who'd escape the wrath of their parents—girls against early marriages, and those who'd defy circumcision—as far as from the neighboring Luhya community. There were girls who were forced into early marriages and had refused, girls looking for a better future, girls who'd turn down forced traditional doctrines to embrace Christianity, and another bunch of girls who'd crave for a better sustainable life, better education, and respect in the society. They were taught simple life skills—cleaning and textile. Skills they'd only grabbed, felt, and expressed within a short stint. They'd learned to bathe, to splash water on their scaly faces, and look at the tiny mirror. They'd learnt to straighten their tangled hair. They'd wanted to shake away traditional beliefs and customs. And Mrs Muller would suggest for an additional staff. The workload had grown to pedigree level; thus there was the need for more personnel in a rushed decision. Some of the local hardliners would pent-up their anger against the growing progress. But Mrs Muller wouldn't listen to any of that. She didn't have to. In this manner, the likes of Timothy Omondo from Yimbo were selected. Reuben Oyamo from Nyakach and Daniel Ogille Okolla from Alego Seje later joined to help achieve the dream of Ng'iya Girls Primary School. It's paramount to note that the current Ng'iya Girls School revolutionized from such simple yet deeply thought idea, discussed from a seating of a boardroom meeting in United Kingdom. Resting just a few meters from the church, away from where the current school stands, all the buildings were simple grass-thatched houses. The sub-standard *one* and *two* were actually grass-thatched cubicles while *three* and *four* were tin houses. Some of the buildings still stand out. *Bwana* Orengo's main house was later brought down to pave way for the building of bishop's house, but the kitchen still stands strong, to date. Every morning, as the sun peeped at the kitchen from between dark-colored clouds, *Bwana* Orengo is remembered. The church is still expanding and is opening its outside doors to people of all walks of life. And the church is named St Paul.

Bwana Orengo went ahead to start Nyang'oma Primary School in 1922 on request from Colonial Sub-Chief, Rajula, and the *council of elders* (Many years later, after Onyango had come to Kogelo, he was part of this council. He'd remembered the *council* that planned to dispossess him of his property and then kill him in Karachuonyo. And now he was part of another more civilized council.)

By that time, colonial chiefs were that powerful entity that not only whipped those who caused mayhem within the community but also ditched the traditional beliefs and supported the whiteman's ideas.[11]

In this very later years, in this matrix, were Chief Rajula, a powerful figure, Headman Odera Kang'o (who was later made chief of Gem) and Onyango

Hussein. Though, Onyango wasn't a chief by any chance, all the other chiefs sought his advice. And he'd counseled them appropriately.

In a nutshell, the famous Chief Odera Kang'o of Gem—a close ally of Onyango Hussein—in 1940s brought missionaries and made sure that every young person was going to school; the no-nonsense chief had built a traditional prison where he kept those who defied his orders. Even parents who'd forced their children out of school were purely reprimanded. After all, he was the chief with immense powers. This is why Gem and the areas around it are credited to have produced the best brains in Kenya. It is one of the areas that is highly developed and prides with the best academic excellence in the nation; for instance, the powerful Ang'awa family and the great Magoha's families on the Eastside. One of Magoha's sons, Professor George Magoha, is a renowned academician and the vice-chancellor of University of Nairobi (UoN). The Former Royal Technical College Chancellor has offered platforms for various world leaders, especially the then Senator Barack Obama (2006), the Vice-President Joe Biden, former President Clinton, and Secretary of State of United States of America Hillary Rodham Clinton among others, who'd give powerful speeches. The Gem Academic giants were Isaac Kero, Ombaka, Professor Bethwel Ogot (Chancellor of Moi University), whose wife Grace Ogot was mentored at Ng'iya Girls School, Argwing's Kodhek, who later became the most sought-after shrewd politician. He died in a tragic accident. Most people believed that his tragic death was politically motivated. The Economics giant Donde's family resides here. Other natives at Wagai, just at the junction to Sawagongo leading to Kodiaga and Aluor on the West, are the Jakoyo Midiwo's families (the coalition government's chief whip in the eleventh Parliament), former political bigwigs and rivals, Otieno Ambala and Horace Ongili—the two were once Barack's good friends whom he played with at Ng'iya playing grounds. And the three had a psychic link that connected them to Ng'iya. It is prudent to note that Horace was later assassinated at the epitome of his political achievement in 1985 (three years after Baracks' grisly death), and many of his friends were arrested on suspicion of involvement or that they had a hand in his death. Ambala was gassed in Kodiaga prison after Ongili's fateful death. He was sent to a political oblivion. To date, no one can tell who killed Horace. While Ambala is resting in peace after his remains were retrieved from the infamous prison and buried at his father's land, dust never settled.

At Nyagondo and Ayowa, at the boundary that separates Gem and Alego, are farming communities, with expansive fertile farms. Living here is the Wagwer community—the feeding basket of Gem and Alego.

Still there is Rogo Mandulis' paternal family and Chief Rachier's family to include, and others who we couldn't mention.

From all that analogy, one would basically conclude that this community valued education. Apart from their biological backbone, education became the skeleton of their welfare.

Apart from their biological backbone, education became the skeleton of their welfare.

Nyang'oma Primary

Albert Wright, popularly known as *Bwana* Orengo, the white evangelist, arrived in an entourage of Land Rovers, something new to the native. *He* was such a self-starting individual, an Englishman, who exercised upon ambiguity and change. He managed to serve the people with a timeless strength, a changeless attitude—prejudgment and prejudices aside. He was able to connect with the inhabitants, of course, through a translator-turned freedom fighter whose life was later gone awry, bludgeoned to death by colonial forces. His particular friend, Molo Otieno, and translator, Ogosa Odek, were great fighters; Ogosa was an ex-warrior of the remnant of infamous Luanda Magere troupe. He fought the Lang'o tribe and therefore, in 1920, he met Lawi *wuon* Awilo, a Kamreri police officer in Kisuma under British rule, who helped establish the relationship between Molo, Ogosa, and *Bwana* Orengo, when the latter was initiating Ngi'ya School at the Mission center, before he could come to Nyan'goma Primary. And the people were in dire need of legal aid through the Whiteman's complicated system. Ogosa was an interpreter with a sarcastic speech and spoke with dignity, sympathy, and pity. He was a strict convert to Christianity. He served the colonial government with no reservation. Being a brainchild of Young Kavirondo Association, he later became an accuser of *Ingereza* (colonial rule) with a changeless attitude. He violently questioned the right and morality of exploitative colonialism, but he didn't question the 'superiority' of the civilized European, the 'inferiority' of African, nor the British imperial rule in Africa which was justified by its 'efficiency'. His very violent accusation of colonialism and sympathy on Africans was held by the degradation and suffering of the Africans living in Seme, Alego, Ugenya, Yimbo, and the upper side of Kamagambo. These atrocities made the spread and preaching of gospel almost impossible, particularly the evangelist found it hard to redress the injustices crafted by the colonial government. To convince the Africans, *Bwana* Orengo, Molo, and Miruka Rajula then the Colonial Assistant chief of Alego sat down together with the *council of elders*. Within a few days, a dream was hatched—continuous meetings hatched Nyang'oma

Church—African Church Mission. Miruka Rajula was a colonial chief at the time, manning a large area of Nyan'goma, part of Ng'iya, and the borders of the current Siaya town.

From makeshift ramshackle hut, the community joined hands, in sheer determination, to build muddy classes, looking a bit cautious in this newly found treasure—education—something Europeans didn't offer to the African children. If it wouldn't have been for *Bwana* Orengo, Africans here wouldn't have even smelled it. This became the first school around Kogelo. Closer home.

Days went by, and later, a dream was hatched; a church stood, and a school (Nyang'oma School) was beside it. The current Nyang'oma Primary School became a conglomerate of education for the thirsty band of African youngsters. This is where Barak would later, in 1946, start his Sub-Standard A, for the *third* time. 'The first being Gendia Primary Mission Phase I and Phase II,' Hawa says. Meaning, he started, dropped, and started a second time. With sounds of bugles, drums, and hammers, high pitched, resounding gong, fused with clanging cymbals ranting the air, the children cheered themselves hoarsely and pompously and were merry-making thereafter. The school had started even before Barak was born.

'This year saw a number of school-thirsty children taking an oath to join this path till death do them apart,' an elder asserts. They knew that education would be the sole source of power and freedom.

In the shadows of the building were groups of young women and grandmothers adorned in traditional *regalia*, enrolling their children in the new school. *Bwana* Orengo was one man who'd dealt extensively with juvenile delinquency and vagrancy, what he was partly facing, not an exception. His folks obviously surged to lend a hand after his first-time breakthrough.

And where would be the comparison?

Or what was the school's significance?

Years later, in this very school, Obama would read eloquently in either English or *Swahili* and translate it in the native *Dholuo* after a short stint, far ahead of the rest.

Meanwhile, factors such as diseases and calamities were devastating. Effects of malaria, plague, jiggers, smallpox, and sleeping sickness were rife. White doctors volunteered to help in appropriate measure to attend to any medical call of whatever nature, from rabies to meningitis, malaria to cholera; barefooted-band of African children benefited from proper medication, from the Western science, an exercise well-accomplished under the stewardship of *Bwana* Orengo. This kind of sporadic disease outbreaks prompted the missionaries to initiate the Ng'iya Health Center. It served women profoundly well. They found comfort during delivery, and it made the black inhabitants appreciate the importance of Albert's good missionary work. Today the center still operates, but mismanagement is almost eating up its operations. It's in a sorry state of disrepair. Though, all the operations were accomplished with a landslide success and a ridiculous speed, Kogelo people—being those living interiorly—either walked to this facility or would get a free medical camp at Nyang'oma Mission Church—a semi-house and a small tin-house—what they called the bishop's office. Here things were completely different. Peace prevailed like an undisturbed ocean . . . In some parts of the nation, it was turbulent. Rebels would attack mission centers, attacking and killing missionaries.

And Albert would describe them as 'those who sinned out of ignorance'.

Albert received calls, big calls from high places. And graceful letters started streaming in. Their effects were almost instantaneous—some from authoritarian colonial chiefs criticizing him of running a project 'in this Dark Continent'. They believed that Africans were uncivilized and deserved nothing less than slavery. While some were encouraging messages from unlikely sources. One came from the then district commissioner and others from government authority. This particular call came when teachers and parents were held in a meeting. One aging elder, a Mr Omollo, is categorical about it. He could marvel at how people could easily link up with those at a distance away and still discuss matters so amiably.

'And Albert's phone rang again . . . ,' he says.

The head principal of the school also concurs thus:

> '*Bwana* Orengo walked into the new tin-roof shackle late that afternoon. Arindo Origa, a black Parent Teachers Association (PTA) teacher had received his rare phone call. Phones were most sought-after commodities.'

He said, '*Bwana* Orengo, someone is on the line. He's been calling all morning.' He was reluctant, and then he said, 'OK, Origa, I'll take it.' He went right ahead and picked the telephone. Origa later said that the two gentlemen spoke at length . . .

'Hello, Albert. Congratulations!' He remembers.

The parents kept waiting for the conversation to end, and of course, they could hear them talk and even translate for each other through whispers! (For those who could understand English.) Although, *Bwana* Orengo had learnt Luo perfectly well.

'Thanks. And whom I'm I speaking to? Hello?'

'Hey, is that Albert . . . Albert Wright?' a caller bumped. The authorities were able to reach out for their 'colleagues on the ground'. Origa later said that 'the DC's voice was hazy, deep, and authoritative, symbolizing a highly built monster, tall, and robust.' According to one of the former teachers, the conversations were deemed appropriate because they opened the floodlight of exposure to the rather dimly cultured community.

'Yea, yes . . . I'm Albert Wright,' he answered, 'and who I'm speaking to . . . ?'

'I'm the new DC of Kisumu,' the caller replied. His voice would have been hissing against the blowing wind. 'I've reviewed your project files, and I wanted us to work together in regard to the projects you've initiated in Alego.' The head teacher says, 'That was the genteel behavior of the ruling elite. They sought one another and support was always guaranteed.'

'I had met with Mr Owen, and he briefed me of the plans.'

'Oh yes. Thank you for that recognition. I've been longing to get support from the government but to no avail. Hope it's high time now we realize our dreams together through these initiatives . . .'

Albert and his newly found friend talked for long, discussing a number of issues. Strangely, with unbelief, government's response was timely. And his friend from Ngi'ya, one Mr Owen, made several journeys with *Bwana* Orengo during these activities.

The ground was then broken, 'bituminized' to pave way for Land Rovers, trucks, and other automobiles ferrying in facilitators, including lumping even the Afro-centric lot as expatriates and incorporating exotic amenities for construction.

The recalcitrant *Bwana* Orengo had the determination and believed strongly that this wasn't going to be a Whiteman's' country anymore someday. Initially, every force in him seemed destructive, yet many years later, he longed to build. Within the terrain of the arid thorn-scrub of the savannah land, he longed to drive down to provide better education, that which was so pleasant enough, that which was wildly needed, and there was no cheerful welcome for the return to giving up.

That was the vow of the young children regular in classes, to learn and to be the pearls of this sleepy society. With no character defect to show off—the young lads believed in dignity and faithfulness to the Western ideas to restore a little sense of purpose to their lives, seriously digging into their history, because they had no defense against the shield of vulnerability, without adversity.

'Where the children had no confidence of the world, the school offered the opportunity and put the world of confidence in them,' the head teacher asserts.

The long drive down to provide better education was pleasant enough, but there was no cheerful welcome for the return to giving up.

Being born in this part was, maybe, the greatest setback in secular judgment. Instead, it became their greatest point of strength. From Kamreri to Kasgunga, Nyamsare in Gembe to Sidho, Kondele to Alego Usonga, children went to school from the best to the rest, those who were just being forced, making no mistake to quit. It was all devalued in the making, never to be dispossessed of the newly found deal even at the point where a painful spasm ran down their steely spine or plenty of wax sealing their ears. They plunged into education as duck is to water. And the gamble later struck the right cord. The dividends would later payoff. Barak wasn't left out either.

In later years, things had changed a lot; Ng'iya had grown to an Intermediate School from a Sector status. To be specific, the government elevated it in 1953. And that's where *Bwana* Orengo came from before expanding interiorly to start Nyang'oma Primary School. All the students of Nyang'oma would join Ng'iya for their Intermediate.

In line with this, Chinese premier Lai later predicted this about Kenya 'as a country ripe for revolution, where the gap between rich and poor is about the highest in the world.'

This is how it started; people, especially Kenyans in particular, and Indian technicians working on the railway line, in general, were already seating a stride in a ticking bomb. Besides, the Kedong massacre of 1895 loomed fresh in mind, in which a trade caravan of Scotts and French men clashed with the Maasai and other Kenyans resulting in a huge casualty. Several *Agikuyu* and *Swahili* traders died, and about 100 Maasai Moran slained to death.[12]

As a country ripe for revolution, where the gap between rich and poor is about the highest in the world . . .

Father Albert, the industrious guru, worked tirelessly with the majority inhabitants (if not all), who were already too willing to join the mission. He was there in the fields, grinding corn with them, herding and hunting with his dog and a bunch of locals. He helped those injured by treating their wounds, removed thorns from their flesh, and pulled rotten teeth. He'd re-taped and bandaged the open wounds. Sometimes he'd suck snake poison from a blister, those bitten from African cobra. Every morning, Father Albert would duck into catechism class. He'd taught all ages the Lords' prayer. Convincingly, it sounded unfamiliar. He distributed clothing after the classes and was watchful enough, so no one would go without a cloak. *Bwana* Orengo liked Molo because of his easy way of story-telling. He'd named him *Omollo wuoda* (Omollo, my son). And the two would talk on various issues ranging from land to politics, Christianity to traditional custom. Molo had donated a large piece of land to the missionary and the three—including *Bwana* Orengo's dog, Bibery, otherwise named *Bibi wuod Orengo* (Bibery, son of Orengo), were a formable group. They'd enjoy their free time together. He particularly listened more attentively to the story of a mysterious woman Nyamgodho. Molo would begin:

> Once there was a famous legend called Nyamgodho, the daughter of the great lake . . .

The story would end with great laughter. The tale would trace *Simbi Nyaima*—a saline lake in Karachuonyo. The traditional fictional understanding of its origin almost surpassed its real formation.

Bwana Orengo wasn't left out either; he began his story, the stories of apartheid rule in South Africa (SA), when the white masters prevailed upon the blacks. An elderly man says that *Bwana* Orengo liked to talk about his father and particularly the stories from South Africa. Maybe, he would begin (according to Oketch Ogwari 'bad boy') thus:

> '. . . Or the stories of a wounded Hintsa. The King of the AmaGcaleka of Xhosa was shot dead on command of Harry Smith in 1835. This

is when he realized that his gun had malfunctioned whilst trying to shoot. The poor Hintsa's ornaments were thrown out and then looted by the soldiers who proceeded not only to abuse him but to cut off his body parts as trophies . . . (and apparently his severed bleeding head was taken to England).'[13]

Many stories came about, but this particular one never gathered much laughter. It was painful and portrayed the rot of the white man's misrule against the black subjects; the story that gave them gray hair. Molo couldn't understand why this kind of misrule flourished and why the white man suddenly started acting so badly! Why some nations started to rot from head down!

Bwana Orengo's father, Albert Wright Sr, lived and worked in SA, during the harsh colonial regime, in that poor country that would get their hard-fought independence last in the whole of Africa. She was like a whore of Africa, prevailed by foreign policies until it was too late. Though it was like a blessing in disguise for the gold-rich country. They attained independence at a time when they really needed it. At a time the bells of apartheid of the higher office came jingling, alerting the chiefs to take appropriate action whenever there was a curfew or a state of emergency. And these were some of the stories passed down to his son, Father Albert Wright Jr, nicknamed *Bwana* Orengo. And that passed down to many other generations up to that of Oketch Ogwari—from Pretoria to Alego and from Jo'burg to Nairobi.

Albert Wright—The first provost of Nyang'oma.

He didn't work alone; his closest friend and fellow white man was supporting him all through—his name was W. E. Owen. The inhabitants around Ng'iya talk fondly about archdeacon W. E. Owen. His filename, they say, 'Walter Edwin Owen'. He was a missionary in a great call. His belief in politics and trust in religion was, to him, one solid aspect of life. They're packaged in one aspect. Owen was a politician, economist, and a 'man of the cloth'.

He managed to nurture many Africans, such as Ezekiel Apindi and Okwiri, the latter through the Young Kavirondo Association. Apindi was one of the pioneer boys of Ng'iya School. He later became a teacher and a bishop.

Owen's famous decorum saying 'when you are presented with two evils, choose the lesser evil' was remarkable.

In his preaching, he'd raised the issue of John the Baptist, with a rich, deep voice. Ng'iya Sector School was becoming a doldrum of worship. Maybe, education and worship were intertwined.

'Your weakness is trying to talk you out while our God Almighty wants to birth victory in your heart, in your family, and in your community. You got to believe it before you see it. That is, by faith not by sight. For believers in Christ don't only own the kingdom business but also the process. Remember first that motivation, self, is based on reward and secondly contributors', the faithful, focus on the value addition to that kingdom. That is, what I'm standing for, be it successes, it's going to be mutual.'

Motivation is based on reward and contributors normally focus on value addition

1945, Death of W. E. Owen

Kisumu Park was filled to capacity. It served as the tomb of Walter Edwin Owen—Archdeacon of Kavirondo. Many tycoons around Kisumu town had given out the land to be used as a memorial. The Colonial Government had spent a lot of money and a lot of thought had gone into it. Owen had instructed the church 'to bury his remains at Ng'iya'—in honor of the institution.... But the 'will' was later altered when he died. The requiem mass was undertaken against a large surging crowd in Kisumu—the town remained—the only option, as his last resting place, the place chosen—Kisumu Park. It'd been fenced with ornamental Kei apple and had three entrances with paved sidewalks. The perfect barbed wire (and wrought iron) followed the fencing. To many people today this is no big deal! Especially to, maybe, a teenaged couple arguing on a bench or school children streaming into the park and roaring around a fountain—very few would recognize the epitaph of Owen. A great man is lying peacefully in this park. The scribbles on a concrete statue block, in upper case, and translated in more than three languages—English, Luo, and Luhya—Owen's grave reminds of the struggle of the black man. He was like 'a white blackman,' for he was a white man in a hot pursuit to champion for the black race. As the lives of manicured shrubs surrounds the grave, with encircled bed of beautiful withering flowers, the scribbles reads thus:

In Memory

Walter Edwin Owen
Archdeacon of Kavirondo
Born: 7 June 1878
Died: 18 September 1945
A philanthropist and human activist
He devoted his life fearlessly to the fight
for justice for all and to the care of the sick and needy.[14]

On this very spot, the plaque read Owen was born in the nineteenth century and died in the next century, twentieth century—the lucky man tasted the fruits of two centuries. 'That day the bicycles rode carelessly on the streets of Kisumu town,' an elderly man explains, 'just like at the speed at which the news of Owen's death ripped through people's mind, and what the medical expert had explained on post-mortem that the sixty-seven-year-old succumbed to tropical cerebral malaria, leaving behind a distraught widow Lilian Olive Owen.' The elderly man would ask, 'Why the dreaded disease claimed the life of Owen?' Or as the firemen retrieved the remains from a gutted property, when they'd arrived too late to rescue a thing when incendiary small bombs (made by schoolboys) created an inferno that almost totally destroyed the city in the course of one night—the white man had run his race. And not only won his own fight but for others as well, the people who'd shaped the lives of others without a penny to claim, who had shaped the life of Barack, the life of late Jaramogi Oginga Odinga, Apindi, Evans, Ooko, among others, and hoards of other prominent personalities in the volatile Kenyan society. Because his presence here, and not somewhere else, was hard to miss, he'd enjoyed the breakthrough he'd left behind. He worked in languid summer and cold winter that the Western corridor of the country would gaze back and see the transformation that came through the hands of a harmless evangelist.

Molo's grandson, William Ogwari Mor, an oral history thespian nicknamed 'bad boy' by the girls at Ng'iya Girls School, where he works, says that his grandfather told him of his friendship with *Bwana* Orengo. That 'he was indeed a friend, an irreplaceable friend, and he'll only meet again in "heaven".' William confuses everything in English—I receive the impression he did the same in *Swahili*, but he explains his burning story in *Luo*. A language he understands best.

'The two never parted ways,' he says. 'They'd spent time together, eating wild berries—And the white man would adopt a series of African ways.'

Mor says that they used to play football at Ng'iya with Barack. 'His eyes said what his mind had decided, well when on the ball, he'd bounced the ball twice or thrice.' Barack was remembered for his ability to drive the penalty kick into the back of the net. 'He was a known football legend at Ng'iya and a great dancer in the traditional costume. He could challenge the best goalkeepers, and his prowess was overly visible; he provided a more earthy and brilliant display. He was the antidote of those famous cunning goalkeepers—wizard goalkeepers—those who've never conceded a single goal in the season. He exploited all chances to score, however difficult the play seemed to be. And the teeming fans would sing heroic songs; as we dethroned the legacy of the best teams, we'll shut them out of the competition.' Mor chats quite affably for about three hours about this man.

'Even at Maseno, the man was given a jersey, and he'd played against tough teams—Homa Bay Secondary School, Mbita, St Mary's, Ambira—"the rough as usual teams". His strong presence in the team was detectable; surprisingly he would go for both the legs as well as the ball,' says the joyous Mor.

One day, Sara confronted Beckton before the sermon, explaining her family's fate and expressing her desire to receive the grace from this new '*God*'. This was the theme of her approach to the clergy. Of course, Barack was largely present, next to his stepmother, full in youthhood.

'Beckton . . . ,' she paused for a moment, without mincing her words.

In her own words, Sara is more dramatic about the description. The approach was kind of humiliating due to the fact that she was a Muslim.

'My name is Sara Anyango Onyango, daughter of Ogwel of Karachuonyo,' she said, with ritual and symbolism, teachings, and faith of this new religion being a balm to her wretched and wounded soul. The name Beckton was super easier to pronounce unlike *Bwana* Orengo, whose real name, the natives of his time, found rather amusing. No difference anyway! '. . . And this is one of my children, Barak Obama. Children are my future, Father Beckton, and the future must be protected,' she joked.

At this point, the tension grew large, from troubled to terrified. Sara was a strong woman though. Indeed, she was up-to-date. None of them knew what Beckton would answer. Or the foggiest idea whether he would respond because his Luo understanding was very raw, emotionally yes, but mentally not certain. They listened with a hand break on for response, Molo helping in translation. Provost Beckton finally had something to tell them. He found himself wanting to talk, to say anything and everything . . . 'I am happy to hear from you. It's a pleasurable moment to receive innocent souls on behalf of the Lord. For tonight, I tell you, the angels in heaven will rejoice,' he said, with a heavy blend of English and Luo languages. 'A language is a dialect with an army and navy, so they say . . .'

Sara wasn't perturbed for Beckton was growing older . . . and most of missionary work was carried out by his successor, Evans Agolla. For once, leadership was crawling into a black man's hands.

Agolla and Beckton became the clergymen after Albert's retirement.

'Let's pray . . . ,' he commanded. Sara says, 'Barack wasn't happy.'

'Prayer? Now what are all these? What've I put myself into?' Obama wondered.

This was Beckton's prayer to all who brought their children to join Nyang'oma Mission School. He just read it out, taking no chances to recite: 'God is going to restore all that the evil one has sealed. He's going to shake off your disappointment before the end of the day. I confess that his love endures forever. I declare victory upon victory for your many children, in all difficult situations and good as well. Our creator will open floodgates tonight upon your household; your oneness shall be an integrated wholeness. This is my encouragement. Receive him, today, for future victory. Perfection is all yours. The great providence of completeness through his supernatural grace shall be upon your generation today and the generation to come. Your house will be a house of prayer. Maybe your forefathers feasted on dinosaurs and strange things, thrived or survived or flourished on fetishes, magic, and charms, but Jesus Christ washed away all this at the cross. His blood was that powerful. First, be free from your mind before you relieve yourself from the bondage of physical religion and gods of the shrines. There is blessing in one's name and victory on another; yet anointing on another and favor and strength on the one regarded as the least. Your name shall be in the scorecard of great minds of this world. World leaders and leaders of the world shall agree whenever your name is mentioned.'

Beckton

The prayer is hanged on a yellowing frame at the school's administration office.

Beckton was a prayerful man, and his prayers gathered masses . . . most of his predictions were damn right. Some people felt he was a prophet. Maybe, he was one!

And when Sara Onyango caught up with him at Nyang'oma . . . when she took Barak for admission, he looked kind. And there was Hunter helping with the translation and prayer. Hunter's action was questionable. They didn't know much about these people.

And people wondered why. Why was he so concerned about the people's problems and misfortunes, more than the people themselves? And why didn't he pray for himself and forget about other people's lives?

Your house will be a house of prayer.

Sara sighed. Things had come over the wires. Now, there was something being brokered in her heart.

'It's never too late,' she believed.

The church preached it openly—plain and square—it caused more confusion than that which education could cause. 'Does *Jarachar,* white man, have a clue that his idea of religion and *God* isn't necessarily our idea of "God" and religion? Does he have understanding?' Obama later said. He believed he'd a religion but no education. So he was in speed to achieve education rather than religion.

Your name shall be in the scorecard of great minds of this world. World leaders and leaders of the world shall agree whenever your name is mentioned. He got to his feet from kneeling.

'*Minwa*, Mother, let's go back to the village,' Barak confided ignoring the *mzungu*, white man.

'I'm not going to let him frighten us with his God,' he thought defiantly. This didn't mean that he was a religious rebel. And neither was he a religious threat. He spoke right with his knowledge, in the best moral tune and in the pedestal of faith. Just in line with what Jesus himself would have wanted him to say!

She was frightened too. It seemed like discussing the matter with the abandon.

'Let's give him more time, Son. You've got to listen to other peoples' opinion,' Sara commanded him, exasperated. In a change of tone, she said, 'We aren't going to leave even a hoof. Each of us, tonight, shall dine with the Lord through baptism of souls.'

Nyang'oma . . . 'And, you young man, Barak Obama . . .' Beckton could not pronounce the names pretty well. 'Your life from now henceforth will never be the same; you shall live your responsibility. You're going to face challenges with a will and intent to succeed, in a show and demonstration of a relentless sense of purpose. If you don't know where you're going, then, any destination will do.'

And Hunter was full of quotes. This actually distinguished him from Beckton. *He that loves the holy book will never want a faithful friend, a wholesome counselor, a cheerful companion, an effectual comforter: by study, by reading, and by thinking, one may innocently divert and pleasantly entertain himself, as in all fortunes.*

Research points to this from a poet and great author Isaac Barrow. Therefore, *Grand thinking started in smallness*—he advised.

'In the diary of Hunter at Ng'iya, his comments would drive you to reading history even though you might not be in the fun,' Mor asserts.

Sara says that one morning Agolla would call Barak Obama from where they were chatting with his friends—in the church building; he'd been keenly observing them share their dreams and aspirations. He looked determined to pass a critical judgment. 'Look here, young man,' he said, while he drew closer, 'a new plan can surface.'

Sara believes that the missionary had identified something that she can't exactly pinpoint but something very unique according to him. 'I know you got no proper roof over your head as you retire home every sunset, sleeping every day on the naked moist ground, which you share with goats while doing homework. And I pretty know well that several brothers and sisters are always on top of you. Barak, you use moonlight as the only source of light for your revision. You need a home as much as you need lessons. Work hard. You hear me? Work harder to change your destiny.' Maybe Sara thought that he was driven by the pressing need to get hold of pupils' unique destiny. Then it was a timely responsibility to groom the future leaders through true reflection and a firm dedication.

This statement was a clear indication of acute inadequacy of essential facilities; it was delivered with a concerned voice and laced with stabbing connotation. It wasn't a botched delivery.

They plunged into education as duck is to water

The Life after *Bwana* Orengo and Owen

It saw the institution of Ngi'ya Teachers Training College in 1953. The pioneer boys were Shem Odhiambo Mbago and John Okumba—Barack's classmates. They'd sat the same exams at Ng'iya. But Barack proceeded to Maseno Mission School. Maybe they'd like to be teachers—for most people prided themselves as teachers despite the fact that it was one of the professions with the most meager pay on the land . . . but service to the community was equally important and brought better tidings (such as job satisfaction).

The head principal had been endorsed by the missionaries—Arthur Mayor—He became the first principal of the TTC. Although, due to expansion of the facility, especially the girls' school, the college was later moved to Siriba to pave way for a girls' institution, the current Ng'iya Girls School.

The famous *agenge* football pitch still existed. This (agenge) meant it was rocky and rugged. Barack was one of the pioneer boys in this pitch. The boys would just play barefooted in here.

CHAPTER 6

Nobody in the world can take the place of persistence. Persistence and determination are supreme.

The *now* moment was looming large though not over yet. People were in rout, persistent to achieve the unknown. The church became the source of inspiration. Christians here didn't want to stay small; they wanted to grow, to increase spiritually, in this instance, like descendants of Abraham leaving the misery of Egypt for milk and honey of Canaan. And education wasn't left behind, either. It was the time for examination. And the Competitive Entrance Examination was around the corner.

Obama already prepared for the Competitive Common Entrance Examination in the rapidly growing school and was doing marvelously well. With this good performance, the anticipation was over. Most school-going pupils would have wished to do their best to join the much-coveted Maseno Mission School or St Mary's Yala, Alliance School or the few Indian-run schools within the bartering Kisuma (Kisumu) town. These schools only chose the best. Therefore, others opted for Kanyakwar or Ambira and other smaller upcoming schools before maneuvering to get a chance in Maseno or St Mary's Yala. In this case, Kanyakwar wasn't a small school, after all. But was black dominated. The colonial chiefs and the missionaries therefore initiated other school projects to reduce the upsurge of admission. In this era, a few schools existed; a number of them like Sawagongo, Ambira, and St Mary's Yala Township later came into being. In the south were Homa Bay, Mbita, and Kisii schools.

The mood at Nyang'oma School, then, was just a competitive one. Competitive Entrance Examination that year wasn't an easy one, but Beckton and

Hunter and the then two PTA male teachers running the new Nyang'oma Primary courtesy of the African Anglican Church Mission, insisted on good performance and that was what they were up to. The teachers were Olali Opany and Arondo Origa. The two assisted Beckton and Hunter in the logistics of school administration. The attendance included Barak. And the Competitive Entrance was supplied. This particular village school was later integrated to include Intermediate classes in 1960. Its first head teacher was Ooko D. Oundo, a former classmate of Barack at Ngi'ya. Through him, hope came to a bunch of pupils who couldn't overcome the hardship of braving chilly cold to Ng'iya on daily walk—for instance, the blind, lame, and those who'd become too lazy. Barak held his hands closed because he wanted and was looking forward to a stunning performance. His thinking?

'I've to pass these papers. This is my life . . . I've to place my rather tiny face on the world map. Though not easy, but I've to. Promise? Promise,' he assured the environment around him.

The examination consisted of a written test that tested the ability to write, understanding, visualizing, and interpretation of facts. That was a challenge to many students. Of course, all papers were tough. The other segment of the examination was the oral one. The oral examination tested the ability of the student to speak foreign languages—English and Swahili—flawlessly. Sara convincingly says that this was Barak's favorite. 'He could speak eloquently, exploring facts and discussing issues very comfortably and he was the class favourite.' Many students in other schools, Arabs, Muslims, Whites, failed it alike. Some whites could speak with ease, so well, but they lacked the knack to discuss various fundamentals.

The purpose of this examination was to enable students to compete for few places available for Standard Six. What Barak described 'as a world map!' The wait for results then started . . .

'I've to place my rather tiny face on the world map; though not easy, but I've to.'

For indeed they were few.

Sara could still recall some of their conversations with Barack during the heydays at Nyang'oma Primary.

'How were your exams?' Sara asked.

'Very well, Mama.'

'But why aren't you happy?'

'I'm fine, Mama.'

Hawa says that Barack wasn't happy. And he'd started hiding his frustration too early in life, maybe due to lack of better means that seemed impossible to come by.

'Forget about Hawa. Is there . . . anything wrong?'

'Not exactly.'

'And why are you looking pensive, Son?'

'Mama.'

'Yes, Son.'

'If I passed that examination, what next?'

'Is that what's causing all this worries, huh?'

'I mean, no . . . yes, that's what is causing all this. I don't know what to do next. I would have wanted to continue with studies. I've seen your courage to take me through all these. We've struggled a lot, Mama, and I want you to rest. Maybe, I'll get some job.'

In short, Sara couldn't believe him. How? Why is he all of a sudden shortsighted? And downtrodden? His road to success or to self-recovery had just begun?

As years went by, Barak was done with Nyang'oma and the results were impressive . . . Sara had traveled many miles to look for any intermediate school for him; his extreme thirst to join Standard Six, the current Standard Four, couldn't let him rest. Her determination was fiery and hot in the heels due to competition from life's hardships. Schools weren't there, and if there was one, then it was miles away with very few Africans in attendance. They were mainly white dominated, while others such as MM Shah Intermediate (primary) was Indian dominated. There was Aga Khan for Muslims or Highways for Arabs and strict Muslims. She went as far as Kanyakwar and even to the far west Asumbi School, miles away from Alego. She passed through Ndere to Bondo, on the other side of the land, traveling day and night, relentlessly, in search of a school. She seemed to be the only mother from the entire village of Kogelo struggling with education matters, seeking for a school with sincerity, which some might have admired but which African purists would have found alarming.

'Now where will I get a school for my son?' She asked herself. 'I think I need to consult Hunter or Beckton. They can surely help!'

Sara trekked back to her husband's village after the fruitless long journey from Yimbo, where she failed to get a chance at Usenge Sector School, due to the long distance and also because there was no close relative around the school to stay with Barak. Some of her relatives in Yimbo were still in a big slumber; they'd never understood or valued education, but not all.

Beckton and Hunter came very early one morning. There were teachers too: Ordained Bishop, Ezekiel Apindi, Teachers, Evans Agolla, Eliud Oguna, and Ambrose, and Ondong, a much junior teacher. The Christian gathering was enormous. It was a warm morning indeed. During harvest season, people were particularly happy. The granaries were bursting with bounty harvest. The gospel according to John was particularly favorable for that season in time: the season of harvest, the fishers of men.

With them were the fellow missionaries, Mrs Muller and Esther Lola; they were also at the helm of Ng'iya, at the time, the principal assistants of Ng'iya Mission.

Nyang'oma School falls under Ng'iya (so is Hono Primary and Usingo Primary schools). The two doubled as teachers, clergy, and reverends. Ng'iya had grown relatively fast. It had both the preliminary classes and the sector school. The majority in the sector class were mainly boys. Most girls were married too early, but a few managed to join Ng'iya Girls Preparatory School. Of course, their world was changing slower than that of boys, and something was to be done about it. The parents wouldn't know the romantic side of their girls' lives, so you'd find a twelve-year-old girl already married off to a much older man in his fifties or sixties, or to one with grandchildren and their dreams would have been shattered. Again, most parents never had a clue that girl child's education was as necessary as the boy child. Anyway, the world was still changing. The eternity still farfetched!

This was briefly after the common entrance examination. He'd come to celebrate the appointment of the first head teacher of Nyang'oma, Absalom Obewa. The new officer (Obewa) had been under training in Ng'iya as a community teacher and mobilizer. He would assist *Bwana* Orengo to coordinate the work in this particular institution.

According to the locals' description, Beckton and Hunter wore similar dresses: a green jacket, a pair of faded blue jeans, and a light yellow shirt with a darker blue silk tie that matched the trousers. The jacket had leather patch elbows. In his foot were polished, custom-made shoes just like a Texan ranger or some actor in Robin Hood American movies. But here was a man with good intent—fishers of men. He longed to convert everyone to Christianity, something Barak found so funny.

Beckton was in charge of the mission and his assistant, Hunter, made sure that nothing was going wrong, a role he played so well. Later, when Beckton left, he took the helm as his successor.

In their numbers, they were preachers and that was what it meant to be called a missionary. Beckton would preach.

'Yes . . . ,' he said, in earnest, to speak about the subject of baptism and its significance, radiating stillness and dynamic movement, John the Baptist being the man behind the success story. He mentioned the burden of apostleship, the great prophets, the Shepherd, and the sheep. And he also spoke about the woman of Samaria. This story particularly was Sara's favorite; she always had it in her heart, the burden to serve and to serve in great combination notable with the woman of Samaria.

He quoted the words of prophet Isaiah:

> A voice of one calling in the desert: 'Prepare the way for the Lord; make straight in the highway for our God. Every valley shall be raised up, every mountain and hill made low; the rough ground shall become level, the rugged places a plain. And the glory of the Lord will be revealed, and all mankind together will see it. For the mouth of the Lord has spoken.' (Isa. 40: 3-5; NIV)

And he came to spread the gospel in Nyan'goma—something that became a habit, especially after realizing that there was influx of students to Ng'iya from the area. Something he had to propagate by the mere fact that he was a missionary.

Some locals were new converts, especially women in brightly colored *lessos*, those 'receiving Christ' for the first time and those who succumbed to sorrow and broke down at the dismay of many.

> *God, in my darkest hour, in illusion and pain, in my sorrows and tribulations, in my anguish and mistakes, I will indeed forever humbly rejoice in success.*

Sara says that people prayed hard. And hardships made them pray even harder.

In constant motion, as if agitated, shaking hard—that was their prayer—short and to the point. They poured their heart out. In that spiritual enthusiasm and confusion, some women actually attested to their unbounded distress amidst growing burden of raising children alone, husbandless. No joke. Could it be that her husband Onyango Hussein succumbed to that wide expansive cruel sea that had swallowed millions of Africans? Onyango had made friends with many Arab merchants and Muslim traders. His name being Hussein and strictly a Muslim convert made him go to long marginal lengths with the foreigners. He was conscripted to the colonial battalion and sent to Burma. On transit to different destinations of engagement, she couldn't neglect that question, pondering deeply comparing one fate with another. Horrible! Or could he be a victim of those selfish chiefs who hunted down humans, herding them, selling them off in exchange for filthy *luxury*? History was on the move. The doors of no return donned on her, and the children followed suit. And armed with this, she dismissed religion slavery; she moved to serve the living God by neglecting the ways of *Chik*, symbolizing her last exit. What a good idea! The new religion was straight in its doctrines unlike the other religion that showed conflicting reasoning, horrible in its description than the other, that means it was either manipulated, muted, or suppressed, having ulterior motives. Under the umbrella of all that memory, now, in sparkling bright white robes, Beckton and Hunter conducted the most awaited baptism for the entire converts. It was a big celebration; people celebrated their hearts out, shouts of praise, shouts of joy, ululating throughout the whole night till daybreak. They wore white robes and handkerchiefs on their heads. All received baptism in the name of the Father, the Son, and the Holy Spirit. The provost would have talked hard and striked a reason for everyone to emulate the doctrine of Saint Francis of Assisi.

A victim of those selfish chiefs, who hunted down humans, herding them and selling them off in exchange for filthy lucre?

Life in Ng'iya in 1947

When Evans Agolla Ong'injo was ordained the bishop of Ng'iya Mission, the new head teacher was chosen. Ambrose Ondong' was his name. He was the one to mold the destiny of the school—handwork notwithstanding. With lines on his face or not, to kill the school would just be another shocking blunder. Whether frozen under a layer of ice or not, Ambrose had to fit the big shoes left behind. Maybe he'd called Owen, his mentor, and left word for Hunter that he'd not be there to see his failure. That wasn't going to happen: the names and the figures by those names were no more. The Alego villager, with one unique scratchy voice—from a shadowy murky image (a symbolism of civilization), was a vague outline of a man who'd shape the life of Barack. His highly built body was spectacular.

The Ng'iya Boys Primary School motto: *Better your best* was a simple line that drove adrenaline down the horny nails. And under the exotic eucalyptus and cypress canopy, Western taste was piercing through the African darkness.

Barak finally landed in an expanded class—the Sector Class at Ng'iya Boys Primary School—for the first time, barefooted. The Standard Five class had seven boys in total. And Barack, Zadock Otieno, Dishon Ooko Oundo, and four other boys (whom we can't trace) made up the class. Zadock has since died. While the short, sturdy, brown-complexioned former staunch educationists, Ooko Oundo, is now living a quiet life at Ng'iya. He asserts that 'we were just a handful of boys. Barack became my friend, and in most cases, we shared lunch together.' He says that 'our lives were conscripted'. Shoes didn't matter anyway. With shoe or without any footwear, village boys on one side and girls on the other side, across the footpath, found themselves learning. What the white man brought to us is amazing. And I'm so delighted to be part of this groundbreaking history, especially installing Barack, the President of United States of America, 'as one of our sons, doing amazing things out there, and especially on behalf of my best friend, the late Barack Sr.'

Since the time he retired from active employment (about ten years ago), the man has never stepped outside his compound—he concentrates most of the time in his tiny, rather modest dusty library—keeping records. The soft speaking old man—one can't actually tell his age from the looks. He looks quite young. He displays the successes of his sweat. This is the man to tell you about Barack.

From Sub-Standard A, B ... onwards, uniforms were allowed, a khaki shirt and blue shorts, for those who could afford. And others who couldn't afford, Beckton didn't chase them away. Nyang'oma School was just a stone throw away. It rested on the land donated by Onyango himself and Rajula's family. But Ng'iya was far away. A distance that they managed by carrying some roasted potatoes or corn. Sometimes *ugali* would do! Whenever they got exhausted, they'd eat the food amidst the bad weather... rainy seasons was the worst—the paths became muddy and impassable.

When he was enrolled, he'd made friends, and a few are surviving to date. There was the late Zadock Otieno. That particular class saw him make one lifetime friend, Ooko Oundo. The short sturdy brown man became his long-time ally, one of the elders who until recently prayed for the President of United States Barack Obama Jr when he visited Nyang'oma Village.

In Ng'iya the overall head principal was Hunter; he'd taken the helm from Beckton who'd since left for London, for he'd fought a good fight. Hunter liked Barak so much because of his fast pace in understanding, both in school and in the service within the school. His English was so perfect, way ahead of the rest. Mastery in memorizing and comfortable recitation of the Nicene Creed was a necessity to any student whether Muslim or atheist, traditional or civilized. It was a necessity.

We believe in one God,

The Father ...

The recitation continued. The 'congregation' looking rather amused, prayed without ceasing. Some had their eyes closed, others standing, others kneeling... yet others confused and had nothing to say, just gazing at the new roof or some unknown. Their voices could be heard clearer at this point ... in a single mellow voice:

> *Who proceeds from the Father ...*
> *With the Father and ...*
> *He has spoken through the prophets ...*

Amen . . . [15]

According to an old resident, Reverend Owen would repeat ÅMEN and the crowd found themselves responding even louder and harder.

'Amen'

'Ameeen'

'Hallelujah'

'Hallelujah . . . eh . . . Amen'—some confusion here and there. They would close with a bigger thunderous Amen . . . confirming how the verses were dear. And they'd break into a song.

The Rock of Ages Cleft for me . . .
Let me hide behind the—

This was a popular song already translated into a native language Luo. 'The mellow tone at St Pauls' Anglican Church could still be heard—something that has become a permanent feature' the larger-than-life clergy retorts.

Nicene Creed wasn't only meant to be recited, not to punish them, but also to prevent them from falling into 'sin' and protect their faith in a rollback plan. Sara was as successful as she was unfortunate—something that was far in too many hearts, for far too long—now the radical of faith became clearer, tangible to the eye, being a good cheerleader, never giving up even when the doors of V I C T O R Y were closed, and inherent victory hardly banging the doors of giving up. Apart from the Holy Nicene Creed passed down to the students of Ng'iya and Barak being part of the folk, conversely for learning purposes, Hunter offered a chit of paper to Barak and what did it contain? He called it 'the *will*'. Taking no great exception: *Always remember that all the freckle forces that play upon you buffet your life!* Life in Ng'iya was one interesting sort of campsite. It was as hard as its distance from Kogelo.

Barak found himself at the top of the class, competing with Arabs, Whites, and Muslims alike from other schools in various common tests for that coveted number one or for the best student from the region—Nyanza region. Father Hunter was largely present, helping the pupils realize their dreams. School life became so appealing that he forgot the allures of colonial discrimination. The purpose of excelling became the doldrums of life and the opium of beating all odds, gunning for excellence.

One day he returned to his mother's hut happier . . . smiling helplessly. From a distance, almost at the Nyang'oma School periphery, Sara would see him through a tiny hole.

'What is it? Barak seems so jovial,' she asked herself. 'There must be something. Let me wait!'

Within a short time, he was closer to the tiny hut, bending to get through the door.

'Mama, are you there?'

'Yes, Son, why are you late today?'

'The school is fine. Lots of friends . . .'

With that assurance, she knew quite frankly that he'd hit the right chord with studies. He'd already been assimilated.

'I know that, I'm proud of you. See, you're one of the boys from the entire village who has taken studies seriously.'

'I know most of them don't want to study. They keep on laughing at me, whenever we meet, saying I'm aping the white man.'

'Don't listen to such opinions, Son. They'll poison your mind. You know?'

'Yeah, I do know.'

He explained the origin of his happiness; how he's happy that he has struck the right chord with education . . .

This was quite motivating for a young lad who has been performing extremely well at school and was hoping to receive a letter of admission to a prestigious Maseno, Alliance, or any other Mission High school in Kenya. Ng'iya life and the sector studies were over. The long trek from Ng'iya to Nyang'oma in the morning, and back, wasn't an easy task. Everybody knew pretty well that it was indeed an uphill task.

A few boys at Ng'iya Sector School couldn't afford uniform and would put on a blanket instead, in the name of uniform—old and tattered, dirty, and smelling sour milk. They wrapped the garment around their shoulders and then extended a knot at the waist. The white man had distributed the blankets. Other parents would send their boys to Ng'iya on oversized cut trousers reduced to knee size. Ooko Oundo says that 'Ng'iya opened an opportunity that he couldn't imagine was possible.' The boys would put on the baggy trousers—the waist way too large—and would tie it to hold using a piece of string. They looked cowardly on those attires. Behind this mask, were gentle, broadminded, dedicated, and thirsty souls, who believed fervently in the benefit that comes with education—men unselfishly devoted to good cause.

In 1949, Barak sat for the Kenya African Preliminary Examination (KAPE) at Ng'iya Sector School. All the graduates were warming for a place in Form III. Maybe boarding school now will do. Barak was prepared to join Maseno High School. The KAPE was over and the best had plenty of opportunities to continue with education. Ng'iya was in a romp as the results trickled in . . . the losers and the successful lot. Though with his grades, he'd opted for Alliance School or any other prestigious school of his choice as others thought of going to Maranda Mission School, he set his soul in Maseno. There could be a better school then, but he only knew of Maseno. And like other village boys, a lot of preparation wasn't necessary. They didn't know what to purchase in the first place. Only the prerequisites held in a letter wrapped in a manila envelope. At the time Principal Ambrose was as influential as his position in the Diocese of Kisumu. And when he was writing a joint recommendation for his students, he knew that they shall be true leaders of this country and beyond.

> To the Diocese of Kisumu,
>
> Re: This Year's Intake
>
> I am writing in regard to the above subject. I have twelve students at Ng'iya Mission School who need to proceed to the next class at the end of this year.
>
> Kindly work on appropriate plan of placement.
>
> Yours faithfully,
> Principal
> Ambrose Ondong'

'In December 1949, twelve students of Ng'iya Mission School got their results,' Oundo recalls. 'We got our letters of placement—or rather the admission letters. It was celebration time.'

Sara says, 'Barack's letter came in handy. I found out that things were running too smoothly, and I wondered why.'

The letter read thus:

> Maseno Mission School,
> Private bag,
> Kisumu Diocese.
>
> To Barak Obama,
>
> We are delighted to inform you that you are one of the few selected to join Maseno School this year. You are welcome to School. It is indeed one of the Christian-based schools in this area. Remember to report on the specified date that shall be communicated to you through your former school. The uniform would be provided at the school. Also, accommodation guaranteed. The fee quoted is minimal, and we believe you can clear it with minimal pain. The school would take care of other expenses except a refundable caution money, traveling expenses, and some pocket money for personal use. We're looking forward for your arrival. Stay focused on your books when you come and always remember your kith and kin back at home.
>
> Principal A.W Mayor
> Maseno Mission School.

That was the letter to Barak at the start of 1950. And he challenged himself to do as required. That was the reason for his happiness and huge smile. Concerning the school fees, he would supplement it by working in the school library or in the school farm during the holidays, so there was no reason to worry, the letter indicated. In a few days' time, they were to set everything ready for Maseno.

Chapter 7

My father was a foreign student, born and raised in a small village in Kenya. He grew up herding goats, went to school in a tin-roof shack. His father, my grandfather, was a cook, a domestic servant to the British.
(President Barack Obama)

In 1950s

At this time, Sara was expected to be pregnant with a child, that never was, and it gathered some fiery criticism.

In Luo custom, one is expected to sire after every three years or less. So in six years, she was supposed to have been far ahead of the pack.

And her case was therefore under scrutiny. She says people started complaining 'Why I'm not playing my role as a woman?'

And before long at the first daybreak of 1950, a lot of happenings came to the fore. One, Onyango and many other anti-colonial critics were released from prison after the intervention by political activists—Oginga Odinga, James Gichuru, Ronald Ngala, Tom Mboya, and many others... After this landmark release, he went straight to Kogelo to see his wife Sara, although, with serious injuries, he meant to count the losses at his 'door'step. The 'door' here was just a rugged wooden structure wrapped with wild papyrus reeds that closed the entry space. The city's atmosphere was just too much to bear.

After this landmark release, he went straight to Kogelo to see his wife Sara, although, with serious injuries, he meant to count the losses at his 'door'step.

The first child Omar, in Sara's hard-fought fold, finally was growing real fast about six-years-old; to be precise, a bouncing boy who was mature enough to look after the goats! Happiness filled the tiny hut. And neighbors would troop in to greet Sara and to see her and the six-year-old baby. The boy had a very strong resemblance to Omar—Sara's stepfather, an ally of Onyango. 'Of course, for men out there, at some point, your father-in-law becomes your close friend, in any case something goes wrong in your marriage, you may definitely find a soft landing—in solving the dispute or in ironing out the differences or a misunderstanding,' Sara advised. Onyango agreed with the name Omar—Omar Onyango Hussein. Calm stripped him asunder . . . a son was far good enough. And he could brave the physical pain to look for raw milk for his son. That was life. No hospital, no medical care, but a definite traditional care, using herbs, in case of an ailment. Then life continued.

Another group that was overwhelmed with joy was Barak and Nyaoke. The two couldn't hide their joy . . . 'Another one of our own,' they said to the neighbors. Barack was about to report to Maseno. Nyaoke's education had been dwindling by then. Hawa hadn't started and wasn't about to. She was either in Kosele or back to Kogelo to visit. But her love for Omar was undisputed. Already Barack was ahead of Nyaoke in class despite the fact that she was the eldest. Omar had a lovely disposition and really wouldn't even hurt a fly. Sara Nyaoke kept by his side all day and all night, soothing him with sweet lullaby, every time the mother went out to the market or fetch firewood or when working in the family *shamba*—farm. She assumed the role of the mother. And Hawa was crawling all over there to help her sister with simple chores like fetching firewood or water; the role of babysitting forced Nyaoke out of Nyang'oma School.

Sara Onyango and Barak had been busy the whole night preparing for the following day's journey—the journey that would take them to Maseno School.

He filled his metal box with a few belongings that obviously included few plastic utensils, a blanket, a spare khaki short, and an unironed T-shirt. 'The school shall provide the tailor-made uniform'—the admission letter had promised. He put his documents safely in a waste paperbag. They included the admission letter, the recommendation letter, the handwritten letter bearing his date of birth, the name of the parents, and the location of his origin.

'I think we'll be leaving in the morning, at first cockcrow so that we reach Maseno in time,' Sara suggested solicitously.

'No, Mother. That would be too early.'

'Why? I think that's the time your father starts his journeys.'

'See, that's he. At around *two o'clock* in the morning, wild foxes are still roving, and we might be devoured, Mother!'

Those days, traveling wasn't good either, and one was likely to tumble accidentally on hostile pack of wild animals, both during the day and at night. The savannah land was wild and untamed. Kogelo was still a jungle land with dangerous snakes and other wild animals wandering at will—crepuscular—and it was a remote land without proper roads; there was no power or cell phones, a world isolated—but the exploitative world was definitely coming to them—a world anxiously coming on a tidal wave of demand for a faster, affordable means of transport, other than walking.

This argument continued until they settled for 4 a.m. The agreement reached in stillness and no lament. They were held responsible for this history, and they would one day tell their grandchildren, the genesis of such epic journeys, for their life was atomized. That morning they will trek to Maseno, about forty miles away from Kogelo. Determination wouldn't allow them to relent. The two, showing electrified energy. Barack went to his *simba* to have a nap. The *simba* was built a few meters from Onyango's *duol* (hut). For those who have been in Kogelo, it's the improved building on the right of the main house. The routine of the day had sapped his strength, and he was looking for a deserved rest.

Shortly before dawn, the actual time for starting long journeys, the cockcrow was deafening—used as time indicator . . . the third crow made him wake up, earlier than he thought and the first one to suggest early departure! He staggered, in the middle of the night, out of his hut and made his way to his father's hut. Anxiety wouldn't let him catch more sleep.

'Open your eyes, Mother. It's time. Let's start for Maseno early enough, as you said'

'Barak, I'm already awake.'

They were finally up. It was still very dark; Barak had hurriedly gone to the neighborhood to awake his cousin Joseph who was also joining Maseno. Within a short while, they packed, started walking, sure-footed—only those in savannah land could dare that chance, that coarse terrain on barefoot. The dewy grass slapped against their swiftly moving legs, their shadows dangling in the moonlight. Hyenas seemed scared, a little, from the disturbance of their whispers and the commotion of their shadows. The pack of animals, a *mzungu* would have drove into a game park and gave them care there, other than ten African women in dire need of medicare. They crossed river Yala. Traditional bridges that people used were too delicate and most frequently washed away by the torrent swelling rivers. To find one intact was a chance event. Most women were up by 4 a.m., fetching water before it was muddied upstream by massive human activity—revealing how people were losing their heritage to modern invasion, in a rush to chop the forest. Water was scooped from grassy streams and drunk pure from the calabash.

Before they got to Sawagongo, the present day, Sawagongo Market or before Luanda, there were assemblies of barefooted bands of cattle rustlers, shaved from broken pieces of pots, wielding bloodstained iron-tipped spears. They seemed less dangerous. People were living in the outskirts of the colonial society. That didn't deter their walk. Other villagers around Sinaga and Luanda emerged from the rather quiet rain forest, like some sort of prehistoric hunters and gatherers forgotten and passed by time. Like people living close to raw lifestyle, hordes of village youths scampered to the treetop to savor the raw honeycomb, bees docile at the wee hours of the morning. However, all these didn't matter to them; they continued with their journey, Sara still fit as a fiddle.

Around 6 February 1950, for this was the season of reporting in the school calendar, as the day bled the night away, Barak and Sara were among the first to arrive in the expansive Maseno. The school had attracted an army of people ever deeper into Africa's primordial blackjack-thronged jungle in search of education at an astonishing rate. People were voluntarily forced into accepting its benefits. Maseno forest (in the rocky hill called Mabungo, where Mabungo stream meandered to the plains) was ripped apart amid soaring population growth, and the open space was quite a spectacle—dotted with tin-houses, a few blocks of blue gum, and a rare pool of stagnant water, *something Sara was introduced to as a swimming pool.*

'A swimming pool?' she asked the guard. 'So the tribal setup has a modern touch?'

This particular pool had its own history. 'In the year 1927, Stansfeld made a resounding fundraising, and Maseno built one of the first swimming pools in East Africa,' the guard offered. He stopped the narration thinking he'd exhausted the story, but Sara didn't know what it's for—'Maybe drinking water for cattle!'

It was situated in a murky grove where two streams flowing down Bunyore hills met. It has since shrunk, though the other can vaguely be seen at the valley near the school forest by the school games pitches. The forest growing emptier by the day! It's reported that currently Maseno School has no pool; yet, it sends swimmers every year to the national swimming competition for schools.

Reverend Stansfeld, otherwise nicknamed *Bwana Hornbill,* was behind the school's dispensary after initiating, successfully, the swimming pool project. *He was the darling of the students. Maybe because he introduced good diet and being a clergyman—the spiritual man here!*

Parents with their children trooped in. The older boys and prefects were in arms to assist the new entrants. 'The school captain was giving very stern orders as if he was a junior teacher! He was in charge until the principal arrived,' Barak later said sadly. The luster of being a captain has since vanished. First, they lined up for uniforms at the tailor store. 'It was called Oriyo Shop—named after a tailor, Mr Oriyo—who'd since left to Alliance School . . . together with Carey Francis, a former principal, in 1940,' the school captain noted. The uniforms—two pairs of khaki shirts, two shorts, a tie, and a colored cotton open-necked T-shirt. The white color was also an option. Additionally, white garment drill pants were given, which served both for outdoor activities and for sleeping. Health records were also kept: the weight, the height; surprisingly, shoes were unheard of, not provided. The number rose steadily over time until there was a permanent presence of a sea of humanity.

Barak's admission was as follows:

> Name: *Barack Hussein Obama*
> Index Number: *3422*
> Class: *B.*
> Hostel: *Willis House.*
> Study zone: *Scots' House.*[16]

The name 'Barak' quickly changed to 'Barack', maybe due to clerical error. Who knows! And that was it. Of course, there was no error. That would be the correct name.

The new student, Barack, was to study at The E-shaped brick house. The Willis dormitory was rather silent, unlike the Tucker dormitory where bullying was the order . . . and keeping mum the law. The late Oginga Odinga was once appointed the junior prefect of the Willis dorm and, later, Tucker dormitory, as a senior captain. Maybe that's why there was some sanity. Since there was shortage of classrooms, students were forced to maintain the same class until Form VI. This study house was built by the Scottish missionaries and has since been occupied by the current Form IV students up to date.

Maseno had struggled from shortage of staff dating back from 1926; then it had only three European teachers (but this number increased subsequently as more Europeans streamed in), three senior African teachers and six junior African teachers attending to the needs of about 190 students. And in 1950, there wasn't any big difference.

In a short while, as witnesses would have it, the Principal of Maseno by that time, a Mr A.W. Mayor emerged from his office—a brick-stoned block—flanked by four teachers. Mr Mayor was a stern-faced Briton, with a strong sonorous voice. His presence could be literally felt from the way he occupied the central spot of the parade. He welcomed the students and their parents to Maseno. First, he'd offered them a photo session, parents smiling happily for the camera. He then released them and particularly thanked them for bringing their boys. Sara was there; hours later, she was still trekking back to Kogelo. She joined other villagers, who'd brought their sons, and those who were going toward Ng'iya, Luanda, Sinaga, Siaya, Bondo, or Lela on foot. 'Better join a crowd than a lonely walk!' she said, affectionately. Stories and laughter flowed freely. They'd shared their experiences. Villagers were overwhelmed by similar burdens and hardships. There'd shared the hot sweltering sun but soon each branched, one after the other, back to their huts. The crowd shrank moments later.

Principal Mayor, in a brown khaki suit and well-groomed hair, introduced his staff before commencing the long narrative of the school's history . . . . An elderly man from the outskirts of Maseno says that Mayor would narrate the story as if he was part of the history-making process. Indeed he'd risen to the occasion as an ingredient.

It was mandatory and almost customarily important for the principal to narrate the history of Maseno School, especially to the new entrants. It was like a proverbial saying—each sitting principal was mandated, by law, to tell the history of Maseno just like it is.

'Maseno School was started in 1906 . . .' he began. The innocent souls stiff in their black skin.

Reverend J. J. Willis was the founder of Maseno Mission School. He was a missionary statesman, a man who'd broad humanity and deep love and tolerance for Africans. He gave the people of *Ramogi* the first impetus for education; he was a multi-talented missionary with a convincing touch doubling as a teacher, translator, and pastor to the people of Maseno. This institution was one of the bedrocks of many works started by Christian Missionary Society and back then, great emphasis was laid on manual and technical training. Skills taught included carpentry, building, printing, tailoring, clerical work, and telegraphy that stretched out to practical activities in respective fields.

Reports available show 'that the five solid classes you see serving to date were used by the school apprentice from bricks made from the school. In 1912, he became Bishop of Uganda after Bishop Tucker. At his consecration, JJ was described as a 'leader—young, dedicated, and debonair—to whom fellow missionaries could rally.'

Indeed, this came true for several missionaries who steered the school over the years to innumerable successes' succeeding him.'

He continued, 'In 1917, the third principal was Reverend J. Britton who rose from a senior teacher. He'd risen to the helm after Reverend Willis and Mr Pleydell had left.' Mayor narrated standing at the central assembly hall near the present Old Mackay House.

Many other missionaries had served as principals before Mayor took the post from Mr Edward Carey Francis who'd served between 1928 and 1940. Mr Carey Francis had inherited it from one Mr Canon Doctor Stansfeld. Carey Francis had left in 1940 and moved to Alliance School in the same capacity.

It's recorded that Edward Carey Francis spoiled the party for redundancy or rather reluctance and introduced academic excellence at Maseno then, and later, Kenya as a whole. The late Jaramogi Odinga, in the book *Not Yet Uhuru*, records that Francis was

> 'a man of great simplicity who did everything side by side with us. He was good at football; he wrestled with us; swam with us, like us, without any clothes; when we worked in the garden he stripped to the waist and dug beside us; he even ate with us . . .' [17]

The man's fluidity in leadership and his revolutionary skills took Maseno to tremendous heights in academic performance. His tactical efforts on academics put Maseno into good books. He reshaped the school to become an academic giant up to date . . .

Mayor took calculated steps to explain the tenets of the school.

That it's built in the motto: 'Perseverance shall win through.'

To date the motto still stands *'Perseverance shall win through'* . . . It became the 'national anthem' for any living soul.

The school was built for Africans, and the earliest pioneer students were Orao, Owiti, Odindo, Onduso, and Osare. Others were Omondi Aloyo, Ezekiel Apindi, Oywaya, Omino Dan, among others. Jaramogi Oginga Odinga, the doyen of official opposition politics in Kenya over years, the father of the current Prime Minister Raila Odinga, was once a student of Maseno School, and his influence was still very strong! Names of Odongo Omamo, Ojino Okew, Apollo Ohanga, Achieng' Oneko, Odhiambo Thomas, Ogot Bethwel, Ndolo Ayah, and many others—lingered high in everyone's lips by 1950! Omamo worked in Maseno, during Barack days, as untrained teacher. He became one of the mentors of Barack; he took him under his wing. Under his tutelage, Omamo saw a future in Barack and encouraged him to take athletics and soccer as his 'pastime' but concentrate in mathematics as 'a way of life'. However, his stay took only one year.

The school rallied on the mission, 'Foster and promote holistic education and to train students who are capable of contributing competence to global development,' Mayor said.

'Your new school shall ride on the vision, "to be the National School of Choice that shall mold your character,"' he said unwaveringly. Barack was pensive. Of course, the rest were drowning in the narrative. Overzealous and the speech wanting, the Form III students were in high spirit, and Maseno School was such a good new home. The narrative took long, and he felt as if he'd already spent one year. It was both a mental and a physical fatigue. That day ended with the Mayor putting a lid on the core values, retrieving the reasoning of his predecessors—that Maseno is built on fundamental pillars—academic excellence, outstanding performance in—and out-of the class activities, exemplary discipline, leadership, environmental conservation, and voluntary service—and up to date these values still stand. Maybe breaking any—or going against—would have been suicidal; a slap in the face . . . And Mayor seemed one who'd give out a dismissal verdict in a flash at any slight indiscipline or unimpressive behavior. They were at ease, standing straight, arms behind them as if they were soldiers waiting for honor. Mayor caused laughter when he led the students through the now 'Old Boys song'—*'Aparo Ng'ang' Maseno'*. Mrs Britton did this particular song in 1920 when her husband Rev. J Britton was then the principal. It was sung in the tone of 'Isa Gwine back of Dixie'. The funny Mrs Britton would conduct the song, waving her hands in the air, as a choir master, and she would be deep into the Luo Music as if she was just one of the natives. She would leave her audience in stitches with her humor. But her gaffes sometimes went to extreme length, gaffes that became fodder for her students and black teachers. While Mayor led them to a cheerful and a thunderous clapping and they never wanted to stop applauding, through the entire speech, he wasn't only addressing the theme of nationalism, but he'd degenerated to poking out a more parochial speech to the Maseno lovers—'Aparo Ngang' Maseno'—the love of Maseno. The path that Maseno shall offer was an eternal piece that they all needed. Third formers were the laughing stock of the compound, but above the bullying, they could still share their own stories in small cocoons. The boys from Luhya tribe would tell tales of their initiation as a right of passage. Of course, there was nothing much to share apart from different diversity in customs and beliefs . . . the stories that would proliferate into dorms. 'They'd said that during their initiation ceremony, at the age of ten to fifteen, they would be covered in blankets—not to be seen by women—and taken to the forest at freezing temperature, a prickly mist would be falling (during very cold season or winter) and sounds of drums would be heard from a distance. The drumbeat was a real therapy. The young souls would be taught by selected guardians (about the world of manhood). The selection of a guardian was particularly done with great sensitivity—men of good report, men above reproach, and with good rapport with the *council of elders*—The Luhya boys would be painted, using red ochre, the hair in any section of the body shaved to a smooth touch, and then they'd be smeared with sludge of clay and white paint on their forehead. When the clay dries, it really felt awful on the smooth body! The boys would face the cut—at the wee hours of the morning—their skins discarded, the foreskins would be buried—a sign that they'd shed youthhood. After the cut, they would be kept in groups, in different huts, as they prepare their mind psychologically on the coming task, trials of manhood. They would learn how to eke out a living. Meanwhile, the blankets and other childhood paraphernalia would be destroyed or rather burned to mark the end of the transition. The 'men' would leave the chilly forest—singing songs and praises and dancing—for a party at the homestead, approximately, ten miles away. At this stage, the 'men' could differentiate which was freedom and which was independence. Conversely, *Ramogi* people, where Barack belonged, would simply initiate their girls and boys by removing the six lower teeth. Something he gave a wide berth. The Luhya boys would scoff at their passage, wondering the significance. In Maseno, students would wake up for morning devotion—the sermon, boring at the wee hours of the morning. At 6 a.m., the boys would run to the nearby stream, river *Mabungo*, when there would be water shortage, to fetch that precious commodity in a bucket and later taking the cold bath in the congested washrooms. A long snarling queue would be seen. You'd tear the guy up if he took too long inside the bathroom. At 6.50 a.m., they'd assemble for porridge and soft bread, the butter-less bread proving hard to swallow. Only a few, a handful of students would sneak in butter and keep it in their lockers. They'd carry it to the dining hall, applying it sparingly for it to last over a term. 'The butter would be stretched to elastic limit,' they said. Barack and a multitude of other boys would take it dry, the matter tasting nasty in the mouth. Lunch break would be another disappointment.

Years quickly passed, maybe three solid years, without major incidences. Maseno School wasn't a favorable place, after all. But being in Maseno was 'godsend'. Barack managed to interact with the whites, Indians, and Arabs of Orient descent, and made it to the athletics, football, and hockey national teams. Maseno students played hockey. And swimming was a major event. They would maul the neighboring schools in the preliminary hockey matches during the tournaments. This is just one of the many sporting activities that Maseno excelled in, the other being swimming competition. Playing against European schools, for instance, Prince of Wales, now Nairobi School, was one of the interesting events ever. The Maseno boys would move all the way from Kisumu . . . traveling all the way, on a bumpy, dusty road, to Nairobi and would be asked to relieve themselves before they got there. Yet, they were always on top of the game despite all the frustrations. Sometimes they would be taken straight onto the field to avoid using the special facilities. During the games, the Maseno boys had good timing in their runs, electric pace. Some of their scorers were so superb that a yard away, they would break from their opponents, and no one in the world would be able to catch them. The wasteful opponents, in a disastrous start, too nervous to score with rushed movements, unfounded lack of cooperation, picking the right ball but not capitalizing enough—they thoroughly lost the chances too easily. The Maseno feat in the game would surprise the white boys because such chances would open their minds, and they would play to win. Of course, they would show no signs of nervousness or tiredness. Their late blooming would leave the Prince of Wales boys with limited options. And a thunderous applause from the cheerful crowd wound it all. The game would sometimes become so rough that students would find themselves literally hitting one another with the hockey stick. The field would turn so ugly that it would call intervention of the schoolmasters. And the game would be stopped, ending prematurely before halftime. Immediately after the game, they would be rushed onto their lorries and then sped away. Nairobi and Maseno were two worlds apart. The boys would later talk harshly—disappointed about this—over supper that was obviously served early to pave way for preps, or complain nightlong. It was some sort of racial discrimination. Barack didn't like it. The complaints were endless. After all, he'll remain a *Luo* at heart and also at all that pertained to life's contradictions. And the wrong-headed remarks kept coming, ruining the good spirit of love. All that left him a bit provincial. To extradite the bad feelings and start afresh.[18]

In the same book, *Not Yet Uhuru*, by the late Jaramogi Oginga Odinga, this frustration was eminent; he would pose:

> '. . . On our way the White teacher stopped the lorries and eliminated two of the reserves. A teacher we were traveling with, Mr Gilbert Odawa, the team, and me left the lorry in disgust and walked to Maseno by foot. The white teacher drove past us and rushed to report me to the principal. When he saw me coming to the principal's house to give my version of the incident, he left the principal's house by the window.'[19]

This symbolized the uncertainty between blacks and whites. However senior a black man was, he couldn't just automatically differ with a white man.

Maseno became a campsite of a few white aggressive whiz kids with raging adrenaline and very harsh attitude toward the black folks. Newcomers, like Barack, were known to emerge from the 'hood'. By that they meant the 'bush' and found the rather cozy Maseno an abrasive settlement. He found himself in trouble, in running battles with the administration, and the rich kids obviously were very obsessed to frustrate the blacks, as if cursing their future, instead of blessing it. As if the world was fast going round, and they were struggling with acceptance.

In 1951, there was a change of guard; Mayors bowed down to his successor, Mr Bowers. Change was eminent, positive change and negative change . . . that which favored whites and that which subdued 'some blacks'. Any reader should know that this was colonial period, and oppression was the order of the day . . . even where it wasn't necessary—whites still forced it.

In this oppressive bandwagon, notably, was Principal Bowers, a white man, a man with a pale skin, with a face that was thoughtful rather than beautiful, face that reflected pride, courage, and sensitivity. Mr B.L. Bowers, or 'Boaz spider' as he was popularly known among mature students or 'BL' among new entrants, a Briton who took little of students' naughty lifestyle. Good and bad omen befell the two cousins—Barack and Joseph. Bowers promoted Barack to a more proactive stream A (It was regarded as one of the best; the best students emerged from there). Despite the changes, he'd maintain his *Willis hostel*. Joe fell on the wrong side of Bowers's thinking, and just a single hitch sent him to the bad books. He was shown the door and went home in full frustration blended with desperation. No one, including the elderly man who volunteered to give the information, could single out or avail the reason for his dismissal. 'Boaz spider or BL,' maybe, prided in details like that. The end of role reversal, for he was a 'naughty' student and that was him. He decided to take another flank and plan in life—'stay at home and maintain patience, waiting for the bleak future to come'.

BL noted Barack at a glance, a stunning-looking boy; there he saw evidence of stunted development, of independent resolve, growth, and internal discipline. Maseno School wouldn't accept such individual in its community. The dream of schooling would one day come down tumbling. 'The story of Barack, Joseph, and BL was exceptional' as Sara would put it. Barack argued with BL at length, knowing very well that it was commonplace for a whiteman to call a black man to perform a chore—and even accuse him of negligence and still complain that it isn't performed to 'standard'. 'But, sir . . .' Barack tried defending his brother after that bloody dismissal letter. The report read this way:

> . . . Had a history of inciting racially motivated violence at Maseno School. It is thus decided that he would pose a threat to public order and that he should be sent back home for the school to maintain peaceful coexistence . . . He was met with critical force.

'Overruled. No buts . . . remember, it's obvious that interactions of skill and knowledge lies squarely within your heart, sometimes combination of all these gets thick, you may not know that you need to listen.'

The statement showed the difference between the civilized and those in savagery. Sarah says that it wasn't an easy way, after all, to unblemish a black student—when a white man spotted vagrancy in him. The white man was regarded damn right.

'Let me tell you this, Principal BL,' he said, jabbing his fingers in the air. 'He's never been involved in any form of running battle or riot here or outside. Period. I don't know how to say it any more clearly than that. Never involved. I'm bloody sure.' He lost his temper. In persuasive messages, he managed to make a comeback to the 'hearing desk', to argue his case afresh. But he lost entirely. They could've labeled him with dozens of crimes ranging from murder to mayhem, but no one came out to ever be able to prove anything. Though, this was much better. Why?

In some areas, there was no room for questioning the legality of a case. How about those who were taken from their huts in the middle of the night by colonial powers, tortured, and murdered by anonymous assailants, for undisclosed reasons, in the wee hours of the night? An atrocity after atrocity, bestiality after bestiality was the order of the day. Maybe for not paying hut tax! 'It's a good idea that you go back to the village, settle, and put up that 'ability' to sacrifice. Know what you want now for what you want eventually. Not all who show capability have capacity. This decision I'm making here was amiably put in a pedestal for public scrutiny and reached by the entire school administration,' BL added without blinking or twitching an eye. The former guard at the school compound narrated the ordeal. He says that Bower was stumping his authority as the new head of the school. Without hesitation or making any mistake, he meant that

'It's not me being blind to your frustration.'

Barack was looking confused and prevailed, looking like a player who has lost or blundered in a crucial deciding match. He'd shown frustration as if he was the victim. BL was a great teacher and undisputed administrator. His judgment didn't come too soon. But when it knocked the door, then it was the final verdict synthesized and structured, true to his words, and conclusive. But caring and observant mind goes well with such intricate overtures or rather dismissals or suspensions because unless taken care of, it might severely affect one's limited options. For all that we obtain too easily, we esteem too lightly; it is dearness only that gives everything its value. Only heaven knows how it puts a proper price on its goods.

Basically our character is a composite of our habits

'You've qualified as the enemy of this school. And it is our pleasure to relieve you so that you can exercise your brutal force elsewhere, maybe, back in the village. Thank you for coming . . . to Maseno,' (Extending his handshake to

Joseph, of which he denied to accept) '... Over to this center of excellence,' he added. Barack turned around in humiliation, but he wasn't done yet. His cousin was going back to the village. Malik says that 'my dad couldn't stand it. How can an innocent man be put into such shame?'

BL, a no-nonsense administrator and a strict disciplinarian, forced Joseph out of Maseno Mission School barely two years before completing his studies. The poor African was proceeding to Form Five, an audacious effort, anyway. Apart from being efficient, humiliation at hand, or truly effective, making right choices remained his best prerogative in any way. It was time to back it off partly and hit the road.

That one glorious year was marked by good meals: donation of bread, confiscated vegetables, and fresh fruits from unlicensed hawkers in Kisuma (Kisumu) market, a source of that precious menu. Empty cans and soiled paper bags made footballs for the young boys—of Maseno. Oxymoronically, he didn't fail to connect the dots to eminent problems ahead—the cruel kindness, the false truth. It was ripe time to discover himself and learn greater respect for other people. The high moment of puffing away was over for the binge alcoholic lads. Reality was fast crawling in... Local brewers were facing a setback. Revelers were 'mourning' a best friend, a lost friend. In conscience and a bit conscious, Joseph was the unsung hero, at that moment only. For once, making life a function of the way, he was treated and entering in records mingled with platitudes, a human lampshade. Plunging his name in a litany of cases of indiscipline from the most decorated status of dedication and honor to a laughing stock, that which lifts the lid of the rot, opening a can of worms, underlying a lifestyle of youth living life on the fast lane reaching in a cumulative all-time high. Youth was driven by bigotry, overly and overtly, inconsistent with this kind of arrangement. Principal BL was assertive, a Briton with a firebrand politics, addressed the first assembly... He took the leadership of Maseno with an iron fist, with unpopular image for the urge to positive change. Behaving like some head of crypto-Masonic—the rumor doubtlessly silly. Running the school in a manner resembling a cocoon of odd fellows, templar, do-dah cultists, and free masons. This in itself was a sorrowful reminder of their human vulnerability to division or fragmentation or degeneration of self-goodwill. He singularly behaved like an epithet of an extraordinary being against the black subject. Back into the inanities of colonial injustice where a black student was an easy prey, or assumed easy prey, when it comes to discipline and trust.

The year 1951, life cooled a little bit. Education calmly took over from chaos. But this was a temporary replacement, for without chaos, Maseno boys believed that life wasn't normal. To create 'some normalcy', something had to happen, maybe massive bullying. Bullying here was in the form of forcing new entrants to fetch water from the stream with leaking tins or to wash the seniors' clothes and wait for them in the scorching sun, while standing, till they dry. Then fold them and take them to the 'master'.

At Maseno, Barack was a humble student, keen in his work, did it with diligence and accuracy. Lending a hand to other students stuck in calculus or statistical data representation, to some others in congruence and quadratic identities, while to still others in geometrical deductions and applied linear equations. At dusk on Fridays, especially when BL had traveled or was out of school, the boys would sometime sneak out, unnoticed, and head to Kisuma town, miles far away in search of 'fun'. Here, they would meet their girlfriends from the village or just those they meet in town. He was indeed very popular, particularly and especially to girls. He could drink silly and later a sizzling, wild romp would follow in a world filled with magic and beauty. It was when plunk music started to get into people's head; it almost overtook glam rocks. Self-fulfillment was the only option. At night, during nightfall, Barack transformed into something else; Maseno boys had a past—he loved music from his early age. He went to raucous parties that almost became a permanent fixture in his life, a fun loving cocktail rock and roll guzzling dynamos, roaming through the dark, a dimly lit town, cackling through the dense night, drinking, and dancing. Just boogying. Kisuma town nightlife was awesome: full with ambience and beauty. He caught up with the cat-women in a break dance—those women, distinctively sassy with 'drop-dead gorgeous look', formidable assets to their advantage. Girls just wanted to have fun! The school life was a bit stressful, and white discrimination, maybe, was part and parcel of the cause.

They caused breathtaking scenes; shocked young men made endless parade to watch them shake, as they took to the floor, shaking their tush on the dance floor, gyrating their curves away. Notable were clubs packed to the rafters. White men and black women lost in the music and drinks giving way to promises of pleasure, huge wheels rolling away under the dim streetlights. To seal the deals!

This particular establishment pioneered the culture of raves, the in-thing of town. Yet it was filled with the iconographies of Mary, the mother of Jesus. The town being the government empire here, the allures of city life drew many people from the villages of On'geche, Kolwa, Nyatindo, Rateng' . . . It was mistaken that anybody who went to Kisuma, maybe, had some business with the government or with some local authorities. Later, they'd find themselves in the streets' bingo. Bending the rules of character, *students flocked the joints in droves*. These self-respecting night owls had their own base—a dog-eat-dog world. Barack was far 'too busy' to think about a serious romance; again, he'd no qualms about the whispers that followed him around, back in the village.

This lifestyle never went unnoticed, and punishment came in its way. Some students fell on the growing list of Oluande K'Oduol who was expelled way back in forties. A situation that angered many black teachers, such as Richard Arina, Bukachi Webungo Akatsa, Odawa Gilbert, and Omondi Timothy. Then, Oluande was a pro-black lifist. The activist of change didn't like the way black teachers and the white counterparts treated each other and the way they treated students.

In 1951, for instance, a white teacher would be made to supervise a black colleague and literally scold him for not doing one or two things during the lesson. The humiliation, which made the white students laugh while the black ones gazed in shock. And BL would say nothing whenever a complaint was raised. The black teachers would look odd and scary in their jackets, shorts, and long stockings. The socks were multicolored. This was also a bone of contention: dress code. These arguments infiltrated in time immemorial, causing jitters both among the parents, black teachers, white counterparts, workers, and other staff. The students disapproved. Some caused a go-slow.

CHAPTER 8

In the Year 1952

Omar, now growing pretty fast, the eight-year-old son of Onyango started schooling at Nyang'oma Primary School. Life was lonely though, but Sara Onyango pulled a surprise to the family: a baby girl. The bright day of 29 May 1952 sent a gift, a shooting star to the family yearning for a daughter. And Onyango couldn't hide his joy 'For a home without daughters is like a spring without a source,' he repeated Ogwel's belief.

Onyango named her 'Abong'o' after a distant grandmother of his. This was incredible. An Old man reserved such a name for his 'most loved child'. And true to his words, Abong'o was the darling of the old man. After frustrations from Nyaoke, due to her unstable marriage, Abong'o came at the right time. It was indeed good news even for Barack. He'd learned of Abong'o's birth while in Maseno. Finally, a companion to love and cherish. The joy lasted for a short while only. In May that year, Barack wasn't on holiday because he'd taken part-time job at the school compound. Clerical work. 'A sister at last,' he said. But Omar's joy was overwhelming. The little boy would try to carry her, who was three-quarters of his weight. But the weight was too much to lift; they'd tumble down to the ground. Onyango wouldn't stop at Abon'go; he 'initiated' her into the Islamic world. The name *Zeituni* finally settled firmly on her.

The newborn was indeed called Zeituni Abong'o Onyango Hussein. But Abon'go remained the traditional name. The number, in the family, was on the increase. As fate may have it, Sara was a happy mother. The days of Halima were cruel, to her husband, and it seemed she'd finally brought the happiness back to him. The wishes had been confirmed. Although, this was just the beginning. The little girl, then, started growing up. Not knowing a lot shall unravel in her dear life. Or what the poor country was going through.

Hawa says, 'Barack worked so hard that whatever he worked for, not only paid his school fees, but the money would find its way into our household—for domestic use. I confess that Barack made me put shoes under my feet. And whoever is complaining about Barack . . . is just annoying. When he came to the village, for a short break, he took me to Siaya township for shopping at an Indian store to buy a footwear, and he also bought a small goat (as part of his savings) and me a pair of plastic shoes, a new skirt, and a khaki blouse. 'Those trendy, fashioned garments!' she jokes. Did I tell you that the shoes were good? And the village girls envied? The only disadvantage was that they really roasted my feet on a sweltering sunny day. This man, Barack, was a caring brother. We talked a lot on our way back as I kept the newly found fortune in my home-made weaved basket. He didn't like this issue of not going to school. I wasn't going to school then. And Barack didn't appreciate this . . . he wanted me in a classroom. Sometimes, while in Maseno, Barack wrote us letters—letters we could barely read; remember, I'd never stepped in a classroom. One particular one that he wrote to us thus:

Mar Hawa Auma kod Sara Nyaoke,

Amor ahinya ka aparo ni uthi maber. Ageno ni ungima! Anbe angima mogudho. Somo emaomaka ngang' ei Maseno kaa. Ti nende ok na bi dala nikech atiyo ei skul mondo ayud solro mar pis. To kata kamano anabi bang' ndalo matin mondo anenu.

E an owadu.
Barak.

(For Hawa Auma and Sara Nyaoke,

I am happy that you are doing well. I hope that you are well too! I am also well. However, studies at Maseno is taking toll of me. This coming holiday I won't be able to come home because I will be working to raise additional money for school fees. However, I will make effort to come over.

It's me, your brother.
Barak.)

These letters would reach us through messengers who traded their goods at the Mission or those from Kogelo who worshipped at the Maseno Mission.

Of course, we never replied. I didn't even know how to hold a pencil. I warned Nyaoke not to try writing anything because it would have turned out weird. She still insisted to write, but I doubt whether she wrote something in private. Barack became our handwriting tutor, especially after realizing that we were growing older without basic education—he taught us spelling, word usage, and pronunciation of one English word a day.

He wrote in a tattered piece of paper:

> *Bi kaa*—Come here.
> *Adwaro*—I want.
> *Wana rom*—We shall meet.
> *Musawa*—How are you?

He wrote either on the red earth or on a piece of paper.

On 20 October 1952, *five* months after the birth of Zeituni, politics took toll of Kenya. The Governor of Kenya, Government Officials, wealthy white settlers—Government Advisors such as Sir. Charles Markham, Captain Briggs, Lord Francis, and Sir Michael Blundell, held an emergency meeting—within a few hours the country was under a State of Emergency, arising from the *Mau Mau Uprising* led by Field Marshall Dedan Kimathi, General China (Waruhiu Itote), General Tanganyika (Muriuki Kimotho) and General Mathenge, against the barbaric colonial rule. It was stirred by the arrest of KAU officials—Jomo Kenyatta, Achieng' Oneko, Kungu Karumba, Fred Kubai, Bildad Kaggia, and Paul Ngei, in what was named 'operation jock stock'. In a seating judgment, a University of Nairobi social scientist said that Judge Thacker Ransley convicted them for conspiracy—the poor Judge had received a bribe of Kshs 2.800,000 from the colonial government. The miserable men, awaiting hard labor and torture, were tried and sentenced to seven years in prison at Kapenguria, in the northern part of Kenya. The hottest part of the savannah land (later they were nicknamed Kapenguria Six). This is a similar torturous experience Nelson Madiba Mandela and his accomplices suffered at Robben Island. *KAU* was a party that started in 1944—as a group of Africans in Nairobi—from a 'student' organization, KASU—with its leader being Harry Thuku. Later, after the arrest, a new breed of leaders emerged: Tom Mboya, F. W. Odede, Joseph Murumbi, W. W. W. Awori, Oginga Odinga, and C. M. G. Argwings Kodhek. After some time, the following year, *KAU* was banned.

But at one time they took the Kenyan banner to Lancaster in London in search of *Uhuru*—Independence. One would ask, 'Who was Dedan Kimathi?', 'Why was he named Field Marshall?', and 'What made him hate the white people so much?' The generation to come would be told: 'Dedan was born on 31 October 1920 in Karuna-ini Village of North Tetu (Nyeri District). During his time, education was mandatory, and he'd joined Ihururu School and then Church of Scotland Mission at Tumutumu where he could only afford a Fifth Grade (An equivalent of Standard Seven). He didn't finish his primary school and was, therefore, expelled in 1944 for being a troublemaker. Dedan later joined the army and posted to Ndarugu where the Italian captives were kept. Here he learned how to use short-gun and rifles—but he wasn't allowed to use the weapon past the store's doors. Something he'd not agreed with. He'd sneaked the material out to try his skills. That he found to be perfect. His life treated as a scavenger—cleaning, sweeping, and digging pit latrine whenever one was filled. He'd only dressed in short trousers, a closed collar, and a jumper coat. He fled to the forest and became a freedom fighter.' And the generation to come would be amazed. And this particular generation that Zeituni represented would ask, 'What happened then, after he'd fled to the forest?' The anonymous historian would continue, 'He fought so hard and marshaled hundreds of soldiers, mainly the *Kikuyu* tribe (the vigilante group—the *Mungiki* emanated from this sect and is causing mayhem up to date). He would wear a leopard skin. Walked like a leopard. He used this as a decoy to blind the white soldiers. In the process, the 'leopard' would shoot to kill. This never lasted. Kimathi was captured and maimed to death. His remains were buried at unknown place. The controversy surrounding the whereabouts of his remains still haunts Eloise Mukami, his wife, who has sought every solution as to where the husband was buried . . . she has filed a court petition against the government—it still remains a puzzle to her. She wants to bury the husband's remains before her time of death comes. Many thought, and still believe, that Kimathi's remains were buried in the expansive dreaded Kamiti Maximum Security Prison compound, but where exactly? Maybe if the government excavates the whole compound and maybe run a DNA test to verify whether the bones they'll find (of course they will come across hundreds of pieces of bones) belong to the former freedom fighter. These are some of the past injustices that need close attention—especially the attention of the sitting government. The torture victims of colonial administration were never paid even a cent following their suffering; their lives were soaked in a fresh gall—bitter to their very flesh. Onyango passed through this kind of mistreatment and was never compensated. He later died a bitter man. In the following year, 1953, there was Barack, Hawa, Omar, Zeituni, Sara, and the aging Onyango; the pillars of Obama's family. Surprisingly, Nyaoke would call in from Karachuonyo, *Kaluo* Village where she was first married.

Her home bordered Dorsila's homestead. Dorsila would complain 'why her niece continues to roam like a witless sheep. She keeps walking everywhere.' Maybe due to troubled marriage. Her complains wouldn't stop at that. They were endless and hard to solve. The old man would agree that there was indeed no immediate solution to her marital woes. She'd escape and even go as far as seeking refuge in her mother Akumu's new home in Kosele . . . which, of course, was far much nearer than gathering her pieces to Alego. In some instances, during holidays, Barack would visit her, at least to know how she was doing and to get to know who'd married her—The brothers-in-law and that shaky extended family—the family he wanted to know more about. He would eventually go ahead to see his 'lost' mother Akumu in Kosele. Above the backdrop of this, the Kenyan politics wasn't left behind either. The Maseno boys came to know that the Governor of Kenya had requested and later obtained British and African troops, including the King's African Rifles to attack Africans (especially the resistant tribes who'd group into small war-groups and the *Mau Mau)*. They'd begin counter-insurgency operations. In May 1953, General Sir George Erskine took charge as commander in chief of the colony's armed forces with the personal backing of Winston Churchill. The students knew pretty well that it wasn't business as usual. They would 'riot' silently or rather a go-slow. The white teachers would get mad as the black counterparts joined in support of the mini-rebellion. This was a major confusion. BL's hair, maybe, started falling out, his complexion sallow due to 'scorching effect' of the growing rebellion. To him it's a trying period of a lifetime. Later, this would remain just as bad memories. Despite all the ugly incidences across the country, the detention without trial, the fights between *Mau Mau,* and the British insurgence, the politics, violence due to colonial resistance; The Duke of Devonshire would send pleas for calm. The heartening conclusion was that Kenyans wanted independence! For the damage was too great. Barack's reputation then, and indeed, other students' as well were appalling. That was according to the administration. They were summoned; the list of endless 'crimes' was then laid on the table. They couldn't defend themselves. The reason is that it was a colonial era and winning a case against a whiteman was a daunting task.

Meanwhile . . .

As he tinkered with the problem. One day he would confess:

> 'Why my favorite pastime was nothing steamier than alcohol. It was the denominator of all forms of pleasure.'

Written on BL's doorway was the wise saying thus: *Sow a thought, reap an action,* He told Malik that 'it was the time he saw darkness merge with light.'

According to Malik, his father read it so well. It sunk and reminded him of what the great physicist wrote:

> We are what we repeatedly do. Excellence then, is not an act but a habit (Aristotle).

A symbol of the perfect defeat of his life. It was like going to look for trouble when it doesn't come looking for you!

On the walls were radiating framed autographed pictures of George Washington, Lyndon Johnson, Franklin Roosevelt, Abraham Lincoln . . . .

All America's former heads of state. Why?

Why my favorite pastime was nothing steamier than alcohol. It was the denominator of all forms of pleasure.

One thing turned into another; Barack felt unwelcome in this new society. How about his 'lost father' whom (according to) rumors had it that he was hurt in the capital or in Zanzibar, working—*or according to the report he has been a staunch supporter of anti-white revolution?*—Or maybe to the fact that he was a Muslim—*worshiping another religion?* 'What the hell went wrong in that Zanzibar? Poor Papa!' Barack wondered. Malik says that all these 'became issues he'd grapple with'. And some of the frustrations that finally culminated to his current problems. He noted in defeat what had happened in the wonderland of Zanzibar, Burma, or that country or city where his father was?

Malik says that 'the man was disturbed'. 'Are Africans condemned—how about my prodigal father?' 'Is he condemned as well? Condemned to a future of poverty, disease, and premature death?' . . . Maybe that would later become his own prophecy!

The prevailing perception of Africans and their capabilities never transcends the confines of their so-called limitations. To understand this, remove the blinkers and see Africa beyond aristocracy, authoritarian rules, or barbarism. Whites turned the black into beasts to be maimed, chained, and enslaved. In remembrance of all these, Barack was downcast, nothing else came close. Not even his Kogelo Village where he was condemned. He bemoaned the loss of his heritage and the peace that it came with. Beckton once told him, 'In trouble, know that Africa is a tough continent . . . where life becomes tougher by the day. Embrace positive change and never relent in working hard. Every time we're ripe candidates for a big fall! Don't neglect any situation. For you're reared to assume responsibility. It may be your beginning of the turning of tables.'

And he would nod in satisfaction. Barack clutched to his feet, faced westwards, and left Maseno for Kogelo Village, the home of his forefathers.

In considering the lukewarm faces of the oppressed, Barack told his son Malik that Kenyans were in the verge of giving up. The white administration had gone too far in admonishing them. 'Is the white man making fame out of human misery?' he asked. 'Behaving as laissez-faire leaders who are too laid back to make fundamental decisions, only riding in oppressive notion that which has forced them to a political abyss.' Malik would add that these were 'some of the impediments that brought shame to his inner heart'. *A laissez-faire leader too laid back to make fundamental decision.* 'And he could talk fondly of his father, Onyango,' Malik adds.

'I think my father was a great leader, a self-appointed genius who went out to look for the fast-changing future but lost the very future,' Barack continued his pestilence against the truth. Father-like-son attitude encroached his peaceful heart, causing the thoughts to scatter, limping-off like a rabid dog, and detaching from himself. Only a few years back, Barack was a hero, a celebrity, now, a black sheep in the neighborhood. And having known this, too well, with an awful certainty that there was no escape to remain undercover and keep his name out of the gutter. He was a chap with an expertise in evading justice or injustice, whatever it was. This time he was not lucky. 'I believe the case is closed,' the arduous principal stated as Sarah was having her way in the office accompanied by his embattled son for retrial. BL had prepared the case with meticulous speed; he made sure that he had the full evidence, cleaning up every loose end. 'No . . . eh . . . the case is still open. As I'm concerned, it's just the start. I want justice, Mr BL,' Obama interjected. 'And I want it now.' Looking a bit conscious and careful, Sarah wasn't fully inside yet but could hear the heated exchange. 'Where is the evidence that I'm wrong? Where, Mr B.L? Above all, I'm surprised at all these outpouring condemnation. Behavior in that context,' Barack continued his case, trying to hang tight to his sentiment.

'Look, Barack, in a world you surely had no power, you chose to give yourself superpowers.'

'And it's like you "kill mankind" and ask, "Why are you here", huh?'

'That's what you believe?'

'Aren't you a man enough or some sort of phantom?'

'A future man can't depend on you, Barack.'

Sara says that, in the middle of the exchange, she felt a strange sunray piercing through the narrow hole of BL's cedar-made window on her glittering face. The glass window already gathering dust, symbolizing the last time it was washed. It was BL's window, and no one ever touched it except BL himself.

BL was fluent in *Dholuo*. And one thing that particularly perturbed most people was the fact that the senior white teachers would speak effortlessly in local dialects compared to the locals learning English.

To Sara, BL bemoaned, 'Tell me, why you would come down here, trekking long distances, to defend a vagrant?'

Maybe he thought the father would have come, instead. But Onyango couldn't make it to Maseno due to illness. BL, maybe, thought the father was some sort of a tribal chief carrying a spear and a shield in either hand, maybe dressed in traditional attire with a leopard headgear, matching the one hanged over his shoulders, maybe a man black as coal, with his bare chest sweaty and hairy, or maybe a man looking intelligent just like his son. He got some right some wrong. He'd reserved his comments.

Sara was mesmerized and confused. Clutched onto an old sofa beside a wooden chair—that she wasn't invited to sit on! The BL office was a small, uncomfortable-looking room containing a battered desk. It appeared deserted.

'It pains to see a son in such a predicament,' she replied '*Japuonj* (Teacher) I'm laying my belly down on this case, for bargain sake this is what maybe they've adopted as a way of life,' she apologized, her voice quivering with indignation, later calm.

To her these were mere teenagers causing havoc.

'I know you're facing trouble handling these children, but there must be a constructive criticism. Naysayer and "I wish you worst" will call it a bluff . . .

but let's build a consensus. This is the uttermost hope for these young men. And that is what we must support. We should learn to arrest getting upset for differing in opinions, create benchmarks, and a strong order in the sphere of judgment.' She was indeed resolute. The man could not hear any more of it. He was incoherent with rage.

'And you, Barack,' Sarah said, 'get some lesson. It's time to get the lessons right. And can you please tell us what happened beyond the bounds of stupidity, now that you seem to be the one responsible for the largest tragedy?' as she started for the door.

'I . . . everybody seems to be the enemy,' Barack answered.

'You've not made a name for yourself. I think this burden hasn't made you a hero, anyway,' BL interjected.

'And you think you almost fetch a great win?'

'I see . . .'

'I'm not rude in any way, BL.'

'What's that suppose to mean, then?'

'No. I just have some sort of morbid curiosity. If you're candid with me, I'll be frank with you, in return.'

'If you can change, it'll do you good and for the whole country, a lot of good.'

'My pleasure, but there's nothing to change,' he said injecting some pace into the accusation.

'I'm acting tough. You don't expect a soldier to wield a broom or some olive branch instead of a gun in a bruising battle. Never.' Mr B.L played host to other boys, according to a former cook at the school. The elderly man says that a number of students were expelled under unclear circumstances. Or under the disguise that they'd not completed their school fees. As BL turned to direct a venomous look at prime victims (Barack's ilk in this battle), they lost hope.

Obala Alego was a chap who believed that 'there's always a tomorrow'. He was declared 'unruly and disobedient'.

In the penalty row was Owich of *Muthire* Village Gem in a cutthroat assembly, patiently waiting to argue his case; the case in question was airtight. Ochillo Ng'on'ga of Kochia—a twenty-seven-year-old whiz kid who came to Maseno with an interest to specialize in physics and mathematics from Kotieno Ambiju, along with Obondo Oromba son of Otange Aguko of Nam Lolwe and, Kiambi Muchiri, a boy from Murang'a are 'also on the chopping board'. The poor son of Ng'ang'a was 'naughty and not ready to learn', the report read.

There was absolute tension, hopes dashed, although amorphous calm quickly picked up to replace sectarian mistrust for a while. Barack said dryly to his friends caught up in the dragnet, 'I'd seen it coming, friends, this kind of intimidation and even more threatening than this . . . look, victory, shall come beforehand. We got what it takes to lift ourselves from this type of misrule. These are lives of people reduced to ethnic enclaves.' Barack was particularly bitter about this kind of mistreatment, although, it was just a tip of an iceberg.

What if their charges read like this?

'Arrested on a mugging charge, served a sentence for hacking a warden to death, caught attempting to carjack in town, picked up for raping elderly women, or just pimps?'

'What would be our fate, and yet it's not true. What would be our fate?' He later told Malik.

BL's judgment was concise, a militant piece.

'You obviously got a buzz, a thrill from *bilking* fellow students and the administration out of their peace . . . ,' he said,

> '. . . but they hadn't found it funny and neither do I. Go home and start your own school.'

Not dissuaded at all from their decadence. There wasn't time for more argument. '. . . I can't take any more of your sheer arrogance. And sloppiness . . .' Looking agitated, BL quickly left for another office and moments later, he walked over to Barack and handed him a large *manila* envelope.

'. . . I'm sorry. You've no place here, sir.' That was BL speaking.

He stood there, holding his breath, clutching his hand protectively, willing his mother would get hold of him and the envelope and carry him back to the village.

Barack saw this as a memorable day: a moment to forget fast; a haunting period; a day that will live in infamy; a dreadful day not worth a dime or a bet or a psychopath. That day that never gave way to a give-and-take arrangement, a day to give and forget, and a day to give and let go and an exercise in vanity.

'Vanity is the devil's mirror,' he said. He hoped he was invisible. *An exercise in vanity. Vanity is the devil's mirror.* BL engrossed a sensuous treat, an irreparable damage or rather an ethnocentric passion. It was the last chance that ended in futility when Barack stepped his best foot in Kogelo. These were dying minutes in his life. He thought it utterly senseless to argue with BL—it was pointless and benefactors' tone invited no discussion. So he'd sent his life back to Kogelo to rest the matter for a while. No matter how long it would take for justice to be realized. He started to dwell on other issues. Politics was rooting strongly.

The State of Emergency declaration was still in effect. And in 1953, after the State of Emergency was declared by the colonial Governor—Sir. Evelyn Barring marked the year when things started changing at once; The Secretary of State for colonies, Oliver Lyttelton, came to Kenya to listen to the grievances of KAU Party. Barack would receive news from his father, both bizarre news and tantalizing news as well. Onyango Hussein, once prodigal father, was alive and cultured. He thought wryly in a glow of euphoria. This separation had instantly affected her 'more than he would have believed possible—from the side of his father'. In Kogelo where people concentrated on farming, herding, and creating a stronger brotherly bond—that united the entire village. He resumed the old life of Nyang'oma, a totally different life story giving way to boredom. Life clashing him: one to nothing, two to nothing. And later a hat trick to nothing. A confusion tossing you around like a ball, picking up the pieces and waiting for a verdict from Maseno School! Sara Nyaoke now spent most of the time at home after separating from her second husband.

And Joseph was about to have his second-born (The firstborn, Acholla, had died of cerebral malaria). He'd abandoned education and was in the verge of making a fortune from farming. Barack and Joe found themselves tight again—close together as brothers, using an ox-sledge to plough the terraineous land—tilling it for millet plantation. Hawa says that 'they would use bulls, the African zebu, two of Onyango's and two from Joe's father—Ndalo Ayus. The bulls had designated names. Surprisingly enough, the animals would respond to these names. Some were Odongo, Ojwang', Oseng', Obura, among other names, while the 'milk givers' had more feminine names such as Sela, Atoti, Dorsila, and *Nyar Suba*. The funniest of all was the white bull named *Jarachar*—to mean a white man. The industrious, heavily fleshed bull was a crowd puller. His strength was reliable. Barack would be forward in a bullfight—he was a bullfight addict.

And Onyango, maybe, happy that Sara had kept the kin and kith well, protecting them with hope, sweat, skin, and blood. Although, no wrap-up news from his household at Nyang'oma being rumored at first, and later, openings finally surfaced. Now the two worlds started cohabiting, with one another. 'Outside world' communicated with Kogelo, and Kogelo, in turn, sent echoes and lamentation to that 'outside world,' and it ended in commensuration with each other.

However, Barack wasn't a happy shot. He found himself in trouble with Onyango—reason? He was supposed to be in school, for his last year. Indiscipline had caused him back home. One thing that actually made his father relent was that he'd also faced the wrath of a white man, the thorough beatings, and the imprisonment at Kamiti Maximum Prison. The case of Barack didn't come as a surprise, though.

In the year 1953, Ng'iya was elevated to an Intermediate Mission School by the government following request by Mr Hunter, and toward the end of the year, Barack sat for his Form *Six A-Level Examination* at Maseno, albeit the expulsion. It was known as the Kenya Advanced Secondary Certificate Examination (KACE) or the Cambridge School Certificate. They were examinations that went all the way to United Kingdom for marking. Later, the results would be brought back to Kenya. The examination was nicknamed 'the blue paper'. Barack would later tell Malik that 'I sat my blue paper in 1953'. This was an examination that accompanied the city guild-training certificate either in carpentry, tailoring, and clerical among others that Maseno offered its students besides the National Examination. He, therefore, specialized in clerical work. Something he'd done as part-time job in his heyday at the school. Shocking statistics shows that in 1950 only sixty-one African boys sat for the certificate; in 1953, there were eighty-five boys in the whole country (Barack being one of them) and no girls in both cases. However, in 1955, 245 African boys and seven girls would sit for the examination. It is reported that white schools such as Prince of Wales (Nairobi School) built in 1931, and Duke of

York (Lenana School), and the Kenya Girls' High School (Kenya High School), which were later built in 1940s, attracted the largest number of blacks, doubling those in African schools. After this education, a few proceeded to the university abroad . . . and the first Kenyan to obtain a university certificate was the late Peter Mbiyu Koinange, in 1938. He'd got a master's degree in Education at Columbia University, United States of America. Even then racial discrimination prevented African students from getting overseas scholarships or loans. As Barack graduated from Maseno, the first lot of educated young people, about twenty Kenyan students, graduated from Makerere Technical College. Back in Kogelo, with a certificate, life had started for another sprint. He juggled between voluntary teachings at Nyang'oma Primary School where the head administrator was none other than Hunter—and the overall Ng'iya fraternity. On 29 December 1953, the Ng'iya fraternity was hit by a deadly 'catastrophe'—death of Lilian Olive Owen; the wife of Walter Edwin Owen died at a Kisumu Hospital. Her death was unexpected—a few days ago she was instrumental in the coordination of the examination at Maseno School and other schools that fell within the Maseno Mission fraternity. She'd come during prayer day at Maseno prior to the examinations. Sara says that 'she was a woman who had touched the lives of all generations in different ways before and after the death of her husband Owen. 'All the students were once again assembled at Kisumu Memorial Park to witness the sending off ceremony of an iron lady whose husband died eight years earlier (later) after the husband's departure, when all was done, life came back to normal. And overall, Principal Hunter was a busy man; he would fish out the best former students and offer them 'some work to do'. He made Barack the math teacher for the lower class cadre, a job he'd enjoyed very much—a teacher, he was, now in arithmetic class. While Hunter would go as far as convincing him to take teaching course for it'll be a way of giving back to the society. At some point, he'd made him teach catechism—but he dropped it; he was a Muslim. Again, something else he wasn't keen at was a plain teaching profession. He knew pretty sure that teaching wasn't his calling. Second, the missionaries were so domineering that you'd easily be lured to Christianity. Of course, he was a Muslim by birth, and working among the Christian believers wasn't an easy ride. Maybe that's why he'd preferred teaching nothing other than arithmetic. One, it was his favorite, and second, the issue of religion was never taught in mathematics. He would connect pretty well with his pupils much faster due to the fact that he knew most of them right from the village. Some were his cousins, others, nephews and nieces. Others called him 'uncle' because most of his peers had already married and had approved parental care with several children to look after. To him marriage wasn't in his list of priority then. In 1954, in Nairobi, the Royal Technical College of East Africa (now Nairobi University) started its operation following pressure for higher education by Africans. This year also marked the capture of Warihiu Itote (also named General China) on 15 January 1954, and the subsequent interrogation led to a better understanding of the *Mau Mau* command structure. It was the time when the not-so-friendly Native Land Rights Confiscation Orders were announced, and many people would lose land to the white man due to their inclination in regard to *Mau Mau* Movement. Barack was traveling to Nairobi amid chaos and restriction. He left Nyang'oma for an evening train. Onyango had made an arrangement with his friends and cousins in Nairobi. And John Ong'inya, a neighbor who was then working in Nairobi, had come to the village and told him on how they would meet when he gets to Nairobi. Hawa says that 'my father had lots of friends and his immediate cousins always came to his rescue. As much as I can remember, Anyim Kanyindha and John Ong'inya had been working with him. And John, particularly, jointly owned a plot with my father in Kariokor and Huruma although they'd lived in Kibera, Lang'ata, for most of their lives. Kibera wasn't as developed as Eastland. But there wasn't any shanty in view. It's unbelievable that the place they lived in is a stone throw away from where his grandson, then Senator Barack Jr visited in 2006. In that year, Barack got a foothold at John's tiny wooden structure. Another friend was Henry Mumbo Komuodo. He was from Kogelo. They were so close that their friendship was unnerving. They'd met in Kampala, Uganda, in the army. It was hard to get to the city and start hassling without a contact person—either a relative or a friend—maybe to provide shelter. Food wasn't a problem. Someone would get it once he's started working. A relative would tell how to start and whereon or else you'd find yourself behind bars. And the state would be so reluctant or just unwilling to release you sooner. The State of Emergency was in effect. Kenyans traveling to any destination were thoroughly checked at designated points; the famous checkpoints arose as a result of such quarantine. When he got to Kisumu Railway's main terminus, it was a hell of human activities (going on). The fare stood at Ksh 3.50. Onyango had sold one of his bulls, named Akech, for Ksh 10.00 so that his son could find his way to Nairobi. He'd used part of this money and kept the rest. The journey was far from over. And the folks carrying raw fish to Nairobi or a bundle of guavas to the city consumers caused discomfort and thus a major commotion. This kind of train had been compartmentalized—maybe due to economic status of the people in the country. A sane white man took the first class. No African (however rich you were) would find a ride in this class and bearing in mind that the country was volatile signified an additional entry of racism card. Barack was pushed to the third class, unfamiliar territory any way. His first voyage to Nairobi had been by bus. The Maseno School bus, which had some sanity of traveling. And now he was bundled in a rather congested third class. The second class comprised the Asians—people who'd capitalize on the Africans' rebellion and had struck a right chord with the whites. They won their hearts and were able to access plum jobs as supervisors and tasked with all clerical duties with higher pay as compared to the Africans. They could get a job offer for their sons. An inexperienced white would be the overall boss. The Asians were able to get ostensibly lucrative tenders from the whites' government. In this manner, they were economically stable; they started several businesses, rose above Africans, and plunged into politics. Later they'd be major financiers of the government. Due to this kind of regrouping against a common enemy, an African army of estimated 17,000 formed a formidable combat that caused mayhem. Every black man was part of this army in his or her smallness. Barack later said that 'the country was going crazy. Gunshots and tension palpable enough to force you back to the village (a more peaceful place)—due to fear of dying.' He added that 'he was part of the army because it was the Africans who were the victims here.' The colonial government responded by sending out over 30,000 soldiers to counter the insurgency. Maybe that's why Barack would describe the city 'crazy and draconian'.

On 24 April 1954, the Operation Anvil came up, after weeks of planning by the army, with the approval of the War Council. The operation effectively placed Nairobi under military siege, and the occupants were screened. The captured *Mau Mau* supporters were moved to restriction camps otherwise called detention camps. Many of the soldiers who were hiding in the forest were smoked out as well. The Home Guard formed the core of the government's strategy as it was composed of loyalist Africans, notably foreign forces, like the loyal British Army or African recruits called King's African Rifles—which Onyango had worked for. Many people, innocent or not, were forced out of the city. Murder and massacre came into effect and thousands died at the wake of a head count (by the end of the State of Emergency, reports indicate that the Home Guard had killed 4686 *Mau Mau*, amounting to 42 *per cent* of the total insurgents). At the end of the war, the mortality rate among Europeans and Asians was a paltry fifty or any other meager number, by all standards. This kind of guerrilla war-like operation is similar to what took place recently in Mt. Elgon, when Government of Kenya laid ambush on the outlawed Sabaot Land Defense Force, killing a number of its soldiers including the mastermind "Major" Matekwei.' The government combat chased them till deep into the forests. And they were killed when they'd nowhere else to run to. The dusty train left them at the Kenyan-Uganda railway terminus headquarters. And John Ong'inya had been waiting to receive him, a bicycle in handy. He was one of the few lucky Kenyans to not only own a bicycle but also have the privilege to ride on it along the streets of Nairobi. The weary-looking Barack had consumed enough dust—he looked dusty to his eyelashes, the hair completely dusty from the red earth . . . in a short while, they were speedily meandering the streets, Ong'inya on the wheels, to a destination he knew little about. The streets were chaotic—people moving west-east, upstreet, and downstreet. Unfriendly faces, people wearing a face of perplexity and unfamiliar color all coming from all walks of life. People dressed in better suits and ties . . . better behaved and moderate. People in a rush. One would wonder where they were going. In the book, *Moi: The Making of an African Statesman*, by Andrew Morton, he describes Nairobi streets more vividly. This is the best description ever and actually pinpointed the rot that was there—Africans being on the receiving end.

> . . . to the busy streets of Nairobi, a city which, though multi-tribal, was clearly racially divided, was a distance measured not just in miles. Indeed, the color bar was so well-defined that in some main streets, for example, one pavement was reserved for whites only.[20]

Oops! Racially divided, although, some element of integration was evident. The whites, Asians, and blacks were able to mingle freely but conscious not to be too personal. Awino, a neighbour, later said that 'Barack was a responsible man who'd embraced his coming of age with good attitude, and he wasn't confused to the allures of city life. He came to start life afresh and that's what he was then looking up to.' Maybe his energy was awesome, evident of someone on the road to make the rough future smooth. After miles from the city center, they rode quietly, a long distance, through bushes. By then the surrounding environment was still bushy and untamed. The now Nairobi National Park harbored wildlife that easily crept to the roads and pathways. While driving, one would stumble against a speeding antelope or a monkey that would jump like a mad cow to the opposite bush in a spin. The people living interiorly had complained about such wild game, particularly the lions and cheetahs which'd kill their domestic animals, eating herd boys. A tin-house in the middle of nowhere, a secluded neighborhood in Pumwani, marked the next homage. Awino had lived here for sometime 'as a home civil servant with no portfolio,' according to how he later described himself. He manned some of the tiny segregated pieces of land that they jointly owned with Onyango at Kariokor and Pumwani. Nairobi life was better and balanced. But he was still a novice.

CHAPTER 9

The Steps of the Determined Person

> There is no real excellence in this entire world, which can be separated from right living.
>
> (David and Jordan)

Now is the time to develop a strong commitment to reality, skeptics toward life, early lesson in devotion to duty, and respect for reason. Civilization spread with railway speed, penetrated rapidly into the unknown depths of Africa. Barack, now in formal dressing, surpassing the traditional type skin-ware, decided to marry. He didn't want to pass down the attitude of failure or defeat to the next generation.

He would later tell Malik that he'd gone through hell in his life. And that 'the son should know that things weren't good at all with Daddy'.

'For failure begets failure.' He later said to Malik, 'Can God put some fire in my spirit? That those children of separated parents are likely to have a failed marriage? Or is it that abused children often become abusive parents? And forget his lost mother?' He stood firm to set a new step.

Marriage not left behind, he vowed not to lean on his own understanding. He was taking a bold step. Never to listen to tales of African women who died during their pregnancy and left no children. Or any story of the sort. He wanted change, but he won't say what change he was looking for. Or did he miss something? Folks, he wanted to marry Kezia Aoko, the lady he met at a function in Kisumu and later East Karachuonyo—a native of Konyango Village around Gendia Mission. The village is a few miles from Mawego

Township. Back in the days, during the good old days of schooling at Maseno, he mused. The lady whose dressing was in finesse . . . , that which extols the values and virtues of the rural Kenyan woman with a modern touch—without any preference of secrecy. This was quite a different turn of event, especially where arranged marriages were still deeply rooted in minds. There was no probing, no digging into each other's history or background. It was evidently unique. He wanted to live his dream, more in need of a vision or destination and a compass to map out the next road to take.

Kezia was fascinating; their meeting was one amazing experience. Her liking to Barack increasingly gained momentum. She threw love into a spin and never backed down in loving him. And she wasn't about to begin. To her, it was highly impossible to let him go.

As Barack showed indication of the scion of hope, Kezia beat odds and logic together, with a soul of mixture of passion and romance though she remained tight-lipped, completely oblivious of the facts covering love. Through their courtship, suspicion and suspense and chivalry and rivalry stalked them everywhere they went. All these trappings never limited their options. Barack's love for Kezia was deeply rooted, but he never provided her with any assurance whatsoever, especially that which involved love and marriage. Maybe buying time! Now where was his delight? He mused, smiling but his tone not altogether friendly.

He was in battle with himself just like an accused homicidal felon on the rampage, running from the hands of justice. Better be safe than sorry or sorry instead of strong or thinking of a ceremony that never was! No—he was going to marry her, through traditional way, with a biblical intent and create that ability to suffice one another. Kezia continued waiting. As if waiting anxiously for the lead to burst out or volcano to explode. A long wait that almost soothed life's worries! 'Dying' in suspense!

Sad memories of colonial government actions lingered high. The colonial masters shamelessly dragged Luo and Kalenjins in droves to Lambwe valley and left them at the mercy of dreaded tsetse flies—causing sleeping sickness, claiming lives of hundreds, if not in thousands. Grouping and groping in darkness for an open launch of attack!

'Why didn't they want to make peace with the colonized? Why?' Barack wondered, 'If peace is a good thing, if peace is rest, it keeps us from fighting, anxiety, and harassment.'

Peace and love is used interchangeably. But power attracts love more, though peace provides the climate for their existence. The world will know peace when power of love shall overcome the love of the power. That's best. Clinging to the least possibility and attracting abstract possibility.

'People want peace that passeth understanding, and I want the understanding which bringeth peace.' Barack cooled according to Sara, descending on the landscape of decision making, in an intense battle on marriage procedure. No wishes to stress. Of concern, he was no free loader, anyway. It is always painful to encounter (with the hard times at the best moods or nasty moods at good splendid times). Or who can be ashamed of his origin? Or struggle to hide anything that might disclose this fact? Barack sensed from the start that Kezia was the woman he'd been looking for. He put a demand in his faith imperative to making a move. Intuitively, he would make very bold statements, but not of dissatisfaction—every weeknight and nightfall, turning ways into will and inabilities to abilities.

'I know I can't do the ordinary and the extraordinary, the natural and supernatural,' he thought, with an obstetric conviction, in a conventional sense. Again, he never believed it is possible to have it all.

He wanted to ask Kezia anything because he had the freedom to do so, but there was nothing to ask anyway. Having Kezia like a friend was a blessing and having her as a wife would be the source of all blessings. He was unswervingly determined to pursue her—operating on an accelerated time line. That's one of his biggest faults. He had had enough. Enough faults. He was giving himself another solace. Sara agrees and says that things were tough . . . And, as Hawa puts it, Barack would say thus:

'My spirit is a sickening spiral, escalating every day. I don't know what's going on around my life.' She recalls her brother's behavior. 'Barack doubted, his esophagus contracting and tears coming to his eyes.' The confidence to marry descended from elation to bitter lament. Thoughts took toll of him, and everybody suspected that his zeal had no limit. Maybe, he walked in his sleep, waking twice at night with screaming nightmares.

Malik would agree that his father poured a lot for him . . . 'He could even tell me how he kept dreaming . . .'

'Do you hear what I say?' Barack would ask himself in deep sleep. 'No. I don't want to,' he would reply, feeling melancholy in the dream.

'If you open something, you'll surely close it,' Barack once told Kezia in another dream without explaining what he meant.

'But how about if you break it? Will you close it back?' Kezia would joke in one of their many steamy conversations. Barack was neither off-putting nor able to resist any longer, sustaining their wait for power of love. But how was he going to redress the growing imbalances in his family?

Traditionally, marriage was solemnized just like in the modernity, although the former had a (great) number of rituals that accompanied it than the latter. Onyango Hussein, who married in pomp, in a traditional classified, the prodigal father, was not here, working in Nairobi, and sometimes had gone abroad. No family reunion. Barack had at one time struggled to seal the void, compounding their souls together—but careful in accepting the things he couldn't change. Sometimes, a confluence of factors would surface: practical, psychological, and emotional. Indelibly, causing more confusion with a heavy heart, he replied to all these woes. 'I give myself time to do the simple things. And I plan. I choose the easiest route that looks good but with a minimal fuss. I know that fear of discrimination is a powerful motive for keeping quiet. Denial, deception, shall keep me going!'

'It didn't last, to be honest, for long, but it was a medicine.' Kezia would later tell Barack, without a backward glance or bad cheer.

'. . . I'm seeing you going down the road of self-criticism, but then, you don't have to! Or are looks just too deceiving?' Kezia threw a jab. Barack had nothing to confess, but had a reason to contemplate about deep in his heart, clock fast ticking its long hand away. Upon which they had to start counting. Barack often referred to her as Grace. 'My Grace, the love of my heart.

'I don't have the abundance of love in my heart. Let me enjoy the little I have. Yes, I don't want a lot of it. It's poisonous.'

Malik says, 'He thought dating was taking root; it was a world of unknown, world on its own isolation. My mother used to warn him to be wary of love. "It's infectious,"' she said.

'Look here, Barack . . . ,' she advised, 'people have used you. And you don't just let them do it over and over again.' Hawa says Kezia once poured out her soul to him. 'Do you like it? You actually like it? You'd rather be abused than pay attention to the people who have tried to care about you? Why put yourself to this shame? You need to list all what you want before you take time to do them: it is necessary. It's a passionate appeal.'

'Barack and Kezia loved each other,' Hawa says, 'and love actually accepted them, connecting them together. No rush. They weren't about to tell anybody about it. They couldn't understand what they were going through.'

From a distance, Kezia knew this pretty even. 'You'd rather be abused than pay attention to the people who have tried to care about you,' Hawa comments.

Without asking, she suspected that this union was about to end even before it started. 'Maybe Kezia found so many men coveting her. But that was not enough to worry her. She wanted Barack to pursue her, in fact, with an ardor that he first found embarrassing. With an abandoned presence,' Hawa concurs.

Sara thought, 'I suppose it's the spirit of the era that makes her want to soothe this awkward boy, dark, and full of secret woe, whom, she knew, her parents would regard as less than she deserved.' Recollecting all these trimmed up situations, her personality changed with a manifested ferocious intellect and other virtues that remained remote.

Now who knows? Who knows what's going on in a woman's heart? She can change her mind. And if she changes it, she would let him know. A feminine influence! His heart was burning everywhere and anywhere, with a favorite passion quickening in expression of love. He'd to live and labor for the fragility of humanity, enthusiasm of marriage, and fire of God. The glow of youthhood able to define the thin boundary between deception and persuasion, capability, and capacity. Maybe the age was too remote for accurate guess? The entire anticlimax left both of them depressed.

'I think she suggested it would be better if I didn't mention her name,' Barack thought, at least, according to Hawa. 'No wavering but drowning in fear,' she says.

'And what can shape a boy into a man, his reluctance? Giving way to interest? Or interest to fascination?'

'The surrounding situation was an eyesore and details in her mind were scanty enough. Hurting indeed. Secrets that can cause mass exodus of people?' Hawa questions.

'Hope he's still in one piece,' Kezia said, for she found herself thinking about Barack constantly. She'd talked to him once, yet she was unable to get him out of her mind. She could not explain it even to herself. A feeling she had never had before, an attraction she had never felt for any other man.

Kezia wasn't a village girl after all; she was sleek and sophisticated with the polished aura of the wealthy socialite, irresistible. She would be combing out her hair and tying it back with a red ribbon every evening, in a new style and fashion never seen before. Perfumes and variety of colognes were a big hit in town, the in-thing. Kezia would close the wooden door, cramped, leaving behind a fragrance of rose or jasmine, just like a twilight girl looking for a fling! She did it in the heat of the moment, her energy shifting and favoring the idea. She had a deep passion for fashion—every thought was a composite of a physiological advantage in her mind—pitting her over the edge.

Prodding questions began to arouse memories, good riddance. Malik believes that his mother wasn't at ease at all. According to him, that was going to the next destiny she'd been waiting for!

'Why can't he come out so that I can give him savage beatings if he doesn't want love, huh? Hopefully yes. He needs some thorough beatings. He's elusive or guilty of "murder," plain and simple.'

He wasn't in the mood to talk or think much about it. She once looked into his eyes and saw the despair there. 'Could this be the reason why he's taking too long to respond?' She belonged to him, body and soul. But she wanted to coil the mixed signals together—to appear indifferent or infallible. Stubbornness captured him like idolatry, with compelling truth pedaling the process.

'Now how can the strength of a man's virtue be scaled, should it be through special extortions or by his habits?' Kezia thought. 'Oh—hail the power of stubbornness.'

Time allowed him to bring out feelings in her that she had suppressed wild, atavistic passions, that she'd been afraid to let loose. Never to throw it down his throat, only pleasure—pleasure Kezia hadn't dreamed possible. Pleasure pulling her from the brink of giving up!

Nairobi

Kenya

CHAPTER 10

The whole life is but a moment of time. It is our duty, therefore, to use it, not to misuse it.(Anonymous)

In 1954 and 1955, Nairobi

The village was torn. At a time when hunger, thirst, hopelessness, and frenzy gripped it, he came to Pumwani; this was the convergence point of most Luo job seekers. Pumwani wasn't teeming up with a warren of shacks, open sewers, and dirty alleys—like what you see today. And it wasn't a home to over one million people, now living in abject poverty, where there is no shred of hope or self-importance.

Pumwani was Nairobi, and Nairobi was Pumwani, a city of danger and fortune, a place where one could translate his meager knowledge, that is, from poor peasant to an all-time wealthy socialite. It was a land of opportunities, a city where traffic became denser by the day. 'Where do all these come from? And who owns them?' a short, tough, squat, little man asked. Tall buildings, sophisticated mansions, unlike the tiny huts of Kogelo! Nairobi was 'a place of cool waters' like some sanctuary detached from the wild savannah land. Through Pumwani, slum boys would sneak contraband to the city. In most cases, they'd not succeed; the colonial police (called *Afande)* and their supervisors (*Nyapala or Nyapara*—depending on your pronunciation*)* would hit regularly, in running battles with the youths; the gangs sometimes masquerading as police officers would bombard unexpectedly, and a battle would ensue. Conversely, the *afandes,* in a brown double-breasted suit and a tiny brown pair of shorts, would dress like women in scarves and raid illegal liquor dens, making huge arrest and recovering lots of liters of illegal brew. The police boss, in a wide brightly colored tie, would assess the aftermath and wonder 'What's going on?'

Barack would go out there to look for employment. Those days manual jobs were in plenty unlike what you see nowadays. Just a paltry number of Kenyans had left their villages for lucrative jobs in the city. They would work in a construction site; the building sometimes would come down due to negligence and poor workmanship. The rubble pancaked on top of them. He worked so well considering his lack of experience. Life was hard enough. The gangs that masqueraded in the informal settlement slum, sniffing for valuables—then the life of criminals. And the residents dreaded their return. Perhaps a great number of people were still waiting, in futility, patiently, for independence. He'd met Mohammed Suleiman who gave him tips on job hunting; Suleiman had been very close to Hussein, and they worked both in religious matters and political activism. Two people—so unalike—agreeing fiercely on a future. Malik believes that he was an intelligent man, advanced in age, kind face, light in complexion just as different as Onyango, looked more religious—dressed in a *khanzu* just like the *Indian coolies* who worked on the railway line. *A coolie* was a derogatory term describing Indians and other Asiatic people—from the Orient. From his looks, he seemed a very social and exposed man and talked fondly of his white employers; he was 'a cook supervisor for a senior colonial official'.

There were people mending the railway—a folk of Indians wearing funny little round hats, oversized working suit pants, and a windcheater with elasticized ankles. Barack would work on the railway line just like anybody else doing menial jobs. But his diligence was evident.

Malik says that 'they'd dogs, with white markings, and head, the size of a basketball, the biggest pit bull he'd met in the continent, serious looking animals wagging their tails like a rag doll. The animals looked very harsh, that they could sink their poisonous teeth deep into the bone. Then crunch the bone, leaving their victims in a bloody heap. And the job seekers were to meet employers or presumed employers who were so reluctant and would continue to stir their coffee with the arm of their spectacles, looking strangely at their vulnerable victims—"a bushman" they'd called. And you'd continue to explain yourself hoping he's listening. They'd throw you out to some manual work. It's like slamming the desperate man to a break, in a short skid distance.' They continued to behave that way thinking Africans were least candidates for the available jobs. Of course, it wasn't easy to get that lucrative job in a silver platter despite the fact that they were in plenty. The damage they inflicted on the Africans was too much that would haunt them for decades. It'd be hard to clean up; Barack vowed not to allow giving-up get to his script, for life had bruised his heart red, and the white man had scarred it to a premature misery.

When trouble arose in Nairobi on 21 January 1955, barbed wires were erected all over the capital. British soldiers kept vigil from rooftops of high buildings, their rifles roaring to shoot at any African who would dare come closer in an attack; the soldiers would sometime corner a daring civilian—they'd not stop beating him half-way until he died. From a low-flying aeroplane, in residential areas, leaflets were dropped. Sir Evelyn Baring, the Governor, and General Erskine signed these leaflets—at a time when the *Mau Mau* influence had reached the heart of the city.

It read thus:

> The Kenya Government has offered all the Mau Mau Freedom Fighters a chance to surrender to the security forces. His Excellency the Governor Sir Evelyn Baring has given a general amnesty to all persons who have committed crimes during the Emergency up to 18 January 1955 . . .' [21]

At the end were signatures belonging to the governor and the general on both margins of the paper that cheered up the information.

In disguise, it was a scheme that was meant to capture the vulnerable culprit. Many people were caught unaware, arrested, and convicted. During such a swoop, Stephen Oloo, an ex-policeman, was detained; David Oluoch, a KAU member, and Reuben Demesi, all were close friends of Onyango. They'd been arrested before in a protest, charged, and taken to Kamiti Maximum Security Prison. In this case, the three were taken to Mageta Camp headed by a 'rogue' white man who talked of Treaty of Westphalia that ended the thirty years war in 1648. One would wonder why he talked about it frequently.

This was their second arrest.

Apparently, Onyango would have been caught as well, had it not been that he was nursing back his fast-slipping life, the wounds of independence struggle—a freedom fighter that never received a medal? And if he received one, then it was stolen or misplaced.

In the book by Caroline Elkins, *Imperial Reckoning: Untold story of Britain's' Gulag in Kenya* (Pg 143), this particular island is described by the author in more critical view. It served as a concentration camp deep into the turbulent waters of Lake Victoria.

> '. . . camp to find nothing. This seems to have been the norm for the remote camps, like the one on Mageta Island, in Lake Victoria. There the batch of detainees arrived in shackles in the cargo hold of a boat . . .' [22]

On 15 March 1955, the year scrabble became a game; Sara Onyango got a baby boy. Onyango's happiness couldn't come out, especially in public but deep inside he was a happy man; in private, he fought down joy. The boy was named Yusuf Onyango; one neighbor couldn't pronounce the name properly and continually called him Yusup and that name eventually stuck—Yusup Onyango.

In the Year 1956

The capture of de facto leader of *Mau Mau* Dedan Kimathi on 21 October 1956, south-east of the capital, Nairobi, in Nyeri, a town at the foot of Mt. Kenya, signified the ultimate defeat of the outlawed *Mau Mau* group and essentially ended the military guerrilla offensive against the white man. In this year till early 1957, substantial governmental changes to land tenure occurred, the most important of which was used to punish the *Mau Mau* adherents. Swynnerton Plan rewarded loyalists and reprimanded *Mau Mau*. So there was also the Operation Anvil. The plan was completely hard to predict. All these happened against the backdrop of marriage about to be 'solemnized' between Kezia Aoko from Konyango Village and her long-time friend, Barack Obama, from Alego. At this point or in this age in time, people started celebrating marriage in a different way; this wasn't an exception. And how would Kezia put it?

Malik narrates how Kezia fondly talked of their meeting. 'It was at a dance in Kendu Bay, my hometown. Barack was there on holiday with his family,' she later said.

'I went to the dance hall with my cousin William, and I saw Barack entering the room. I thought, "Oh, wow". He was so lovely with his dancing, so handsome and so smart.'

Malik says that his mother was a born Christian in a family of boys and several girls; among them were Kezia and Jane. They would sneak with her friends, never to be noticed by their stern father, to dance to the tune of *orutu* (a traditional lyre) and *nyatiti* (a harp). The musicians would skillfully play the harp accompanied by *bunde* (drums), gourd flute, and *ongen'go* (metal rings) in a traditional outfit called *ohangla dance*. Their mother, Perpetua, would realize that the girl and her cousins had sneaked out, but she'd remain numb to avoid instability. Probing them would be a recipe for chaos. People, old and young, would emerge from darkness, whenever the musician launches a hit song.

According to Malik, his mother says that 'We went to a local dance ground near Kendu Bay. It was a notorious dancing arena where people assembled early enough, both for an afternoon jig and a late-night party. There were bonfires all over, like some sort of a jungle party. See, it was a great experience. We met people from everywhere. That's where I met Barack. You know, I'd already known him before?

On December holidays, it was both pomp and merrymaking and that's when youths' got time to intermingle and have fun. It was commonplace therefore to meet abruptly or plan a date. So I was off school. Each day Barack and my cousin would stop by the house. Every time I looked, they were always there, trying to convince me to go with Barack to Nairobi.

About a week later, William and I took Barack to the station. We were going to say, 'Bye bye, see you next time,' except that there was no bye bye. When the train arrived, William and Barack said, 'You are going to Nairobi,' and I obliged.

If Nyandega had got a clue, he would have instructed the station manager that 'if a girl fitting her description comes with a boy to buy tickets for Nairobi, he must turn her away. However, the boy is free to go! Have no business with him.'

Hawa says, 'The two had developed a tangent for each other. They both felt a great relief so much as feeling cut adrift. A strong hint then came out that they might try their best for one another. Kezia Aoko (daughter of Perpetua Adera and Mzee Nyandega) had escaped to Nairobi's Ofafa Jericho. The sprawling Jericho was one of the middle-income-earners estates that actually constituted the civil servants, well-to-do city council officers, clerical workers, and a number of civil society staff. The spectacular identity of Jericho was the city council houses that attracted even the nonstaff—the 'ghost' tenants. Ofafa was an acronym of Eastland Townships named after a priest Ambrose Ofafa who, as was mentioned, was assassinated by an unknown vigilante group. Ambrose, while he was alive, would walk throughout this township condemning the atrocities that were being committed by the *Mau Mau* against the *Luos* living here. He met his torturing death together with his friend, Tom Mbotela. Therefore, there was Ofafa Jericho that came after Makadara, the oldest estate in the area. Although some other estates sprouted, such as Maringo, Lumumba, Mbotela (named after Tom Mbotela), Makongeni, and Shauri Moyo among others, the most notable was Ofafa Jerusalem commonly known as 'Salem'. It'd the highest population. So there was Ofafa Jericho; Barack lived here—Ofafa Mbotela, Ofafa Maringo, and Ofafa Makongeni . . . as earlier indicated all these had a joint acronym Ofafa. One of the government houses was situated in Makadara, then the part of the nerve center of government business. So commuting to town wasn't necessary or wasn't a big hassle. Something that Barack preferred. He'll just walk to work. This government house was later turned to Nairobi Law Courts, the current Makadara Law Courts. The old railway line connected it to town center. Most notably were Thames, Austin, and Ford-made vehicles that plied here ferrying the government officials and well-off Africans. (Ford V8 was the most outstanding and later Ford Escort). Due to this, people living in Kaloleni, Bahati, and Makongeni moved en masse to occupy better houses put up by the Nairobi City Council in the neighborhood, Jericho city, although they knew not that it's a government project. It wasn't easy to differentiate the two. Later, maybe after months, the Commonwealth Development Agency built Buru Buru Estate. And Eastland was a complete district altogether. Currently, and politically, Eastland is 'a city within a city'.

Back to the story . . .

Malik says, 'My father had secured a house Number 445 built by the Nairobi City Council authorities with support from the Central Government—those tiny tin-roof "self-contained houses" built on postage-stamp-size piece of plot. His smoky paraffin lamp would be an asset when darkness falls. Dirty paths posed danger by the heavy dust that billowed up the surface. The dust causing danger settled on the not-very-good-looking pieces of furniture he possessed. These houses had a small kitchen that fit only one person at a time and a toilet on the backside.'

Barack would land in this house with the help of an initiative of Tom Mboya, who spearheaded a housing scheme. This came under the transforming and upgrading system of the Kenya Local Government Workers' Union. His Worship the Mayor, Reggie Alexander, had been defeated in a highly spirited case filed by Tom Mboya and Karebe to stop the project. It's the time when Mboya represented the poorest in the country, living in slums and dilapidated neighborhood. He would run most of his affairs at home or meet his friends—Barack being one of them—at the Civil Servants Union in Kariokor (the current Starehe Constituency). Barack later became a life friend after joining this Union. This is where the dream to learn and get Western exposure was hatched. Meanwhile, Kezia started her cooking, a job she liked most, with great cooking skills—the man, after work, would sit, read his newspaper, taking in the sweet and savory smells from the boiling pot in the kitchen. The married couple enjoyed the companionship. His neighbor, Morris, an elderly who worked at the Public Works Department and lived with his son (while the wife stayed in the countryside) was happy that his closest friend, Barack, had finally 'settled down'. Though, as others celebrated his achievement, and Barack hopeful and mightily proud that Kezia accepted the settlement, it wasn't a good riddance to some people, notably Nyandega, Kezia's father.

This marriage particularly angered Mzee Nyandega; he marshaled his sons, William Odiawo Nyandega, Shem Nyagaya, and Solomon Nyandega to the city to bring her back. Awiti Nyandega was too young to go. Odiawo was a no-nonsense and nonentertainer. He died last year, aged seventy-five. Surprisingly, they'd made a deal with Barack to sneak Kezia out! Of Kezia's brothers, Shem died long time ago but Awiti is alive. The man talks positively of his nephew, Barack Jr, the President of United States with a warm smile. 'He is a man with high integrity. I wish we would have him here.' Awiti lives with his wife (a businesswoman) and three children. Although he is under treatment from unknown ailment that has twisted his arms, he says 'I've been sick for a while, but I'm improving so fast.'

On the issue of Kezia's sudden disappearance, he says, 'My father had probed the issue and rejected the timing. He thought "it would have been better if Barack had added more cattle to the fold before thinking of snatching her away—unceremoniously." He did not meet the demand. And that's why they had stripped him of every opportunity to keep her. Of course, later, my father relented.'

When Mzee Nyandega contacted Onyango and failed concerning the early unprocedural exit, he decided to go after his daughter . . . 'To take the bull by the horns.'

The journey to Nairobi was kept secret so that news of our coming wouldn't reach Barack before we got there. And the old man was smart enough to find him unawares. There was no much talking. The irate father, flanked by his furious sons, baying for Barack's blood, whisked off the young lady from cohabitation. It's good he wasn't around. Hawa says, 'If he were there, things would have turned nasty. He would have made a mistake of fighting them.

When Barack came from work, in the evening, he heard sundry and irritating stories . . . an empty house and neighbors' housewives gossiping, more willing thematically to tell it all. It burgeoned and sent deadly tentacles into parts of Kogelo and Konyango villages. Villagers from both clans were indeed remorseful.' Morris, a lean man who'd use no excess words just as his inexcess weight, an incisive thinker, who had no tribal tinge that characterized other non-Luos, consoled him and told 'to stay focused and look for alternatives'. He became his mentor in such times.

'Just take it like a real man, Barack. You have to face it off without fear.' This is characteristic of what some societies practice—honor killing—where a woman is stoned to death for infidelity or any form of 'immoral behavior'. *Ramogi* people didn't apply such form of punishment. They literally took their daughter away. But still it was severe. Barack had to rid himself of fear.

He couldn't listen. That was a weakness. The following day, he'd pressed his supervisor, Mr Wycliffe, for two weeks paid leave and maybe an increment in salary since he had a lot of issues to sort out. All this bombarded on a deaf ear except for a one-week paid leave granted. He headed straight to Kogelo, maybe that he felt traumatized and debilitated, shadow-boxing with the issue at hand, to look for a means to 'solemnize' his marriage to Kezia Aoko. The family wasn't against Barack, but the way he took their daughter wasn't mature at all. It was too casual. The rituals were absolutely absent . . . that was rather a matter of concern . . . shame that the old man was trying to avoid. So Kezia was back in Konyango Village, and not happy at all, though; she felt cheated, and no piece of comfort would have made her stop crying—the cry of pain and that of pestilence. For Barack, caught in the jam of neglect, like an African goat suffering unnecessary cruelty in the hands of unprofessional butchers, the butchers doing their thing badly, this was bad news. He made an emergency stop at Kogelo. Onyango was fuming like boiled yam in spite of his physical pain. He'd found it rather amusing—the route Barack's life had taken, before it even started. When all had been discussed, two men were sent with fourteen cattle to Konyango Village—the birthplace of Kezia Aoko—in Karachuonyo—just around Gendia. Sara had prayed and given her blessings for journey mercies. The custom was to dictate the rest.

Onyango forked the cattle. Barack was to follow the troop the following day. It was marked by wit . . . the renegotiation wasn't easy. To add insult, there were job pressures back in Nairobi. 'He was needed to report back to work and juggling the two became so tricky but what could he do?' Hawa asks. Between

1954 and 1956, the number of jobseekers had doubled, and Nairobi felt larger than it had the day before.

January 1957

Kenyans were haggling for political supremacy; one of such Kenyan was Barack's old friend and a mentor, Onyulo G. N., a Maseno High School graduate who worked with him in his formative years in Nairobi. Onyulo was working at the Judicial Department as a clerical interpreter. One thing that distinguished him was his oratory and the knack of language skills. Also Kadima JGW who graduated almost at the same time as TJ from St Mary's High School, Yala, grew to become a serious politician. He would defer with Barack anyway, saying, 'See, Barack, your ideas, especially of "accuracy" is, I fear, somewhat different from mine.' Maybe he felt that Barack was somewhat independent minded. And maybe Barack felt that he imposed philosophies on other people although the two would still consult one another before sunset.

The same beginning of 1957 was marked by awesome love and marriage celebrations. It was still very volatile since the declaration of State of Emergency in 1952. Even traveling was still a complicated affair . . .

The scars of the battle were finally over.

Hawa says, 'The Konyango Village played host to Barack and his other three cousins, Ndalo Ayus (named after Onyango Hussein's brother), Alfred Obambo Lodi, and Samuel Abon'go. Ndalo was an expert negotiator from Kogelo who'd been consulted whenever such duties called in. He died when he was down to 'a single tooth'. The late had come of age and was known to quell tempers. Barack picked him for this role. His namesake had accompanied Onyango when the latter went to marry Sara Ogwel. He had since died. Samuel Abon'go was just three months older than Barack. He played the central role of negotiating the bride price for he was recently married to a much younger girl. Malik says that they (Barack and Samuel Abon'go) grew up just as brothers. He lived and died at K'Obama Village in Kanyadhiang. He said that he'd encouraged Barack 'not to begin to entertain the idea of second marriage. That he'd been in trouble before—sneaking Kezia to Nairobi. And marriage woes had been written on the palms of his hands.'

Samuel Abon'go talked of Barack, saying, 'He (Barack) later told me a lot of things surrounding his life. And what many people say about Barack is all wrong! That he'd inordinate pride in his appearance, that he soaked his life in a port of wine. That he'd drink too much . . . I never saw him so drunk to stage what people say about him. That he committed suicide, that's not true!

'The hosts were so different contrary to what they'd done before,' Samuel Abong'o recalled. We went there, shaken, in the pedestal of fear. And I thought, 'What if they attacked us? But we remained positive, Nyandega and Perpetua, very happy that their daughter was ceremoniously married. I believe that my brother, Barack, did the right thing.'

Malik emphasizes that 'Traditionally, suitors were sent to the girls' homestead to negotiate. Remember the case of Sara Onyango, my grandmother, where rituals were a composite of the marriage ceremony' . . . In this case, during the material day, Barack joined in with three friends and set foot in Karachuonyo for a hand in marriage. Previously, some cattle had been sent to Nyandega. 'That was called *ayie,*' Hawa concurs.

She's very sure that Barack married at a time he needed a companion.

'It finally happened between the year 1956 and early 1957 due to the fact that it was elaborate enough. Barack took in arms to make sure that his marriage wasn't going to fail at all, and his father, Onyango, present then, was supportive and literally ordered Sara to release the herd of cattle for Barack's marriage. He was no longer outside the country then or working for the British government, maybe, in Burma and Zanzibar, and no longer trotting the world as the white people led them from one conflict zone to another troubled zone: from Burma to Zanzibar, Tanga to the interior of African violence-marred Continent, and back to Europe. He longed to be with his son at Konyango; he'd wanted to choose for him the best bulls from the herd, toward this course, but that didn't happen. He was nursing the wounds of colonial masters, grounded in his hut.

He was outside the country then, working for the British government, maybe in Burma and Zanzibar

True love and the glamour went abode. They rivaled everything people said or had done against them. After the negotiation, the old man had called Barack aside, 'Kezia is all I got, Barack,' he said, his face remorseful.

'I see.'

Malik says that his grandfather, Nyandega, was a strict disciplinarian; he had educated Kezia in a world against girl-child education. Nyandega, an Adventist, would be very sure that Barack was the right man for his daughter; he'll give him all the blessings . . .

Samuel notes, 'I got wind of their conversations. Nyandega had warned him thus:

'I'll be watching over you,' he said. 'You better make her happy and warm. You know what I mean?—Happy!'

'Understood, Papa. We'll be a great couple. Moreover, Kezia is great,' Barack replied.

'No fights or wagging fists, no quarrel, no anything . . . I mean no bad things, son.'

'Understood, Papa.'

'Kezia is polite and a great cook. Make sure you're there for her food. You're going to be a son-in-law we're proud of! Right?

'You have to make sure you take good care of her, huh!'

'I promise, Papa. I'm going to do everything you said. I'll be a great comforter.'

'Promise me, Barack!'

'Promise. Sure, I have to apply some fresh eyes to this marriage, in the meantime, and we'll surely have plenty to talk about!'

Samuel says that good friendship was arrived at and a promise made . . .

'Agreed, Barack?'

'Agreed.'

'I'm not through with you yet. Now that you're part of my family—"royal family," maybe, we need to talk sometime later.'

'Good chap. Don't go breaking her heart. Now you can go right ahead and join your colleagues?'

And he had walked away, leaving the old man and Perpetua, who'd joined him, staring after him.

He thought himself a baby, getting stern instruction.

Samuel adds, 'Old men were particularly harsh on their daughters. Barack found that the sun rose and set on his eyes. He was a lucky shot. He had dwelt on marrying Kezia at graphic length, never consumed with fear or intimidation.

Of course, intimidation from rival suitors! Yet he didn't brag about it.'

'Barack held the efficiency in climbing the ladder of success, while Kezia Aoko kept a keen eye on the ladder leaning against the right wall. This is how they suffice one another,' Samuel says.

'Both didn't depend solely on how much effort they expended but on whether or not the effort they expended was in the right jungle.'

He thought himself a baby, getting stern instruction.

Samuel understood Barack so well. He thought, 'I'd taken the task, in marriage, and no one's tears will prevent me from succeeding in it,' Barack promised. His eyes set on the ultimate goal and the ultimate price: *Successful marriage.*

He told Samuel, 'People would retreat in fear or go forward in brevity. But my compassion for Kezia shall never swing. It'll remain steadfast.'

'And who will keep me from falling?' He equipped according to Malik.

Barack called, with intensity, 'Never to be a doubter but a believer, a perseverer and not a quitter.' Hawa says, 'The mystery in marriage was a hard nut to crack.'

'And it was his chance, in time, to choose.'

Hawa says, 'When the two finally settled at Ofafa Jericho, working as a clerical officer, earning $1 a month at Kenya Railways Headquarters wasn't a favorable waiver from life's hardships. If the boss parted with a paltry 160 shillings, what of a clerk? The poor men would be broke every day, all year round. Their family would suffer out of this. Maybe making a facelift from soft loans—which sublimed before it got to its intended purpose. The pay was so meager that one wouldn't admire keeping a pet. The exercise meant an additional expense from the already overspent purse. Overburdened pocket—but binge, drinking alcoholics faced the grim picture with solitude. Drinking was inevitable. There were domestic front misunderstandings, slips in providing for the extended family . . . that he would take away at the famous Driving Inn Pub in the neighborhood Kaloleni Estate. This was a notorious pub at a corner. The whites streamed in, some with their wives, others just wanted some peaceful fun—the cold evening biting the dark faces—desperate for change. Barack would come late—at the middle of the night—banging the metal door at 10 p.m. or 11 p.m. That was life. It'd to go that way, avoiding it—a major eyesore. And life would have been so real. Something he'd not faced head-on. A stupor would be prevailed with a cold shower, taken from a basin, in the morning. As the hangovers were washed away—he would rush to work, a bit late, the sway of alcohol still strong. The man looking a little confused from the weekend allures. The pub was a beehive of activities with people finding themselves in a rather precarious state with their seniors.'

Malik says that his father would tell him of men bumping with their bosses' wives on the dance floor . . . 'Look at the story of Odanga. The night owl saw a lovely woman on the dance floor. And he asked her for a jig. The woman agreed and got into his two arms, and he then commended her on how great her footwork was. Odanga would ask her 'What's your name?' 'Mrs Thompson—Tom Thompson.' He paused for a while and thought, 'That's my boss's name.' Odanga dropped her and literally ran away. 'I almost passed out,' he said. He left the poor woman in shock and disbelief. The white woman, dazed and dejected, looked down and went to the husband, who'd been watching closely. That was the wife of his boss, Tom Thompson. He said later that Odanga almost wanted to sink beneath the floorboards. For humiliation was too much to bear. When he reported to work after the weekend spree and incident—after spending sleepless night—he sheepishly went on with his chores. Most of the time his head was down. At one point, he heard Tom shouting, 'You're a rogue. A big bastard . . .' He thought the world was about to collapse, looking spent and terrified. Moments later, he'd realize that Tom was shouting to an unknown receiver on the other end. For one, life was revolutionizing—from ash age for whitening teeth and blue detergent to bathe to real social climb—dancing, Scotch whisky, water-flush toilets, and showers. From roasting birds in open fire in the field, grazing cattle, eating roasted corns, and listening to fables from older folks to boasting about good pay . . . And a great car!'

For Kezia, living in Eastland was an eye opener. And whenever she visited Kogelo, Sara would advise her, 'Open up your eyes. Start your own business, sell clothes, and hawk goods to supplement your husband's meager income. Or else, you'll become a prisoner of insufficiency.' The same sentiment echoed by Perpetua, her mother.

The man would deflect criticism from Kezia—the pay wasn't good enough, squeezing it against the needs of a multitude from Kogelo to Kendu Bay back to a single room in Nairobi's Jericho. Barack wasn't even a working class. The poor man's life was painted red with frustration: money issues. First, Onyango's purse was wide-open enough to swallow the whole income. Second, there was litany of accusations—of being lazy and not working hard enough. So many people would come, neighbors, relatives, still in their local dialect, streamed in whenever Barack visited the village. Handouts came out freely—another channel of expense, and expenditure sheet was growing mightier and larger.

Omar needed another pair of shorts or shirt—the ones he'd, had been bruised by event, patches more than the original garment. And Nyan'goma Primary second PTA teacher—Samson Chillo—was against tatters, so Omar would be sent home to get a new attire. Barack, the real man, the responsibility lying squarely on his head, would provide. Zeituni was happy that the elder brother is around, promising her that 'he'll take her to the city'.

'I'll take you with me to Nairobi—to the city.' And Barack would be a king. Showers of praises would adorn him all day long. But keen to avoid demystifying how city life was bitter. Sara Nyaoke was in Kendu Bay, Kaluo Village, to visit her mother Akumu. And Hawa Auma had come back from Nairobi and had gone to visit Barack, and Onyango wanted her back next to him. Hawa says that her father would complain 'you don't allow your daughter to rove all over the city like a lost creature.'

In July 1958, prosecution of AEMO (African Elected Members Organization) who included its Chairman Oginga Odinga in a Nairobi Makadara Court caused a major pitfall. Barack and many other young men would protest. They held placards and large banners written as follows:

> *To hell with the Lennox-Boyd Constitution*
> *Freedom and Justice for Kenya.*

The government was flexing its muscle and condemning them for riots and incitement. The same government was not supportive enough to listen to their grievances.

* * *

Meeting Tom Mboya (TJ), at Kaloleni Hall was a blessing in disguise.

At his residence in Ziwani Estate, Barack would meet his friend there, no more than once, and they'd hatched a scheme to have, at least, an office in Kariokor. This is where the flurry of activities and connections started. Barack had known TJ following his friendship with Pamela Odede from their old days at Ng'iya. Hawa says that our relationship with the Odede's 'was purely through inheritance'. So TJ knew Barack just as a brother. 'Barack and TJ then hatched "a cordial cohabitation" because they shared one vision'. Hawa says that the piece of plot that TJ lived in was part of Onyango's land that they'd bought as a joint group with other friends that included Leonardus Ndiege, TJ's father.

The confident trade unionist was meeting workers within his docket—The Kenya Workers' Union. It was at such occasions that many dissatisfied low-income earners would air their grievances to a confident trade unionist. Coincidentally, TJ had traveled widely and was enjoying massive support from various stakeholders in trade industry, and those keen on workers' plight—the so-called human activists. They included blacks and white folks in equal share. He'd made a dozen of friends—from Kenya's landscape to the entire Africa region, from Johannesburg to Cairo, from Nairobi to Accra, Ghana. He'd shared platform with Kwame Nkrumah and Nelson Mandela. TJ created a good rapport with the Americans and the Russians alike, Kenyans in Diaspora and Africans in high offices around the world. In his footsteps, Barack followed.

This inter-connection would lead to a constant stream of whites to his tiny office in Kariokor, from J. F. Kennedy's family to other philanthropists devoted to change 'a rather bad situation such as oppression and racism'. People's lives had hope on the flipside. Senator Robert Kennedy would visit this office—when he came to Starehe Boys Center—in his company was Geoffrey Griffins—the principal of the school. This was the time TJ was elected the patron of the school, a position he served until 1969 when he met his cruel death. Later the senator addressed a gathering at Kaloleni Hall.

The hall would be packed on Sundays—when Kenyans, confined to informal settlement by the ruling class, made a persistent cry against poor working conditions and meager stipends. And TJ would step in, into big offices, and plead their cases. Some bosses would promise better terms when protesters caused mayhem; they'd promise 'we'll see in to it'. The seminal influence wouldn't allow them stop the deceit.

TJ's meetings saw an overflow of humanities. The people would gather to listen to him, others would climb trees (as if he was some sort of Jesus of Nazareth), and some others would knock a branch off a tree that struck those beneath. This meant they'd taken issues more seriously than they took most things. The old high and dry situations were dire. Their target and, indeed, worry wasn't against anything but on those who cruised on Ford V8, those they worked for millions of shillings yet didn't plough back a fraction to the work pool, those on high-waist shorts, and on long-patterned socks and a plus eight snickers. Their children clutched onto their hands on an outing or evening stroll—the blue suspenders ran down the waist. They were people who'd nothing to hide and hid nothing—purveyors of determination and hardship.

Many pundits would call it a drunken decision made by outrageous, arrogant, and inferior blacks, who'd wanted money to blow. No, it was no mean cry—the colonized had learnt the money 'prudence', and their demand was as reasonable as those of their immediate counterparts.

Barack met many white people, from trade unionists to educationists, Americans, and Britons. They'd started various projects through the banner of TJ office—a shabby one to be precise.

Barack got wind of some short courses that would enable one to gain entry to any university overseas—a boy was born on 15 March 1958, his name was Roy, at the now Pumwani Maternity Hospital, formerly known as Lady Ainsworth Maternity. It was one of the first World War Hospitals; others were in Kisii District, established in 1916, which dealt with the treatment of extremely wounded soldiers. Lady Ainsworth was a 'first class hospital'—a reserve for civil servants, its first stone laid by Mrs Lady Ainsworth, who gave hope to those who couldn't afford King George's Hospital, the current Kenyatta National Hospital, or the European Hospital (currently Nairobi Hospital). It dealt mainly with emergency birth cases. And the shock is that you'd see convalescing mothers sharing beds, while others slept on the floor. In this hospital, mothers would be discharged prematurely to create room for others who'd be at the verge of labor. More than forty children would be born daily. Although, earlier on, it was for the spouses of military soldiers, before it could be opened to the public.

In March 1959, Barack had sat a Correspondence Course at Nairobi Royal Technical College, and TJ was on a tour in the United States organized by the American Committee on Africa (ACOA). Here he'd addressed Senate Foreign Relations subcommittee on Africa and spoke to stakeholders and individuals—Hubert Humphrey, Stevenson Adlai, Martin Luther King Jr, John F. Kennedy, and Roy Wilkins. In April and May alone, TJ was promised over forty scholarships. And the first few would join in August. This could be why Barack traveled in August 1959, although the money was not enough to cater for all the expenses. He was therefore forced to look for two alternatives—one, a convenient, appropriate university, and two, an additional source of income. Malik says that although Barack traveled to America during the Tom Mboya Airlifts, it was through his own efforts and smarts that he managed to get there.

Barack took the correspondence courses certificate. With this, he'll qualify for an admission to an American university. People ducked to these courses to grab the competitive opportunities. A number of them were offered through the Nairobi University—formerly Nairobi Royal Technical College.

Upon completion many students crossed-over to Makerere University in the neighboring Uganda, while others would use their Cambridge School Certificate to secure a scholarship to Russia and India through a programme initiated later by the late Jaramogi Oginga Odinga, especially when the Makerere option seemed oblique.

During all these processes, he came across two American women who were on missionary work. According to Malik, the two were Ms Elizabeth Mooney of Maryland and Mrs Helen Roberts of Palo Alto, California. They also taught at the Nairobi Royal Technical College on voluntary basis.

Barack then traced them to Mombasa—the coastal town of Kenya—250 miles from Nairobi. Malik puts it thus:

'When he got wind of the two, my father sought the two women in Mombasa when they were on vacation. Later, when they came back to Nairobi after the holiday, they advised Dad to photograph all his documents and attach them together with various testimonials including the ones they wrote for him.'

One of the two was an international literacy expert Elizabeth Mooney Kirk from Maryland, who'd been in Kenya for quite sometime. She was on a mission to work in East Africa with her major concentration in Kenya. Meeting Elizabeth was just a chance event. She encouraged Barack to write applications to various universities . . . of which she advised that they're no guaranteed chances but with faith he might land into one! The man got lost in the entertainment of writing applications—According to the letters addressed by Barack to one of the universities—his son, the President of the United States of America, Barack Obama Jr, emphasizes in his book, *Dreams from My Father* that 'Mrs Roberts advised him to write to President Calhoun'. Malik agrees that letters that were written by his father shows how young people struggled to get to American universities. One of the letters written by their father and is in his possession reads thus:

> Dear President Calhoun,
>
> I have heard of your college from Mrs Helen Roberts of Palo Alto, California, who is now in Nairobi here. Mrs Roberts, knowing how much desirous I am to further my studies in the United States of America, has asked me to apply to your esteemed college for admission. I shall therefore be very much pleased if you will kindly forward me your application form and information regarding the possibility of such scholarship as you may be aware of.
>
> Barack Hussein Obama.[23]

The president of the United States, in his memoir, *The Dreams from My Father*, also emphasizes this particular letter.

Time was accelerating so fast, and in weeks, there was no sign of success. Malik says his father later told him that 'it was not easy. Many weeks had gone by, and I'd not seen a thing'. But he had toyed with the idea of an eventual surprise. Malik agrees that 'it was a carefully considered choice. He never chose the path of submission or giving up'.

In April 1959, he managed to secure admission at the University of Hawaii (UH), Honolulu, after applying to over thirty colleges. He wrote the letters and forgot about them, waiting for any eventuality.

When all seemed promising, he'd applied for a passport. It caused him mayhem. For political reasons and for logical issues, getting one was truly an uphill task. Most of the colonial government's offices were housed at Gill House. One, Mr Gill, a Kenyan businessman, born of Asian origin, owned this particular building; he'd rent the premise to the government and later sold it to the same government. He was such a powerful man that he would move hundreds of wealthy Asian businessmen to a meeting with top government officials, rally loyalist Asians to help fund the government budget against *Mau Mau* and other negative elements. At some point, Asians would meet at Caledonian Sports Ground opposite the Cathedral (now All Saints Cathedral) 'to strategize business.' This doesn't necessarily mean that Asians made the British hate Africans, but they were also protecting their businesses. And the government was desperate for a loyal partner.

Gill, as it's normally called, was situated between Government Road and Victoria Street, the current Moi Avenue and Tom Mboya Street, respectively. McGeorge's House flanked it—that served as the National Broadcasting—that's former Kenya Broadcasting Corporation Offices. The Immigration Department—that has since moved to Nyayo House—was situated at Gill House. Road licenses, LPOs, among other documents were being issued here. That has since moved to Kenya Revenue Authority at Times Tower. These are some of the buildings that Barack criss-crossed as he sought that elusive document—the passport. It was a 'white man's document' that caused the saddest feeling in the world, and only a few black people in high places would get hold of it more easily. An ordinary man, like Barack and his folks, had to run up and down, before accidentally stumbling on it. One would think of wearing a white-faced mask to guise identity and bad feelings. It really brought worst in men. Behind that mask, he'd wanted to break down and cry. There was Mr Anderson and Mr White—Immigration Officers at the time. After a few days, Mr Anderson left. And Mr White was reinstated as the Principal Immigration Officer.

The search was intense, and in a joking manner, some officers would ask whether he'd paid hut tax now that he wants a passport or whether it's his birthright—such annoying questions. The questions, indeed, were like a foot-in-the mouth. Maybe corruption had started crawling in slowly. The Immigration Department roasted applicants like hot potato in the name of interviewing. The interview was a grueling one, the officer would ask the following:

> *Name:* Barack Hussein Obama; *Age:* Twenty-three; *Occupation:* Junior clerk; *Employer:* Kenya Railways . . . and many other miscellaneous questions.[24]

The officer would attach a recommendation letter from the employer written by his immediate supervisor, a Mr Wycliffe, and correspondence examination scores, the Cambridge School Certificate, or the KACE. Mr Wycliffe was from Devonshire. He'd brag about his town: 'I'm from Devonshire, a native of sky blue city in the heart of the kingdom.' The coward juniors would be scared to death. But Barack once refuted: 'That man wasn't from Devonshire—or whatever he called it—he was nothing but a domestic labourer in England, trying to hoodwink us with lies.' This description only came when salary was delayed. At that moment, people would be classically annoyed. Others would abscond from work. When asked why, they would remorsefully say, 'It really rained, and all the log bridges were swept off.' Sometimes, it was purely a dry season.

Barack got a recommendation from Mr J Omollo. He worked with Barack earlier in 1956 and later became the General Secretary of Railways African Union. He described him 'as a real worker who never backed down at the thick of work. He performs his duties within the required spate of time. And the work appears just excellent. He was a team player and mobiliser.' Omollo, a trade unionist who later worked with TJ, had encouraged Barack, and he'd say in worker's union meetings, 'I unload all my worldly possession because I want to help others and myself.'

The process went smoothly, and after three months (What Sara would call the third moon!), the passport was out. The passport No. 84764 had the name *Barack Hussein Obama.* And details appeared clearly as he'd been promised. In some cases, efficiency was evident, while in other cases, there was no hope. Most of applicants at the start of the month would be lucky (when the officers had been fully paid). The work would be smooth. But immediately after, at the close of the month, there would be sluggishness. Reason? The immigration officers are hungry again! The incomplete passports would rot in the drawers, a dangerous liability that had to be shouldered by the desperate applicant to grease the hands! This tradition has since faded off.

Armed with a passport was a sure chance of getting a visa. The American Embassy issuing American student visas was at Ambassador's House—a few meters from the famous Gill House. When he stepped in this particular embassy in April 1959 (reliable prediction), and according to Malik, unlike the passport, visa wasn't a problem, though. Maybe due to the fact that the university had communicated to the embassy and convincingly put forward his case as a priority.

The year 1959 started in a good note. There was the wife, a son, a passport, a visa, and an admission letter to UH . . . air ticket . . . he could afford a smile.

But chaos rocked the city when British soldiers and those supporting them launched a brutal attack on African prisoners, beating them to death at Hola.

The Hola massacre is remembered by the institutionalization of Mau Mau Memorial Girls Secondary School, built in the remembrance of the massacre. The nation was at its deathbed. It was being mismanaged at a hurricane force, one of the efforts mounted to scathe the resistance forces—a pawn hatched to bring down the spirited effort—by African freedom fighters. During this time, the nation was almost declared a 'rundown'. It was a boot button to sink the continuous attacks against British soldiers. This conflict brought another gem to the already marred relationship between blacks and whites. Zeituni grew up at such tumultuous time—when conflict ruled—bloodshed, fear, and horror reigned. Maybe, the hovering spirit of death landed on her—upon her birth and never let her heart free. Fear gripped her even before she barely got going—growing in life.

Barack would tell her, 'My sister, you were born at such a bad time, when people fought—a time when blood was shed. And the country was on fire. Hope this won't shake you in life.'

Malik said that his father would read through, repeatedly, the university prospectus to ascertain that he was indeed going to the right place and talked fondly about the university, and sometimes asked him to read it for him. The pieces of information that still fills his archives read this way:

History

'Founded in 1907, in the State of Hawaii. UH is situated at the splendid, beautifully curved valley of Manoa at the outskirt downtown Honolulu. A flagship campus in Honolulu town on the Island of O'ahu.

The regular classes began with the president, John Gillmore, at the helm and five freshmen, five preparatory students, and thirteen faculty in temporary quarters near Honolulu's Thomas Square. In 1912 the newly named college of Hawaii relocated to a 300-acre site in Honolulu's Manoa Valley soon afterwards and the first permanent building—known today as Hawaii Hall—was erected amid pig farms and Kiawe groves.

The school is a sea of humanity of, not only the Hispanics but also Caucasians, Mixed, Asians, American Indians, Hawaiians, Pacific Islanders, and African Americans . . .

We offer bachelor's degree, master's degree, and doctoral degree in over hundred fields . . .'

With the addition of the College of Arts and Sciences, it became the University of Hawaii in 1920 and has since grown into a nationally and internationally respected institution of higher learning. The Territorial Normal and Training School (now the College of Education) joined the university in 1931. The university continued to grow throughout the 1930s. The Oriental Institute, forerunner of the East-West Center, was founded in 1935, bolstering the university's mounting prominence in Asia-Pacific studies. In 1939, the first student union building was erected through financial contribution from the community.

And there was this picture that he made up and pinned on the wall. He'd say, 'These are the pioneers of the University of Hawaii. Do you understand, Malik? They are the founders.' And I'd seen him smiling to my mother—a quizzical smile that prompted my mother's attention. It was amazing seeing them hug afterward, as he retired to the wooden chair. To me, I didn't see what was funny about the words—the many words that he read repeatedly and loudly like a Holy Koran or some famous Bible verses. I came to realize that the words made a lot of sense to him. And they formed the integral part of his dream. This picture is still lying as part of his souvenir.[25]

Also, Barack had old letters, notebooks, and private papers that listed all his visions. With all these, at Maseno High School, they reviewed the novelettes titled, *Thuondi Luo* (Luo Heroes)—a literary work that brought to light the culture of Luo and recognized the community's driving force. The booklet had been published in the 1940s. He said that the novel buttresses the position of self-satisfaction and that the book communicated the growth of collective bargain and the fortified village model of administration. He believed that whoever wanted to know much about Luos, when one understood that narration, one understood the entire community. Many students had lulled themselves into the conviction that community strength was such a huge structure.

He would peruse the department of choice . . . And read it aloud . . .

Department of Economics

The Department of Economics is one of the fourteen academic units in the College of Social Sciences, which in turn is one of the four Colleges of Arts and Sciences. The department is housed on the fifth floor of Saunders Hall, a building shared by a number of social science departments and program . . .

These include the improved version of what Barack received in the early May 1959. According to Malik, a lot of contemporary writings have emerged and descriptions have changed over time, but the original idea has remained. All these occurred at a time when a cook killed the employers' son, the same cook who had passed by, carrying the baby on his back only the day before;

or is it an Asian who spat into his workers' eyes—just to annoy him?

Or is it the banishment of loud African laughter and shouts in the European kitchen?

Or is it a settler slapping his worker—and the victim fighting back with a machete?

This tells you how Kenyans had a whole crucible of discontent.

He believed that it was going to be a life-changing experience, though there wasn't any trace of an African mentioned in the lists of Hawaiians, Islanders, American Indians, Asians, Caucasians, and Hispanics. It caused him some jitters. It was a matter of concern. Will he be the only African among the other 'tribes'? He meant to take chance that which shall not lead to more disappointments than solutions. His attitude was damn positive.

To date Barack has made a mark in the history of UH. In the official University of Hawaii records, Barack's life is featured prominently.

> Patsy Mink, BA, '48, former US Congresswoman
> Kenneth P. Moritsugu, BA, '67, former Surgeon General
> Bob Nash, Bed, '84, UH Warriors basketball coach
> Ken Niumatalolo, BA, '90, US Naval Academy head football coach
> Barack Obama Sr, BA, '62, Father of US President, Barack Obama
> Richard D. Parsons, BA, '68, Chairman of Citigroup
> Cheryl Castro Petti, BA, '94, CNN Radio network anchor
> Ann Dunham Suatoro, PhD, '92, Mother of US President, Barack Obama
> Jay Shidler, BBA, '68, entrepreneur and benefactor of the Shidler College of Business

The news was good. It meant that upon completion of the studies, lucrative jobs should be availed when the colonial powers were leaving them for Africans.

CHAPTER 11

When Life Gives 100 Reasons, I Show It That I Have 1000 Reasons to Smile.(Anonymous)

The Airlifts – 7.30 p.m.

On the evening of 5 august 1959, the music was not for ordinary ears—it wasn't satire either. It was the second turning point for Sara Onyango and the first turning point for Barack. Journalists and picture lovers on the thrall, in full force, were rotating their lenses, taking memorable shots, holding precious lives in a thrall.

Barack sat at the waiting lounge, surrounded by a battery of aircrew dressed in conservative suits. He was casual, almost to the point of indifference. The sight of very busy people visiting Kenya: tourists, businessmen, ambassadors, students, or those deporting was very evident and awful—a sea of humanity. He'd never felt this way before.

The students had a cocktail, under yellow translucent light, at the Old Embakasi Airport (this particular airport was constructed in 1948 for the colonial army aircrafts. And in 1958, it was formally opened for commercial use; other planes belonging to the Ethiopian airline made a brief stopover, but the first Boeing 1789/09 took off on 6 September 1959 in the history of Kenya). Ethiopian airline was the oldest in the region. The Ethiopian airlines had been plying in the route. This was the oldest airline in the region. The turbo-prop aircraft took off with Kenyan students in its belly under the banner of BOAC (British Overseas Airlines Corporation), the famous Tom Mboya's Airlifts.

Meanwhile, Barack, just like the rest of the students, who would, months later, travel through the same airport for the same purpose to United States, threw a bash for his lovely family. It was a kind of competition, of supremacy, who'd throw the heaviest. Kezia was very happy yet upset—Roy, his doting son, pensive and teary, was gaining composure to live life without limitation, while Sara kept silent for the better part of the 'ceremony' for she'd seen a lot unravel firsthand, and also because of her wisdom, she wasn't moved. From the look of things, she was in deep lamentation, the reason being not known. Onyango Hussein, maybe, was on his knee, praying, 'Allahu Akhbar, praises to Mohammed, the holy prophet.' Onyango had requested Sara to accompany their son to the airport for he was left in the custody of the homestead. Sara complied, knowing how dear the situation was, at that moment, for each of them.

They had dinner at a seafood restaurant, one of its kinds in East Africa. One of the waitresses had sent them a bottle of the rare champagne, on request, also the rare one in the region. And Barack and Kezia drank a toast. The party had begun; the dishes never stopped coming thereafter. It was celebration time, maybe the last one between the couple!

'I'm very happy, honey . . .' came from Kezia.

'I . . . I don't know how to thank you. And I don't know what to offer you. Maybe, I'll first thank you for givin' me this opportunity. It's all you people who'd accepted me to leave for studies abroad. It's really kind of you.'

Kezia was pleased, very pleased, but the burdens began to get more and more. Maybe, she declared him an outlaw, the time he opened his mouth to speak, appreciating her with that irresistible passion although his kindness and generosity was not farfetched—at that time.

She thought of a husband—in America—'Would there be no more binge drinking, no more cigars, and no more late parties? I mean a cry of the dispossessed!' She was dead lost.

'Why don't we have the world do it? The world's taking too long to reveal the truth in life.' She testified 'the world running in reverse.'

Barack was listening . . . Roy says that 'he was this man who'll speak when it matters most to keep quiet or keeps quiet when it matters most to speak.'

To the unborn, he said, 'My child—what am I goin' to do with you? You know how Papa cherishes you. How awesome you are?' And he said, 'I love you all.

I don't know what to tell you now, but I'll surely write and call, whenever possible, later. I'll let you know everything when I get there, to America.'

The three just found themselves laughing at his jokes, jokes that later turned real and which later 'separated' the family.

A sigh of relief quickly rented the air. This was a strong parting shot for a family that is not only grappling with domestic complexities but also the trappings of religion and cultural beliefs.

'Papa, see we'll be locked in our own little world, a world that we can't see a trace of you, as we're used to,' Roy asserted, 'don't forget us.'

'Yeah, Son. I'll remember all of you. See my love for you is much greater than the fear of death.'

Roy would ask this kind of question 'coz of the nature of picture he'd made toward the father. The stories they had shared together came back frame by frame.

'In my youthful days, Son, my friends and I, ambitious lads, would take women to all-time high . . . luring them to . . . when they became mad in the drink and dance.

'And why my favorite pastime was nothing steamier than alcohol? It was the denominator of all forms of pleasure.'

Sometimes he'd encourage Roy, 'If you can't take concern on your life, then do it on your son.' And he'll finish by saying, 'Roy, you're my son, and I'm your father, you are the head of the family'—his head deep in the stupor, buried in a state of confusion.

If you can't take concern on your life, then do it on your son.

Barack's life was now a series of compartments: There was America, his family in Nairobi, grappling with joblessness, and those waiting in the village, ready for handouts 'like a dangling carrot', and there was the escalating news of 'Kenyans for freedom', a course to seek alternative options or for just other alternatives, worlds that needed immediate inclusion. He was torn. It happened so gradually that it didn't seem to be happening at all. What was happening in his mind? A mind-boggling question:

'Will America come to accept this black cache of Africans'?

There was a difference—a big difference, although his head wasn't wrapped too tight with this fear.

'Will Americans suck them whole unto their social network?'

'And is the social network just?'

In my youthful days, my friends and I, ambitious lads, would take women to all-time high . . .

Sara was silent. She kept silent for the better part of this phenomenal departure. She had no option but to accept how she was going to miss him. You couldn't tell whether she dreaded the moment or considered it enormous, whether Kenya would be a stooge of USA, Britain, or Communist USSR imperialists, or an emblem of hope of Africa.

Barack was looking apprehensive; he wanted to 'approach' this new life, instead of 'attacking it'. 'That would be tactless.' He had clarity of vision, which baffled—which he exercised at his own volition.

'Oh yes, we're flattered,' Barack yawned. 'How could such cruel people exist, the colonialist, like some aliens with no "screw bolts in their brains"?'

America's life was completely different, they said, life consolidated, unlike the fragmented African society. But here, they were, African students leaving to study in a society they knew little about. They couldn't predict what was about to happen or could happen. One, they had firsthand information of white slavery, crime syndicate, and racism. This was mainly due to European colonial misrule. But America sounded different. Two, Kenyans were still disorganized—no independence—no space available for African experts. Barack froze. He said to Malik, 'What's the essence of goin' to study—then . . . ?'

There was a bursting eagerness in his quest to unravel these two critical issues.

Kezia was there as well and the young boy—maybe growing up so fast—Roy—wasn't amused by the events; of course, he didn't know what was going on! He was a toddler. The father was going too far away. He won't be coming back sooner. The name America was mentioned several times.

Definitely, he was going to another country, in a continent that he'd wanted to know some day.

Maybe if he grows up to a more mature fellow.

'My plane is about to arrive, mum—I'm restless,' he said. Roy could listen to his father; the last words of the old man sent him to some sort of frenzy. Though he was still a child, he could grasp a few. And he lives to tell it.

Looking on, with despair and tears, was Aoko. Roy was only one-year-old. But Kezia Aoko showed some signs that another baby was on the way. Something Kezia was pretty sure of. They knew this was the 'end of their physical contact', and they wanted to affirm it to append their belief and signature. The father, they have barely known, was going to a world, apart from theirs. For the young Roy, Dad was his king and he the prince. The shining star was leaving. Painful as it was awful. They felt an emotional connection that quickly dashed off sucking them into a life of desolation and loneliness. Not a soul with the father figure shall care about them or would be able to fill the vacancy he was about to create. Their fears were real. Kezia was traumatized; no proper income inflow but stomachs to fill. It was a tall order. She felt the breeze of husband's departure, with a blind optimism of overcoming it, but it lasted forever patched in her inner heart, in a state of panic.

'When are you coming back?' She'd asked this question several times and found it new every time she posed it, again and again. Roy said that his mother would always want to have some assurance . . . 'Hope you'll be communicating to us. Remember you have left us with nothing to cling on . . . so go work hard,' she affirmed. Roy says that his mother was absolutely concerned, asking many varied questions and registering the answers with shock. Barack was frail to answer any of these mandatory questions. They were hard questions—questions that needed technical promises. And answers to which he couldn't take claim. Coming at a time, he couldn't even able to erase the hard realities of his family but to promise optimism. He didn't have the liberty or powers to promise anything.

'I know this bond is unmistakable. We'll be communicating, honey.' He assured her with a champagne breath—hint of hard-earned lifestyle, holding tight to his shirt.

'And are you sure . . . ,' Kezia wondered, 'I'm sorry, I doubt that very much.'

'No. No cause of doubt. It's pointless to doubt now. Take some chicken pie. I know you would love them.'

'Your departure is going to give us a life of hell.' A conversation Roy noted.

It was a dark moment for her and the kid, including the unborn. But they'd to face risk and bombard uncertainty for a better, vibrant future, the future that lay on the bedrock of conviction. The future he knew little about. Now every day was going to be a day of emotional connection with an arousing belief in fluffiness and love and that which shall ignite hidden remnants of infidelity. She found herself trembling as though she was in a butcher's apron with blood spattered all over her body and face bleeding slowly. She felt uncertainty, unreality, a deep sorrow, and an ineffable sense of loss. Unhidden fears came into her mind because she knew with certainty that the days of sweet smell of the tobacco were over, the slow puff of the pipe from Barack.

All right, she felt agitated.

'Could we get this over with?' She sought composure whenever it could be found. 'You've to accept it and not argue.'

Barack was making a journey that almost (took) left his family into chattel slavery of desire that condemned them to endless labor without pay and disconnected them from the seminal influence of their departing father. Barack had never before had a reason to think of himself in terms of what kind of a person he was, but now it was necessary.

Malik asserts that 'he sleepily mumbled and waved us a good-bye.'

'I'll miss you all. I love you. You're my family, and I'm torn between wishing you good always.'

'Be good too,' Kezia would reply. 'The memories of our joy shall never part my heart. How about you, Barack?'

He kept quiet. Malik asserts that he wouldn't respond sometimes, and you would wonder why!

The future had been closed to Kezia right at her face. Ruefully, she could imagine life ahead as a real hassle like some loads of genetists racing to sequence all genomes required to create life or a medicine holy grail clandestine to beat time.

Meanwhile, Sara stood and then sat looking spent as if the baby and the bath water was about to be thrown out, her mind repackaged and warmed the cockles of Kogelo's hinterland. Without blinking an eyelid, she watched the mad rush of young Kenyans seeking further education in foreign countries with awe.

In this entourage, it was no exception that the student—Barack—happy and despondent, symbolized the future of Kenya, the future with definitive charismatic leaders and lieutenants, eager to trigger the delayed birth of a new-African society and radical departure from the colonial labyrinth of injustice to the effect that there would be an extraordinary change.

The most arresting question would later be 'What was the so-called change for and when will it occur?'

The answer would be, 'Don't be sorry, be strong.'

Radical departure from the colonial labyrinth of injustice to the effect that there would be an extraordinary change.

9.45 p.m.

Barack's departure, and in fact, later, the entire Tom Mboya's Airlift—student—beneficiaries weren't just for him or themselves respectively but for the healing and posterity they thought they could bring to their country. It was a burning ambition—a stark contrast from what many people thought.

Their open mindedness seemed strange even to their families. A white journalist asked, 'Is the future oblique or vibrant? Do you think this voyage shall bring or rather create another dimension for Kenyan aspiring young talents and the society at large?' The other was rolling her wide camera.

'Yes yes. I think this opportunity has opened dark corridors that seemed oblique, and I believe everyone is in high moods, ready to move to America,' Barack replied.

Roy says that his father was categorical about this information, and he wanted to dish it out without failure. He would pose thus:

'I know the sleepy village of Nairobi is awakening and is redeeming itself from the slumber. We're quite a number who'll make it to America, and this number shall represent a new heritage for transformation albeit at rapid pace.'

At the airport, the journalists were asking every kind of question.

'What do you say concerning the politicians detained in Kapenguria—In Lokitaung' Prison . . . ?' The politicians were named the Kapenguria Six of Jomo Kenyatta, Fred Kubai, Kungu Karumba, Paul Ngei, Bildad Kaggia, and Ochien'g Oneko. And one of the convicts, Paul Ngei, later described the prison to the press as 'St Lucifers' Monastery of Lokitaung'—he meant they were starved of all sorts of pleasure—alcohol, cigarettes, and most prominently women.

'. . . bearing in mind that they were top politicians here in Kenya?'

The journalist questioned the importance of this exodus and the significance they'll bring to the society. Though the subject was too painful and risky to discuss, the answers came out timidly, feebly, and with less assurance.

* * *

Malik says that his father would remember what Beckton once advised:

'Your life from now henceforth will never be the same, and you shall live your responsibility. You are going to face challenges with a will and intent to succeed, in a show and demonstration of a relentless sense of purpose. If you don't know where you are going, and then, any destination will do'—a phrase that he wrote in his diary as a reference and an advice, an idea that he should adopt as a young man.

Beckton was 'an angel in disguise', on the eyes of suitors, just like Sara was, during her marriage. As a matter of fact, that was what he wanted to hear, without pretence.

Resonating sounds of *Uhuru! Uhuru!* would rent the air in a short stint and later, with a compelling portrait of nation building. Sara, Barack, and Kezia were major composite of this change and nation building, enticed by fast-growing opportunities—that 'change' was about to open or had already slightly opened good tidings. Many senior black citizens had already left to study abroad, either on individual basis or through government-enhanced study funding for the loyalists.

Back then, the notion of clamor for change was a fodder by itself, which broke the fear for prison and boosted the popularity of defiance. The call against oppression was therefore a reliable yardstick to this change.

They'd to struggle with the *Mau Mau* fears. The Lari Massacre was one horrible experience!

Barack's shrewd thinking was something that was insidiously un-American about him. As described by Philip Ochieng', he was an intelligent chap. Philip has risen to become somewhat one of the best writers/columnists. Hope he isn't given too much credit, though!

He wanted to do something, but he didn't know what it was yes,—his favorite book; he unzipped the bag quickly, searched it through the many clothes, and pulled one out, some nonexistent New York bestseller . . . or the Shakespeare's King Lear—the famous book during that season with a blaring title. In 1959, King Lear was the hit book, though. And Malik asserts that this was a book of his choice. He had a hard copy of the book. What was his motive? Ruffled copies of this book are gathering dust in his cupboard—but I pick this particular conversation in an inked underline by my father:

> EDMUND: I will seek him, sir, presently: convey the business as I shall find means and acquaint you withal.
>
> GLOUCESTER:
> These late eclipses in the sun and moon portend no good to us: though the wisdom of nature can reason it thus, and thus, yet nature finds itself scourged by the sequent effects: love cools, friendship falls off, and brothers divide in cities, mutinies; in countries, discord; in palaces, treason; and the bond cracked 'twixt son and father. This villain of mine comes under the prediction; there's son against father: the king falls from bias of nature; there's father against child. We have seen the best of our time: machinations, hollowness, treachery, and all ruinous disorders, follow us disquietly to our graves. Find out this villain, Edmund; it shall lose thee nothing; do it carefully. And the noble and true-hearted Kent banished! His offence, honesty! 'Tis strange.
> *Exit*
>
> EDMUND:
> This is the excellent foppery of the world, that, when we are sick in fortune,—often the surfeit of our own behavior—we make guilty of our disasters the sun, the moon, and the stars: as if we were villains by necessity; fools by heavenly compulsion; knaves, thieves,

and treacherers, by spherical predominance; drunkards, liars, and adulterers, by an enforced obedience of planetary influence; and all that we are evil in, by a divine thrusting on: an admirable evasion of whoremaster man to lay his goatish disposition to the charge of a star! My father compounded with my mother under the dragon's tail, and my nativity was under Ursa major; so that it follows, I am rough and lecherous. Tut, I should have been that I am, had the maidenliest star in the firmament twinkled on my bastardizing. Edgar—

Enter Edgar
And pat he comes like the catastrophe of the old comedy: my cue is villanous melancholy, with a sigh like Tom o' Bedlam. O, these eclipses do portend these divisions! fa, sol, la, mi.

Fully engrossed in the book/story . . . he said, 'He was interrupted by the loud speaker.'

'Attention, please. Attention'—it blasted. 'We've taken off safely from Nairobi's Airport, and now we're approaching the Atlas Mountains. Therefore, let's remain calm and composed. The weather is very rough. I repeat, the "weather is rough"', repeating it with much more strength. 'Hope you'll all comply.' Barack was disturbed, he told Malik. This was his first air travel, and therefore everything was new. The crew made a short commotion that made the students stick to their seats in compliance—with the new rule.

'I knew things would come back to normalcy,' he told Malik in the process of trying to convince himself.

'Would you like some drinks, sir?' he was interrupted again, this time by a beautiful model, an airhostess, six feet tall with an attractive broad smile. Malik narrates every aspect when his father later brought the storyline detail by detail.

'A glass of juice, sweetheart,' Barack replied. His eyes roving, following her shadow until it disappeared into the closet. Malik says that 'he was good in this department of persuasion. And he excelled greatly. Again, fresh fruit juice was his favourite.'

'She is damn gorgeous. That's a true African beauty—impeccable.' He would relax to let the words sink and the world around him to calm.

'Here is your juice, sir,' a soft voice finally whispered in his ear after a short while and another broad charming smile. The lady had brought the glass of juice, and she really smelled nice apart from her great attire and figure.

'Thank you,' Barack said, in honor of her skin that was good enough.

'Anytime,' came the reply. It echoed again and again in his tiny African brain.

Everybody looked to his direction. Curious and nervous to know what was going on in his mind. He absolutely sighed off.

The lady who'd served him juice came in handy.

'Can I help you, sir?'

'No, thanks.'

'Do you need something?'

'Thank you for your kindness, girl.'

'Maybe you take some sleep or visit the washroom for a relaxation. They're just around the corner.'

'Thank you again for your concern.'

'Anytime.'

'Anytime is a strong word to me, anyway!' he thought.

He'd tell Malik that he finally fell asleep. He thought of the story—*Edmund* never found his true identity. That he felt a villain, a fool, and lived in an environment of liars, drunkards, and adulterers—they were cut out from the real world. *Edmund* comments that *we make guilty of our disasters*. Malik says his father felt that 'this was a perfect template of his life and his society'. It was just a story. A story that looked real as he looked back at how life has climbed its ladder. Malik says the plane was in Europe. 'It was a typical example of a problem that he was partly facing—a problem to know his own identity—the story of a man at the verge of collapse. He may not be sure how tomorrow will be, each day with its own confusion, its own mysteries, and its own disadvantages. He felt a loser in the winning side—Barack felt how discouraging to fly miles across roaring oceans and seas in order to learn better skills of life, to be educated in a foreign country when his country still wallowed in deep slumber.

'The plane first made a brief stopover in Rome, Italy. It was amazingly a surprise interconnect for one who has never gone past the Kenyan borders. That was amazing, isn't it?' Malik poses.

After another couple of hours on air, past Spain's airspace to France . . . these were the times a plane can gas twice in a single journey. Barack later said that, 'it was a great experience, though. However, one felt as if the feet had wheels of fire. Maybe the plane was just slower.'

'It touched down at Paris Orly International Airport, France.

Barack in Paris, France, August 1959

'The Orly International Airport of Paris was enveloped in the lush velvet of artistic and cultural heritage of the French-speaking people, situated on the southern end of the capital. Orly remains as the overall airport in terms of passenger boardings. It has two terminuses West and South. From the airport—radiating to the interior—the country enjoyed the most secreted heritage of all times. This is the reason why France remains an exotic tourist destination. Men were in straitjackets and leather straps, women expressing their French culture in unique dressing and jewellery. France and Paris had already grown into a stable economy unlike African nations,' he said. The country's culture was too rich to be dismissed as a mere expression of heritage.

I had to spend over eight hours in Paris due to delay in the departure time. I had food at the Kyriad Orly Airport Hotel. It was this old hotel that has improved its catering over time to become one of the best in France. Overlooking the Eiffel tower, we left the hotel, courtesy of AirFrance by the airport shuttle at exactly 1600 hrs.

Kyriad Hotel is an exclusive hotel with a myriad of exclusive international cuisine. The Notre Dame Cathedral flanks the hotel and from the geographical perspective, École Polytechnique forms the integral part of this hotel.

The air traffic was also evident—AirFrance airline offered the linking pad to a growing world-class travelling solutions. The airline was already giving a mouth-watering challenge to the rest of the regional airlines. The bruising battle of supremacy wasn't any closer to ending. One thing that accorded AirFrance international status was its improved passenger comfort and a cut in the travel time to half, and the losers were fighting back tears. 'I took the turbo prop airbus to America's New York JKF Airport at the Paris Orly Airport south terminal. At the time one would choose Lockheed Super Constellation, depending on the departure schedule. 'AirFrance was one of the leading and world's largest airlines.' Barack told Malik. And Orly was the main airport of Paris. Although later the construction of Charles de Gaulle International Airport meant that most operations shall be transferred to the more expansive space. The journey was quite entertaining by the fact that we were joined by other passengers from all walks of life. The French nationals, the Spaniards, the Turks, and Germans (who had boarded the plane from Berlin) all enshrined in one journey to the United States of America. I believe the rush of the ocean was canceled out by a roaring hum of the airbus. I started to realize that this country, United States, was, maybe, one amazing continent for those uprooted from their comfort zone, searching for a sense of belonging in a foreign land. The AirFrance flight covered the route in just less than eighteen hours. It was a brief stop, though, and no major incidence occurred in Europe. The AirFrance turbo prop plane, finally pulled off to America. In a short stint, the plane hovered across Pacific Ocean to the vast land of United States of America; New York's Kennedy Airport was calm but cold. It was, maybe, winter season. There was freezing temperature, way below 5°C. Barack says that it was unbelievable. The city was damn cold compared to what he used to experience in Nairobi—Maybe 20°C at most, forcing the blood vessels deep into the body and the muscles twitching against the soft black flesh. Signalmen waved the two semaphores they held, guiding the Boeing toward the waiting ramp. They wore oversized earmuffs and large yellow fluffy jackets with blue and silvery white stripes. The pilot was adamant; it was a long journey, though, from Kenya's tiny airport through Rome and Paris, Orly to New York's Kennedy Airport. It was 9 August 1959. The giant plane pulled up to a stop making a fixed circle.

The lanky AirFrance plane finally brought hundreds of Africans to a new world. Barack later told Malik that inside the plane, one of the cabin crew shouted over the loudspeaker:

> 'Ladies and gentlemen, hope you've enjoyed your journey to America. We've landed at New York's Kennedy Airport at 1600hours. The crew are extending their gratitude for your patience, love, cooperation, and great enthusiasm. A further announcement shall finally come to you in a short while.'

Today such announcements may be taken lightly or mistaken for a mere noise. To Barack it was his first time, on flight, and every moment he noted down. Perhaps to us it would be silly or amazing, but to him it was a great opportunity. An opportunity that lifted him up the shackles of Kenya's urban landscape, with nothing promising, to a land with a different cast, so the loudspeaker became an abstract map, the guiding map to the United States of America.

There was no commotion, but in a short while, true to the voice from the loudspeaker, the ramp team finally opened the door of the Boeing. He was prepared to leave the rather exhaustive plane, the plane they'd booked in *old* Embakasi Airport, Nairobi. With his bag tight on his hand, he was indeed ready to start a new life. His independent life in a foreign land, trotting the vast land on a student visa, began with no one to mark 'him'—the security, the FBI. He said nothing, but his mind was busy. Again, one of the cabin crew's voices came over the loudspeaker.

We're pleased to inform you that you may now safely disembark. All your luggages are arranged neatly at the waiting bay. Please grab yours and leave at your pleasure.

Everybody disengaged from the plane and trooped out—headed straight to the reception where their luggage streamed out. They walked through the expansive airport, looking in amazement, the beauty of United States—skyscrapers, huge planes, tall buildings, and beautiful people—and right ahead was a closed glass door with a golden-lit plate written 'Reception'—the reception area. The friendly guards, men and women, glanced at their documents before directing them to the luggage depot. The security wasn't as tight as it is in recent time, maybe, due to the fact that there was nothing like terrorist threat. Though, watchful security eyes couldn't get off him. This was going to be a routine exercise, the view he'd get used to hundred times on his way to various States. The rooms extending from the reception area were styled in apartment settings with expansive master en suite, maybe, the VIP section, superior suite, deluxe suite, and the executive suite. This was just a taste of States. The restaurant on the rear served delicacies. And some of the travelers ducked for pizza, others pasta or McDonald's hamburger—away from Kenyan's dishes, mainly fish and *ugali*. In a short while, Barack had taken another plane, as planned by his organizers, to Chicago—the new home. The city, Philip would later nickname 'Windy City'. He confronted huge homes—with all-day brasserie, a lake-view pool deck, a lounge, and a piano bar terrace. Some had, in addition, elegant treatment spa, a gymnasium (fully equipped), not forgetting sauna and Jacuzzi.

His life was a phenomenal one, a fairy tale that emanated from rags to opportunities, from disappointment at Maseno to a land of opportunities in Nairobi. How did it happen? This is a ten-dollar question. That calls for clarity, a story that has spiraled various channels before emerging as a fortune in disguise.

Hawaii

United States of America

Chapter 12

In 1959 and 1960s

University of Hawaii, Honolulu,

When he landed in United States, he felt that a lot of solutions shall be found to many hardships back home—the connection, the ideas, the right people, the papers, the means, and later, a wife! Malik says that when the old man spotted Hawaii a lot rung in his mind. 'He saw the face of Hawaii, and he felt everything. One, there was nothing magical about the city, but inside him, he saw opportunity. Two, his life, which was torn into pieces, shall be sewn once again, this time with a foreign piece. Three, it was a trying time that would test his tolerance in ways that he couldn't then have imagined.'

According to Sara, while in Hawaii, Barack found it a place where he had a house and no home . . . it was indeed a better settlement . . . a home where he had a house but no home. Friends were definitely made.

His life wasn't about being inadequate or adequate. And it wasn't about anything—close to his wife or academics. It wasn't a major downfall or a letdown . . . It was all about looking for an ideal identity.

The cars were one of the sleekest, fastest creatures around. They'd offered a pretty appearance to glance. The sports cars were hot—brilliantly designed, leathered, steel-made, gorgeous, and splendid on the driveway. They affected him in ways he didn't anticipate: Catwalk women, tall, strikingly attractive blue-eyed bottle blonde—those in modeling and those in acting. Life was defining everything he'd ever hoped for. Kogelo wasn't mentioned. It was an old-fashioned name. He talked of Chicago, Indiana, Ohio, Chicago, New

York... the white-dominated States; the affluent Hispanics dominated States, the Caucasian States... It was United States of America where there was jitterbugging, shagging, and line dancing—a military hairdo. Some sort of a commando hair cut. Young students below thirty years of age branded such form of shave. That made them resemble some sort of mimes on hyperactive steroids. The students may be hell-bent on ruining their lives. Students who've never seen even a cow—that is a live cow or an elephant. Some would say 'one little monkey sitting on a ledge'. The problem of feeling black in small towns and big towns—in streets and alleys—wasn't going away too easily. Back in Kenya, there is this famous writing:

> Leadership
> *Pillar 5*
> Nothing is Black or White.

Those who've never experienced the mysteries of the African jungle, or lived and survived, they can't afford such an imagination.

He'd not wanted to be described a poor African. He hated it. But he hated it proudly. Back in Africa, Kogelo, in particular, there were still hopeful souls that braved the heavy gust of dust that hit them on the face like water-starved mongoose. And there were people living below the poverty level, people who'd possess large tract of land but lacked the machinery to till it.

Chapter 13

I believe in a slight change of priorities—and values that Kenyan child will have a shot at life. And doors of opportunities shall remain open to some, if not all. But we should stop and ask ourselves. What do we want for Kenya? And never stop there.

(Tom Mboya Airlifts)

Shankardas House, 6 September 1959

The office of USIS (United States Information Services) was packed to the brim. Those watching from the Kenya Cinema would actually define the mood *incognito*. Politicians, notably, the late Ronald Ngala, Gikonyo Kiano, and the late Jaramogi Oginga Odinga, among others, were absolutely present to grace this occasion. A car would move slowly up the drive, make incomplete arc—come to a halt, igniting off with a bowl of dust—at the double flight of stairs leading to the Shankardas USIS offices on Government Road. The late Jaramogi sprang out of his car. He would wave his flywhisk, taking steps up, and walking briskly. A small crowd had gathered beside the area condoned off by the hawk-looking security men. Other prominent personality hopped from their cars. *Jaramogi* was a brave leader, who didn't know that a lot would unravel against his brevity. Surely it didn't take too long before it blew off—his world came down tumbling against the backdrop of 'anti-Odingaism' in the independent government that he fought for. The toil, the sweat, the blood, and the tears of the late Jaramogi later turned to remorse for toil, regret for sweat, mistrust for blood, and loss for tears. After a short while, the late Jaramogi was a frustrated man whose friends and allies were assassinated in cold blood, Pio Gama Pinto (1965), JM Kariuki (1975) . . . by the unknown assailants, or maybe government forces he fought for and now turned against him. During these times, the armed security kept vigil, their arms resting on their laps. That was going to be the norm, and Barack knew it pretty well. It was indeed a bad piece of information. The busy *Moi* Avenue (formerly Government Road) was condoned off for the public due to security reasons and by the virtue that a number of government officials were largely present. Powerful speeches flowed freely with politicians thumping their authority in a supremacy battle. In political dispensation, Mboya and Jaramogi had a strong contrast in their demeanor.

The latter, a go-getter urban socialist than the former, enjoyed a massive national support in all corners of the divide.

It served as the meeting point for the students. The students would answer . . .

'See, these loads going to USA are the future of Kenya. The current predicament is quite awful. Though the obvious will come out, the earnest self-seeking style of colonial leadership shall end.' Barack's colleagues would reply in September. 'What could this exotic misrule earn in Kenya?'

Tom Mboya was born in a sisal estate in Thika to Leonard or Leonardus Ndiege—a sisal worker in a white farm belonging to Sir William Northrup McMillan at Kilimambogo, a short distance east of Thika in the heart of Central Kenya. His mother Mama Rosalina was a housewife. Nobody noticed Mboya's intelligence at his early stages of growth except his mother. He was born on 15 August 1930 and died from assassin bullet at the tender age of thirty-nine on 5 July 1969; even when he was growing up, his presence couldn't be felt. But he was a man, shrewd young man, who turned the lives of over 800 Kenyans into huge success story. Mboya joined Kenya's hot politics with a vision—a revolutionary vision, which was misinterpreted as mere arrogance. The rather conservative young man from *Rusinga* Island had a dream—a passionate dream to steer Kenya into a new paradigm shift. That gave it a turn-around without recounting the loss Kenya had experienced from execution to ritual killing: detention without trial to disappearance of vocal activists; the dispersal and regrouping of sectarian tribal warlords to killings of *Mau Mau* fighters. All these took part in the struggle for independence. The independence that was so near in 1959 yet so far in the minds of many desperate, yearning for change.

TJ, as he was popularly known in political circles, was chosen—a man who embodied the best this country had to offer. He wanted to eradicate the slander that says 'a black youth with a book is acting white'. He had ambitions transforming to a disease or death. At one time, clear-eyed Tom, with an easy smile arrived in a joint party at Shankardas House to hear for himself from the young who'd a burning desire to change the course of history of a nation that was slowly crawling from the ravages of colonial mistreatment. Of course, with the help of the outside mission, notably the US State Department.

'We must hold our values against a hard reality and see how we're measured up to the legacy of our forbearers and the promise of future independence'

Applause . . .

'I believe in a slight change of priorities—and values that Kenyan child will have a shot at life. And doors of opportunities shall remain open to some, if not all. But we should stop and ask ourselves, "What do we want for Kenya?" And never stop there!'

Applause . . .

'Do we expect the British Government to solve our problems—which they created for us?'

Applause . . .

'This is an awakening call. We should all move from the dangerous option of remaining in our oppression. And search for that elusive independence by insisting on equality, freedom, and justice.'

The upcoming iconic figure, students watched him in disbelief. Indeed, TJ was a mentor, who rode in the wheels of politics with courage. TJ was a great man, with him a young American entrepreneur and Jazz maestro Scheinman William X, both conceived the Airlifts to America. And it never took them long to compare notes. This was an unusual partnership. Harry Belafonte, in his foreword to *Airlift to America* wrote about TJ.

'In 1956, I met a remarkable young man, my age, with a revolutionary vision that would change the course of history. His name was Tom Mboya, a labor leader with a passionate dedication to rid his country, Kenya, of the shackles of colonialism. He detailed for me a wide plan of Africa that inspired my commitment to its struggle for liberation.'

He continued:

'Tom sought me out, and through his eyes, I saw the harsh ugliness of colonialism. I met extraordinary young, determined to live a life free of the prison of colonialism. Kenya, like Tanganyika and the other East African countries, then had no universities. There was only one college, Makerere in Uganda, and it was a technical school. The fear was that when *Uhuru* (Freedom) came to Kenya in 1963, there wouldn't be enough people prepared to take over the many civil services, diplomatic and teaching positions that would be vacated by the British.'[26]

All these players were connected to the spirit and period of change, in the historical significance and moral imperative of the liberation struggle in Africa. TJ feared he would not live to see the fruits of his vision due to first, the fact that the political dude was seriously polarized, and second, he created 'more personal enemies than friends' within the political divide, 'for his oratory mien, strategy and witty handling of political dynamics'.

The names of Robinson, Harry, and Sidney would forever ring in the minds of Sara and Kezia, Hawa and Nyaoke the true sisters, Omar and Zeituni, and indeed, Kenya as a whole. These names opened new doors of opportunities for their son and husband, respectively, for someone they regarded as the apple of change in their family. But despite all these outpourings, the strong tirade of disappointment was hanging in the balance—political upheavals between Mboya and some first Lancaster Conference Kenya representatives arose. They argued that young talented Kenyans should study closer home and attend Makerere College University in neighboring Uganda, instead of taking America's offer. In this bandwagon, some *Legco* luminaries and members also supported the point in the premise to derail Mboya's vision and influence, later, due to political reasons . . . a year later KANU, in 1960, the National Political Party, was formed; that was in May 1960 to be precise.

'Kenyans were ambitious, playing conspicuously well to gain independence, and he believed there shall be no tie for ambiguity. Kenya is ripe for change,' John Kang'ethe added, with a composed default mode written on 'his' bright face.

John Kang'ethe, Fred Geke, Philip Ochien'g, the late Pamela Mboya, Collins Odinge Odera, and seventy-six others were in the quest to take the most published flight. A total of eighty-one students went off to United States.

'And who were they? Do ordinary Kenyans know who they were? Who can tell them so and we've kept quiet—so those in the 1959 TJ airlift? This list is meant exclusively for ordinary Kenyans and the world of good will . . .' John says.

    AliVIONZA, Grace
        Howard University,
        Washington, DC
    BOIT, Dorcas Chepkemboi
        Spellman College
        Atlanta 3, Georgia
    CHANZU, Said Ambongo
        University of Pittsburgh
        Pittsburgh 13, Pennsylvania
    CHEGE, Henry Rigil
        Cascade College
        705 North Killingworth St
        Portland 17, Oregon
    DALIZU, Fred Egambi
        Lincoln University
        Philadelphia
    GATHONI, Gladwell
        Diable Valley College
        Concord, California
    GICHOKI, Rose
        Clarke College
        Dubuque, Iowa
    GICHURU, Mary Nyaguthi
        Newton High School
        Newton, Mass.
    GITHURU, Simon Makau
        St Francis Xavier University
        Antigonish
        Nova Scotia, Canada
    GICUHI, Evanson Ngiobi
        Diable Valley College
        Wilberforce, Ohio
    GITATHA, Samuel Kinyanjui
        Conrad State College
        Wilberforce, Ohio
    INDAKWA, John
        Lincoln University

Pennsylvania
ISIGE, Jackton Ngunyi
> Wisconsin State College
> Steven's Point, Wisconsin

KABACHIA, Vincent
> LaSalle College
> Philadelphia 41, Penn.

KAIRO, Simon Thuo
> Northwest Missouri
> State Teacher's College
> Kirksulle, Missouri

KAJUBI, Johanna Mwangi
> Howard University
> Washington, DC

KAMUA, Elizabeth
> Diable Valley College
> Concord, California

KAMAU, George Gachigi
> Diable Valley College
> Concord, California

KANG'ETHE, John
> Roosevelt University
> Chicago 5, Illinois

KARUGA, Cyrus G.
> Iowa Western College
> Mount Pleasant, Iowa

KATUNGULU, Regina
> Skidmore College
> Saratoga Springs, New York

KIMATHI, Titus
> Houghton College
> Houghton, New York

KIWINDA, Ellistana
> Philander Smith College
> Little rock, Arkansas

KUN'GU, James G.
> Diable Valley College
> Concord, California

KWASA, Shadrack Ojude

Howard University
Washington, DC
GITHANGA, Francis Lewis
Diable Valley College
Concord, California
MAGUCHA, Joseph Burn
Greensville College
Greensville, Illinois
MALOYI, Geoffrey M.
Central College
IOWA
MASEMBWA, Solomon M.
Northeast Missouri State, IC
Kingsville, Missouri
MAUNDU, Daniel
Philander Smith College
Little rock, Arkansas
MAUNDU, Philip
Morehouse College
Atlanta, Georgia
MBAYAH, Mungai
New School for Social Research
66 West 12th Street, NY
MBITHI, Johnson
Tuskegee Institute
Alabama
MBUGUA, John Paster
McGill University
Montreal, PQ, Canada
M'MUGAMBI Andrew P.
Georgetown University
Washington 7, DC
NJUGUNA, Beatrice Wairimu
McKinley Contonran High School
Berkeley California
MUGWERU, James Sir
Brighton Young University
Provost, Utah
MUNGAL Arthur Wagithuku

Bowdain College
Brunswick, Maine
MURAI, Stephen Macharia
St Q. University
Prince Edward Island, Canada
MARATHA Nicholas Muge
Western Wilson College
Swanan, North Carolina
MURUNGI, Robert Wallace
College of Idaho
Coldwell, Idaho
MUTISYA, Samuel
Philander Smith College
Little Rock, Arkansas
MUYIA, Harrison Bwire
Wayne State University
Detroit, M.
MWALOKI, Dickson C
Simpson College
Indianola, Iowa
MWANGI, Charles
Damson's University
Charlestown
Prince Edwards island, Canada
MWANGI, Joseph Wanyoike
St Thomas College
Charlton, HD, Canada
MWHIHIA, Kathleen
New York University
Adult's Education
New York, NY
NABUTETE, Frank Habakkuk
Philander Smith College
Little Rock, Arkansas
NGUMBI, John Mutua
Jews Christian College
Hawkins's, Canada
NJOROGE, Raphael
St Mary's University
Halifax, Canada
OCHIEN'G, Adonijah

San Francisco State College
1600 Halloway, Ave.
San Francisco 27, California
OCHIEN'G, John
Simpson College
Indianala, Iowa
OCHIEN'G, Philip
Roosevelt University
Chicago 5, Illinois
OCHOLA, George Philip
University of Chicago
Chicago 37, Illinois
OCHOLA, Samuel Akumu
New Palace State Teacher's College
New York
ODEDE, A. Pamela
Western College
Oxford, Ohio
ODERO, Boniface
Manhattan College
Riverdale 71, New York
ODIN'GE, Odera Collins
Northern State Teacher's College
Aberdeen, South Dakota
ODADA, Patricia
Howard University
Washington 2, DC
ODUAR, Benjamin E.
Central State College
Greencastle, Indiana
Wilberforce, Ohio
OGESSA, Silvanus W. Onyango
DePauw College
Greencastle, Indiana
OGALA, Boaz Harkean
Morehouse, College
Atlanta, Georgia
OLEMBO, James Reuben
Purdue University
Lafayette, Indiana
OMONDI, Raphael

St Mary's University
San Antonio, Texas
ONYUNDO, Aaron
Tuskegee Institute
Tuskegee, Alabama
OTIENO, Olero Samuel
Morris Brown College
Atlanta, Georgia
OTIENO, Jackson
Morehouse College
Atlanta, Georgia
OTONO, Elisha Otieno
Saint Mary's college
PO St Mary's, California
RABALLA, Nicholas
Tuskegee Institute
Tuskegee, Alabama
RAGWAR, Jennifer Adhiambo
Spellman College
Atlanta 3, Georgia
RUENJI, Arthur
Durham High School
Durham, Connecticut
DAMMA, AbdulRasul M.
University of Massachusetts
Amherst, Massachusetts
SANTIAGO, Francis Anthony
Harvard Payne College
Brownwood, Texas
THAIRU, Daniel M.
Virginia Union University
Richmond, VO
WACHIRA, Peter William
Ishaza College
Ishaza, New York
WAGEMA, Grace
Howard University
Washington, DC
WARUI, George Mbuthia

> Oklahoma City University
> Oklahoma City S. Oklahoma
> WASHIKA, Nathan Fedha
> Wisconsin State College
> Superior, Wisconsin
> WATATUA, Solomon
> West Virginia Wesleyan College
> Buchanan, West Virginia
> WOKABI, Angelina W.
> Clarke College
> Dubuque, Iowa
> New York, NY[27]

Authors have repeatedly shared that *Fight doesn't reward prudence,* they concur that the meaning is shrouded in confusion.

John says, 'Pamela and Philip, among other students, were in our travel.'

'Philip and I were going to Roosevelt University while Pamela to Western College for Women (Oxford, Ohio).'

He talks fondly about Barack.

'Barack had gone earlier, to Hawaii, to the University of Hawaii,' he charged. 'The same city my friend and I were heading to before making our way to Hawaii and before heading to Chicago (The Windy City). And we met black students from Kenya, and we represented Africa.'

At his Ngei Residence, John would display a Sunday, 4 January 2009, Daily Nation Opinion written by Nation Media Columnist Philip.

And he explained thus:

> 'Of all my fifty high school classmates (1955-1958), JC ("Jesus Christ") Kang'ethe—who hails from Meru—has been my closest friend, the one I know best. And it was not fortuitous. From Alliance, we flew together (in one of Tom Mboya's airlifts) to Chicago in 1959.'

Indeed, other students would live with Ann S. Kheel and Ted. The two had helped extensively to organize the airlift and again hosted some students at their house. They finally set up a TASK Foundation that provided funding to the project.

The students met African American Students Foundation Committee and other actors supporting the programme—People like Eunice Kennedy Shriver, Malcolm X—he was a jovial man; there was Jackie Robinson, George M Houser, and Senator Hubert H. Humphrey. Also, on 9 September 1959, when they landed at the Idlewild Airport, New York, they met two gentlemen from the Foundation, Cora Weiss and William X. Scheinman who welcomed African students to United States. The following day on 10 September, a playwright and a brilliant scholar Lorraine Hansberry gave a powerful speech during one of the orientation days. Her confidence was awesome. This particular session took several days. There was Sidney Poitier, and their best day was when one group of the students met Martin Luther King Jr. He was a real man, who never shouted obscenities.

The celebrated columnist continued thus:

> We shared a room in the house of a black pharmacist called Charles Thompson, his wife Jackie, and her mother Ethel. We enrolled at the same one-block but high-class Jewish University in Chicago's 'Loop' called Roosevelt. And, for four years, we painted the 'Windy City' completely red.[28]

According to the *Washington Post* . . . Malik recalls:

After the success of the 1959 Students' Airlift, Mboya decided to expand the program in 1960 and to include students from neighboring African countries. This time, he raised $250,000 for 256 students. Universities and colleges promised scholarships worth $1,600,000, but Mboya still needed money for the airlift itself. His American friends suggested that he approached Senator John F. Kennedy, who had just launched his presidential campaign. In addition to chairing a senate subcommittee on Africa, Kennedy controlled the Joseph P. Kennedy Jr Foundation, named after his elder brother, who was killed in World War II.

The two men met at the Kennedy compound at Hyannis Port, Massachusetts, on 26 July 1960. Kennedy later said that the family was initially "reluctant" to support the program because of other commitments but eventually agreed to provide $100,000 because it was impossible to raise the funds elsewhere.

Despite all the successes of these programmes, one man wasn't at peace—the president of the Republic of Kenya, Mzee Jomo Kenyatta. In the book, *The Reds and the Blacks*, published later in 1967, the then American ambassador to Kenya, William Attwood, had difficult time at those moments—like any other high commissioner, there were threats from head of state against his association with Mboya, which wasn't a big surprise. The president questioned his intentions and the continued traveling arrangements he organized for the minister and the support he accorded for his plans. His association with Mboya was already soaring, and he felt that the cabinet member was too ambitious.

He didn't give up and softly continued with his country's policies.

He hosted Barack and a handful of students, who were leaving for United States in August 1959, a month before the highly publicized TJ Airlifts.

Out of annoyance and persistent success stories along with this, the president warned: I want to see to it that the flow of these funds stopped.[29]

1960

University of Hawaii
2500 Campus Road
Honolulu, HI 96822
4 October 1962

Dear Mr Barak H. Obama:

It is a real pleasure to inform you that your name has been placed on the Dean's Honor List for your outstanding performance of your academic work at University of Hawaii during the Spring semester, 1960.

Your selection for the Dean's Honor List is an accomplishment of which you can be proud, for this honor is bestowed on those students only whose grade point average for the past semester was 3.5 or better.

Please accept my heartfelt congratulations on this achievement, and my best wishes for a successful academic career and a happy future that lies beyond.

Sincerely yours
Dean, UH

He had qualified for inclusion in the exclusive *Phi Beta Phi*, *Phi Beta Kappa* fraternities.

Chapter 14

> It is in the past that most of our injustices lie.
> (Anonymous)

On a beautiful Sunday at the onset of 1960, moments stirred up issues.

Every issue came up for a moment and that turned out to be an element of change. Rita Auma wasn't only born, but she ended up joining the long list of Roy (her brother), the eight-year-old Zeituni, Nyaoke, and Hawa, and Omar: aunties and uncle, respectively.

Above all the births that occurred at the start of this year at Lady Ainsworth Community Hospital, Rita was already born and her life started. Kenya's politics was growing by the day—torture, violence, discrimination, and stalking became the day-to-day major ingredient of governance. And the grip of the colonialists onto power became more and more determined and defined than the day earlier.

A year had passed since Barack left Kenya; Kezia was shuffling up and down—life changing wild enough—too much bills to pay, no proper income, as if all the world's problems and hardships were settling right at her household. Most of businesses ended in futility. She and the children would go to visit Perpetua *Nyar* Gem (Kezia's mother) or Sara Onyango—both were adoring grandmothers, in the rural home—to ease hectic situations. In the countryside, life was bearable unlike the urban hustle, parching from one lifestyle to another, from one job to another, without proper settlement or adequate payment and selling anything—using second hand clothes and plastic utensils in the name of profit and to make a living. She couldn't trace when she last wore a proper suit. That she'd given up. One thing she knew was that she wasn't going to change Barack by the virtue that he was away, but she could do that to herself, to her family, and to the children, to make them understand that life had changed from the time her husband left, and to help and prepare them to live without a father figure now that their father had stopped communicating directly barely a year later. She'd to help them understand the money she didn't have, and do something for the children who needed upkeep badly. She'd to get the guilt out, change the language, and move on to gain foothold in the midst of hard times of need.

On the other hand, as the only African student in the economics faculty, Barack was in regular contact, therefore, with white folks—he'll adopt their liberal values, incubate their ideas, send tributes to their lives, and support their dislikes, and attend classes with white students, discussing with entirely no black figure around, except residents of the Hawaii neighborhood. Maybe there wasn't a racial prejudice. The class consisted of young men and women who'd form the vanguard of the core of politics, of business, of social networks; wives and husbands who'd later explode in debates and national broadcasts, make profound decisions in banks and other financial institutions, in governments and conventions, an elite class of great leaders to reckon with.

America wasn't a good place for a black folk. A racist society where there was Africans-only bus, Africans—and colored-only State, Africans-and-Hispanics-separate foods, only townships, only trains . . . It was a world and country with basic white laws and regulations to stop you from being aggressive, from knowing your rights, whether you should own property or not. All the laws were a culmination of fantasies that came to a white man's understanding barely or rather profanely about when they'd have thin information about the black man. The changes that took place, profoundly, radically altered his principles—from a man who left Nairobi, left an expectant mother, and left a son and from a man who knew little about the world to a man now vexed by the continuous misunderstandings of the new world coupled with the responsibilities he'd not want anyone to ask him. He, therefore, wanted to mix the waters of the two worlds. The rather colder American waters and the warmer tropical African waters merged. He was in a path to self-realization or maybe departure from that reality. Barack believed that all these successes weren't small occurrences after all. Because of the easy share of how things came up—pursuing a BA Economics Degree at UH at Manoa was a surety that he'll be able to restore his fathers' legacy, repair the colonialist damages, and reverse the long-lost hope. Later, with a master's, he'd be an African elite savoring above and the world below his feet. He wished to convince his mother Akumu to decamp to Alego, to restore the hope of the Obamas—the *Jok'Obama*—the dream that seemed within reach—he didn't want to remain a fraud in the eyes of

Onyango after receiving a crown in a foreign land. He wanted to rest his case by getting a plump job back in Kenya and would be the pride of the ailing old man. Barack told Malik that his father, Onyango, 'was a person he couldn't despise. He was a great man who longed to live to see the prosperity of his lineage.'

Meanwhile, Onyango was then frustrated; he'd worked while seated... bathed while seated, and found it hard to walk around due to physical pain and perhaps paralysis, proving cruel on his body. Sara would be with Onyango in every step of his suffering. A role she fitted so well. He'd stopped to go swimming at river *Worungo* though he liked it. At the river, there was a deep section where men would assemble at 10 a.m. with their younger sons to swim. The older teenagers would come in the afternoon. Upstream was a secluded spot for women. No man would dare cross this path, and no woman would pretend to swim downstream to the men's territory. Both the old and the young liked this sort of entertainment. The old would, particularly, swim like teenagers, their toothless smile depicting how dear they liked the game.

Obeid believes that Onyango was perturbed by the fact that Barack went so silent. Maybe the letters he wrote were actually showing some traces of misunderstanding. How come he talked of marrying a white woman? He asked Sara, who was equally confused. The setting at home was sombre. The inclusion of this emotive issue in his letters was the center of the uproar. Barack stated that he's married and that he wasn't going to change, at least at the time he was drafting the letter. In the letter, he wrote that he had actually married a Kansas girl. Her name was Ann Durham. And that remained simply as that. He also mentioned the fact that he was proceeding to Harvard University. Onyango knew basically that Harvard must be a white-dominated college and with a better or higher chances of achieving good education.

1963, Independence Day

On 28 May 1963, Kenya was a changed state. The guard of honor had changed hands across the race from a white-man rule to the black-run government. The new governor, Malcolm MacDonald, invited Kenyatta, other political luminaries, Oginga Odinga, Tom Mboya, and other political icons to form the government. Jomo Kenyatta was made the first prime minister of Kenya at Uhuru Gardens, (now in Lan'gata constituency). During the polls, Kenya Africa National Union (KANU) had beaten the rival party Kenya Africa Democratic Union (KADU) at the polls in the first democratic elections.

One thing that caused other's concern in the first Kenyatta's government that threw observers off balance was nepotism in the ministerial positions and other powerful positions, especially positions given to those close to him. Mbiyu Koinange, a minister, was his brother-in-law, Dr Njoroge Mungai, a minister, was his nephew, and Charles Njonjo, Attorney General, his cousin. Confusion arose and mistrust started smoking out. A Luo, Jaramogi Oginga Odinga, was later appointed the vice president. And a myriad of other Luos were appointed to the cabinet. Achieng Oneko, Tom Mboya, J. D. Otiende, Samuel Ayodo, among others.

With these unbalanced appointments, Jaramogi could discern some mischief. He smelled passivity, and the prime minister, later turned president, wanted submissive cabinet ministers, those who must be ready to be squeezed at their nails and never complain. Those ready to be stepped on and still smile. These developments he (Odinga) could not accept, and his devotion started to wane away.

This struggle was unremitting. In the process, professionals appointed in the various positions in the new government felt the same and many would resign in protest. So the government was just a one-man show. And that was the comical mistake from the side of the president. He was overzealously disorganized. But power is addictive, and any innocent soul may be poisoned when the strength of power swept them away. They get confused and good leaders disregard the massive dignity that was formed after independence. A few discreet observers warned that 'the new government was likely to collapse after nepotism was introduced to it. And that the gentility of the masses

could at times be diluted by this. That it was a government that was fitted for failure. A crowd of thousands of enthusiastic Kenyans had ushered the new dawn. And the speech, the powerful speech drafted by Mboya and read by the prime minister, Jomo Kenyatta, was indeed the key to that elusive dawn, as if they had been living in a bottomless planet. And they would escape distrustful eyes of a white folk that amused arrogance.

But Kenyans were not lucky, their leaders wanted to amass wealth as fast as possible. They wanted to be land barons, under the crystal chandeliers; they wanted to be real-estate managers, to own personal banks under their names or in their interests: the oil interests, the drug interests, and many other money-minting interests. The trick was how to execute to achieve these many interests. Corruption and impunity remained the only options, as if the country was piously not ready for independence and its leaders jaundiced by power, excessive power, to be precise, lacking the pragmatic determination that actually brought them together, and the squabbles finally replaced the old-time harmony that bonded diverse political opinions.

Most politicians felt frustrated. The air had been taken out of them. They were remorseful of their failings. The government was therefore a terrible monster, a fascinating devil. The same government they served strangled them. Maybe they would easily vote a death penalty against the government of President Kenyatta. This is the kind of government that awaited Barack. As the ululation songs of *Uhuru*, for freedom, rented the air, the prisoners were granted conjugal visits and petty criminals were pardoned. And as a chain smoker finished the last piece of a cigarette and thumped it on the ground, independence became a hot topic in Africa as a whole. It was like an extra piece of toast over and above elegant benefits that came their way upon the defeat of white-man rule.

Kenyans were on the crossroads; some cried, and others ran. Confusion was finally over, and they could not wait to shout, and they shouted endlessly.

The leaders had been disintegrated by the seminal influence of vision, pragmatism, ambition, and logic. A government that was in blends with deadpan wit. A subculture that continually grew to the epic level.

The 1959 TJ Airlift was the perfect replacement for the jobs that would be available after independence when the whites left. The return in 1962 and 1963 was a landmark.

For instance, a large team had been sent by the recruitment agency to the United States of America, the Secretariat was then sitting at Jogoo House (under the Secretariat official Lugonzo)—their main work was to recruit all Kenyans graduating from the American universities and colleges to the ministry. The able Ministry of Planning and Economic Development—he might be lucky to have been picked by the minister himself. The minister was none-other-than Tom Mboya, the shrewd politician and economic tactician. They were to be deployed to different departments within the expanded government system of the independent country—within the ministry, government parastatals, and schools—as administrators, financial analysts, and security personnel, etc. They'd stepped in and said 'they're the ones to take control'.

Of course, not all brought back their feet in the country at a go. One such person was Barack who'd proceeded to Harvard University for a master's degree.

He divorced his wife Ann Stanley upon setting his foot in Harvard. And the dreaded divorce papers followed almost immediately. The divorce 'was one of the lowest moments in his life,' he later said. It was something un-African, which evoked bad blood, and went against the traditional customs. However, in American settings, that was the custom. It showed the differences in ideology—between the two beliefs, between the two races, between the possibilities and the impossibilities . . . That Onyango had condemned repeatedly and concluded that 'his son was no more. His son was 'lost'. That's when Ruth surfaced—when she came into his life, the son of Kogelo married once again. Another of 'arranged marriage'. Maybe he'd defined marriage as 'a consensus'. No one would tell what transpired between the two—but there was a couple. The process of losing by the left-hand side and gaining the same (or even lesser) with the right-hand side was phenomenal. One wouldn't actually know that he'd lost anything. But Barack felt pretty robbed—that he'd lost somebody significant. Someone he'd loved and a son he'd cherished. Now that he'd been a loser, everything was now a chance event—like a headless hen planning for an escape, which he can't find. And maybe he felt as if waking up from a disorienting dream. Or someone forcibly inserting a canister in his ears. Since his decision was rushed, maybe his friends—white folks or blacks—would have thought him 'ignorant and rude—or dumb as hell—no one can tell.'

And Ruth's arrival was such an event.

The Airlift came to fill all the vacancies left after the British took off. Some of them found themselves in high positions wielding immense power and having superfluous authority.

Odinge Odera Bios

He was born in Kanjira Village, Yimbo Location, Karachuoyo, schooled at Usenge Sector School in mid-1942, joined Maranda School in January 1950, and sat for Cambridge school certificate in 1956. In 1953, he worked as a clerical officer at Kenya Police Headquarters in Nairobi Industrial Area and later as laboratory assistant in the material branch of Ministry of Works in January 1958.

He sat for the correspondence courses at Nairobi Royal Technical College and later started applying for American colleges. After a short start, he received admissions to Northern States Teachers' College (Aberdeen South Dakota, US) and a college in Mexico City.

Through the help of Jaramogi and Tom Mboya, he was one of the beneficiaries of 1959 Aircraft.

In USA, he was enrolled at the Northern States Teachers' College, and later University of Dakota, Vermillion, on a transfer as a journalism student. Upon graduation, Kenya had got independence and when a recruitment secretariat agency went to the USA, his first job in the independent Kenya was as a District Officer of Kapenguria, West Pokot.

Odera has been an editor, author, and a father, self-confessed adviser of Jaramogi Odinga. He has survived political intrigues, imprisonment, and political persecution in Nyanza.[30a]

His latest book, the best selling novel, released in 2010, *My Journey with Jaramogi: Memoir of a Close Confidant*, has received good sales in the global market.

Philip Ochieng'

He grew up in the village, like Barack, studied in a rural school, and moved to Alliance High School in 1955. He completed high school in 1958 under the fiery reign of Carey Francis (we've got a glimpse of his life history earlier in this book).

Philip benefited from the TJ Airlifts in 1959—just like John Kang'ethe. Philip says they met with Barack, for the first time, at TJ's office. But he was already in the final stages of flying out—ahead of us.

In September 1959, he and John were enrolled at Roosevelt University, Chicago; other students joined them in 1960 in the subsequent airlifts.

The students, though in different universities and colleges, met more often in the United States. John says, 'I and Philip lived at a block along 5210 South Kenwood Road. Later, I remember Philip moved downstreet in a separate apartment.'

John Kang'ethe says, 'My friend Philip is a good writer, with a precise perfect command of the language.' During this interview he brings various pieces of Philip's literary work. Ranging from political analysis, heydays at Alliance, and what actually happened in different generations of politics.

Among the interviews and literary works carried out by different authors, Philip describes Barack as 'charming, generous, and extraordinarily clever. However, Obama Sr was also imperious, cruel, and given to boasting about his brain and his wealth.'[30b]

I get no comments from John, anyway. John says all of the students got a perfect opportunity and were perfectly good candidates in all the spheres of influence. I agree how Philip describes his social aspect, and I would be privileged to add that he was exceptionally charming as well as adept with having pretty good fun.

'He was excessively fond of Scotch. He had fallen into the habit of going home drunk every night. His boasting proved his undoing and left him without a job, plunged him into prolonged poverty, and dangerously wounded his ego.'

Philip believes that at some point, people may make drastic explanations to their current predicament. And he talks more boldly about his kinsman.

'You bring a woman from far away, and you reduce her to pulp. That is not our way.' He had many extremely serious accidents. One of his limbs is fixed with crude iron.

'I know Barack was just like Mr Toad (from *Wind in the Willows*), like many of intellectuals in the field—very arrogant on the road, especially when he had whisky inside.'[30c]

John adds, I was surprised when I learned how he died. A freak road accident! That was a sad incident. Though, it was great time having drinks with Barack. A drinking pal who will keep you laughing; at times, we'd realize that it's already midnight. One thing I know, according to my opinion, Barack wasn't a heavy drunkard. But he used to take his time with the scotch.'

Malik says that all this time until the Obama name became famous, Philip Ochieng' and some of those listed as close friends of Barack had never been seen or known to him or the family. Maybe they were casual friends who would meet in wine joints for a toss and to remember the old days they spent in America . . . The Cottage Grove, 95th Street, The Lake Side Drive, The Gold Coast, Hyde Park, The Michigan Avenue, Buckingham Fountain—rekindling old memories and now coming out of the woodworks because of the newfound fame to claim kinship and closeness to Barack.

Pamela Mboya

Born in 1939 to Mzee Odede and Owila, Pamela Arwa schooled in Ng'iya Girls' Sector School. And in 1946, she met Barack there—who was then across the school path at Ng'iya Boys Sector School. He was then in a senior class. Barack later said, 'We called her Nyar Owila or Arwa'. In 1950, Barack went separate ways upon completion of Kenya African Preliminary Examination. He joined Maseno while Pamela later went to Alliance Girls. She said, 'I met that gentleman at Ng'iya, and we never forgot each other. I kept in touch. I can't tell when or where but around this time . . . I also met Mboya. In Alliance Girls', I sat for the final examination and joined Makerere in 1958.' She dropped out and joined the TJ's Airlifts—a man who would later marry her. The girls that included Patricia Odada, Damma Abdulrasal, Cathleen Mmwihia, Angelina Wokabi, among others. While in Nairobi, their friendship didn't die out, and Barack treated her like his own sister. They would visit one another and that was what Nairobi life was all about.

In the United States, she joined Western College, Oxford, in Ohio for a BA. This is where she met him again after he had left a couple of months earlier to United States. Barack was one of the organizers of 'Only black Kenyans Ball party'. 'We held a number of get-together parties, the condition allowed us for learning and socialising,' she said. Mboya had asked them to consolidate together and to encourage one another during their stay in a foreign land.

On her return from the USA, she worked in several institutions. And notable was her marriage to TJ—their colourful wedding attracted the attention of the Pope and the Queen of England. They went to receive blessings from the two personalities on the eve of their wedding. Pamela's tumultuous time came following the assassination of her husband. At the time she said, 'I felt the heavens coming down and consuming me—as if I passed through slime and never came out of it.' After the conclusion of the burial ceremony, Pamela appeared before the Murder Trial Inquiry—a dejected personality—'an inquiry that never bared any fruit.'

Pamela served as Kenya's Permanent Representative to UN—Habitat—from the late 1980s.

In February 2009—Pamela Mboya died—aged seventy. John Kan'gethe says, 'Pamela's death was unexpected. She seemed strong, cultured, and just jovial as usual. She died in a South Africa hospital due to cancer—forty years after the death of her husband. She was flown in from Johannesburg to Nairobi

Chiromo Lee Funeral Home. At requiem mass—at the exact spot where her husband was laid—tribute filled the cathedral—but there was a peaceful crowd. Far different from what happened forty years ago when her husband died.

Mrs Anna Tabaijuka—Executive Director UN—Habitat said,

> 'Mrs Mboya was not only committed to the success of UN—Habitat. She was determined to help the agency find solutions to the problems of providing housing for urban poor everywhere . . .'

After a couple of days, from Nairobi, she was flown to the Lambwe Valley rural home in Uriri Constituency by a government chopper to an airstrip. Pamela had moved here from Rusinga Island and settled fifty miles from her maternal home. Those on board were family members and included her children, Mboya Jr Maureen Odero and Susan Mboya. The hearse picked the remains from the airstrip in a snarling convoy—prominent personalities witnessed Pamela's arrival. The Suba District Commissioner Odino Ojuko—who was in charge of the security detail, was present. Politicians, Miregi Okuku and Orwa Ojode, graced the occasion. During the burial, a teary reception greeted other prominent people—Rt. Honourable Raila Odinga and a number of cabinet ministers arrived during her sendoff. Raila spoke of a woman he knew as 'a unifying factor'.

Pamela was laid to rest having worked for as a chairperson of HelpAge International, member of Kenyan Women's Political Caucus, among other organizations, having worked tirelessly for mankind. Pamela was the woman who knew Barack so well; they all laboured through hard times . . . through education . . . through disappointments and sorrow.

John Charles Kan'gethe

As the echoes of the singing women filtered through the thicket of Meru Forest and was quickly taken up by a strong wind that crashed it on the rocky hills of Kenya (hills), John Kang'ethe was born on 30 November 1940.

In the 1950s, Meru was gripped by a tumultuous period when the Mau Mau freedom fighters made a strong resistance to the determined and mindful white solders. John joined Mulathankari Primary School between the years 1947 and 1951. At the end, he sat for Common Entrance Examination.

He then went to Kaaga Intermediate in Meru and passed Kenya Africa Preliminary Examination at the school in 1954, making it to Alliance High School, Kikuyu in 1955-1958. John sat for Cambridge School Certificate and scored Division I. A first class in contemporary grading, it was time to move out—he made it to Roosevelt University, Chicago, Illinois, through the Airlift together with his friend Philip Ochieng'. In casual attire, John says, 'I joined a bachelor of arts degree (Economics and Political Science) class in November 1959.'

John remembers his contact with many other students when they'd a party in a Chicago Restaurant or in the streets or when some students shared great achievements; especially when they made it to the Deans' Honor List. It was during the Spring Semester, 1962. Philip later left the university back to Kenya before completing his degree. See, when I receive the letter from Otto Wirth, the dean, It was time to work more harder and to stay in that list as long as I'll be there in the university.

This isn't John's words but as an author, I believe with this kind of achievement, I strongly believe it might have been real partying for the black elite. The results trickled in around 5 October 1962, a day after John received the letter. Maybe, Barack had been in the Dean's List earlier as well! Twice or thrice! Who knows! And I think he wasn't ready to be struck out. 'I will never be shown the door. I'll stick there as long as I was out in UH: Because there's where I belonged. The dean's list,' he said.

It was believed that in 1962, Barack was already in Harvard University for his masters, and Pamela was arranging for her wedding with TJ. A former airlift beneficiary who was enrolled at university of Hawaii says he met Ann Durham twice in a local pub together with Barack, and he was the only one without a babe beside. When he met Ann, she was a little young lady about nineteen years old. She looked amazing, and I believe he loved her. We shouted in deafening voice of Niagara, a black student enjoying the luxury like slaying the dragon and battling the backlash—obligingly celebrating hard work. During these parties, I sensed the pragmatic love of education if still not obvious truth, and I think it paid to me that we felt patronized by the most liberal support, the support that would have been abridged into sentences, into opportunities. We celebrated the achievements with doggerel glee.

We had taken away fear, and I remember Barack reciting a song. Or a poem, whatever it was. I think he had copied it in his mind and was burning him down. The praises of the Marion!

The old gent will hustle for it,
The old lady will rustle for it,
The small boys will tussle for it
The old maids will bustle for it.
And all unite saying, 'it is the best by far'.

I asked him what he meant by that 'its education' and he answered—as he picked a tot of cold Vodka, the only remaining on the table.

The boogying and boozing was interesting; we had aspects in common. Same demeanor, same vision, same model—ooh! Same origin. Did I tell you Barack was a great dancer? The man would simply take things a bit slow at first and climax into a body twitching dance. His dancing reminded me of Mboya, who'd similar moves. When the party was over, we dispersed. Barack told me, 'It was interesting trying out your party. I think you upped it a little bit. I like celebrating our culture in an unfamiliar territory,' he said.

A very simple and dignified speech!

Did I tell you, I fixed them a meal; we ate so fast because of lack of time and started off down the street. 'I'll miss you,' Ann waved back lazily.

The Recruitment Secretariat—sitting at Jogoo House, recruited most of the students while they were still in the United States. Lugonzo headed the Secretariat. For instance, John worked at the Provincial Administration Charter—as ARGA, *District Officer,* between 1963 and 1965. Already Barack was a much senior man—appointed to work for the government, especially for the upcoming Sessional Paper No. 10. He says upon return to Kenya, he and Philip met Barack. 'Whenever we met, he asked our views concerning what we would like to change within the government or implemented. I knew him as an econometrician, a shrewd and hardworking econometrician. The following year, 1966, I moved to the private sector, getting employed in Pfizer Corporation, as assistant pricing coordinator in its regional headquarters for Africa. I coordinated their operations within the East African region from Agip House. Here we worked for more or less like consultants. Later, I resigned for a more challenging assignment.'

When changes hanged over Central Bank of Kenya—John managed to secure a job there following a vacancy announcement. 'It was in April 1969—when the bank employed me as superintendent in the research department, I found that a lot needed to be done, and these were some of the highlights that we discussed with other banking experts at graphic length at the city hotels or other meeting joints. I moved to a senior position on promotion in 1972.' He says he worked with Joab H. O. Omino. Joab had been a senior official at the bank. A former student of Alliance High School, he was later elected a Member of Parliament, served as the Kenya Football Federation (KFF) Secretary General. He's deceased and his remains lies in his rural home of Kisumu.

When Barack passed on, John was an assistant principal in the Foreign Department of the central bank. 'I was shocked (and everyone was!), and John doesn't know how to describe the death of a friend so dear. Many friends converged for burial arrangements, up to the time he was laid to rest.

And by 1990, I was appointed the principal of the bank in the Foreign Department. Promotions crawled so slowly—something many employees condemned, including John and Dr Obama (they'd been complaining about it). I tried raising my voice but was shut as a pulp. John remembers applying for outside jobs.

Another close friend says that at one point Barack asked me about the African Development Bank and I told him that it was a successful bank doing so well with a large clientele base. So when he applied for the Addis Ababa-based bank, he succeeded as a financial advisor in Africa—but he never went there.

As trouble brewed at the bank—John retired on 30 November 1993. At around this time multiparty politics was taking shape, and the government was already feeling the heat of all-inclusive opposition in the parliament.

I went back to the private sector and assumed the role of a financial and administration director at Samaki Industries Limited between 1993 and 1996.

In 1997, Tropical Food Products hired me for two years' renewable contract as a finance manager, a job I took without delay.

One thing I know was the fact that Dr Obama had a bright future ahead of him. He might have risen to a permanent secretary or an equivalent. His brilliance was unmatched.

John says that 'Starlight Night Club served cold whiskey—the Scotch whiskey.' We wined till late. But Barack was always the first to stand up to head home. The setting had good ambience. We had chilled out whilst sipping sundowners; there was a stretch of restaurants and promenades. There was partying, eating, and an all-age ultimate vibe at the opposite pub. And nothing was more spectacular than the face of Kenyan night revelers. This opposite pub had a share of its wonders—at nightfall, revelers would swarm in—they moved in with haste. They had joined in a jamboree that never died out so easily. Some sat in round tables, drinking soup with their hands. These were the times when the illicit brew took center stage and was beginning to take more victims than gunshots from a machine gun.

Another reveler notes that at one time, the pub opposite Starlight had experienced a real earthquake or maybe poor workmanship and people were trapped inside; one victim would narrate the sad story thus: 'I was lying on my belly next to a wall, wondering if it would fall. And the exit seemed congested with corpses. I had felt chunks of concrete coming down. A solid piece of a concrete rock had hit my cranium. I thought it had broken it apart. When the rumbling started, the drunk patrons and the waiters were all committed to escape—a stampede that caused an immediate standoff.' He said shaking off the dirt from his clothes.

The pub—within a radius of few meters—had a reserved interest—the epicenter of fistfights—as if the revelers converged to settle some scores. There could be certainly a camaraderie that culminated to a dangerous fistfight. The scene I had only witnessed in Chicago. In a society that I first saw, a reverend with a Bible passed by a pub and a catechist romping alongside. I don't think they glanced inside and looked like some historians dispatched into different directions—some to the future and others to the past. Maybe some of them rode on muleback and others on horseback to bring that elusive history. Others went through the air like a squadron of warplanes.

From the dreaded opposite pub, back to Starlight, Barack spoke with gusto. Always our discussions ended in a note of optimism. As he shared a stick of cigarette, he had fondly talked about various aspects—the economy and stroked over to the stories of failed marriages, the tales of nagging women, and the struggles to break from the comfortable confines of conformity—the essence of a just society. He spoke more like a peasant expressing his anger. And the music? The hippie days involved great traditional music—a pure mimicry of the white settlers' waltz.

As the wining continued—the story of my father lingered on. Of the men slithering down the forage-grown paths to aim at the poor enemies in the fight to realize independence. They had worked filling sandbags, packing them along the slit trenches to form a formidable barrier. They had hung their revolvers from a wire hook on the wall—the King's African Rifles servicemen fought for this freedom; and for me, we'd started abusing the very freedom. They had worked through harsh terrain jumping up the thorny shrubs that even a goat would not relish. The servicemen would count their losses—some of them lost a foot during the war.

Ministry of Finance, Planning, and Development—1964-1969

Entebbe Airport, Uganda, 1964

Barack stepped into the tiny East African country for a job at Makerere University, now in 1964, it had grown to a fully fledged university. At that point, jobs were available but only for the educated, Barack being one of them. Entebbe Airport was like an ant's nest—currying travelers, wailing babies, and blaring loud speakers announcing, 'For local trips, take left corner and for International travelers, go right ahead.' The voice echoed with a heavy blend of Bugandan accent. And the unsightly view of arrogant black police officers—those who hadn't even been civil—maybe because it was independence time.

A job with full medical cover, handsome allowances on traveling, housing, and recreation. Makerere was a serene university with beautiful banana trees shading the smooth roads. Makerere was the school (college) of choice. African professionals found refuge here. 'Barack would invite his brother Omar to Kampala. Omar had sat for the A-levels at Maseno Mission School. The boy was to join Makerere University at the start of 1965, and preparation was, therefore, at top gear,' at least, according to Sara. 'My son, Omar, joined Barack at Makerere,' she says. Sara had worked so hard to see her son Omar follow in the footsteps of Barack. They were both enclosed in a cavern of changing their destiny and the destiny of their family—'as if they were at the bottom of a deep crevasse, that they'd to face or sustain a few bruises by living in a foreign country,' a country that had hardly celebrated their first anniversary of independence. Hawa says that Barack later told her 'that by living in Kampala, Uganda, he felt as if he lay in a tomb; this is where he'd fall and lay trapped because he was not meant for Uganda but Kenya. He wanted to deliver! And Kampala would be the last obstacle on his way to Kenya, in a hectic pace to join the Government of Kenya.' Omar, therefore, during this stint, started applying for overseas universities (in the steps of his brother). And impatience often got the better part of him. '. . . inked each application with a quick fix, with great expectation to try a different taste of education system up on the other end.'

Behind all these developments was the first African student to attend the University of Hawaii. Many writers had described these as a CIA-afflicted Airlift Africa project to gain control of them and their countries of origin Tanzania, Kenya, Zanzibar, Uganda, and Rhodesia (South) to encounter similar programs established by the Soviet Union and China in the region.

In Kenya, Jaramogi Odinga had established such a project. This kind of argument was a tussle between the west and the pro-Soviet and pro-Chinese African nationalists where Jaramogi belonged.

Working in the faculty of economics in the University of Makerere, 'just as an economics lecturer,' according to Malik, 'was a milestone achievement.' Few Kenyans, who had worked there, as dons, made it big in Kenya, for instance, a fellow economist Mwai Kibaki (the present Head of State of Kenya). He taught economics class for a while before being recalled by the Government of Kenya. Barack would later work under him at the Ministry of Planning when he was the Permanent Secretary. John says he also remembers Barack working under either Duncan Ndegwa or Philip Ndegwa. I chose to be quiet here! Although, I set foot into the bank to know exactly when the two gentlemen served the bank.

The first black Minister for Information, Broadcasting, and Tourism in the independent Kenya, Honorable Ramogi Achieng' Oneko, phoned Barack in November 1964 and promised him a job. That—only in the premise that my father had Western-honed skills—which he really needed at the ministry. He was this black man (a Young Kavirondo die-hard) who had been in constant touch with serving ministers and assistants, associated or allied to TJ—all directed by TJ to fill the vacancies with professionals 'those within and in Diaspora'. Achieng' Oneko, the boss, would later link Barack to the Department of Finance in the upcoming Kenya Tourism Development Authority (KTDA)—a job he never took until later. Oneko was born in 1920 at Kunya Village, Rarieda, Bondo District. He grew up in the remote hinterland of Kenya. Just like Barack, he was village-grown and schooled there and joined Maseno Mission School. Then, he was recruited to a political movement, Young Kavirondo Association by Owen. In 1963, he was elected the Member of Parliament for Nakuru Town constituency and later Rarieda constituency in 1992 during Multi Party Politics. Oneko died in 1997 due to heart attack—survived by his widow, Jedida, who died in 1992, and Loice Anyango. He had eleven children—seven sons and four daughters. He was one of the 'Kapenguria Six' freedom fighters and quit the government in 1966 to join the opposition politics as a member of the Socialist Party—Kenya People's

Union, KPU, when the president they had suffered with in prison for nine years turned so nasty. He had painted signs and slogans praising KPU progress and solidarity for the better part of his political life, later joining Ford Kenya.

'Barack resigned in December 1964 and had crossed over to Kenya by road to Kisumu where he met Honorable Oneko. Omar came home with their few belongings three weeks later. Barack had taken up his new job in an oil company, the American Shell/BP at the institution's headquarters in Nairobi,' Hawa says. She quickly adds, 'He never took the KTDA job immediately due to technicalities.'

When Barack received his appointment letter from Shell, located in Agip House, he was pretty sure that it was a reply to the many job vacancies he had applied. He had posted various job applications to various government departments and corporations.

At Shell, my father was in charge of all the petrol stations at the Hurligham area and its environs. One particular one is that at the roundabout along Route Forty-Six, where he pitched tent while on his supervision round-trips.

In bits and pieces, in plots and episodes, the life in Kenya started in earnest. Ruth came, and she met a man 'far-fetched and unreliably as it sounded, her future husband.' Barack was going to settle on another marriage with a woman, Jewish woman, older than him in the heartland of Africa. Amazing!

His coming to Kenya, through a flurry of individuals, was awesome. Barack discussed the upcoming job with the minister in Kisumu. There was something that quickly flashed. Oneko advised him to wait for a while as the vetting period was still on the offing. And the Shell/BP (American) Oil Company job came almost immediately. Working at the oil company at Agip House sixth floor—adjacent to Esso House—the new economist settled at Rosslyn Estate, a coffee plantation settlement where cooks, gardeners, and a driver was part of the pay package. Malik says that 'it was a life, a very good life worth living.' And education was my father's first priority. I was enrolled at Aga Khan Primary and he dropped me at school every morning; he had enjoyed his work following the enthusiasm that he showed. Now we were living with our stepmother, Ruth, without my mother; then she was living away from us, but the two intermittently met at Rosslyn. About eight months later, in 1964, we moved to Hurligham Estate, the posh estate a few miles from the city. It was rather amazing. This was a complete mix: Auma, Ruth, the old man, and myself. And Omar was working his way out of Nairobi to study overseas.

My father worked for the company, the American Shell/BP oil Company, as a manager. It was just a temporary job that warmed and enhanced him to join the government through the Kenya Tourism Development KTDA—a job he applied for but never took until some time later. Here, at KTDA, he had been employed as a junior economist but rose steadily to a more senior position. At this time, I felt the efforts of his actions—to feed a lot more people, to dig out to fulfill the desires, the buzz, and excitement of all who needed help. And I could see an enclave that started opening up, the role of a polygamist. I remember my grandmother, Sara Ogwel, coming over, especially when Omar was in his last preparations to fly out.

But their squabbling was evident. Ruth, a white woman, was not at ease. The racial aspect was a real stumbling block. The village life was so unforgiving, at least, according to her.

My grandmother did not like the marriage (arrangement). 'Why go far with these foreigners?' she asked, in a rather calm deliberation. Maybe she had advised Omar to 'watch his steps' while in America—maybe he had heeded the advice. And Sara wanted the advice be permanently tattooed on the back of his mind. Omar Onyango left that year to America, and he never looked back. He has never stepped back to Kenya. As if he was cursed, condemned staying away from the very family who worked out his travel. Sara says, 'I would like my son to come back and build a *simba*. I've no problem with him staying in Boston but as a Luo; a real son of *Ramogi* must have a *simba* in his ancestral land. He cannot separate himself from that fact. It is a changeless business deal that he must accept.' Omar was a man with a refined demeanor, utterances of a round orator, cool looking and soft tempered, a detailed son of Onyango—and not in a hurry. He had inherited the wit of, maybe, his great-grandfather Sigoma or someone of that generation—unusual child, big for his age. He had his legs flapping around loosely to the great awe of everyone. He'd to follow in the footsteps of his elder brother, Barack, who passed through Maseno and then to the United States of America on a scholarship.

Sara said to him, 'Go there and behave yourself.'

She consented.

'Do not behave like a child still cuddling "like a child in diapers"', she joked. She knew that the mess that African scholars find themselves in, in the West was unbelievable. The USA, a country she described as 'commonplace', a country she would know well. From the stories of Barack's life, the squabbling from

Onyango depicted to her that USA is a country that had hope and confusion in equal measure, especially for the black race. For the Kenyan students, a country where crime always seemed most real. Kenyan students struggled with agency at the brink of finding voice, the voice to silence those who doubt. And that voice that should translate to Kenya to fight grand corruption at the local authorities and voice to sound truth at the hostile Police Department in United States of America.

And it was necessary to talk and reason especially for someone who'd grown up in a hostile countryside and is waging a strong move to a different capital, a more sophisticated capital. And it was not a wish that he never missed on any spot. I joined Nairobi Primary School at the start of January 1965, almost at the time my father was starting his doctorate on 'An econometric model of the staple theory of development.'

I was very young, but this man, Barack, my father, explained these concepts of African Socialism. He had talked of jargon on socialism. I did not even know what he meant, but conceptualizing these facts to our way of life was something I came to accept. They were very much applicable. Maybe these concepts held him responsible for all his household needs. Back in Kogelo, life was growing a bit complicated; the number of dependents was on the increase, but the country's economy was all right and pay package was good. He managed to pay for me the rather expensive school fees, Zeituni's education, and Rita Auma's baby classes. And there was Ruth still trying to settle in Africa, and Kezia, my mother, running errands to keep her afloat. In the midst of these entire debacles, there was a man, a responsible economist providing every penny to every need.

Omar was settling well in Boston and had joined the university, studying just like any other student out there; doing some jobs menial, to be precise, to suffice his staying (there). 'Omar enjoined living in America with practical unanimity,' my father said. Malik recalls the initial stages of Omar's life when he telephoned from America. Sometimes, and perhaps several times, my father often phoned him, and they conversed for hours.

'Hi, my brother!'

'I'm fine, Barack. How is home?'

'Everything fine. We're building the nation.'

'That's OK. It's a responsibility.'

'And remember you are an American now, but you shall remain in our heart anyway...'

And my father would break into a torturous laughter.

Omar on the other side broke into a roaring laughter, and the two talked for long.

These two gentlemen were building a solid background for us. And, therefore, whenever my father telephoned, either at home or while in his offices, I knew good rapport was lurking in every quiet corner of their heart.

On 16 March 1965, TJ telephoned my father. And they met at Hilton Restaurant. It was and, still is, one of the exclusive hotels in the town, known for serving various delicacies—both exotic and native cuisines—from French fries and steak, taken with dry gin, to Kenyan Coffee. At the time a white man—a highly energized individual, full of snappy stories, headed Hilton. This made him occasionally assume the role of a waiter as a public relations exercise. He had a prominent fox-face look, a magnetic talker. He demonstrated 'high-class confidence man'. These attributes attracted both prominent and less prominent people to Hilton. His PR skills were just amazing. Mboya had initiated the Industrial Relations Charter—about three years ago—in November 1962 when he was the Labour Minister. And along these lines came the Industrial Court. When they sat to discuss the progress of the court and how they could introduce its tenets into the Sessional Paper No. 10, nobody can tell the one-to-one verbatim of their conversations. However, the initiatives that followed were glaringly beneficial. They discussed the idea of a *social security fund*—and Cocker was appointed the Appellate Judge of Industrial Court with Ocholla Makanyiengo—a community mobilizer and a trade unionist, fighting hard the culture of impunity against the workers. Ocholla George Philip alias Makanyiengo was an Airlift beneficiary. He attended the University of Chicago (Chicago 37, Illinois). And through him, Cocker would push and be convinced to protect the workers' grievances against the exploitative employers—mainly of Asian origin. He managed to hand down great benefits to the shortchanged and oppressed workers. One such ugly incidence occurred in 1964 when COTU, FKE, and Cocker were embroiled in a tough battle, the CEO of Federation of Kenya Employers refuted claims by Robert Ouko (the Labour Minister)—that workers must be lenient to the government. A lawn tennis player and a pro in hockey, Cocker was a popular judge among the dock workers. He couldn't make fatal mistakes in his judgment—the country had its ears in this one.

Mboya, including other bosses, under whom Barack served in different capacities—agreed to his great ideas. That's why they'd called him time and again to consult him or offer him a job.

Recommendation letter

SHELL/BP LIMITED
EAST AFRICA HEAD QUATERS

TELEX . . .   Agip House.
TEL . . .   PO Box 30340.
                                                         NAIROBI.
                                                               KENYA

                                                      1 April 1965.

                     To Whom It May Concern

This is to certify that Mr Barak Hussein Obama was an employee of Shell/BP Corporation, East Africa Headquarters, Nairobi during the period 14 December 1964 to 30 March 1965.

We are pleased to state that Mr Barak's conduct and performance have been satisfactory at all times and that he was always appreciated as a colleague.

He left the Company of his own accord.

Director of Manpower Development

Telephone: Nairobi
When replying please quote

Ministry of Planning and
Economic Development
Lt Tumbo Avenue

Ref. No ... PO Box 30464
And date Nairobi

18th April 1965.

Mr Barak H. Obama.
Shell/BP LTD
Agip House.
PO Box 30340.
Nairobi.
Kenya

Dear Sir,

With reference to your application for a post with the Ministry of Planning and Economic Development I have to offer you an appointment as a Senior Economist on probation subject to your passing a medical examination, which will be arranged by the Ministry.

The period of probation will be one year and your conduct will be reported on periodically. At the end of the year they will be considered by the Board of Directors and if they are up to the standard required by the Ministry of Planning and Economic Development and your health remains good you will be put on the pensionable staff with effect from the beginning of your probation. Your salary will start at £1180 on a scale rising from £1140 to £1300. All increases will be subject to satisfactory work and conduct. In addition to salary you will receive a Nairobi allowance equal to 15 per cent of your basic salary but this will not be included for pension purposes. Leave and other conditions will be subject to the general conditions of service in the Ministry, a copy of which will be handed to you should you accept this appointment. I must emphasize that this offer is not final until you have passed the medical examination. If you accept this offer we would like you to take up our duties as soon as possible. Will you please let me know whether you wish to take up this post on these terms?

Yours faithfully,

Principal, Personnel Recruitment Committee
Ministry of Planning and Economic Development

Lt. Tumbo Avenue
PO Box 30464
Nairobi
Date: 20 April 1965

Barak H. Obama,
Ministry of Planning and
Economic Development
Nairobi
Dear Sir,

Confirmation of Appointment

I am pleased to inform you that the Permanent secretary has authorized translation to permanent and pensionable establishment retroactive to the date of your first appointment to the service of the Ministry of Planning and Economic Development.

The Ministry's Pension Scheme is still in process of being finalized and as soon as this done you will automatically be entitled to benefit from it again, retroactively to the date of your first appointment.

Yours faithfully
Principal, Personnel Recruitment Committee
For: Permanent Secretary

Barack had been a priority to TJ. And maybe he'd felt embarrassed when his friend worked out of the country, and his surrounding seemed so foreboding.

This year marked the coming of Ruth Baker. Malik says, 'My stepmother, Ruth, also came over. By then, my father had gone to the village to see my grandfather. He found it hard to explain to the people who she was. But the people knew that their son "had gone west in marriage."'

The former Jewish teacher came to Kenya to seek for Barack.

Hawa had said that Thomas Mboya, 'son of Ndiege', helped my brother Barack a lot of times.

Not only once but a number of times.

Maybe they'd talked. And she was therefore coming over,' Hawa said.

Now they'd share more than what divided them: the racial card, and the long distance that separated the two nationals wasn't important. And we had to accept that.

'Upon his return to Kenya, Barack landed a job at the ministry after trying Shell/BP and KTDA.

Malik says as follows:

> 'On 3 July 1965, my father published a paper entitled, 'Problems Facing Our Socialism', in the *East Africa Journal*, harshly criticizing the blueprint for national planning, 'African Socialism and Its Applicability to Planning in Kenya', which had been produced by Tom Mboya's Ministry of Planning and Economic Development. The article was signed by 'Barack H. Obama'. My father was one of the few critiques chosen in the East African Journal Office to publish in line of their views on economic trends in Africa dubbed Kenya's Sessional Paper No. 10 on African Socialism. Among those shortlisted included Hilary Ojiambo, Gabriel H. M. Nyambu, and Gus Edgren'. Also Dharam Ghai, another critique contributed his thoughts on 'African Socialism for Kenyans' in the *East African Journal*, (June 1965).

During this time, Barack was working on his doctorate dissertation on 'An econometric model of the staple theory of development.'

Gabriel H. M. Nyambu, according to the documents in my father's archive, describes him as a friend with great knack of feature writing. The record shows that he worked at the Kenya Ministry of Information, Broadcasting, and Tourism. The man did a finesse work by introducing a different flavor to the readership of his writings. The man had gone an extra mile to introduce pertinent points that few could explore.

The record, folded carelessly in a dusty brown envelope, describes that Dr Ojiambo worked as a consulting physician to Princess Elizabeth and Kenyatta National Hospitals in Nairobi and also as an honorary consulting physician at the Aga Khan Hospital. The family friend worked on the question 'Does witchcraft have a place in modern medicine, especially in Africa?'

Gus Edgren worked on the 'Solutions to the problems of unemployment and underemployment'. He'd met Barack in Makerere, although he worked in the research section of the Labour College, Kampala. He had been a consultant for various Labour Ministries in Central and Eastern Africa. He'd also worked closely with TJ at the labor conference forum.

Barack's Doctorate Dissertation

The handwritten piece of paper was just a culmination of facts and figures that translated into a real implementation policy. That hit the headlines in ministries and the media, in the corridors of financial institutions, and in the minds of various think-tank groups.

The facts contained in dusty pieces of papers—partly eaten at the edges by mites and moths—talk about 'Problems facing our socialism'. The browning papers with the write-up, quickly fading off, contained the brain of an African scholar and speak the mind of a typical African most-sought economist. A search on top of a cedar-made cupboard revealed an old briefcase, also containing my father's personal documents, the passport, and the curriculum vitae, among other documents—the divorce letters, and Ann Durham's letters. And the place has become a hiding corner for many three-grams-plus size cockroaches—their eggs roaring to hatch. They speedily race into hiding like millions of ducks flying away from a pond. Some items have been saved but many lost to deadly termites. Others were stolen during robbery in Rosslyn.

Within the economic think-tank circles, he was a far popular figure who worked with a tacit like-minded people, such as Hillary Ojiambo, Gabriel Njambu, and Gus Edgren, among others. They were the branded class of policymakers. No one would step forward to dispute that fact or drift it to some criticism. Some of these traits were hereditary and a true inheritance power from the generation of Owiny to that of Opiyo, from Kisodhi to the generation of Midiwu, to that of Obama. This was a long-standing inheritance. In the backdrop of these dreams, hope, and policymaking, Barack strived to form a circle of technocrats who'd shape the country. In the discussion of the dissertation, the handwritten pieces circumvent the reasons why African socialism suffers. It reads in part:

> Since many of the African Countries achieved their independence, there has been much talk about African socialism inter alias communism.

Barack argued that 'there has been no individual or country that has at any time defined socialism'. He talks on the advantages of socialism as a gadget of trade, of international relationship—a way of bringing every person, group, company, country, or trading bloc an inch closer so that every aspect of togetherness in trade, in tradition, and in socializing is realized, and mutual, based on respect, nonracial, and prospering for both partners. Malik says, 'My father contributed his thoughts on a paper that realizes that, as is true of any country, we must encourage international trade, foreign investment, etc.'

He talked more objectively on policies. It not only specifies the objectives by which this country should be guided but states the policies through which it hopes to fulfill these objectives.

Barack's understanding of politics, in his discussion, also prompted aggressive search of the true self of these power brokers. He wrote, 'If it is accepted that it is the leaders of a country who usually formulate and define ideologies, then the only source for this definition would be to get it from them either through their speeches, press reports or papers, or through their actions.'

He talked of the absolute powers that the politicians misuse and the speeches well derived, but lacked the lustre during implementation. He said, in part, 'So far the statements made by such leaders as President Nkrumah, Nyerere, Toure, etc., have not had much in common. Likewise, the actions of these leaders while diverting a little from the capitalistic system have not by any means been directed toward any particularly defined ideology, be it scientific socialism *inter alia* communism. That Africa was open for business. That Africa has overcome tenterhooks and was now a trade partner—and not just a tabloid or a rubber stamp. That Africa wouldn't take the monarchic question anywhere, instead, shall be flatly against the royalty; he knew Africa has revolutionized from the belief that it was "just another dismal wreck". In his dissertation, he offered two choices of defense. That people of the world, especially lagging behind in economic growth or development, "wanted a just settlement in the economic disparity so much as a quick settlement to end of corruption which had become a world conflict." In the economically stable country, even some sort of armistice peace can replace chaos for over three decades, and the new government could continue living in peace with a better or rather new plan. And without this fact, these circumstances continue and their people wouldn't build a good fleet, no matter how hard they try. 'And those big nations shouldn't mishandle the ideals of the small nations.'[31]

Many authors have written about socialism. Some say 'the only answer to communism is socialism, not reaction.' And the big peasant problem was the very peasant, who wasn't interested in hearing about socialism.

And the politicians, who were representatives of the peasants, traded accusations—whether they should adopt communism or choose socialism and whether Kenya would be a military area or a democratic country.

He believed that communism was an old story—an old idea that was absolutely blown away by increasing demand for a truly socialist state. Communism inherited an ancient tradition of violence and illegality. He said that this country was suited and much more ready to adopt socialism than were our grandfathers or recently our fathers. All his arguments were sensational.

Critiques in support of B. H. Obama:

Tom Mboya's speech in support of Sessional Paper No. 10

From the book, Mboya, *Challenges of Nationhood*, pp. 73-104:

Many critiques for communism were also asserted, and Mboya was compelled to highlight the tenets of African socialism.

He called them prisoners of foreign propaganda and described them as 'politicians who never tire of blackmail'.

He said, 'It was our concern to define a system and to identify policies that will meet our needs, solve our problems, and further our ambitions. Each country has its history, its culture, its inheritance of economic institutions and resources, and its own problems. To impose on a people a rigid system (Marxism) that takes no account of their needs, desires, aspirations, and customs is to court disaster and failure.'

The president stood by Mboya at that time and actually condemned those who supported communism. He said, 'There is no room for those who wait for things to be given for nothing. And there is no place for leaders who hoped to build a nation on slogans.' In this way, he brooded admiration and revulsion in the same measure. He thought they are 'those undermining our independence'. Also he accused the opposition; he revoked critics by saying, 'It is a sad mistake to think that you can get more food and hospitals or schools by simply crying communism.' As far as criticism is concerned, he had gone a full circle.

Barack believed that this paper was for the people who had laid down their lives for the struggle!

The paper received a wild rejection as well. As if they had tested it and denounced it entirely.

One politician was a bald, sharp chinned, Anyieni Zephania, a member of parliament who criticized the use of 'African Socialism'.

An MP and former freedom fighter, Kaggia, was furious about the planned sessional paper. In his trademark bow tie, long beards that touched base with the tie, this elderly gentleman, seventy-eight, of old-fashioned times was comical in his defense. He said, 'I do not mind calling our socialism African socialism, Kenyan socialism, Kikuyu socialism, or even Luo socialism, but I believe that whatever prefixes we use, it must be socialism and not capitalism.'

On religion, Barack advised Mboya that '. . . fundamental force of religion which has been denied in communist countries will be a definite feature of our society in which traditional religion provided a strict moral code. But political rights will not be contingent on religious beliefs.'

Tom Mboya would agree with his intention and argued that the socialism they are adopting '. . . commits the government against a revolutionary break with the past in its attempt to transform society. The general policy—rather—is to build upon and modify the inherited economic and social systems. Mboya agreed and concluded that there are people in the political arena who still live in ignorance in their ivory tower. All the critics described the communist as souvenirs from the bitter and dramatic past.'

Ghai worked with Barack in the implementation of the policy document after being passed by National Assembly with minimum amendment. They complained of politicians who behaved like misguided youth among the crowd, who needed immediate inclusion into the community. Malik says, 'During that time, the Kenyan national radio, newspapers, news agencies, and ambassadors worked to promote the importance of African socialism. And each unit believed that without comprehending that one comprehends nothing. My father believed that the African socialism would guarantee every citizen full and equal political rights.'

Other politicians even formed defense groups; others had coined the name Capricorn Contract to push for agenda of change in the political scene. And they were held by that paradox of collaboration.

When the paper was finally adopted, with the relevant amendments, he sat close to a window in his large mansion with a lush garden overlooking the Nairobi landscape. I felt the smile and the confidence that came from my very own father. In a light note, this is the day a petty thief kept rapping on the very window oblivious of anything when my father stuck his head out. He saw a man escape in a runaway with a few statuary things that he had picked from the neighborhood. Ten meters away, the man was caught and wrapped at a corner by the security guards completely deprived of intelligence. He appeared somewhat fatigued.

Obeid says as follows:

Barack convincingly noted what he thought a Kenyan should be: 'One need not be a Kenyan to note that nearly all commercial enterprises from small shops in River Road to big shops in Government Road and that industries in the Industrial Areas of Nairobi are mostly owned by Asians and Europeans. One need not be a Kenyan to note that most hotels and entertainment places are owned by Asians and Europeans. One need not to be a Kenyan that when one goes to a good restaurant he mostly finds Asians and Europeans nor has he to be a Kenyan to see that the majority of cars running in Kenya are run by Asians and Europeans . . .'

When my father met his long-time friend, TJ, it was time to move to the Ministry of Planning and Economic Development. TJ was transferred here from the Constitutional Ministry as a minister and following that meeting, I often saw him coming to visit my father, in an official ministers' Mercedes Benz with the Kenyan flag hoisted on its nose. He parked the Benz just on the left side of our house. They would joke and drink until late in the night. I came to learn that he shared a lot in common with my father, the brilliance, the eloquence, and the confidence, and the jovial son of Ndiege, a sisal cutter, was a true nationalist who reviled ethnicity and dirty politics. He confessed to serve his country. The greatest dancer of all time and a friendly comedian, he was a man with different personality. The same shadow that lingered on my father's face. I saw the same statement flash on his eyelashes, in his smile. Ruth served them food and drinks. TJ would leave at around midnight for his home, his Lavington home, chauffeured by a black chubby-looking gentleman.

In the Ministry of Planning and Economic Development, my father would have various assignments, both in the country and outside, in Europe, China, Ghana, and South Africa. And he followed in the footsteps of Onyango.

At the Ministry of Planning and Economic Development, TJ spearheaded the order of promotion of the professional staffs at the Ministry of Planning and Economic Development; they were properly paid—Economists, and Statisticians, which included Barack, who enjoyed huge benefits, attractive schemes, promotions, house allowance at the Staff quarters. It was not comparable to what he'd earned when he was only a clerical officer before independence. That was just a drop in the sea. A senior economist was six grades below a minister—in the civil service hierarchy. This made it absolutely rare or unnecessary to access the permanent secretary, but Barack found it easier to access the gentleman. He was consulted again and again by the two principals. Working under Mr Emilio Kibaki, the Permanent Secretary (PS), (Now His Excellency, the President of Republic of Kenya) and TJ, the minister. Barack participated in the enactment of various legislation of the ministry and affiliated government institutions. At twenty-eight, and TJ (the boss), at thirty-four, the 'Young Turks' were reliable to the nation; they were great levers that drove the economy to where it was supposed to be. The results were equally impressive. The Gross Domestic Product (GDP) grew by more than 7.2 per cent annually in real terms and 10.1 per cent in nominal terms. The country's economy was equally at par with that of South Korea and other economies; Singapore's was far below this mark. Currently, the story is different.

At the time, government revenues grew by 20 per cent p.a. in nominal terms. And in 1970, the ministry enhanced the highest primary school enrollment to nearly 100 per cent—a record mark since independence. That means the economy grew at the same record mark of 3.2 per cent annually.

At one point Barack said, 'What was bugging my boss was not the economic growth but the increasing slums. A situation that was right in his Kamukunji Constituency, which he represented in Parliament.'

Mboya, together with his advisers at the ministry (that of course included Barack), agitated for family planning in Kenyan urban dwellers, especially those in the informal settlement. The Catholic Church had fought down the idea. 'It was against the teaching of God,' they claimed. Then, the head of the largest religious movement in Kenya, Cardinal Maurice Otunga (would discuss the idea with ministry officials) and later took a rather approaching method to solve the stalemate. Here Barack, Njenga, and Kamau were some of those making the negotiation with the ministry and were too willing to start implementing the policies. Adoption of the policy came in handy. And that was a success story. It was a concern of the populace.

It seems senior economist saved his 'little world'. And the world was raven by ideas of senior economist. Barack was a Kenyan Luo, an African economist. He single-handedly wrote the Kenyan economic plan and statistical survey report. It showed how tenuous was his position, and it was like a journey through a pain barrier. But now he'll be ever remembered as the father of the President of United States of America.

In the start of 1965, Barack and others, through the directive by the Honourable Minister, TJ, came up with the social security fund policy that was implemented by the National Assembly with minor amendments, what is now called the National Social Security Fund (NSSF). It is a state corporation established by the NSSF Act (CAP 258) Laws of Kenya in 1965. This corporation, in their records available, states, 'Our key mandate is to register members, collect contributions from members, and prudently invest contributions, and to pay specified benefits according to contingencies stipulated in the Act.

In our quest to be a world-class center of excellence in the provision of social security, NSSF has embarked on a number of initiatives aimed at transforming and repositioning the fund to be a leader in the pension industry.

The Board of Trustees recently adopted a new organisation structure aiming at enhancing organisational performance and improving the quality of services provided to its members. It is against this background that NSSF is now seeking to recruit result oriented individuals with drive, vision, and creativity to fill various management positions in the fund.

These positions will support the senior management in providing strategic leadership and driving the change.'[32]

From Obeid's own words: 'Back in the estate away from the national scene, my brother had a share of his responsibilities' . . . Obeid says, 'Good neighborhood was something that contributed a lot in our lives. At Upper Woodley, we lived with top-notch prominent members of Kenya, politicians, and a number of powerful families. People and families we called our own. There was Chesoni family (the former chief justice), Honourable Achieng' Oneko (a freedom fighter and a minister), Onyango Midika (later member of parliament), Nyando, the Konchella's (a former member of parliament), Mulu Mutisya (a minister and Akamba politician), Jerry Osodo, Ambassador Maurice Omwony (a former Kenyan ambassador to Germany), Okot Bitek (a renowned author and poet), Washington Jalang'o Okumu (a diplomat who brokered a peace deal between the Mandela's ANC and the opposition party in 1994). Washington shared a lot with Barack, and they were to produce a strategic plan for the development of Western Kenya. There was S. M. Otieno (a lawyer by profession whose burial caused a furore and hit the headlines in the national television. A tussle erupted that pitted the Omiya Kager clan in Nyalgunga and the widow's Kikuyu clan), Ouko Njenga, Odeny Toney, Manyisi, Charles Mukora, Akatsa, Dr. Meshak Oluoch, and Boaz Ogolla (a former registrar at the University of Nairobi) whose brother Yaya Ogolla was a good friend of mine. At the far end was Mr Schwatts, a Boor Africana (originally from South Africa). His son, Peter Schwatts, lent me his motorbike most of the time. Roy and I learned riding using this motorbike. He also had a grand piano where the estate boys flooded the house to learn a trick or two. Mark, particularly, frequented his house; he'd loved playing the organ. After a short while, he bragged to be a talented pianist. Mark would secretly tell his father that he needed a piano of his own. Indeed, he considered the request and insisted that he'll purchase him the organ. Having only good neighbors wasn't enough. Do you know that later when Honourable Minister for Tourism, Information, and Broadcasting, Achieng' Oneko, was arrested after he had resigned and joined the opposition and, since the arrest was politically instigated, no one came close to his family? Everybody distanced themselves. Barack went there and enrolled the former minister's children in Kilimani Primary, where his own children, Roy and Auma, schooled! He said thus:

'Our children can't be on their way to school every morning while the minister's stay at home, peeping through the window. Tomorrow (the following day) I'll take them to school. We can't allow the politics of the day affect the lives of innocent souls.'

People wondered what he was up to. He didn't care what the government authorities said thereafter. Of course, they said so many negative things:

> 'Barack is insulting the government.'
> 'Barack is fighting the same government that puts food on his table.'

'Barack seems to know a lot pertaining to oppositions' under dealings. And he seems to be part of that opposition.'

All that went on record. Although, he remained adamant and avoided being drawn into that controversy.

1968

This is the year Samson was born. If you like, you can call him Abo. The amiable-looking youngster was amazingly friendly. And I knew that it's a great pleasure to have somebody to call a brother, although he did not grow up with us in Woodley. From the looks—I knew he would one day boast of a self-made man. When I visited my grandmother in Gendia, Kendu Bay, I would carry him up my shoulders, and he would giggle gleefully. 'You might drop him down,' she said. It was fun. The baby attracted the love of everyone, and they flocked around him. I think he'd smile repeatedly to everyone around.

My aunt, Jane, was the contact person—these were some of my happier moments. And the birth of Sammy made us very happy.

On a sunny Saturday, 5 July 1969, the life of Kenya's powerful minister, plausible politician, and long-time career trade unionist was claimed by assassin bullet outside Chhani Pharmacy, Government Road, and now Moi Avenue, in broad daylight. That day Barack had met his boss along the busy street, between Standard Bank and National Bank—adjacent Grindlays Bank, and they'd talked for a while; they discussed his travel from the United States and made a commitment to meet in the evening for some good dinner in one of the city restaurants. The minister was rolling on his official Mercedes Benz accompanied by his personal assistant and private secretary, Nundu Otieno.

'Let's meet in the evening and discuss it,' the minister assured him.

Reports show that 'there's a lot that was going on within the government, and political mistrust and squabbling was a real threat to its stability. There was no peace'. Maybe Mboya was among the luminaries someone wanted eliminated toward the achievement of that elusive peace. Little did they know that in politics there's no peace . . . politics and peace are two unlike poles that can't come together. Maybe whoever planned it wasn't a wise one after all. When they'd eliminated Mboya, turmoil started rocking the government afresh: the squabbling, the political mudslinging, and the assassination—the endless massacre and corruption. The politicians lived in fear, especially those opposed to the government. A KPU youth leader saw Mboya car passing Grindley's Bank heading the northern lane.

The minister was in a jovial mood, drove away, greeting the public, as usual, shaking their hands from the car with great humor, and a broad infectious smile.

The minister had gone to buy painkillers, and the assassin had been monitoring his movements closely. It was fascinating how he knew the whereabouts of the minister. The bald, short, chubby man with a long nose was later known to be Nahashon Isack Njenga Njoroge alias 'Njosh'. A man, who knew Mboya pretty well and had a shrewd, ugly, humorous face, a typical con man.

The minister bought the drugs from the shop of an Asian businessman, Mr Mohini Schmi, and they'd conversed at length—for about ten minutes. He was heard saying, 'I'm counting on you. I know the drugs will relieve the pain. Isn't that so?' They joked and left the door closed behind him. Those present were Roshan Manjii, Havinder Singh—both are cousins to Mr Mohini and Johnstone Mwangi—an employee. The assassin was lurking alongside the door as if waiting for someone, in a black suit, a briefcase on his hand. He held a little matchstick on his left ear. And known to be a chain smoker, that day he was a man on an assignment, he didn't smoke a cigar! 'Njenga had "careless hard-steamed self-assurance", the wife said, 'and a huge weakness with listening—never interested in listening to anybody because he was talking all the time himself like some sort of right-wing idealist. Many paradoxes accompanied his action. What was the motive?'

A few minutes after the two departed, Barack had no idea that the minister was pleading for his life at the entrance of the chemist as he retreated for cover shouting, 'Don't shoot. Why do you want to kill me?' The fairly big man, middle-aged, thirty-nine—to be precise—fell unconscious, blood spurting out of the frothy mouth—'a speeding motorbike as if in a planned mission hurriedly passed by as a van followed in hot pursuit—the assassin ran toward Queensway Corner,' Manjii witnessed.

As the minister writhed in pain—with the help of well wishers and a handful of Police Officers, headed by Chief Inspector Mr Rowe, who later witnessed as the officer in the scene of crime, and Assistant Inspector E. M. Gathondo in St John's Ambulance, that arrived quite late—he was rushed to Nairobi Hospital (formerly European Hospital) Emergency Wing. Another delay in admission was evident.

The incident was unexpected—it caused jitters, and Barack knew that the man died with loads of information.

The television stations around the world covered the death extensively. Notably, British Broadcasting Corporation (BBC) was in the forefront to announce: *One of Africa's youngest and most brilliant politicians, Mr Tom Mboya of Kenya, has been assassinated.* And the East African Standard Newspaper reported thus: *Gunman Assassinate TJ. A car races off as three shots are heard.*

Barack told Malik as follows:

Flurry of activities took place—The Deputy Speaker E. R. S. De Souza described the act as 'Most Shocking'. While Achieng' Oneko, former Minister of Information, Broadcasting, and Tourism and a Kenya People's Union Official described the assassination 'as killing people's liberty'. He broke down and wept in the streets and was helped to the car by friends. The Provincial Commissioner for Nyanza, Charles Murgor, dismissed Kisumu Agricultural Show—Kisumu was the political home turf of TJ—there was violence and unrest. And the police commissioner at the time, Bernard Hinga, ordered for calm—promising that the Police Department was actually in hot pursuit for those involved. And the Attorney General, Charles Njonjo, held a high security team meeting at the Criminal Investigation Department to dig out the matter.

I and loads of friends were among the first to arrive; the sombre mood engulfed the hospital, and the minute he was pronounced dead, a near stampede resulted and pandemonium almost erupted, people jostled for space to view the body of a fallen hero. And there was the family and friends, Pamela Mboya, Akuku Mboya—those who couldn't believe their eyes—ministers and prominent politicians as well paid their last respect. Jaramogi Oginga Odinga, Robert Ouko, Vice President Daniel Moi, J.M Kariuki, J.D Otiende, and Achieng' Oneko were among others. Jaramogi spoke to the roaring crowd, which curiously composed of Kenya Peoples' Union (KPU) supporters, for calm. He said that 'it was only four years ago that another serious politician was murdered in cold blood.' The bitter 'father of official politics in Kenya' spoke without mincing his words. Gama Pinto, a close associate, had been slain to death in 1965.

The world's attention turned to Kenya. Radio stations in Europe and the USA announced the sad news—the minister had just returned from foreign mission.

The Front pages of Sunday, 6 July 1969, of *New York Times* read thus: A *Fallen Kenyan Hero*, all that was shared by the *Washington Post* and *The Times of London* on that particular date . . .

It was a bitter taste, especially for Luo's electorate who felt cheated in the division of the national cake—the angry crowd, mainly the jobless, the poor, and those who just felt that it was wrong to kill Mboya pelted stones on motorists and to some politicians who they felt were the architect of the grisly murder. This action showed how the ruling tribe was terrible politicians and could not be relied upon, whereas the opposite was true of the Luos. And that's why things went out of hands. The whole country was on fire. The president was reported to be in a hideout. Maybe all fingers pointed at him . . . who knows! The truth will definitely come out. He'll never hide forever—thus, as the head of state emerged from wherever he was, the same way, one day, the truth will come to light.'

On Monday, 7 July 1969, preparations were on the offing. Malik says, 'My father was indeed part of the funeral arrangement both in the Nyanza Funeral Committee and linked them with the Ministry of Finance where Mboya served. This committee consisted of prominent politicians and ministers: Achieng' Oneko, Samuel Onyango Ayodo, Mathews Ogutu, Eliud Mwamunga, Doctor Odero Jowi, and Arthur Ochwada, among others; the Nyanza Provincial Commissioner Charles Murgor and Masinde Muliro. Surprisingly, Barack was selected to assist Samuel Onyango Ayodo to draft the plans. This was the first time he worked with Honourable Samuel Ayodo. They came up with the funeral arrangement programme and most prominently prepared the *eulogy* that was read by Honourable Samuel Ayodo during the burial.

The death of an eloquent, stern politician and the author of *Freedom and After* caused confusion and explosive chaos in the whole country. The following day on a fine Tuesday morning, the President held a meeting at Gatundu (the President's rural home)—to discuss TJ's death. 'Imagine four days after,' he said bitterly. The sorrowful ministers couldn't believe it. One of their own was slained to death. They resolved that TJ was to be given an official send off—A state burial to be precise.

Barack recalled, 'On Wednesday, 9 July 1969, we were at Hilton Hotel to fine-tune all the technicalities that would have inhibited the programme; there was Honourable Ayodo, Honourable Achieng' Oneko, Honourable JD Otiende—and at exactly ten o'clock, after a lengthy deliberations, the programme shifted to Holy Family Basilica Church for a Requiem Mass. I was just another small man with no proper portfolio in the society, but I'd attracted a big attention. For the first time, the President came out publicly. This service finally enclosed all the rival leaders under one roof. It was a tense time. The President himself, Vice President Daniel Arap Moi, and the entire cabinet and prominent personalities attended it. Then trouble started here. The Cathedral Square was littered with pieces of rocks and glasses; the black bullet proof Benz was pelted with stones by the irate crowd—the people out there wailed. The president never greeted KPU party leader, Jaramogi Oginga Odinga. He arrived after everyone was seated and never did the greeting, as is the custom in a state function. The cold reception trickled to every side of the political divide and overcame the prevailing peace in the presence of God. And from this day the tribalistic notion gripped the nation. A foreign banker drove onto a tree and killed himself when a stone boulder brought down his windscreen.

During the Requiem Mass—Archbishop of Nairobi, J.J McCarthy, led the sermon and he said, 'The Lord gave to Kenya TJ, and God took him away. Let his soul rest in eternal peace.' A few people clapped, but the rest kept quiet. The clergy talked a lot about TJ—that he was frequent at the church and couldn't miss a service when in Nairobi, that he was a family man who loved Pamela and the children, and that God had taken away a man Kenya would not wish to lose. The crowd outside smoked, 'God has not taken him a way. Someone has. We want to know them. But we can see some.' They chanted loud and clear.

The body left the Lavington Home for Rusinga Island. And during this time, many politicians took it upon themselves to accompany the body to the rural home while some were still politically engaged and would join them later. Those who accompanied the body included Odongo Omamo, Samuel Ayodo, Minister for Tourism, Oselu Nyalik, Assistant Minister for Labour, and Charles Murgor, the area PC.

1969, TJ's Convoy to Rusinga

Charles Murgor said, 'When TJ's body was being transported to Rusinga Island, hostility, bitterness, and fury overwhelmed mourners.' It was a major setback for a laid back administrator.

The Kisumu mourners, around Ahero, and the entire Kano region, blocked the road, held placards above their heads, and used tree branches and figs as umbrella. They were armed and had spears, axes, and swords (This is the way they mourn). They threw huge stones boulders, logs, and rolled rocks onto the road. They blocked the traffic as the General Service Unit Officers tried, effortlessly, to quell the nation's hostile crowd. The number of mourners increased at every corner, at every plain path, and every bush. People left villages to welcome the body of a fallen hero. And they crowded the hearse carrying the body. Most of the huts were still empty long after the convoy had traveled eighty miles away. People still wandered at the roadside. Barack later told Malik that it was trouble controlling the surging crowd. Our security system had failed even before it started working because we expected large crowd. But the crowd that turned out was much larger. Nairobi had been just the same. Mboya died at the time when his people needed him most. My father predicted more of such incidents. He did not know that he would be the next victim.

Hostile crowd greeted the body. The mourning continued and viewing was impossible due to drama in the muddle of the roaring crowd.

'We lost a friend, we lost a leader, we lost a father, and we lost a politician . . . ,' the crowd mourned in unison. The VOK announced the death repeatedly. No media broadcast house would relay a slanted news or diversion from the truth. My father's investment in this man's life was one particular stern moral message, how one can stand with a friend to the point of death. The National television showed newsreel footage of TJ assassination, a cruel death from the hands of assassin, Njenga. The man later said, 'I m executing orders from the "Big man".' A statement that caused a furore showed how the country was still grappling with political fossils, old-fashioned political gimmick—a country that still remained at the same place as the rest of the world moved on. Malik says his father narrated as follows:

'The casket carrying the body of the Minister was loaded onto a ferry to Rusinga Island at Mbita Point. Mourning took toll of the people, tears rolled, and a dozen of people collapsed. The body was transported across the Lake Victoria from Mbita Point through Sindo Township to the isolated Island where the leader hailed from, the Island surrounded by others as Mfangano Island, Sese Island, and Mageta Island. And when we arrived at the compound (of Leonardus Ndiege), the crowd was uncontrollable. We had hard time once again controlling the rowdy masses. Whatever way you look at it, TJ was mourned by all generation. The old and the young, the rich and the poor, black and white—hope was at peace with him.'

On Friday 11 July 1969, after an overnight stay, my mother, Kezia, joined the mourners at Rusinga; it was a burial ceremony. And Bishop Otunga led the ceremony. He was full of courage—although he had refused to preside over the burial because he was 'deeply depressed by the sudden demise of TJ'.

He decried the bad image that the politicians were creating—the scenery very ugly and notorious. He eulogized TJ as a young man full of vigor . . . a man full of devotion . . . his death is a challenge and a lesson as well as an embarrassment to the people of Kenya. And during the burial day, my father was a busy man putting everything in order, and that day Samuel Ayodo read a moving eulogy the much aviated—a tribute that sent the hero to the grave. Samuel looked gracious as he delivered the eulogy. He said that TJ was a liberal, a man who never lived like a Luo politician, or a Kenyan favorite majority leader, but the son of the world; one of the leading luminaries from the planet. That his life shall remain a living testimony in the minds of the people with positive sentiment full of high-minded ideas; those seeking less political confusion and debate but full of sound mindedness; those not bent on political knuckle. Pamela's eulogy was a moving one. She spoke of her loss. Then mourners, friends, families, relatives, and supporters lay wreath at the grave; later, steady stream of handshakes, hugs, and photographs took over. My parents went to Kogelo that evening. I felt a moving row melting. Their reunion (of my parents) was one awesome aspect. I felt that there are aspects that create peace, reunion, and refresh marriage in a way we cannot understand, and it flows freely like a milk glut. And I think that day they learnt how to position themselves on the issue of marriage. I had to grapple with fact that their separation was not a smart issue. I longed for the day they'll once again live under one roof. Then my mother was not living with us in Woodley Estate. I felt the bad happenings could always be reversed.

Every speaker, one after the other, talked of him as a great leader that Kenya would not want to forget fast.

Odero Jowi, assistant minister said, 'TJ was a sincere and friendly leader of this country.' Masinde Muliro was in attendance and told the mourners, 'It is time for Kenyans to be calm—the country is not safe at all.' During the TJ's eulogy, the master of ceremony, Samuel Ayodo, was very remorseful. 'We've lost a brilliant leader. A charismatic socialist and a proper leader in this era and time—it will take Kenya years to fill that gap. No one in the near future will come out strongly to fight for a common man as TJ did.'

The presidential speech was given out to TJ's brother on behalf of Pamela. No one wanted to hear it. The late Minister for Planning and Economic Development was laid to rest in a grave that was later developed into a mausoleum. Today, next to TJ's body lies another grave of a man with whom he had tirelessly worked to bring hope to the souls of the poor. William X. Scheinman wrote in his will that he'd want his body buried next to TJ's—in Rusinga Island. Today the two gentlemen's bodies are interred just a foot apart.

This shows how the vision of two people can knit them so firmly that even death can't separate them.

After TJ's burial

Miserable stories followed the burial ceremony—*tero buru* dance ensued. Bulls were forced into TJ's house, a ritual to dispel bad omen. And there was dirty chaos as well. A drunken brawl arose. Fights broke out as women and children ran for cover. Of course, it was not something new; traditional mourners have been fighting ever since after a burial ceremony. This was just usual. They were accustomed to unleash terror, maybe to chase the bad spirit of dead ancestral land in that blinding midafternoon sun.

On 25 July 1969, in Nairobi State House, the President of Kenya, Jomo Kenyatta, announced a replacement for TJ—tension had gripped the Ministry of Planning and Economic Development. Who could it be? That was in everybody's lips. Odero Jowi was the new minister. He was indeed TJ's friend—a fellow Luo. But he couldn't fit the shoes Mboya had left behind. He admitted. The announcement was to take place with immediate effect!

This was the new boss to contend with and an inquiry set up; the life was absolutely at its low moments.

My father said that on 12 August 1969, Mboya's Murder Trial began. He said that 'these were the trying times of his life.'

The TJ Murder Trial

During that time, Mr Charles Njonjo was the Attorney General—a man who had worked extensively with TJ when the latter was the Minister for Justice and Constitutional Affairs. 'These were darkest moment of my life, Son.' Malik was only ten years old and a pupil at Kilimani Primary. Auma had joined him.

When the case was opened officially at the Nairobi High Court, the chief prosecutor appointed by the president to investigate the matter was John Hobbs, and he was assisted by John Bell, who was then assistant commissioner of police. The chief magistrate sitting at the pretrial court was S. K. Sachdeva—a combative man who was stern with his court directives. He looked serious and much apprehensive. On the first day, the first witness was brought to stand—Chief Inspector Mr Rowe—who was the officer of the Scene of Crime. He said that he got there moments after the bloody shooting and took the necessary precautionary measures, but 'the minister was still alive. So we rushed him to the Nairobi Hospital Emergency Unit for immediate treatment. I knew we could save his life.' The second witness was Assistant Chief Inspector EM Gathondo; the chubby-looking man with a large earlobe was always exact in his utterances. He looked reserved but intelligent. He later said after the inquiry that 'the government seemed supportive to unravel the matter but deep inside, I didn't believe it.'

This was one of the explosive murder inquiries in the history of Kenya. Otieno Nundu the private secretary to the slain politician and the closest contact person present during the murder said, 'We were in the car when suddenly the minister started complaining of pain. It was unusual for him to complain of such things. He had been very strong of late. And the honourable minister walked in Chhani Pharmacy to buy some painkillers. He repeatedly complained of strained brain following his travel from United States. But he was very stable. The doctor who took charge of his treatment at the scene of crime, Mohammed Chandri, said, 'I tried to resuscitate Mboya—but the bullet had been lodged in his throat. He was a dying man. He died later while undergoing treatment.'

In other testimonies, Mr and Mrs Mohini Schami gave testimonies. 'We believe that Mboya was shot by people he knew and that his death is not a normal thuggery but a pure assassination. Mboya and his family have been our friends and customers for along time now. So this is not the first time he was visiting our business.' Other witnesses included Lavender Singh—the cousin of Mohini, Roshan Manjii, and Easton (Johnstone) Mwangi—an employee at the pharmacy. At the Nairobi Hospital, Doctor Rogoff, who treated Mboya, removed a bullet lodged on his throat and pronounced him dead. 'There was a bullet in his throat. I removed it, but he'd already died.'

During the entire trial period, the assassin's lawyer Samuel Wauhiu was at pain to defend the suspect. And the trial judge remarked repeatedly that 'repetitions made his head swim'.

It came at a time when Barack would be cross-examined by Deputy Director of Public Prosecution, Mr James Karugu. It was a terse time that required one to be extra careful with not only his life but also his words. Barack, Obege, and Okombo all testified almost at the same time as private key witnesses. Also, Omwambo, the KPU party youth leader who was present then testified.

During these trials, testimonies came from other witnesses; among them were Pamela Mboya, the wife of TJ, and Akuku Mboya, TJ's brother. Others were prominent ministers such as J. D. Otiende, while other politicians were questioned both at the High Court and in private.

In all the sittings, the major suspect Nahashon Njenga entered the courtroom with guards and handcuffs; he stood, looking with a composed face. He studied the witnesses for a moment across the courtroom; the slain minister's wife collapsed and dipped her face into her hands, and the suspect looked down. The two could not sustain a one-on-one face-off. Njenga leaned forward on his elbows and muttered something to the guard, then looked absent minded, and the guard pounded his head. Njenga became the talk of the town—a despicable man, and everyone hated him. He killed the inspirer of many, a boss and a political architect. So it was hard to feel sympathetic for Njenga. 'He needed some lethal injection.' 'This man, standing here, needs some cruel death,' one witness was reported as saying.

My father's best day that came amidst the tumultuous time was that day the newly appointed Minister for Planning and Economic Development, Odero Jowi, ordered the printing of the Sessional Paper No. 10. He discussed the document with senior officials and professionals who drafted the paper. There were Hilary Ojiambo, Gabriel H. M. Nyambu, and Gus Edgren. That Thursday of 14 August 1969, my father worked till midnight. And the following day they'd gone to the parliament, accompanying the minister who was going to present the paper to the House. In the House, the KPU MP Okello Odongo brought the House to a point of order and urged the House to adopt this paper, whose implementation was overdue. The MPs knew pretty well that this country was at the verge of collapse, especially its socialism . . .

15 August 1969

From Afghanistan, in the Pushtunistau set up in the free and lofty mountains of Tirah, from Chital to Baluchistan, and from Khyber and Bolan passes to the Kenyan National Assembly along and sandwiched between Uhuru Highway and Parliament Road, the Sessional Paper No. 10 was discussed by those who believed in communism and those who strongly believed that socialism was the way to go in the post—independent Kenya.

During the afternoon-long discussion that easily went to the night, Mr Honourable Okuto Bala, KPU Nyando, seconded the motion brought into the floor amidst shouts from the government side. They continued to shout, 'China! China!' In this era, the Chinese Government supported the communist way of governance and to which most of the government MPs belonged. The communist approach was also supported by Russia (USSR). And Moscow released millions of shillings (dollars) to fund the government which supported their foreign policy. Barack called them 'backslapper politicians hacked from the forest'. The debate was a hot pan of accusations and counter accusations milled around every utterance; every supporter announced at the end of the day.

The ardent KPU stalwarts argued that that was the moment like uncharted morass where socialism and communism overlapped. Therefore, it called for sobriety so that Kenyans were not hoodwinked with nonstarter policies. During the heated debate, the government's chief whip and Kanu (member of parliament) Martin Shikuku joked and threw a salvo that 'some members of parliament are not socialists, and I wonder where they belong because they do not seem to wear the communist cap.' This caused a thunderous laughter. When the day wore on, Honourable Masinde Muliro (Kanu, Kitale East) argued that as much as that debate is worth discussion, it is prudent to know that the country is likely to degenerate to anarchy, that many Kenyans have started feeling the heat of poverty a few years after independence. What shall happen in the next few decades? It caused a gloomy picture at the eyes of many, and even those sitting on the public gallery could agree.

He talked with much conviction never observed in him before and looked around, rather than at anyone. He believed that Kenya was to have an overhaul in land policy and good governance. In support of Honourable Muliro's sentiments, J. M. Seroney, KANU, Member of Parliament for indent said that 'There is no fair distribution of wealth.' That the country is showing grim pictures 'where some, or rather, just a handful of people are rich while majority are poor.' The motion was moved with jovial unanimity.

The speaker announced that the paper shall be adopted if the far-reaching amendments are rectified (implemented). He reiterated that all bills that have been brought to the floor since independence have not been supported the way this has sailed through. He believed that it shall definitely be passed the following week. He particularly talked extensively on child labor, be passed for the following, or those children on hard labour who can hardly reach the cash drawers used by shopkeepers to serve customers—that they do so by standing on a wooden chair, children who had been crippled by arthritis blinded by the red dust, and teeth browning for drinking dirty water. The paper was to be passed for them.

They called him handsome Barack in spite of his defective right leg. From these alterations and amendments, Barack had become a key personality in the ministry. Something that cost him: his brilliance quite absolutely inhibited the way of promotion. It's like it kicked off or blew the bridge to promotion. Although wherever a good office was to be filled, Barack would always be among those mentioned, but it never bore any fruit. Maybe he kept himself surrounded by critics of the government. Odero Jowi, the Honourable Minister, took him literally as Mboya's man, so within his ministry, Barack was treated with scorn. Contrary to the belief that he, Odero Jowi, was a Luo; as a minister, he was to be listening, keeping an eye out. He became their gravedigger, opposed Barack repeatedly, and obstructed his ambition to climb up the ladder. In this process, he lost his grip, and he started giving up. He threw tantrums of hard work into a culvert of forgetfulness, that is, he immersed himself in his work. In a mix of frustration, he thrust his hope into a convergence of job hunting and still lurking away from the blacklisting list that was yet on its way. He thought, 'Could exploitation go down? Humor feigning anger!'

When the minister contributed at last, and the speaker wound up his long speech, he ascended the rostrum and as the applause welled around him in approval and MPs tucked his speech into their briefcases, he made way to greet his colleagues upon which he received congratulations, Honourable Minister! As the seats were clearing quickly, they smiled, some threw their bodies onto others in a hug, and others had a breaking handshake, while most would wait for the start of a procession for a splendid reception at the parliament backyard. There had been clapping, thumping of feet, whooping, and cheering.

Malik remembers some of the ugly incidences after the death of Mboya. 'When my father went to visit my step-grandmother Sara in Kogelo—this was his routine because the family needed him so much that he couldn't avoid the fact of being the head and the responsibility lying squarely on him. Akumu was in Kisumu for a condolence visit to one of the relatives. He (the relative) had been buried, but she had not attended the funeral. So my father went to see her and also to attend a presidential function at Kisumu's new hospital launch. 'On 25 October 1969, the sunny Saturday afternoon turned in to a bloody day,' he told Malik. 'The president went to officially open the Nyanza General Hospital—*Russia*—built by the Russian government through an initiative put through by Jaramogi Oginga Odinga. The President arrived at 3 p.m. and the irate crowd started chanting *Dume! Dume!*—*Dume* is a bull, and that was a

KPU slogan. They shouted to the weather-beaten President *Wapi Mboya! Wapi Mboya!* (Where is Mboya? Where is Mboya?) This was the first time he was stepping in the hot bed of official opposition party at the home turf. He was not lucky.

When he was invited to speak by Odero Jowi, an assistant minister, he stood and charged on Jaramogi (who was silent but equally not happy). The two freedom fighters and powerful politicians sparred.

He said, 'You, Jaramogi Odinga, if you were not my friend, I would have crushed you like *unga (*flour meal*)*. You are rich while people of Nyanza are starving.' The statement sent the crowd silent. But when the tension died out, Jaramogi retorted, 'People are crying because they are hungry. You have not given them what you promised at independence.' And there was a massive applause even before he'd finished. The crowd continued chanting—in deafening tones. One could not tell what exactly they said at that point.

Chaos broke out; the shooting started as the crowd broke ranks with the security team. The Presidential security squad—the men in black suits let out the bullets into the crowd—'Shoot to kill!' their superior said. The bullets brought down men and teenagers, who perched on the trees to follow the ongoing proceedings. And women (both pregnant and those who just came to see the head of state for the first time) were shot at the limb as they tried to flee. Arrests were made, and Ramogi Oneko was the first prominent politician to be arrested. He was jailed without trial till 1975. The year another prominent politician J. M. Kariuki was assassinated—the fingers were pointed at the president.

At 9 p.m., VOK bulletin announced a curfew in Kisumu till November 1969 when calm would return. The curfew was later extended to Awasi Township—a few miles both from Kericho town and Kisumu.

Barack told Malik thus:

> 'I could not travel back to Nairobi—the KPU territory was hot and burning. The police were on the lookout. So many people were being arrested. I decided to better stay safe at my rural Kogelo because I knew I'd be arrested. Traveling was forbidden for top-notch civil servants, especially those serving in the government.
>
> The sad happenings awaited my father in Nairobi. When he got back, he was a bitter man. He could not trust anybody; he thought they were conspirators

and when the president of the Republic of Kenya cracked his whip, many Luo professionals lost their jobs *en mass*. He was not only sacked and his services blacklisted from any employment, but he was to face a pretrial of TJ's death as witness No. 12.

On 14 August 1969, my father was served with various letters; one of them was to be a witness in the murder case of TJ. The home was deathly quiet. I could see growth of small pieces of gray hair on his head. And his face was marred with wrinkles. I saw a different person.

He sat straighter on the couch and pulled a bottle of whiskey, something he had not done for a long time. He drank while his legs pulled up to his chest. And after two bottles, he left one on the table and one on the floor, he slept as if on sleep-inducing pills. He talked almost inaudibly, as if his mind was vaguely absent. I felt for him. Ruth wrapped him in a jumpsuit. My father felt a skull fracture upon himself or rather acclaimed by the delivery of the 'red letters'.

At the start of December 1969, J. D. Otiende resigned as health minister. He read the signs early enough before the sacking letter came his way. President Kenyatta was throwing the spanner to the works amidst resignations and sackings. TJ's death elicited heavy opposition against his government. An explosive death that literally weakened the government and the opposition gained drastically. As president gained his footing, the Vice President Moi warned people to abstain from 'loose talk' in the parliament. The vice president was put into task to explain why there was nothing being done on the murder case. And the legislators accused him of sterile explanation to the House concerning the case. And that the House was not eligible for parole or flipping of position. The able vice president masked it all in a broad smile.

When my father appeared before the Trial Committee sitting at the High court of Kenya, he was already a jobless man and a wanted man who the president had summoned at the Harambee office and warned to be careful with his tongue, especially that investigation was still going on.

That the need to be calm—maybe that would be what the vice president had called 'loose talk' during answering session in the House. Not a long time ago, many people faced the pretrial judge into the death of TJ. And a lot was in the offing.

On 4 December 1969, the minister for health wasn't under pressure to resign, but he did. The day he handed over his resignation letter at Harambee House, the Presidents' Official Office, a handful of supporters stood by the roadside, waving placards: 'We need a transparent government. This government is killing her own people.' They braved the baking sun, shouting. They wanted him to address them. We only waved back and shook a few hands before rolling up the car window. He then sped-off. He wasn't happy with the manner in which the murder trial was conducted. Many, who testified before the court and held high positions in the government, either resigned or were sacked indefinitely. One such person was Barack. At this time, the President turned into something cruel and uncontrollable—at one time, the London's *Daily Telegraph* described the President as a 'small-scale African Hitler'. When Nahashon Isack Njenga Njoroge asked, 'Why don't you go after the big man?' the high court was thrown into disarray.

In the meantime, he was writing a monograph entitled, *Otieno Jarieko, Kitabu mokuongo* (Otieno, the wise man. Book 1).

In his book, he talked about the rising need to educate one, the character, Otieno, who lived a difficult life. His desire to complete studies was driven by the level of poverty that ravaged his community.

This particular book wasn't published, but its second part, *Otieno Jarieko, Kitabu Mar Ariyo* (Otieno, the wise man, Book 2) was finally published by the Kenya Department of Education in January 1970.

1972

In 1972, Barack was a poor man. The trial was over, and one wouldn't dare to offer him a job. His bank accounts were frozen, and some of his properties were confiscated. He was within the prying eyes of the head of state who'd blacklisted him from any formal employment or any business engagement. His passport had been withdrawn. And he could not make any traveling arrangement. So he started living on the pockets of his friends. Life became unbearable, and he resorted to some good boozing. Unfortunately for him, one after another, his friends started abandoning him.

Ruth Obama signed for a divorce and left. She later was engaged to Simeon Ndesandjo, a businessman with trading interest in East Africa. He was living in Kenya but made occasional trips to Europe, Asia, USA, and Latin America. For between the two human beings are chasms of shame, family lies, and secrets—the secrets and chasms that led to bitter separation. After a couple of months of separation, she was living with Simeon Ndesandjo and slowly vanished from the life of my father; her family went out as Mr and Mrs Ndesandjo. Richard Ndesandjo and another boy, Joseph, were born. That was the experience I shared with Ruth Baker. She tried, but at the end, she left.

We stayed at the house in Woodley till 1974. Obeid agrees that some friends can't be trusted at all. 'Simeon Ndesandjo was Barack's close friend,' he says. 'He was a regular visitor at Woodley. He visited them as a family friend. It's surprising that he married a friend's wife.' Let the truth be told, maybe he contributed to the speedy divorce of the two! Or else what can one say? As an elder of this family, I believe Mark Okoth is still part of his family. Before all that 'fracas' came by, I remember I took Mark to school at John Kang'ethe Kindergarten just a few miles from Woodley Green estate. I did a lot of duties; at one point I represented Barack at Kilimani Primary School's parents' day. As I took photographs with the children, some of the parents mistook me for their father. See even by the time Mark was joining St Mary's Primary in Lavington, I was there to support his father. He loved education, and out of everything else, education came first.'

Obeid says, 'He lost his Woodley house. He had been out of a job for a long time on account of injuries from the accident of 1971 along with the differences he had with those in power. Sara and Zeituni ferried his belongings to Alego, and he moved to my tiny house in Ngara Estate. I had a two-bedroom flat that actually served me so well. But when my brother came around, we had to squeeze everything there in one room. And together with Rita and Roy, we all agreed to live in peace and wait for the next day.

The flat was built with bricks. It had a wooden floor measuring twenty-eight feet by thirty-one feet. The single door, facing northeast side of the court, was flanked by windows (glass). The room itself was large enough, however, much smaller for the huge family. Barack had prepared an outside man-made fireplace. (It was not part of the house architecture.)

It served him well despite his battered reputation, living in this rural-like neighborhood with crude, rather burgeoning community, remote and unfamiliar—a far cry from Woodley estate.

One aspect that made Barack just take it the way it is, is the fact that it could still serve his social parties where he treated his friends with whisky toddy that made it have a glittering exception. Life turned into a surest guarantee of downfall against the clandestine of glow and expiration—unhesitatingly by the virility of changing ways of living. In the morning, my father dropped us at the school, and then he had to get back to the new house. See, he had worn a snake-eyed face, that meant, he would allow no room for question. 'Dr Obama, you have not gone to work today.' 'Dr Obama, your car no longer goes for service. It looks wasted. What is the problem, sir?'

When he would get home, my father would not go straight to the house; he would spend almost three bonuses in the car, just enjoying the puff that he smoked from a cigarette, rolling up the car windows to keep the smoke inside. He enjoyed the intoxication, the pollution that kept the car smelling a bunch of tobacco. He blew the strong stream of smoke as if the next minute he would tear someone up.

On 14 January 1970, before he fell ill, Barack was on record, giving his thoughts on the best farming techniques that would bring agriculture into focus and which the African farmers ought to incorporate in order to improve their productivity, improved farming methods—he mentioned the idea of zero-grazing in the throes of collapse, another method other than the unflinching free range, and increasing food crops for the population. Then, he talked on how to make excellent breeding stock. He shared these sentiments in a brilliantly researched and hallowing book, *Yore mabeyo mag puro puothe* (Wise ways of farming). This book got the government into the custom of publishing agriculture-related thoughts like that, which Barack worked out. In the book, he rejected the overindulgence in the archaic ways of farming, reliance on a few scrawny goats for milk, traditional poultry and growing fruit and maize crops in subsistence scale.

1971 saw the birth of Bernard. A couple of months later, he moved from my house in Ngara to Racecourse Estate after a brief stay at the Abbey Hotel. He said, 'Let me try another sanctuary.' At least, the house was a little large—by that, I mean it wasn't as suffocating as compared to my house. The Ngara houses were so small that they looked more or less like maize stores.

Working at KTDA

Obeid says that when Barack first met Jerry Owuor, he worked at the KTDA office. Conversely, he was very close to the Rt. Honourable Samuel Ayodo, who took up the ministry of tourism at some point. Jerry later became one of our family trusted friends up to the time Barack died and beyond. He was from Alego Ng'iya.

The newly found boss and ardent friend Honourable Samuel Onyango Ayodo was born in Kamolo Village, Wan'gapala, Kabondo Division, and became the first member of parliament (MP) for South Nyanza. The influential political icon from Nyanza doubled as the first black MP and minister from this region. His onetime Personnel Assistant Reuben Dete says, 'Ayodo was resolute and strict. Civil servants would stand at ease wherever he telephoned them. Just as TJ, he chose the best professionals that formed a strong web of best managers and head of departments (HODs). 'I saw Barack several times,' he says. 'He was a hardworking chap from Alego,' says the aging old man. The minister used to call him 'Barak *Wuod* Alego' (Barak, son of Alego). In the month of June 1970, he took 'leave of absence' because he fell ill, and from then, he went away from the ministry for treatment. During the stint we worked together, I liked the changes that he made at the accounting section. He made sure that transparency was adhered to—we used to make a huge loss, but his coming was one aspect that changed the face of the ministry. Barack was a prolific worker. He never backed down in solving financial crises. I used to see him leave his office very late in the night, and he served as the financial advisor to the boss. He was admitted at the Nairobi Hospital, and I remember the minister and me passing by to see him and wish him well. He was always in a jovial mood. At the initial stages, he worked from the hospital bed, but the doctors later advised him to take some break, to detach from work pressure to allow healing. My short contact with him was an interesting piece; I found a dedicated character in him, an ardent socialist, and a determined financial expert, whose services were only sought by corrupt-free professionals.

Chapter 15

The grisly road Accident – 1971

Malik says that one of his fathers' friends, Mr Osoro, would advise him, 'Barack, you're drinking too much. Your drinking is too heavy for your lungs. They'll one day burst open and spew all that you've consumed.' Another friend was a medical practitioner, a well-renowned physician, a very decent Irishman, with plenty of gray oily hair and the hair pulled back, forming a poky-tail. A gray pencil-shaped moustache protruded out of his triangular-shaped beard. And he was resolute while saying, 'It's time to stay away from the bottle.' A spell of silence would engulf the air between them, as the tension built up. The doctor wasn't too easy on Barack. And Barack had to accept that. 'Stop drinking and move on.' 'Maybe he'd advised him the country wasn't prepared for a drinking economist,' Malik asserts.

Malik says that he would yell and mumble something almost inaudible. The drinking would continue in earnest. He'd thought of quitting, for drinking covered him in his own mess.

The year marked the bloody takeover of Uganda by the ruthless dictator, Idi Amin. And the western Kenya's neighbor became absolutely ungovernable; heightened tensions provoked a massive exodus of Ugandans to the Kenya-Ugandan borders. And government's priority, top on the list, was to quell the tensions that radiated to the Kenyans' upcoming small towns of Busia, Webuye, Kakamega, and Kisumu. In fact, the dictator would later claim that this was indeed part of Uganda, something that caused jitters to the Kenyatta government. Although, the trouble would later emerge in the same government, away from the external pressures, not to mention the incursions by the guerrilla war (*Shifta* squad) at Ogaden in the Ethiopia and Somalia border. There were elements planning a coup attempt, on April 1971, hatched to bring down President Kenyatta's Government; a freak drunkard man—a CID officer—had carelessly revealed the plot at a country club in Mombasa, and the news reached the president's ear at the click of a button. Within a short time the president acted—The result? Many people were hit by speeding motorists, as if the roads had become death havens or death traps, others jailed, some others mysteriously disappeared, and the president under siege was with minimal options at his reach. In such cases, a shrewd president must act—and Kenyatta acted fast enough. That was the leadership of the time that served that generation pretty well. His intonation of *Nyan'gau* (Hyena) *must be silenced* was loud and clear. And the hysteric laughter of the 'hyenas' went under—a clear indication that his foot was strong on the ground.

As they approached Adam's Arcade, there was a light traffic held by a truck that had overturned and spilled its oil along Ngong' Road. The traffic was completely blocked.

'Pull over to the other side of the road and get your way,'

Muriuki ordered Opere.

'There's a police car ahead, we have to look for another way.'

'Or go up and tell whoever's in charge that I want to talk to him.'

Opere was a police officer—a retired police officer. And he pretty knew Barack. In fact, that afternoon, they had had a cool drinking spree until late at 9 p.m. So the wreckage actually shocked him two hours later. It was unusual to get an accident at that spot. But the speeding vehicle hit the poor man, at the roundabout. A white man, whose pickup was also involved in the accident, died instantly. Though, Barack didn't die instantly, his body was a wreck. Cases of accidents were far much too high in the Kenyan roads, the accidents so rampant and had risen to an alarming rate, while the legislation on the cases of insurance cover null and void—without a trace. Victims themselves or the victims' family would try to seek compensation only to find their footing hanging helplessly.

'This is Barack,' he thought early. He identified him instantly.

'OK, Opere, I'll check it out.'

Muriuki got out of the car and hurried toward the squad car. A few moments later, he returned with a police sergeant. Opere opened the door of the car, rolled down the window, and held out his hand, taking the ignition key from the right hand to the left hand, extending it for a handshake.

'I'm in a hurry, Officer. We have a patient with a broken neck.' 'Broken neck . . . ?' The police sergeant was shocked.

Opere nodded.

'And a limb . . . we need our way out, sir.'

'If you don't mind,' Muriuki added.

Two minutes later, the police car, red light flashing, was guiding the trail car past the wreckage, and the huge crowd was looking at the wreckage 'like some piece of garbage the cat threw away'. When they were clear of the traffic, the sergeant got out of the car and flashed them to go right ahead.

'Can I give you an escort to the hospital, Mr Opere?'

'Thank you, Corporal.'

'I . . . I can't tell you how . . . how grateful I am!' Muriuki thanked the police corporal as they sped off. Opere stretched his nerves on the wheel pedals as if this night would have to last him the rest of his life. And the memories came flooding back.

When they got to the hospital doors—at the emergency room—doctors and nurses struggled endlessly to revive the poor man's life. Their faces were a combination of disappointment and fright. This time, there was no hesitation. Barack choking on some blood as they spurged his ribs, he choked on blood again, writhing in pain—drowning in his own blood.

'I wish I wouldn't be here to watch my friend blow himself to hell,' Opere said, frustration written all over his face. 'I swear to God, this is disturbing.'

'Like a man caught in the middle of a jewellery heist,' the seemingly confused Muriuki mumbled. The doctors tried almost in vain. The ears and mouth flashed out the much-sought substance, that rare commodity—alcohol. Maybe, his life was doomed to end, to be short from the beginning and have unhappy ending. Nurses were in a paralyzed shock. 'Why couldn't he tie the loose ends? Maybe, his life wouldn't be in danger.' Or just noncommittal life—'harping in the theme of enjoying life to its fullest'. If he misses a dose of alcohol, he'll catch a disease with an interesting preposition. He grew intertwined in this rule and got accustomed to it. He finally lost the battle. The regular guy became both the alcoholic and the accident victim—but at the end, he'd remain just him—Barack Obama.

Rehabilitation was necessary. Extensive therapy seriously needed. He'd learn to walk again. Well, the limping was evident. As some of the tendons had shrunk during the many stitchings and when the copper plate was being inserted on his right limb. So there was the limping Barack far from the Barack we knew. Many doctors had recommended an artificial limb to overcome the persistent limping. To allow him stand straight with prosthetic legs? That would have been a different story all together. The affected limb caused massive pain—something he'd not desired. As he lay in the hospital bed, 'he felt as if the limb was on some abstract fire razing it down whole—as if it was connected to an electric circuit. As if he couldn't cope with the limb anymore,' Malik says. He asserts that 'the pain was serious, making his nervous system catch fire as well. Medication did very little. And the embedded metal bar in his flesh served better than the relief he got from drugs.'

He'd stroll in the evenings, along the hospital corridors, enjoying the warmth from a cigarillo. He could try smoking in the hospital.

And he'd gently tap the cigarette on the edge of the glass window—as if it was his last. On the flipside, he was actually recovering pretty well. The man was overcoming the agony, pain, and fear of a broken limb. He was rather obstinate—as a true *Luo* he couldn't let frustration or anger take over him or raze him down. One of his friends says that at this time Barack knew that 'he'd given his legs to this country, working tirelessly', and he'd say, 'Now what's remaining is my life and am at the verge of giving my life too.'

Barack stayed in the hospital for quite sometime with the hospital bills skyrocketing every other night he'd spent in the facility. Malik says, 'We were broke. I was still in Kilimani Primary, and school fees became one elusive factor in my life. The accident robbed him part of his strength, coupled with some sort of bankruptcy; we started wallowing in limitation and endless want. My mother had little to offer—that's the time, the first time, I came to realize that life could be hard enough! The lifestyle changed, almost Homeric in its scope and hard, remarkably in its detail. My father felt like giving up on committing positively to anything in life . . . especially job-related—past jobs threaten the urge to take up future opportunities. The experience ruined him. He decried the occasional glut of mistrust within the public sector. When he brought the notion of moral responsibility in the thick of maddening rule, he failed.

When he felt better, he decided to seek specialized treatment in the United States. Omar was doing remarkably well—and the two agreed to meet when he flew in. But he'd say, 'I'm also going to see your uncle in the United States. I know he longs to see his father. Do you know him, his name is Omar.'

As bannered trainloads passed by, the Midwest remained at 80°C and struck high-level temperatures. The city was sweltering; in the city of Hawaii, heat wave had gone quite high. In the east, women hawkers flooded the market in India with low stiff straw hats; they looked like small huts in African hinterland (from a distant view). Everything seemed (at least according to him) renewed, if not undoubtedly accurate.

Ten years (a decade) separated two important dates; the time Barack Jr was born and the time the other enthusiastic parent, the father, came calling, an older, frustrated, and spent man, contrary to his expectation. He was a man who only bounced around with the most well-kept good humor, with hardly any worry at all, bearing his burden with solicitous energy like some contested reunion. Had he buried himself in the sand, he'd not have seen the light of day, the carnival mood that waited for him in America—the rant (if at all it ever existed), the glimpse, the patronising, the spluttering, and the charm that he brought to America. You could not tell that he was sick just a few months ago. He looked refreshed. Jokes flowed freely amidst the systolic rhythm of cigarette smoke. The two Baracks spent restless nights talking late into the night. They talked on issues of books, politics, predators, and African jungle, political tides, books of history, and law as they sparred on the leather chair; the hilarious laughter poured from their bedroom, and they stood at the doorway, watching the coming in and stepping out of the moon. It was so interesting. He said they tracked down old fables and enjoyed the delicious food from Toots' kitchen. And the time she had offered to prepare it rejuvenated love. Barack was like this man feted when retaining a chieftainship. Toots treated him as one of her lost sons. Here there was no uproar, yell, cat calling, or slipping boos or miscalculated hisses or the colossal chuckles that had dogged him enough back in his youth. The situation that incensed him stalked him into America. To the great depth gavel of United States of America. My father was not a politician, therefore, no longer and never hanged on the coat tails of politicians.

1972

'Life lost its bulwark on which I grew up,' Barack said. It started disappointingly. The decisions seemed not really his. Once he woke up, he did nothing. A man who had been used to putting on excellent suits in the morning and igniting his car on to work, for once stayed home and took off at ten to catch up with the news in the newspaper while bathing in the sun, sandals on, and the sun set on his face while still in pajamas. Prudently he did not like his sorry state, but life pushed him to accept the fact that life was breaking from a half to a stand fill. Maybe to usher in another disappointing phase, maybe the dashed hopes that may translate to raise expectations and the act of staying focused and developing a thick skin, the way to look at staying focused and developing a thick skin—in other words, the way to look at things quickly changed. To analyze the narrow perspective and then never stop at that the broader perspective, the latter provided a variety of factors that were never answered. So the pursuit for answers still continued. Answers to give meanings to the question, what happened to Barack these days? He hardly comes to town! Or could it be that his life is in the wires?

Could it be that he quit his job? Does he frequent his favorable joint? By the way where is Dr Obama? Where did that man go? Malik says that things really changed for the old man. All these questions rung in my mind as I saw his past friends enjoy their liquor. The friends he had been generous to, but now they mention his name and remain at that—Dr Obama. They tossed their orange glasses as huge chandeliers lit their black faces. 'Where is Obama?' No one—I say no one came to his rescue. People need to be their brother's keeper, but his friends knew little about that fact. On his part he had not sought their sympathy. He kept quiet, thinking that he'll rise again and keep his candle burning. My father could not facilitate the dialogue for seeking help; he believed that a man enough should always come and lift his friend as much as he sees him stuck but quiet. Mister that's a friend. Instead, there are friends who only wait until you beg for help. 'Oh my friend, I don't have bus fare', 'do me something', or 'my children are going to sleep hungry, lend me some money.' No, Barack would never lift up a lip to say that. He'd keep just silent and watch because he believed in common sense. Many had thrown their black double breast suits over their shoulders to avoid my father's gaze. And yet some may have been to ridicule him for something Daktari (Doctor) had said—'Can you lend me something? Now that you are a whole doctor, how can you miss hundred shillings in your pockets? What is this pocket for?' Barack lived a seriously pathetic life, but the soul of a fighter never goes off. It continues fighting, continues thumping the blood getting to where it is needed, and the functions are executed. In this manner, the creature lives on for another day and finds how to sustain the lifestyle. My father was such a creature, with many mouths to feed, school fees to pay, bills to settle, relatives to bury, yet still the creature lived on, and people went to school, they were fed properly, bills were cleared, and relatives received a dignified sendoff. That's why the birds of the air feed, yet they are not the legitimate owners of the food they eat. And we lived like birds of the air.

The regular, almost inevitable vigil, and travail by the special branch arm of government; that day, he felt indifferent and talked silly; actually he mumbled something and went for the door. His utterances were kind of few, laconic sentences; for once the government had reduced him to a mere pulp. This condition was actually going to, at least, last for a while: the cynical manipulation, the whirlwind sweeping scandals under the carpet.

Barack walked and talked like a terribly grieved man. His heart was like a smoke-filled room. Malik says that although, he remained strong like a man from his self-admittedly heroic exploits, a man who was trapped but escaped unscathed.

Earlier, after spending weeks in Hawaii, Boston, Nebraska, Chicago, and Oklahoma, having great and sweet time with a son, the man just looked revitalized, after mapping out a well-deserved tour from the hospital bed to a new leaf of life, from the shackles of disappointment to a walk at the beach line of Memphis, well-planned and plotted.

From sparsely populated places with a meager ten electoral votes, through blizzardy and worst of weather, to an ambitious mind that remained filled with private yearnings, my father made hard choices: pursuing serenity, avoiding confrontation through tough confidence, healing, and not nostrums. The first choice was harmony instead of vengeance. When bloom of discontent replaced trust, he actually communicated to himself. And he actually got some right answers. Maybe this time offered him chance to live under the tender feet of his family: my brother, Barack Jr, and the rest of that family, because they simply treated him as just one of them. And these actually made it not to offset his American connection. He actually brought hope to a heart or a troubled soul. He broke the spell that he was a runaway father. He declared that he was indeed involved. And it was clear that he blanketed them with love. He exonerated himself from being an irresponsible father. There was a suitability to visit at this time because it revived extinct love, hope, and family bonding. He did not desert at a time when he was needed most with lavish overreaching in itself. The Christian holy day was well spent. He was now any other conspicuous citizen walking around with his family, taking them to enjoy the Christmas mood, the livid high, the meteors (or the shooting star), the pine tree warped with sodium lights—events that looked a distant possibility now buoyed by the truth and reality.

In 1972 Continued . . .

My father drove me through a narrow, one-lane road, meandering to the top of a hill—in a forested jungle. There were beautiful colonial buildings upfront—and I remember asking him, 'Where are we going?'

'I'm taking you to school—a top national school, Bobby.'

He preferred calling me 'Bobby'. And 'Roy' only came when he was annoyed at me or when he wanted to prevail my mind—whenever I demanded something.

On one side of that sticky path were large boulders and a river—a small stream that drained away industrial waste flanked the other side. There was a bridge just as you approach the front gate. When he drove up, the memories of his jokes came bombarding me. Previous day, when we went for a shopping spree—he was a big spender anyway—he had joked that the shop attendant had to sell the uniform on credit because he wasn't sure whether we were going to secure a chance—we were already late for admission. He bought a maroon and gray uniform. I liked the blazer; it had a cool white rose. My size wasn't there then but he went to the warehouse and got one. I was already a heavyset Form—I . . . weighing seventy kilograms.

And the car broke down. I knew he didn't have money for repair or for purchasing the worn-out part. But he still insisted to see a mechanic.

'Where is the mechanic?' he asked an old woman whom I believed hadn't owned a car or sat behind the wheels before. The woman stared at him and walked away. Moments later his Datsun 1600 SSS crawled back to life, and as we drove away, it left stains of leaked oil on the pavement. I knew that it wasn't in order and needed some thorough repair. A police officer at the gate of the supermarket—with a bazooka on his hands—looked at my father and smiled. I wonder why he didn't smile back.

'How can someone be so sure of his other behavior?' This is the question that welcomed my father and me at Lenana High School. The principal's office was small, paper strewn all over—and the gigantic dark-skinned—a six foot or so heavy set individual, with a mean smile was complaining about a female teacher who had resigned from the school due to her love troubles. She had eloped with around three male teachers that pitted the fourth in a love triangle—nothing was ever veiled in secrecy of confession anymore. She was bending her own rules or maybe thinking fire won't burn her! She was properly scarred.

That aside!

Lenana High School is situated at the leafy suburb of Nairobi—during the time it was jungle land, with wild animals roaming around: the tortoise, the monkeys climbing from one small fig to another, the preying mantis took great pleasure flying on top of a calm stream that drained down to an open swamp. This swamp was mixed up with the Nairobi sewer that polluted it. The weaverbirds were blending the air with smooth soothing sounds and beautiful nests. They hanged dangerously and were rather making swift spins at the doors of their green nests. And they were so many birds. On 18 January 1972, I joined Form One at the school. The head teacher wasn't mean after all, although the first smile he flashed almost misled our guess. He was Mr Ronald, a business studies teacher. The gigantic heavy weight identified my father almost instantly.

'Hey, Dr Obama. This must be your son.' He opened his smile and his lack of two teeth or so was evident—the gap filled with a large mass of red gum.

'Yes, yes. This is my son—the K'obama breed. You see he's well fed,' My father joked.

'The *K'obama* hybrid so you say.'

'The breed wants to join other breeds.'

They let out a loud laughter and a shattering handshake.

And the principal tapped me on the shoulder and mumbled something like 'Welcome to the school.' I tried to figure out what he meant. I tried to decipher how *marijuana* found its way to the school. And why do students take this weed?

I asked myself several questions. And why could they just taint the name of the good school?

The Principal of Lenana School was friendly—though he looked just too strict. A boys' school needed someone like him—because the grandson of home guards needed someone strong enough who can easily turn barbaric dealing with indiscipline. Lenana School had high wrought-iron gate—maximum security to wade off wild animals and intruders.

'Mr Obama, we're training our senior boys to stop the sale or selling of *marijuana*.'

'So it's a cancer here.' My father looked straight to his eyeballs.

'Not only here, but we've realized it's penetrating all the top schools.'

'Is there anything you are doing about it?'

'We are working with the government.'

'I see.'

'You see, Mr Obama—I mean, Dr Obama, this school has come a long way. It started to grow when R. H. James was the first administrator . . .'

'So Mr James was indeed the founding head teacher?'

'Absolutely.'

'And then?'

I was enjoying a free knowledge here. The history was something my father liked to hear or to tell. He had told me of Maseno life and the history behind its formation. And I knew he wasn't going to relent on this one.

'It was meant for the sons of the British farmers. It is a mission school.'

'Then, all my children shall go to mission school!'

'They are taught Christian values—that distinguish these schools from the rest.'

Maybe the principal was too generous with the truth. Or maybe he loved the school such that he didn't want anything else to cross his mind apart from the stark truth. Hopeless, you may say.

The two gentlemen spoke friendlier, as if they knew each other for a while as we approached the admission block. At first, I was day-schooling, enrolled at Elliot House. I was a day scholar or commuter, popularly known as 'day-bags'. Later, when we lost our house in Woodley, I became a boarder. In Block *Three*, there was Carey Francis House with an orange painting—this is where I was to spend the rest of my life while at the school. I was to have joined Block Four were it not that it was already full—this particular block had two houses; my father's choice was the formerly upper junior House or Tom Mboya house, and all these houses were distinctive with paintings—Tom Mboya house had white and two red stripes across and around the upper torso derived from the Flag of England. I realise that the older boys (Or the *Laibonis* as they were called) were all stares from the comfort of their classrooms like a boy of six looking out of the window—they looked like bullies—or some Indian *coolies* mending the railways—and my father talked about them not once. In the heated debate, I heard him mention something like a school motto: *Nihil Praeter Optimum (Nothing But The Best)*. I always believed that my father was a perfectionist. He wanted things best! Best! Best! This school was about to offer me the best he wanted. The man—who I will have contact with for next couple of years talked. The Principal talked about the history—a fact my father asked him. He reminded us that his first day at Maseno was awesome.

'We were told what Maseno was from its inception to what it is today!'

This actually prompted him—he couldn't miss this opportunity.

'Oh yes. I remember when I was at Alliance School. The history was at our fingertips like a loyalty pledge.'

Some wore badges—maybe they served in the scouts' squad. And there were others; two students walked fast, taking long stride across the field talking, ear-to-ear, fast enough. They wore a necktie and a double-breast coat—I knew they were prefects, especially the kitchen prefects. And I learnt later that my guess was right. They had different ribbons worn on the sleeves of the blazer. At Kilimani Primary School, we had a more organized system—there was the school captain voted in by the entire student fraternity; so were school prefects.

The principal ordered the teacher in charge of admission to take up my case—and as I was being interviewed, my father accompanied him to his office.

I came to learn that my father wasn't only investigative enough, but he wanted me to be able to be given a proper education from a top national school.

He asked, 'Can you tell about Lenana School—I know it was a white dominated school. How about now? And I know a colonial governor, Philip Euen Mitchel, started it. That I know.'

The Principal burst into continuous laughter and his huge body was just shaking too fast.

'Daktari, you people know Kenya like the palm of your fingers.' See, all that happened in 1949. It was known simply as Duke of York School. And the students were called Yorkists.

When the admission was over, I was settled for a six-year-high-school study.

Actually, my father was abroad when I joined Lenana. Ruth made all the arrangements; and the headmaster was Mr. Kamunge.

The end of the year was marked with great happenings. My sister Rita had also passed her final examinations at Kilimani School and had passed pretty well. And there was Yusuf who had done well. My father was already reading from a different script. My grandfather called to tell him that he needs to look into the matter. Yusuf was taking his last primary examination at Nyang'oma Primary. One thing that brought headache was money—school fees. His consultancy wasn't paying, and he had to juggle through other means to cater for his growing financial difficulties. John Kang'ethe says, 'At this time he had been broke—can I say bankrupt?'

Dr Obama felt plain broke. He was hassling his way out—this way and that way. I remember him working at the VOK (Voice of Kenya) as a rapporteur. He tackled the topic on 'Wheels of Industries'. This discussion was aired live every Wednesday at 10 a.m. He gathered a rare crowd of listeners from all professions—and those he invited were very known experts in the global market. He once invited me to discuss the benefits of premium bonds and dividends and what they mean to a local citizen. By then the Central Bank of Kenya, where I worked as a principal superintendent, were giving out these services to the common man. From these ventures, he could pay some of his bills and have a bottle of Scotch at the end of the day. One thing I admire about him and that most of my friends don't possess is confidence. You can't know or tell whether Dr Obama is broke or not! He kept smiling, boozing, and partying with his peers.

I saw everything just normal in his life—children were in top schools and, indeed, national schools in the land. Abon'go was in the prestigious Lenana High School, and Rita Auma was on the verge of joining a national School as well. She had passed the country's national examination, and he had invited us for a big party to celebrate that outstanding achievement.

He was definitely happy and showed no trace of discontent or sorrow.

My memory here was a masterpiece:

One thing that still rings in my mind was the time when he sung for me the school anthem.

I told him, 'Dad, why do you repeat the song again and again as if you are the student and I'm the parent? I think you should shun my school politics,' I joked. 'Concentrate on your Maseno School, then.'

Then he mumbled the song more softly—he was changing the car mats:

> *Thought and deed shall bide with tasks*
> *Keep the Rose bright ye our emblem*
> *Sieve the trash dear Lord we ask*
> *For Nihil Praeter Optimum*

He said, 'Can you get me the spanner? . . . And come and listen to this.' I lifted the spanner and as I handed it, he said, 'Listen, Son.'

> *In pride we ride*
> *With rules abide*
> *As all the boys and staff combine*
> *All members here in Lenana*
> *We aim at Nothing But The Best . . .'*

The song was pretty long, but he had whistled the rest of the stanzas in a musical nuance.

1973

My father took Rita to the Kenya High School. I was curious to ask why he chose that school and not any other; he retorted, 'You see what, Roy, the school is located in a quiet leafy Kileleshwa suburb—that in itself is an environment for learning. Previously it was known as European Girls' School and founded in 1908. After Kenya gained independence in 1963, the school's name was changed to Kenya High School. The school is good for your sister.'

Up to that juncture I knew that my father liked the school. He was a scholar, and he knew where to hook a student.

'Kenya High has for a long time been ranked among the best public high schools in Kenya, enjoying outstanding and competitive enrollment from students of all walks of life in the country,' he said.

At first, Auma was day-schooling, but this didn't take long—she was a day-scholar or commuter, popularly known as 'day-bags'. Later, my father didn't like her commuting and convinced the administration that Rita should be enrolled in a full-time basis. Within two days, my sister was at Mortimer hostel; a 'blue rug'—the name of the head of the hostel—directed her to the new settlement, but after a short while, she was transferred to Huxley house. And I would visit her here—not once but several times. I became a regular visitor at the girls' school. One could choose another hostel—by then there was no congestion of the hostels. And there were others as well—Beale, Nightingale, Mitchel, and Bronton—to choose from.

Yusuf was enrolled at Pumwani High School on the other side of Nairobi—Nairobi Eastlands. The first time he came, my grandmother accompanied him; he had never stepped into the city.

He schooled at Nyang'oma, and the country's admission board selected him to join the Nairobi east school.

His sister, Zeituni, was about to complete her secretarial studies at a city college and soon would be working to help my father with the bills.

Meanwhile, my father had settled again with Kezia—my mother—there wasn't any strained relationship, after all. Maybe she was the only one in sight—or maybe because of us—her children.

Life was pretty interesting in Lenana High; my mother came during visiting days or on weekends accompanied by my father. I'd be proud with the arrangement; the reunion was working so well. And I realized that he was much better off, looking jovial and talking less politics. The school was quiet and serene. We played golf at the school's golf course, fed the horses at the horse stable, and watched teachers play cricket from the terraces of the cricket pavilion. I was taught shooting at the rifle range fields; we enjoyed games such as hockey, squash, swimming, and tennis before dinner break.

My memorable day is when we went to mend a bridge. We took shovels, mattock, and spades at dawn, and other students ran for logs from the school store—a lorry had sunk at the bridge, breaking it into pieces. For about three days, there were no studies; we all assembled at the site, every morning, helping construction workers fix the bridge. This was the only way out of the jungle school: The Laibon Lenana School. And with the bridge down and impassable, there wasn't going to be fresh supply of food and water. The bridge was decorated 'Cassandra crossing'—it marked the release of a movie 'ced *Cassandra Crossing*,' a British disaster film on 8 October 1976. In the movie, a terrorist of Swedish origin had contracted a bacteria disease during an attack on the US Mission at Geneva. When he escaped aboard a train from Geneva to Stockholm City, those on the train included Ava Gardner (Nicole Dressler), who was the wife of an arms dealer, a native of Russia—also on board was Richard Harris (Dr Jonathan Chamberlain) and his ex-wife Sophia Lauren (Jennifer Rispoli Chamberlain). Ava fell in love with a much younger heroin trafficker Martin Sheen (Robby Navarro). During this sizzling love affair, Robby was being traced by O. J. Simpson (Haley), an FBI agent working undercover on a priest ticket. Tension gripped everybody—as if it has grown body—especially when Burt Lancaster acting as US Colonel Stephen MacKenzie wanted the train redirected to an ex-Nazi railroad—to isolation in Poland at a place called Janov. The train went past the jungle land and approached a steely shaky bridge—the Cassandra Crossing. The bridge was so feeble, too delicate for the train to pass that it was about to collapse. When disagreement heated up between United States Colonel MacKenzie and Dr Jonathan who believed that the bacteria isn't that dangerous as earlier thought, it was upon the passengers to seek alternative means of stopping the train before it gets to the Cassandra Crossing.

Our 'Cassandra crossing' was finally mended and the school lorry pulled up the murky waters.

1975

Hawa says that during this time her father told her of a dream—in his dream, he had seen a witch dragging him into a cold dirty stream, and that the witch wanted him to die of lung failure—indeed a cruel death for the eighty-four-year-old Onyango Hussein. And after a night of boozing in Kogelo, young and older drunkards could not contain themselves from the effect of the clear liquor, and they would be heard shouting in the middle of the night. 'Hurrah!' Who can dare kill a lion? Hurrah! In that confusion, he dreamed that he was being dragged away by unknown hooded assailants, for unknown reasons, to unknown destination. They came to his hut (*duol*) and wrapped him in a gunny bag and took him a long distance and threw him into a river. One thing that erupted the following day was the disappearance of Onyango Hussein. Sara couldn't contain her grief and anger. It seemed like it might be too much for her to bear. The search continued—an old man disappearing mysteriously? That was also unbelievable.

'It seemed like it was too much to bear,' Hawa disclosed.

'On the third day', Hawa says, 'it was an anonymous herd boy who suffered the major shock upon discovering the muddy body. He thought my father was already half chewed by the wild animals, chilling and freezing from the cold dirty water. The young, shirtless herd boy thought that it was a log dragged by the swelling river. Ooh! It was someone trying to save himself—a rather old man. My father was discovered wrapped in gunny bag tied with sisal ropes at river Wang'pala. The herd boy felt he was dead. When the Police Department in Kisumu was informed, they arrived much late, maybe two hours later. He was hurriedly rushed to Ng'iya Health Centre, a few miles from the river. Sara couldn't take in the news; particularly, she couldn't comprehend the nightmare of the search and the shocking news of his reappearance. She couldn't bring herself to believe or to relay her fears to Barack—who'd been in troubles as well . . . 'People had been on my trail,' he complained. Hawa says, 'Everyone was terrified. Who could have done something so stupid? Something so barbaric . . . I have never seen or heard such a thing in my life! How does someone or a group of people want my father dead? I mean, drowned. To my surprise, I could feel that the rage appeared 'never to die down' or was the family just unaware of what was going on between or around it? Or who was that violent 'friend'—who'd flip-out to kill Onyango. 'So Barack's life therefore was in danger. And it seemed all those he knew were destined to brutal death. For instance, TJ. And why did it start with the father? Or did it start with this man who saw Barack's car approaching and decided to throw himself onto the road? Like some sort of suicidal attempt? And at the hospital, while recuperating from the few bruises, Barack forced him to say everything as to his motive that made him try suicide. And warned him if it happen again, that would be his end.'

'That's a gruesome attempt—a blackest risk,' he told him. And advised him, 'Next time, be careful. Control yourself. You have to control your anger. You almost killed everybody. Do not let drugs control you.'

After about five hours, the man died. 'He seemed just fine—hours before, he was trolled to the morgue,' the nurse in charge said.

Onyango's death, three weeks later, shocked Barack. He asked Hawa, 'Who is this trying to "clean us up"? Who wants to "mop up" *JoK'obama?*'

When Barack grilled the herd boy, 'What did you see first?' He answered 'a cheetah'! And . . . ? 'I knew the animal was going to chew me up.'

And then?

'I wanted to run away because I was scared.'

'So?'

'Oh no . . . I heard someone calling out, "Help me!" That is when I cried out loudly and people quickly gathered. The pack of animals had disappeared into the forest!' cried the shaken herd boy.

To unravel the matter, it was going to take the family a long hard road to sobriety. The water had pushed him into a deep crevasse at the riverbank. And the man still didn't die.

'My brother would be in an agony of indecision,' Hawa says, 'He underwent piles after piles of frustration. He behaved like a man in an asylum.'

'He felt frustrated by the growing discomfort. He would think of hiding under the blood, where the devil can do him no harm,' she joked.

As if frustration was imported—that the white people brought it as unemployment or some unknown thing and carried it like small pox to this tiny village.

Hawa says it was something that crossed her mind as if it was a character assassination. It was as if a tidal wave of a violent, unpluckable hatred that they didn't know its origin had struck. Some witless group was driving this violence. And the big question was, 'Who is this man?'

That was just a dream, a sad dream.

The year opened with a shining sun; drought had eaten part of the country, especially the northern region. This is the time when the famous rendition of JM Kariuki was in everyone's lips. The Member of Parliament of Nyandarua North said; 'It takes more than a National Anthem, however stirring, Coat of Arms, however distinctive, a National Flag, however appropriate, a National Flower, however beautiful, to make a nation.' Everyone sung it—students, villagers, farmers, teachers, colleagues in the August House, street boys, and all sorts of people. It became a famous tag line, almost trouncing the national anthem.

I was in school, and that was the time I was informed of my grandfather's illness. Onyango's health had been deteriorating gradually as a result of old age and a bad fall some time back. Sara had battled with his illness for several years until there was nothing else that could be done. He passed away in his sleep in November of 1975, the cause of death being brain hemorrhage. They say that he had been lured by a witch to the riverbed during one of his drinking sprees and was never the same since then.

When wailing rented the air, Akumu was part of the mourners. Onyango Hussein had died.

She traveled to witness the burial of her former lover, the father of her children. Onyango's death, according to Akumu, came too early. And the nature of circumstances that led him to his death was haunting and believably crazy.

During the burial of Hussein, Sara and Akumu sat side by side. They shared a platform—mourned Onyango—you could see them chatting and sharing one word at a time.

Akumu was particularly hurt. In her eulogy, she said,

> 'Onyango was my first love. He treated me with caution. And he didn't want me to be lonely. Every time we traveled, he always made me feel comfortable. But we disagreed several times on some issues, which to him looked normal. Since we separated, Onyango has never left me suffer; he always accepted my grains, and I have never turned down his ram for feast. He turned up during Ramadhan, and we always made healthy contacts. Even as we celebrate his

departure, let's remember he was full of love and full of life. He loved his country and her people just as he did love his children. I will never forget Hussein and may his soul rest in eternal peace.'

Although people clapped and others nodded, Akumu had several tasks ahead. When Onyango was laid to rest, Akumu stayed for a while and then went back to her homestead, in Kosele, after a stopover in Nairobi. Barack had organized for her stay, and his mother really needed time with him. Barack, through friends, actually footed all the bills left by the departure of Onyango, although, he was jobless at the time.

She stayed in Nairobi before going back to Kosele—this actually gave her a sense of belonging. Akumu believed that Barack was the man on the spot to take care of Amir, maybe later in the future.

When Barack came back from the United States, another half brother Razik Otieno was a teenager. He had a much constant delusion and necessary popularity. And Razik expressed it with a close certainty. Something that has never been any too taxing to him up to date; it was like a boon of knowledge already fixed in his heart: qualified or not, gruesome or chilling, complaining or just mute. Amir and Razik remained his half brothers from his biological mother. Worries or incessant annoyance, Amir would always ask if not financial assistance but also moral sustenance from Barack.

Barack continued to support his siblings; Razik was almost completing his A-levels at Ambira Secondary School. Yusuf was doing very well at Pumwani. Amir later joined in the quagmire of education. He purchased his half brother's idea that without education, there is no life. For people shall walk, drink, eat, and sleep education. A time is coming when highways and superways shall be built by the educated, those who have ideas—an expertise. Education shall be a helpful thing—a real investment.

Amir took these words with soberness; he gathered his disciplines, dusted himself, and took the path to school. Something he never let go. And in this particular school, he came face-to-face with luckster assembly and carefully called village boys seeking knowledge. Boys and girls, who decked out, spilled out their determination in the spurious gaiety of red khaki shirts and blue pants.

And their teachers awoke to begin issuing a series of increasingly unfamiliar topics, if minor, complicated. The A-levels were soon over.

In Asumbi Teachers Training College, Amir learned virtues. The three-year stint proved to him that the issue of education and becoming a distinct scholar was no negligible feat. And the college registered unsurprising increase of attendance; teaching profession became the epicenter of knowledge.

All the support Barack offered to Amir to become a distinct scholar was highly appreciated. Akumu became one happy woman around. She walked with her head held high and believed that achievement comes through hard work and belief. In that, she became the slave of hope and captured joy through the initiatives that he continued to propagate. She believed that nurturing a child has as a big role, as taking him to school to study—and no exception to that belief.

And when Salmin died in April 1977—Zeinab's dowry also came by—twelve cows.

Akumu started a solitude life again. Salmin's second wife—a cowife to Akumu—*Nyar* Oyugis left immediately—two days after the husband's burial. Therefore, manning the whole compound proved tricky initially, but she got used to it. Nyar Oyugis wasn't well known, but her departures caused quite a stir. And she never looked back or claimed anything.

Akumu's life remained lonely. While in this kind of loneliness, she could go to Kendu Bay—forty miles to visit her daughter Auma (Hawa) who was putting up with the husband, Daudi Amuna, in the town. While in Kendu, they'd discussed a lot, and she would spend at her daughters. In the mean time, Barack took care of her, sent her foodstuffs, money, hope, and love.

In 1977, Barack was back to work—for almost a decade, things had been difficult. And he sustained all that frustration—and at times contained with the glowing desire to quit dreaming for a change. Akumu was just thanking the Almighty *Allah* to help Barack find his foothold again, especially after such a tumultuous or rather torturous experiences.

When he came back into employment, he was the favorite with wide experience and tested character. He had served in the ministry, and the permanent secretary, Mwai Kibaki, was the boss.

Obeid says, 'Although, he worked seriously well and tirelessly convinced, while he was at the Central Bank of Kenya, things weren't rosy. His boss Duncan Ndegwa pulled the hell out of him. That's where he got more frustrated.'

Duncan Ndegwa, the author of *Walking in Kenyatta Struggles: My Story*, wasn't in good terms with Barack, and you couldn't really tell whether he liked him or hated him. Malik says that his father would say that people like Duncan Ndegwa were beneath him in intellect and could not or did not deserve to be his boss. He was smarter than all of them. Their appointments were a product of nepotism and tribalism.

Barack emerged from a 'ditch' by his own effort. He is one of the African scholars who may have the benefit of doubt to boast of being a self-made man. He was all this—urged the government to trim the expenses. The opposition, therefore, called that politics. It was like horse-trading—accusations from the public and continual shift of position by the leaders. Consequently, he remained just that—devout and quiet. And still people complained that he was too active. No one believed that there would be a disagreement.

In such scenario, maybe, to some people, he looked stronger—a little bit reposed with a broader mind than anyone else. How about those he had faced and those he would have to face?

Look, what after a hard lifetime, living at the edge with no money to spend? Barack just found comfort in the employment.

That was a reprieve to sort out his financial waterloo. 'He remained taciturn and cool,' Malik says.

> 'The situation wasn't any way favorable—there were youth disgustingly overweight, while others were hit by depression at thirty—and never recovered.'

CHAPTER 16

Nairobi life

Obeid says, 'The raving life was also a share of our planning. And we would assemble at *Starlight Night Club*. It was my favorite joint by the fact that it was away from the buzz of the capital. Most of the respected people in the society felt the magnetizing power of *Starlight*. The proprietor, Mr Armstrong, was a shrewd business guru. He made the place look like a home. And many patrons, at least, those who I know, never went home regularly. It served international delicacies and became the hot topic and simultaneously the trap. Today as I drive along Valley Road to the capital, *Starlight* masked by Integrity House, comes to mind. I could see Barack driving off at 9.30 p.m. to be with his family. Mr Armstrong would be just another whiteman with great wit, a healthy looking and brisk Briton with warm welcome; he made the place look tidy and with a phenomenal ambience. He was one amazing self-confident proprietor and at times displayed a rather rural knowledge of Kenya. That made Africans love his business. A stone throw away was the Sagret Hotel, and on the left side of the junction was Heron Court hotel and the restaurant where I met Barack with some of his friends and particularly met his clients there, and I believe it was his favorite joint as well. He would later stay here briefly with his friend, Mr. Okoda.

I remember vividly the time we would probably have a night party at *Hallians Club* on Tom Mboya Street. This was no child play. We danced rumba from the soothing songs of Bavon Marie Marie. And there was Hi5 Band and John Zanze, a Zambian, who rocked the nightclubs while partnering with Kabaka. Oooh! Those were the times you wouldn't forget. Barack's liking was also centered in the songs done by Equator Boys' Band. Whenever I visited him, at his residence, we would listen to Old Boys—the lead singer—Steele Beautor rocking us over a glass of Vodka. Barack's glasses were really long. Our social lives were one aspect of unity. We celebrated our achievements and that which we were about to accomplish. And we would discuss it openly—the dream of our nation—the self-propelled nonpartisan society. We didn't commit to discuss all these, but we'd find ourselves deep in that discussion. Sometimes I found myself boozing at Grosvenor Hotel—another favorite joint at the outskirt of Nairobi a few meters from *Starlight*. It was a white dominated joint, and revelers thronged the pub barely before 8 p.m. Later the owner sold it to the Department of Defence (DoD). The military revelers had taken over from the civilians, and they turned the pub into a barack.

The husky Congolese bands treated patrons in a rare jazz orchestra. The lead vocalist could play clarinet and saxophone. They called him 'Bavon big money boy', and many other jazz performers came by. The hottest joints played jazz and classical music on weekdays. My father loved jazz and classical music; the sound of violin provoked him. If people would find comfort in music, he was just one of them. And when it came to classical music, he wouldn't lay down any restrictive conditions. In his spare time, he attended various performances by concert violinist.

Obeid concurs thus:

> My brother loved jazz. One day I took him to the Hotel Boulevard near the Kenya Broadcasting Corporation; he bought several whiskies including those for his friend whom we found taking cheap drinks at the famous hotel's balcony. He was a kind man and would want everyone to be feeling the way he was feeling—happy and not complaining. That's how he wanted everyone to be—just confident and unperturbed. The pub section played his favorite tracks—particularly Beethoven's symphony by artist Ludwig Van Beethoven composed by Gerard Schwarz and the Highway Blues by Marc Seales. I particularly loved the latter. We drove to several parties on invitation. And his white Datsun 1600 SSS was a common figure around his friends' gates. Barack also appreciated the great music works by Elvis Presley. The fact that he liked Belafonte music wasn't a surprise; he had met and interacted with Harry more than a couple of times. He purchased a number of signed tracks by the artist. He kept a constant playlist in his car radio and record collection at the house.

CHAPTER 17

1982 – Accident Coverage

At midnight, on Sunday, 1 August 1982, a group of soldiers led by Hezekiah Ochuka, a Senior Private Grade-I from the Kenya Air Force took over the radio station, Voice of Kenya, and announced that they had overthrown the government. Word went round that the force included Sergeant Joseph Ogidi, Corporal Charles Oriwa, Corporal Walter Ojode, and Corporal Bramwel Njereman from the then Kenyan Air Force, Nanyuki Station. They came out to dismantle the Moi government in a gruesome attack. Chief of the general staff was General Jackson Mulinge. The president stayed back at his Kabarak rural home, listening closely to the issues that went in a spin—rebel airmen stormed VOK, what is today called KBC (the Kenya Broadcasting Corporation headquarters), took control, and announced the establishment of a military government.

Chaos arose with great losses; many people were killed and civilians found themselves in a looting spree. It was unbelievably, if not wholly, accidental that the airmen almost took over the government from President Moi. Even at the time, the coup attempt was being suppressed by loyalist forces led by the Army and GSU (the General Service Unit); there were already huge civilian casualties.

The militant force ordered airmen from the Air Force fighter pilots, at gunpoint, to bomb the State House. The big problem was that the pilots pretended to follow the orders—all agreeing—that they had to move more expeditiously to act with utmost swiftness while on the ground, but once airborne, they ignored them and instead, dropped the bombs to Mount Kenya forests.

In swift counter-insurgency, the country was on fire. Before the quick encounter, Lieutenant General Njoroge was heard saying, 'We were planning how to restore President Moi's Government.'

The Special Branch and the Intelligent Unit took charge, led by James Kanyotu—Chief of Intelligence—who formed a committee that consisted Lieutenant General John Sawe, Army commander as well as deputy chief of the general staff, Major General Mahmoud Mohammed his deputy in the Army, the chief of operations at Defence Headquarters, Brigadier Bernard Kiilu, and Major Humphrey Njoroge, who was then a staff officer in charge of training at Kenyan Army.

General Mulinge promised the worried president 'matters would be dealt with at that time.'

In the morning of 24 November 1982, a man bought the *East Africa Standard* to catch up with the latest news on the first development on 1 August 1982 aborted coup attempt. The headline stated thus:

> 'Treason Case Verdict Today'

And there was this other man, Corporal Njereman Injeni Bramwel. The paper indicated that Njereman's case was being handled at the Langata Barracks (Court Martial).

A lot had gone under the bridge since the coup attempt. Many contributors or suspected masterminds were on the run, others were in asylums in foreign countries, while yet others behind bars, waiting death sentence.

The corporal defended himself, 'I obeyed the orders from my superiors.' Njereman denied the fact that he ordered Warrant Officers I Gatuguta and another no-commission officer, to prepare hit rockets and bombs or even forcing Major Mutua to fly an armed FG fighter on a mission to bomb some targets in Nairobi.

That day saw over hundreds of Mathare slums inhabitants suffer, as a wild inferno razed down several houses consuming abandoned sleeping babies as their mothers scampered for safety, trying to salvage a thing or two. Also the keen reader would have come across the notice that Kikomi—a giant cotton miller (and indeed the only factory in the region), the Kisumu Cotton Mills that Barack and other prominent Luos helped raise—went under receivership.

The receivers were Coopers and Lybrand Ltd., and Mr J. Y. Birnie was selected as the receiver manager.

That day the USA planned to deploy giant MX missile. The president of United States Ronald Reagan proposed to deploy huge MX missiles in a stream of Wyoming silos. An ardent reader would learn this operation was at its peak efficiency but was absolutely rejected in the long-run. Reagan would invite the Soviet Union to take loads of joint steps to abate fears of accident nuclear war. Something the Soviet Union never took lightly, and it became a forum of disagreement. The ceramics of life, especially the dynamic ceramics, was changing real fast like corruption eating away the public coffers.

On 25 November 1982

This was the day Dr Obama was involved in a brutal freak accident.

'When my father met an accident a few meters from the convergence of Ngong Road and Elgon Road, the vehicle had veered off the road, and eye witnesses said that he was trying to avoid colliding with an overspeeding white saloon car. My father was not drunk at the time of the accident. When I got to the City Mortuary at the junction of Ngong' Road and Mbagathi Way, the following day after the fateful accident, I found my father "sleeping" peacefully. I got there on a motorbike. My cousin Charles Oluoch accompanied me. The 'old man' was lying on the concrete slab still dressed in his pin-striped, three-piece navy blue suit. The suit was cracked ever so slightly at the crotch but other than that you could have mistaken him for one in deep slumber.

The old man had no blood-splash in his body—no deep cuts anywhere. Then I asked one of the attendants whether he was drunk. He replied almost with great confidence, 'This man is your father?' Then I asked him again, 'What might have caused the accident—was he drunk?' The remorseful attendant replied, 'Not at all.'

According to that statement, it is nonarguably correct that my father never tasted liquor in three or so days before the brutal death. He had arrived from overseas duty, the previous day, and was on his way to Mawenzi Gardens along the usually busy Elgon road (in Upper Hill) to see his family, after having been with some friends. Just as the car was being towed by the Police Land Rover to the Police Traffic Headquarter, as curious onlookers trekking to industrial area to search for jobs watched in disbelief, in the same way the life of an ambitious African scholar was consumed by that piece of metal—the imported Chevy pickup from General Motors. And the life that never recovered from government betrayal of himself and his friends was consumed so easily. The blood—the symbol—of enmity never oozed out to commensurate the bitterness that lay under that black skin. Beyond that façade, bitterness brooded ceaselessly and refused to come out. Across from Kisumu's economic meltdown to Nairobi's ghost town, the isolated road to Upper Hill, Railways Club Road, that morning, Barack's car was a wreck; 'Chevrolet Pickup (a metallic green color) had veered off the road and hit a stationary tree'—a teary witness recorded the statement at the Police Department. Barack had died instantly. It took away the doubt that life of a prominent Kenyan—Barack Obama—was over.

'The black economist's body was taken to City Mortuary. Barack's car wreckage was beyond recognition. The car towed to Upper Hill Police Station (Police Traffic Headquarter),' a friend privy to the family affairs noted at his Mawenzi Gardens. One mortuary attendant at the City Mortuary later said, 'I've never seen a man killed so mysteriously, like the body that was brought in last time.' That was how the shaken attendant commended. The carnage was so ugly, and yet no sign of injury.

Malik says, 'I learnt the death of my father through Sara Nyaoke, my aunt. Jael, my stepmother, also called in by sending someone that morning, and I couldn't believe it. I was in my office at Kenya Fire Appliances where I had a job as a senior accountant just working on one or two things.'

The bulletin on VOK, the anchor, or the coanchor said nothing about Barack. Maybe, they hadn't been supplied with the news. Who cared? Maybe only the family felt the pain more than anyone else. The death, the response, and the mourning—all sent the family into a spin. Nobody recognized the demise of an efficient, brilliant, scholar of economics.

Malik observes, 'I was shocked that suddenly a handful of prominent people came out. Everybody now said Barack was a great friend. I didn't understand why everyone was coming from the woodwork to mourn my father. I don't understand. It is something I've dwelt at graphic length, but I've never come across an answer. He thought some of these movements and surprises wouldn't be resident in my mind—of friends who abandoned him.' Now mourning my father.

Barack kept secrets and shame within himself. The following day, even more pointedly, the *East Africa Standard Newspaper* or *Nation Newspaper* of 26 November 1982 never mentioned anything about this great scholar. So the nation, the people who read Barack's work, those who wondered his wit, or those who benefited from the healthcare reforms or the national social security fund were not informed properly.

How would people know that the man had busted through the government offices, lobbies, and hotel corridors, proclaiming that the best country is yet to come. My father used to say, 'There's only one compromise way to win over corruption and mismanagement and that is to hire qualified people to take over government operations or else the government is just dead. On the other hand, the frequent reader of *East African Standard Newspaper*, 25 November 1982 would be informed simply:

Njereman sentenced to death

He was found guilty of conspiracy. That he supported the 1 August 1982 military abortive coup attempt. The court martial sitting at Lang'ata Baracks found himself guilty. And that he is sent to the hung man.

From the court martial, the newspaper would inform the public that another court across the city ordered arrest warrant for Ugenya member of parliament, Jimmy Aggrey Orengo, then a close ally of Barack. Maybe he didn't know that his friend would be lying at a city morgue the next day. Or could it be that Barack was fast rising, getting back on his feet again. And someone wanted to clip out his wings or was his clipped mannerism obsessive to some people, angry with him and wanted him dead? Or could it be that he was a victim of circumstances that all Luos scholars were believed to be involved in the 1 August 1982 coup. That was mistakenly misunderstood then. 'Barack never knew anything concerning military takeover to start with,' Hawa says. 'Barack, my brother, was not a coward, but a democrat, a man I knew best. Do not listen to the hullabaloo around surrounding his life, coming from the unknown. I knew Barack best,' she says.

On the third day, journalists streamed in; they asked several questions. You see, my father was one of the VOK consultants, and his death meant a blow in the service delivery of the station. When he came, everything fell into its place. The Republic of Kenya learnt of his death with shock and disbelief.

'The funeral committee was set up,' Malik says. 'It was the most trying times of my life. I had to run up and down to consolidate people through harambees (fund-raising), night vigil. And at the same time, I was still at my first job straight out of university. So juggling the two became a very tricky issue. But I had the money to cater for the immediate needs. Sara, my grandmother, had come over from Alego. Hawa, my aunt, also came from Kokal; Said, my uncle, Sara Nyaoke, and all other family members were present. Her brothers, though they were young, were assembled here. The body was still lying at the City Mortuary as the days wore on. And as families streamed in and condolence book kept filling up, mourners dropped their contributions toward the funeral arrangement. Painful, it looked, but we could make little contribution from the small gatherings that we organized at the house.

I had that earnest desire to see things done, and I actually managed to consolidate some support. Jael helped. My mother Kezia was very central here. Her brothers came from Konyango Village. And it was a full house; relatives poured in as they mourned my father. Akumu, my grandmother, was there as well on the third day. She cried and was taken ill. We had to rush her to the hospital. It is very painful to lose a son who has achieved such a great success. A son who'd made you proud, and now you're about to bury him—instead of him burying her. Many contributors were carrying out fundraisers at Garden Square. The ministers for finance, planning, and community affairs, Robert Ouko and Oloo Aringo, were very prominent by then. They helped marshal support from the government and those prominent in all circles of influence.

Obeid says, 'Fundraising was so easy because Barack already had his share of friends who were too willing to contribute everything. I also had a number of various invited friends that came in entirely for all the fundraising. This is the time Honourable Ouko stood and offered Jael a job at the Treasury. It was a great opportunity for a young jobless widow who would lose a husband so soon. To me, that's one of the sterling contributions I've ever seen or heard. On top of all that, he took upon himself to be there whenever we needed him. The minister had worked with Barack on several projects and even invited him as a surprise guest during his graduation in the United States, way back in 1971.

From Onyango's hemorrhage that sent him to the grave to the individual pain that my father suffered, the death of Barack wasn't easy to assume. Akumu couldn't hide her anger.

'She cried all the way from Nairobi to Kogelo.' Hawa says, 'My mother collapsed more than once. She felt half dead. She lost her mind. She couldn't sustain the death of her son after burying my father. She would cry, "Barack, *wuod Opiyo Mireri itho malit. Iweya nang'o?*" (Barack, grandson of Opiyo Mireri, you have died so painfully. Why do you leave me behind?) My mother never stopped at that. She said, 'I won't leave either. Now what will I rejoice if you are dead?' Her cry was taken up.

I thought she'd lost her mind, although she was genuinely aware of what we have both lost. My mind taught me, then, just to be silent. I sobbed in silence. My sister, Nyaoke, followed suit. And a union cry came from every corner of the congested lorry ferrying us to Kogelo. I wished Barack would come out and see how he was loved. The tears of love came out at a time of pain. 'Death robbed me—robbed us of a man we knew in bits, in pieces, especially upon return from America. Barack changed. I could not guess what was in his mind. His death was a permanent daring departure from our lives—a departure from ordinary African life—an illusion. A protracted, curved-away life was taken as if we were wallowing in disgrace and in truth. Barack changed a little bit. I remained a mere spectator as fancy issues took toll of him.

At this moment, echos of eyewitness, following the accident, rung loud enough through my sleepy brain. Of testimony of a car that sped into ditch sideways glinted down Haile Sellasie Street beneath broken tree trunk and leaned on power lines. The driver was trying to avoid an overspeeding car, and the driver in question, was my brother, Barack—my only brother from Kogelo, who my mother Akumu described as *Wuod Mireri* (grandson of Mireri). And that to me meant that some people were behind my brother's death. The plumage of the government had changed. The country was too volatile for existence.'

He helped escape a head-on collision but never succeeded in saving his own life. Barack was not drunk. We all knew that he was a successful drunkard. It is in the blood, you know! But he never thought of using it to end his life.

Barack had emerged triumphant from innumerable clashes—the accidents, the sacking, the rejection, the blacklisting, and the summon from none other than the Head of State, Jomo Kenyatta, and now his life burned down due to these many feuds—many fierce criticisms 'but much had gone into mind: And the mind was already filled up,' Hawa says.

I can't point who actually did these, but the death theory is worth noting:

> 'What was the motive of the car hitting the tree trunk? Then, there was the lack of injuries to kill him, instantly. And who? Or what was the motive? A man died so mysteriously. Could it be that the government was involved? Maybe yes. But ask why was Onyango dragged and later died?

What was the controversy surrounding the government? Is it the late Jaramogi Odinga's political infighting with the government, the abortive coup attempt that may be linked to Barack. But he hasn't involved himself in a coup or any other pure military operation!

If Barack died today, the procession would have been larger; maybe the flag—the Kenyan flag and USA flag—would have been raised at half-mast. And someday, history would have recognized this. His death would have been mourned by UH Alumni, the Harvard professors, the deans, and the entire great University of America—and to reconcile the two countries in a completely complex web. The celebration of his death would have been on a grander scale. The road leading to the old man's homestead was dirty and unpaved. One would easily notice that rain would spoil it completely and the hungry children darting around the muddy path, picking caterpillars, and the malnourished children scampering around bare-chest. Barack's remains were draped with a colorful casket. He'd been a man at ease with all colors, and the farewell organizers made a mix of colors. From the Nairobi City Mortuary Chapel to his residence at Upper Hill, Mawenzi Gardens House No. 345—Roy, Rita, Zeituni, stepmother Jael, Kezia—the widow who'd lost more than a husband—Obeid, cousins, and aunties were all present. The clan got a true representation—pensive and withdrawn. They felt that death has robbed them of a man they knew so well, a man whose time to blossom had just begun. A man destined for great things died at a point when life was at its brink of success, a distance away from its teething stages—a man who'd a bright and serious future and to them he was a demigod. His magic name (Barack) would banish impediments to stay clear of an unbroken rise. The man who took the cruel ritual of succession later found out that job satisfaction was nothing but a ceremony of his rejection. Later, his name wouldn't be mentioned in any corridor of the once powerful planning ministry due to political reasons.

Ideas and wits would later open a new chapter in the history of the world:

'That he fought so hard for accountability and never achieved it.'

But later these fightings paid off. One of his own, his own blood, would sit in the 'Highest Office of the Land'. This character opened a new world to one of his own, a world where people shall be passionate about change. Change to believe in a world of ideas and constructive motives, hope, and genuineness. Another man came up in him who would extol the enormous power of the presidency.

Death/Burial Date 1982

5 December 1982

4 a.m.
Malik woke an hour earlier; he says, 'I woke my mothers, Zeituni and Jael. Already the rest of Kogelo Clan and the entire Alego Welfare Association had arrived three hours earlier. My grandmother, Akumu, wasn't able to sleep the whole of that night—an issue that troubled me a lot. She looked frail and spent. And her mourning made everyone join in wailing. The casket carrying the remains of my father was hoisted onto a bus. In the bus were Jael (with six-month-old George) and Akumu, and many other people. We had a convoy of about twelve cars (Motorcade that later snarled its way out of Nairobi).

8 a.m.
There was public viewing of the body from Mawenzi Gardens, Upper Hill. The cortege set out for Kogelo Village—a lakeside community, 350 km from the capital, Nairobi. My father's coffin was draped in a brown and white robe. His favorite walking stick was placed against the casket. The rose flowers and the yellow sepals were placed on top of the casket.

12.00 noon
In the faulty land of Nakuru in the heart of Rift Valley, the Luo living here thronged the road; the people of Alego living in the town had organized 'a team for Kogelo'. Some of them were his close friends.

3 p.m.
In Kisumu, our convoy was interrupted by irate mourners. They had been waiting for the convoy for at least three hours. Their *matatu* was decorated with tree branches and figs. The buses, including Ng'iya school van (his former school), and other automobiles had red pieces of rag tied on the side mirrors, and the mourners mounted on top of the buses and matatus.

6 p.m.
At Ng'iya market, the cortege was met with a 'larger group of mourners. Old women in brightly colored patterned garments wailed loudly and young women and children jostled for space—all waiting to view my father's remains.

Men wore hooded traditional headgear, while others remained shirtless; young men ran all the way from Luanda Township, holding wooden clubs.

Old men were with blue, black, and white Ostrich feathers; others smeared white clay on their faces, and some spread it on the entire body. As we branched to the murram road—unpaved path—to Nyan'goma, a lead mourner had on headgear and a leopard skin skirted wear that had gathered mud and black jack—he danced and wailed.

People watched from vantage points—from far, others on rocks, and some others were hanging on tree branches. The crowd surged—the elders, the women, and the drum beats throbbing the cow skin.

The distance between Ng'iya and Nyang'oma is short, four miles, but it took us what seems about five hours.

8 p.m.
At the ground on my grandfather's homestead, the bus broke down. There was mud and sticky path inhibiting the flowing of convoy. And inside it, the driver shouted to us that Akumu had collapsed, but stable. Akumu was rushed to the homestead for a deserved rest. The convoy stopped as the scene turned ugly; there were herd of cattle to accompany the mourners; they had sisal ropes wrapped on their long horns to symbolize that a 'warrior' has passed on (that the deceased was a warrior). The bus was quickly fixed amidst the mess, pushed a little, and journey completed.

9 p.m.
My father's casket was placed at the front of his hut. It was a tradition for the body to be kept overnight. A fireplace was fixed, wailing continued as relatives from Kosele, Wagwe Kanyadhiang, and Kanjira Village arrived in the middle of the night.

1 a.m.
A group of religious leaders led by Evans Agolla and Sheikh of Siaya consecrated a spot for the grave, next to my grandfather's grave, under a mango tree. Onyango had picked the spot; he wanted him buried there, according to tradition. (Barack never thought of that—that was the custom.) The clergy led the procession back to the hut.

Young men were contracted to dig the grave, and others pounced on two bulls for curry stew. The number of relatives in the compound was already overwhelming, and they needed food to bite.

2 a.m.
The two bulls were already in the visitors' plates, and the grave was already six feet. The young men took a conscious approach to dig it. There was a large rock beneath and was split by the inferior implements. They sang heroic praises to Barack and took hot soup against the chilling weather. At the end, they settled on liquor; after a few hours, all fell asleep from the influence.

6 December 1982

5 a.m.
Mourning started afresh. Akumu refused to be comforted. She cried.

'Barack *wuod mireri*
Barack *Okew karabondi*
Barack Wuod Hussein
Wouda mageno'

Her bitterness had skyrocketed—the kind consolations from other relatives couldn't do much.

6 a.m.
Close relatives built a temporary shelter. It was traditionally agreeable for his first cousins to erect a temporary shade.

9 a.m.
Homestead was completely full—no parking space—and there wasn't security at all. The tent was surging from pressure from those leaning on its poles.

9.45 a.m.
My father's remains were placed in front of his hut under the Jacaranda poles and maize stalks providing a shade. The viewing continued as there was a long queue of people around the hut. Some cried and others broke down. And still others just passed without putting their eyes past the portrait picture placed on top of the casket.

10 a.m.
The eulogies started. And the nature of burial caused a stir. I wanted my father buried the Muslim way. The Sheikh of Siaya was loud enough to support my argument. The Foreign Minister Dr Robert Ouko called me aside and advised me that it would be great embarrassment for the body to be removed for Muslim burial. To me, I knew he had wanted to be buried honorably, but

I didn't know which one. A short scuffle emerged as I insisted that the casket could as well be taken back to Nairobi. And my father should be buried in the Muslim way. Akumu stood and pleaded, and Kezia, my mother, got hold of my waist and just cried. I expected Mark or his mother—but no one appeared, other than Dave (Opiyo).

Within thirty minutes of discounting, I settled. Zeituni and Yusuf kept encouraging me; it was the longest hour of my life compounded by the fact that the old man did not know what was going on behind the scene.

I sat there as if I had been strangled; I felt weak and spent.

The eulogies flowed freely. One speaker after another spoke sense. Barack's friends, colleagues, and all the people who just loved him and, maybe those he did not know, talked positive things about him pensively. One particular speaker, who stunned the gathering and who could not let mourners rest, was Reverend Evans Agolla. Agolla was the only man of the cloth who'd made sure that Barack was baptized. He baptized Barack at river Ondondo at the shrine where baptism of new Ng'iya Anglican faithfuls received Jesus through the baptism of water—Mor Ogwari reasserted. Maybe others would convince Jesus that mankind wasn't worth dying for. He talked of Barack, whose thirst for education made him go marginal length superseding his own. At one point, about three decades earlier, the Reverend had a hard time explaining to Onyango why he dipped his own son into the water like a lame cow in the name of 'baptism'. Did he have a clue of the faith to which Barack belonged? And who gave him the permission to 'baptize' Barack? 'The father was bitter,' Evans said. But that was there in the school's rulebook. Evans's eulogy was timely. It attracted the most attention because he molded Barack at Ng'iya. Although he was not a teacher, he played the role of a teacher, who kept both the 'girls' and 'boys' schools running.

Evans had come up with an idea of N'giya Health Centre the place where 'we treat and Jesus heals', but he reemphasized that, that was not his idea. It was Barack's and other students' ideas; they complained of ill health and prompted the construction of the health center.

They came to me at my office and said, 'We need where we can cure this malaria. It's too much.' As it came from young people, this statement really touched me. I looked at them and said, 'I'll check into that.'

Evans's grave is encircled in metal rails at St Paul's' Cathedral. It reads thus:

First Bishop of Maseno South Diocese. Rest in peace. Here rests the late Reverend Evans Agolla. Born 1906 Died 9/3/1987.

For I know my redeemer liveth, and that he shall stand at the latter day upon earth, And though after my skin worms destroy this body, yet in my flesh shall I see God (Ayub 19: 25-26).

Evans had been part of this family. His frequent visit to Onyango's home was evident. 'He would spread the word in unfamiliar territory.'

Onyango had told him earlier.

Evans defined himself 'that this family deserved a place in the sun!' Maybe he preached to them indirectly in a way to suggest he had offered two choices of defense, that they had dozens of opportunities to their goals.

He never showed any woeful lack of austerity, and as a result, he never lost faith while he dealt with Onyango, as a Muslim. His faith was an impressive portrayal of perseverance, and when he delivered the eulogy, it was not a sounding board for propaganda. One thing that really stunned many was his strong belief that he could do anything with his high influential office, that his powers as a Bishop would yield some results. And he refused to elucidate.

Evans said during his engagement with the Muslim brothers, Onyango had virtual solitary confinement, that he had adopted some sort of an isolationist attitude, but not a person with irritating qualities. In the midst of all these 'we still plotted a permanent peace—an everlasting coexistence'. He observed that there was a faulty connection between religion and people that required immediate connection.

Maybe Christianity made them look bitter, blind, and reactionary. As if their lives were dipped in a bottle of chloroform, and they were reacting to it.

The friendship between the Mboyas and us never ended too soon. Pamela Mboya had talked of a government unhampered by the vulgarities of tribalism that they executed by killings and hitmen. Her tone bordered on defiance and defense. On the final day, the contribution had been good. We bought a casket and hired three vehicles to be used to ferry the body and everyone who wanted to go home to upcountry. Of course, the vehicles were already full even before the widows found their space. Villagers from Alego wanted to go home, and especially that it was a free ride. It not only became hectic but technical as well to control irate mourners.

One could easily remember the eulogy Pamela gave following the death of her husband (1969), both in Nairobi and in Rusinga. 'That everybody was talking half truths and fabricated things concerning her husband's death. Nobody could say anything positive and anything conspicuous enough to be important. The mystery behind TJ's death went under the carpet. And the government sat on it. The file wasn't there—a case of lost files.' My father's death was just another template but executed differently.

When Oloo Aringo stood to speak, more tears streamed and the women could not contain their grief. He spoke about Barack as a friend and a cousin. A man he had worked with in developments and a man as a matter of fact, 'had great tact in handling development matters'. They have both served in the Alego Welfare Association—an outfit that helped mobilize the community resources as well as coming in—at point of their need. He never stayed back. As the master of the ceremony, he spoke about my father's diligence, skills, love, and how he encouraged people to hold on to hope.

And when he invited the Foreign Affairs Minister, Robert Ouko, to speak, behind that rostrum, I knew that my father was no more. Actually that's when the spirit of reality struck me like a 'wedge hammer'. He spoke of the policies my father had drafted as implementable and had grown of age. He said that my father was a man who would 'bone up on his homework and at daybreak the result would be just too frenzy'.

As the minister spoke, the motley-looking band of schoolchildren watched. And the elders basked in the baking sun, waving frantically. The minister said, Dr Obama wasn't a woolly official—a man who couldn't run away from the work at hand. I worked with him in several occasions, and his determination amazed me. I knew a resilient Barack and a worker who couldn't turn the page on his troubles or, while at the office, would want to be mixed in the internal wrangles. He wasn't a chief of propaganda. He spoke with intense deliberation in times of a crisis. I remember when he was blacklisted by the president, he confided to me, 'I can just resign at a peaceful moment or when one simply cannot go on!'

He later lost his job.

That aside, Barack worked tirelessly with boldness and skill in execution of policies. I always sought him for advice, and he wouldn't disappoint. In issues of economic development, he never disappointed. He understood the warp and woof of economics—the global economic trends. He was the robotlike carrier of public opinion. This actually made him act more of an economist and technocrat and less of a political abyss. And I would define him loosely as 'a man of the future prospects.' He fought for a hungerfree livelihood through his many writings and policy documents. From radio stations to free press, *Daktari* made us realize the need to change our way of living and adopt modern tenets of economic growth. I remember when he longed to forestall the day when there would be an excellent road network to his homeland, the day when air transport would be improved, when there would be principal trunk roads for heavier transport. These were his limitations.

If you look around, *daktari* has left behind a large family including a young wife, Jael.

I know the notorious wife inheritors have started preparing their proposals!

This family needs help. The people of Alego Welfare Association should liaise with my office and see how to help this family. There are young people in the competitive preparatory stages of schooling, and it would only be responsible enough to take care of them.

This was my father's day. Every speaker talked of decorated achievements. And overwhelming praises came by.

He said that my father had carried on alone till the daybreak of his death. Under the immense demands, he persisted on proper plans that overemphasized his limitations and maybe requisitioned his downfall. In essence, his frustrations by the government actually got into our hearts and deeply scratched our very existence. The decline of that existence actually cost us our freedom. Suffering remained the immediate option. Although suffering isn't a choice, it was inevitable.

Jael's Tribute

Jael spoke of her loss. Look at her; she was so young and tender, full of love and yearning to settle down. She kept a rather low profile. To mourners, she showed a strangely wooden smile—a completely restrained half smile. But inside she died of frostbite—exceptionally tired.

There were other mourners who arrived; a far cry landed painfully on the ground on an elbow and rolled away. And there was an endless train of them coming in.

And with a sense of earned relief, the smooth-skinned Jael endeared enormous anger and bitterness. Maybe she felt that she had made a couple of glaring mistakes and that was the danger point. She wore a pair of dark shades and a striking black cap whose net covered her face; the white hand gloves matched her high-heeled shoes. A satisfactory foreign affairs plant. However, death had caused uncompensable damage—an irreversible plight. And the return to normal life is rather slow. Her eulogy was moving, especially from such a young lady; it presented itself as a cyclonic delivery—as a hopeless storm of feeling. And people accepted her cry with some aplomb.

Life is simply an experience. And I'd a share of it with Barack. Despite all that we have faced together, we attempt to go on. I believe it will take us a great deal of time to understand why this has occurred. Barack has been good and at the tail end, he was a loving father—full of promises and energy. I'd ridden with him—and everything seemed to lead to the dark and frightening future. I know my spirits keeled about wildly.

Although he had told me some sort of suffering before, Barack evinced bravery. He had been fixing assignments, and his zeal was unfailing. Even at the zenith of my low moments, Barack still had love for me in the heat of hard times, with a rather abstracted curiosity. We arranged to become real, although we were finally declared couples. In this relationship, it would be hollow or phony if I were to claim that there were no moments when things heated up.

I looked around and saw a sea of humanity. A handful of striped pants teenagers walked about like some youthful naval cadets on a mission. I particularly singled out a boy, maybe thirteen years old, bravely lugging a suitcase along. Behind him was a tall slender-looking man with a long nose and a bulky, heavily fleshed figure that cautiously spoke in pidgin English. He said to a group of mourners sitting under a shade that Barack was his friend. That he heard of his death while on a holiday in South Africa. That he's a Moscow born Russian but met my father in the United States. He said to the amazed villagers, 'You've lost a great man.'

I felt ashamed. I didn't know that my father was all this—a firm man and a good organizer, that he had no big worries that he seemed to be, and apparently was open-minded and listened to good advice. All these were people's opinion.

What I know he stood for—one just didn't show up—and I couldn't tell it at that particular time. I mean there were risks and promises without any rafts of amendments. That became the lynchpin of my belief. And to believe in a father few people misunderstood! My father would tell me, 'There is a drop of greatness in every man.' I liked that sentence; it opened dark corners of my understanding. It is now used by various drinking brands advertisers around the world—'There is a drop of greatness in every man.' I repeated more softly. I felt inseparable from that posture once again. My father said, 'We need to and should stop planning and start acting. The people are waiting for their leaders to act. This is a father who believed that there was no need of pouring money into a leaking bucket—nonstarting projects—or as many developing countries felt the scorching effect of depression or fell under the bliss of economic meltdown, my father would advice that there's no use of pouring good money after bad or that there wasn't good money or bad money. I didn't understand a thing. I thought he was tucked away in some sort of a pigeon hole. And his approaches, I'm made to believe, were so Westernized that most economists (who hadn't come of age) rejected its use.

That my father had people who believed in him and that he was primarily endowed with sufficient diplomatic knowledge to distinguish between bad and good economics—to me that looked like a pipe dream. I hadn't anticipated it. I didn't contemplate the fact that he'd a ubiquitous zeal about the power of determination. To me that was just a mere fact. Some of his colleagues joined the bragging club and who'd specialize in stories beginning with 'I' as follows:

> I made a turnaround at so and so company.
> I was the best in last year's listing.
> I made a massive . . .
> I won the most coveted award . . .
> I backed the fiscal plan . . .

My father served for his community and earned nothing out of it. An exemplary blow that left those with bragging rights gazing, and some of them never recovered. He didn't demand reciprocity after switching on various projects—all ended in a clinical finish.

He served as the secretary general of the Alego Welfare Development Association (AWDA), members of which one was Dr. Paul Oruo. I saw him more committed to this engagement and helped those in need at the expense of his own family. The old grandfather had complained several times that he continues to neglect his responsibility. But you see, he was just doing the right thing. Long time ago, thirty years ago, hyenas and vultures dug and ate the buried in the open fields—AWDA made him a decent burial.

2 p.m.
It was already cloudy and dark; the sky was completely covered by cirrus clouds.

4 p.m.
The procession went on to the graveside—the plain cypress coffin was firmly lowered into the grave.

The clergy from Ng'iya said, 'For Barack came from dust and so dust he shall go back to.' He prayed and Sheikh let out prayer as well.

And as men picked the spade to cover the casket (return the soil), when the grave was halfway filled, I knew, on the spot, that my father was no more. Those who were standing on top gave way. I compared the two graves, that of my grandfather and my father, and I was struck by remorse. Auma and Zeituni already were on their way, wailing toward the hut. Sarah and Akumu followed suit. Akumu particularly took my father's black suit and held it on her shoulder, mourning just started afresh.

I recalled the life we had gone through and looked back at the fresh grave; a man who was to shape K'Obama contemporary history was lying beneath the red earth already. His days in the surface of the earth were over. It was like 'dreams'. That day there was heavy downpour that sent everyone packing.

Twenty minutes later, Akumu kept mourning in the torrential rain. Her patterned *lesso* drenched; she was helped into the hut—a thought of dreams and special feelings about strong prediction or nightmares.

After a week, the home was deserted. Relatives and friends had gone back to their homes. It was a tradition for the close relatives to stay behind for a week or a month—in what they called the cleansing period.

CHAPTER 18

Epilogue

1983 . . . Kosele, Karachuonyo

Habiba Akumu Onyango (NyarNjoga)

In the year 1918, in Karabondi Village, Omollo Njoga was a happy father. The day was just normal, but in the third wife's stable was a child—a baby girl. A local elder says, 'Njoga was out on a fishing expedition at Lake Victoria when Akumu was born. It was at wee hours of the morning, and most men were still pulling the nets ashore. He was one of the fishermen. Immediately after she was born, her elder brother, Acholla, sent someone to go and get him. The messenger told Njoga, 'Your wife has given birth to a child—a baby girl.'

He knew his third wife was expecting a child—he had read the signs, anyway.

But he still asked sarcastically, 'Which woman?'

'Your third wife!'

He replied, 'Are you sure, young man?'

'Yes, I'm perfectly sure. I saw the child myself.'

Njoga abandoned the fishing net and rushed to the village. Actually things were all right.

Akumu's mother was Oleny Obwogi. People called her *Nyar* Toro, daughter of Toro. Njoga married her as his third wife. She hailed from Nyakach, Kadiang'a Clan—the land of *Omieri*. *Omieri* was a mysterious python similar to those of the tropical rain forest of Congo and Amazon that not only would come about during dry season but also would lay countless eggs that would hatch to more dangerous snakes. Omieri was known to live in the massive Odino waterfalls along River Sondu/Miriu. '*Omieri* or the raging water had consumed a number of ambitious tourists who went there,' an elder offered. People almost described Kadiang'a as a 'land of snakes'. The Kadiang'a Clan believed that the serpent brought rain because whenever it surfaced and suddenly disappeared, 'there would be heavy rainfall'. The python would eat goats and consume herdsboys but despite all these, the people still loved *Omieri* because of the rains. Womenfolk called her *Nyar go Omieri (*the lady from the land of the python, *Omieri*).

Akumu had a strong resemblance to her mother. The light-skinned, astute girl was just too hardworking, jovial, and respected her father so much. She humbly grew in this part of the village with good nurture. And always found herself besides Oleny, her mother. They had a lot to share; they learnt about the life that was indeed changing. They heard the stories of white people, and she told her daughter, 'They are mysterious people from the sea—people from the North Sea.'

Akumu grew knowing that whites weren't good people—'You should not meet them on your way. And if you do, run away.' So when they went to Gendia Mission for baptism, she came face-to-face with a snow-looking figure in some sort of waistcloth and without hesitation, she ran back to the village without getting dipped into the water. Akumu wasn't baptized, after all,' Hawa says.

Njoga, though a polygamous man, liked his daughter—at times he refused to let her visit the grandfather, Toro. When the mother complained, the old man would refute the claim, saying, 'My daughter might be swallowed by those pythons.'

Oleny would be dejected. 'You don't seem to understand that she needs to visit her grandfather.'

He would scoff, 'Did you hear that the snake ate another boy?'

'I'm tired of your lies.'

'Why don't you let the grandfather to come and see her, instead?'

Oleny found it hard to separate the two—Akumu and her father. And when a child is spoiled by the father's love, it may actually turn to something else, something almost irreversible.

So when Akumu arrived in Kanyadhiang as a second wife to Onyango Hussein; her role was, therefore, clearly defined. One thing that was completely conspicuous was being a wife vis-a-vis her tender age. At the age of *fourteen*, many pundits will argue that she was definitely too young for marriage. But the truth of the matter was that there were those who got married to much older men—those in their forties and fifties—who narrowed down on a twelve-year-old, maybe as a fourth or a fifth wife.

There was Halima Onyango, the first wife, and the rapport between the two was awesome. They quickly created a formidable sisterly love. And the bond seemed unbreakable. Halima never complained of a crowded relationship or that Akumu has emerged to take up her rightful place or her birthright. No! She accepted the situation as it was and, more so, learnt that it was necessary to coexist. Another point was that in five years, Halima had not given birth. An issue that irritated the council, and they felt that 'this is a taboo'. All these settled squarely on Halima—the unlucky one.

In 1934, forty-nine-year-old Onyango had a baby girl; during her birth, the already aging man found it ridiculous to nurse a child. He was already a relatively old—approaching fifty—but he seemed much younger and healthier. She was named Nyaoke after the grandmother Nyaoke *Nyachungo*. During this particular birth, Onyango was so moved; he had tears on his eyes. Sara was particularly dark-haired with a darker complexion, and her face was round like a potato. One stunning aspect is that she was already a beautiful girl. And as she toured the hut with her young eyes, she was pretty sure that life had started perfectly well—the rest she could not tell. They were just too rudimentary at that time.

She didn't know that she would be, one day, be a veiled woman, deep in Islam, buying wild asparagus from the local market and that on a warm tropical summer night, she will be leaving the medieval town of Kendu Bay for a rural village of Kogelo—when chaos erupts. Akumu brought fortune to the family. She had a large frame, looked convinced and fearless. She made the new family look a bit honoured and organized. Onyango had a say in the Council. In the capacity of a parent, he spoke and his comments were taken more seriously. In his many travels abroad, he knew Akumu would be in charge. She was amiable and not simple-witted, with an astonishing smile from a radiating face, like the map of the moon; she was caged in being responsible—the act that never replaced quarrel, that in exchange for order.

Offhand and repelling aggression, she raised and guarded Onyango's properties with keen interest, with a combat-ready force, especially, when she was the only one doing the administration. The qualities that fascinated many women was her aggressiveness, determination, and reserved character—every character was hard to miss, and it poured out into everyones' soul. And they talked about it all the time. Halima was from Kadem Village—a clan that was still struggling with the traditional beliefs—but she made it up, and she put up with Akumu pretty well. But she left moments later, and Akumu was downcast. Loneliness took toll of her.

On 18 June 1936, two years after Sara's birth, and when Akumu went to visit her mother Oleny, she delivered a child—a baby boy. The custom dictated that Onyango was to bring some goats in exchange for the mother and the child. Njoga stood his ground. So the boy was born at his grandfather's homestead. When Onyango went to negotiate their return, the boy was exactly three weeks old. And during the negotiation nuances, in an extremely frank talk, they all sat in a round circle with a couple of sour milk and clear liquor. The gourd was refilled here and then. They named him Barak—the 'blessed one'. The tradition dictated that after this assembly, Akumu was to stay at her maternal home for another week before taking full steps to rejoin the husband.

Life in Kanyadhiang Village was just pretty habitable until, after the eighth season, Sara Ogwel came over. Life took a twist, and everyone was just too uneasy. It proved difficult for Akumu to find her footing—like she sat on sinking sand, as if terrible fight would start almost immediately, and each swore never to give up on this. Although Akumu had complained of loneliness, this wasn't the kind of offer she was claiming to overcome. This is when Onyango let out anger, and he had disciplined each according to the standards of the time. He dealt with the probable reactions. It was inevitable to give it an insight visibly more eager to maintain harmony. Maybe Onyango feared deeply the potent division that would arise as a result of this quarrel. He begrudgingly accepted his 'blunder'. And this became the main subject of the fights—something irreversibly impossible. And they all descended to hatred, each spiteful of the other. Onyango found it very hard to face the unexpected—many things were at stake; indeed, it was too risky to change anything at that particular juncture. He took his new bride to Nairobi.

Akumu's relationship with Sara Ogwel was something that absolutely caused all the jitters on and on. It seemed like not about to spot any end—like the argument just gone berserk. And there was no efficient way he would stop them. Every inch of their life was a disagreement. Her life was not stable anymore, and this particularly cost both Onyango and the wives. Onyango thought it was not necessary to throw the gauntlet; however, the children felt lonely, and the endless squabbles made them seek second opinion. They felt that the family was too crowded—very much against their expectation. And indeed, they started to plan for an early exit.

In 1943, Akumu had a third born—Hawa Auma. The girl was born at a tumultuous time—during the reign of Colonial Chief, Paul Mboya. The firebrand local leader had set up a tribunal to investigate all the Alego Kamser living in Kanyadhiang Village. His main aim was to look for dissenters and most likely to send them back to Kogelo, the land of their forefathers. Hawa says, 'When they caught up with my father, in Alego Kamser, he demanded his land. In fact, he antagonized him to relent and give up the property. These are some of the issues that contributed partly to my mother's cold feet to embrace this affair, of course, coupled with the disagreement.'

When we went to Kogelo to live there, as our second home, my mother had already changed her mind. I remember her telling Nyaoke, 'We might be soon going back to Karabondi. This is not our rightful place.' Because of the abuse, the disrespectful cowife Sara Ogwel, and the harsh Onyango, who had not only stopped listening to her grievances but also kept prodding her peace. I felt cut off as much as she was isolated, and Barack was even worse off. He lamented and argued with the old man for his insults. It was a commonplace—whenever a new bride comes, everything changes!

One day, Akumu fought with Onyango; they exchanged bitterly, and it marked her exit. My younger sister, Zeinab Atieno, was just five days old. And after that particular exchange, she felt that Karabondi, my grandfather's place, was the immediate first stopover. I accompanied her. The three of us left unnoticed. She didn't inform anyone, including Nyaoke or Barack. And after two days of walking to Kisumu, we stayed at a relative's home for one more day. On the fourth day, we boarded a train to Kendu Bay.

Life just went on.

And living a husbandless life for the better part of her life—for close to one year—wasn't encouraging. There was this man, who used to come to transact business with my grandfather, Njoga. And I remember that he talked much about my mother—how beautiful she smiled and many other things. From the look of things, my mother liked him. His name was Salmin Otieno, a man from Kosele Village around Kosele. After eight months of stay, Salmin brought dowry, although he could not manage the forty herds that my father had paid earlier as dowry. So he brought what he could afford: a paltry fifteen head of cattle!

That marked a third migration to Kosele—twenty miles from Kendu Bay. Salmin was the second born in a family of six sons of Otieno Amollo. She was given vast land to till; she cultivated millet and cassava, and her basket was always full. Akumu would gather herself to work since like it was her last chance to prove that she indeed was a wife of substance. One thing that amazed me was how she became fond of that farming—the millet farming. She always sent me to Kogelo to take vegetables and cassava there. She knew her children were never in good shape and that she hoped to be able to fend for them at all cost.

I took care of Zeinab most of the time; she was always in her fields, chasing a way the birds or fencing the farm off from wild animals.

Meanwhile, I was the key person here connecting her with the Kogelo family. Back then, my stepmother was always anti-Akumu. She hated my guts by the fact that I could go all the way to Kosele to bring grains. I became a conduit. I took an obligation to know what was happening between the divide and report accordingly. My father sometimes gave me some thorough beatings, saying 'Why do you have to run up and down like a pregnant deer. What do you want?' I was indeed shuttling between Kogelo and Kosele—almost after a fortnight.

When Barack had joined Maseno, my mother went to visit him at the school, and I remember the Principal Mr Bowers asking her, 'Are you the mother? Or who is the exact mother of the boy? You look different. The boy looks more of a blackboard than you are!'

I was amazed by how he was able to speak fluently in *Luo*, and his rhetoric was amazing.

She brought him sweet potatoes, porridge, and sugarcane, and as they shared the meal under a tree within the school compound, grief took toll of them. Barack was so angry, and he would shed tears. He knew that our mother wasn't happy and that she was working harder to feed both her children and those scattered elsewhere. They discussed a number of issues, and all ended with tears rolling about.

When Nyaoke was married in Kanyaluo Village, rumors had it that it's Dorsila who made the marriage possible, and from the look of things, my mother didn't like any of us being too close to some of her extended family from the way he was treated. The impression was that you shun them completely. One day, we were informed that Halima had passed on, and we all went to mourn her. My mother, Zenaib, and I went to pick up Nyaoke at her new home. We all took a deserved journey to Kadem Village in the outskirts of Homa Bay Township. Halima had been sickly from what was believed to be a miscarriage, but she was already an old woman past her menopause. How could she experience a miscarriage? I asked myself.

For the first time and indeed, this was my day; Akumu came face-to-face with Onyango. He had come for the burial, and I saw remorseful smile from both sides, the handshake warm, but the guilt was eminent, and I breathed to see each accept one another. It was odd to watch them act so rapacious. They spoke candidly although for a short while because my stepmother, Sara Ogwel, was about to unleash some terror, as if someone was about to take Onyango from her. I still believed in keeping hands free during peacetime. Her rising discomfort was absolutely there. Halima was laid to rest. I like the fact that she died at peace with everyone; everybody came to show his or her affection and love. And as the mourners dispersed, there was little to do or to be preoccupied with. Immediately, we left for Kosele—and the Kogelo people had gone back; Akumu gave birth to a baby boy—Amir Jamal Otieno. Zeinab was four years old. My stepfather Salmin made us a party; he slaughtered a rooster. Jamal was a jovial boy; maybe he had been showered by the blessing from the grandfather—Otieno Amollo.

In her life, she knew that Nyaoke, Barak, Hawa, Zeinab, Amir, and Razik were all from her womb, but with two different men. And that was her strongest belief.

When Razik came, I moved to Kogelo. My father wanted the two of us—Zeinab and I—back in Kogelo. My mother only agreed to release me. My sister was too young to live away from her. I hope she wasn't hardheaded.

The bleeding truth was that when Akumu was introduced to the rigors of being responsible, quietly her attention started drifting from being a child anymore. She could be seen ever busy, herding goats or lifting bundles of firewood from the forest, or a basket of sardine from the shore; in her chores she never gave up doing perfect work. She busied with house duty—it was rare truth to see her playing endlessly like most village girls did. Her timing was spectacular, and she always did her duty with diligence. And this particular diligence made her feel good. And doing her work in time made her feel comfortable.

She grabbed respect, buzzed in understanding, and started looking absolutely beautiful, sprucing herself at thirteen.

Akumu was a full-grown girl then. And Njoga was already receiving suitors in private. But he knew that it wasn't yet time, and she won't go anywhere—the good attributes that almost prompted him to prepare her. It was time to get things ready. A lot of memories oozed out like a fresh cut beginning to bleed again. He was going by himself to protect Akumu from unnecessary early marriage, although she was already showing signs of early departure. At times it was impossible to find the words on which to send off unsuitable suitors. Njoga found it absolutely hard to give reasons or relay regret—amidst those fleeting moments. Oleny kept numb. She forgot everything and anything except what was happening to her daughter. Suitor after suitor, all went back empty-handed—the first one, the second, the third and even the eleventh. The lady had not even reached the proper age of seventeen. Those who came with pounding excitement that went on and on until they were turned down—all went empty-handed. Njoga believed that she would always get someone. And deep in her primordial thinking, she'll not remain a suspect. As if she was a slave to something she had never known, and it was time to learn some of these things. That was an aspect that brought the iota of conviction. They had returned to their homes, shaken up.

Akumu was saddened by the turn of events. Maybe she felt that her father's disapproval sounded hollow.

Four Years Later

Salmin Orinda Otieno and Akumu Habiba had a child. Zeinab was already growing pretty fast. Amir Jamal Otieno was the firstborn in the newly found reunion between the two. Salmin spoke with a rumbling raspy voice. He wasn't at pain to accept her and her two children, Hawa and Zeinab.

Although, Hawa would leave the family at some point in time to join her father Onyango in Kogelo. But Zeinab Atieno remained with stepfather Salmin, and her half brother, Amir, less than nine years old.

Onyango called Auma (Hawa) with convenient assurance of a personal relationship—and with a cool tone. She was his daughter anyway. And he was keen not to undergo life Akumu had chosen—a completely new home.

Njoga died in this year 1955. And Oleny was widowed. The unfortunate death caused outrage and fury in Akumu's heart. Maybe she complained why misfortune comes to her in pulses. Why was there no reprieve in her stormy life? And why herself alone and not other women she sees around?

Onyango knew well enough that he had lost Akumu, but there were some aspects that still connected them—the children, and more so, Barack. Fathers regarded boys other than girls. And a woman with your son deserved respect and consideration that was pretty firmly supported by custom.

So the lucky Amir received his half brother Barack—a two-year-old boy knew nothing about the historic meetings but older people knew that meeting was necessary. Maybe they described it a distant prospect of coming face-to-face with a brother—not a distant relative. They made it rustic awe. Akumu believed that Barack coming together with Kezia was something that will remain like a blood clot in her heart. My mother knew of this union before anybody else. Barack took Kezia to Kosele before they sneaked to Nairobi.

Amir had (close to) a ferret nose for Barack; he connected with his brother, and later at thirteen he lived with Barack in Nairobi.

1988

Hawa says thus:

My mother heard about Barack Jr's coming that her grandson was in the country. She knew that time has come to renew her long-lost hope after her son's brutal death. And she knew her troubled heart would have received an overhaul of hope. And this extravagant desire didn't bear any fruit. Her determination to meet her grandson just went astray. And visibly aware that everyone knew she was just around deteriorated her feelings. When Barack Jr stepped in Nairobi, she received the news that he was to come to Kendu Bay and maybe proceed to see her at Kosele—twenty miles away. This glut expectation came at the thick of exploring ways to consolidate her family. I told her that Barack Jr would visit. I believe her sugar levels had gone down upon learning that the grandson was well received in Kogelo and was enjoying precious time with the step grandmother. Akumu knew that she found the Obamas capable of sustaining meaningful conversations. She attempted to go to Kogelo. But she thought it would amount to a heartening cry to avoid things like heartbreak. Behind the scenes, Barack's visit increasingly pitted Akumu to sham; she felt cutoff and knocked out, which culminated into a series of startling revelations. Her wait descended to disappointment almost mythical, like some slow-burning doom.

My mother felt like a young woman, runaway, whose character is under scrutiny and her intentions under close censor. It made her feel out against the simmering contradiction. The little mother of six almost came face-to-face with her grandson in Kendu Bay. When Barack arrived in Kendu Bay, Akumu was there as well. She saw the grandson, but he didn't sense or had a clue that his own grandmother was three meters away. Akumu kept mum and that was it. The first time she came to know her American grandson. At that satisfying range, her stake went up. She met the grandson with whom she could share a history. In a split of an hour, she went to Kosele a happy woman. And that was a great influence—the sight, because of the delightful latest entry to her life. It became one of her refreshing time in the midst of scaffolding events. Akumu later said, 'I wish I would meet him. I meant to talk to him. And tell him, "I'm happy to see you. You remind me of my son, Barack—who was your father. It is already too late, but I hope it would have been an exciting story."'

Sara Nyaoke told her of Barack's visit at Kariokor. That she would have liked him to come and see her at Kosele. That Barack was indeed her biological son and that her grandson must have got blessings from her as well. Nyaoke spoke to Akumu in a rather intrusive manner, full of bitterness. As if she had stocked all these in her heart for decades.

That night as she held her kerosene lamp, Akumu's happiness was sincerely predictable; for decades, she said, she hadn't felt the same. But one thing kept her firmly triumphant. The grandson was just a stone throw away. And she had the liberty to break away to look for him. In his bungled tight schedule, he could have spared some time to offer her an audience. Hawa shares these sentiments. I would like to meet him before I die. See, my mother, Akumu, tried but failed. I don't want to face the same trauma at the time of death, when death knocks at my door. I think that would be a day of fleeting joy—way above my conventional expectation. My mother's story became a real fable as each bit of the truth unravels. Nyaoke was always on her side, illuminating the essence of staying strong after years of toil and disappointment. It was evident that Akumu had stridden the roughest road ever and wallowed in the pitfalls of hardships.

Some things just happen by accident. Barack visited me at my house in Kendu Bay Township. And everything just smothered so well. He met the biological aunt.

My mother fell ill in 2000. I accompanied her to Nairobi for treatment. Everybody drummed up support to cater for her hospital bills. Nyaoke offered her all her time and money and sheltered her for the entire stay. Rita and all the family members offered funds toward her maintenance at the Kenyatta National Hospital. I was taking care of her at the women's ward—took a sense of responsibility to take care of her; she was eighty-two. Her health became a complex situation as doctors tried helplessly to bring down her sugar level. Despite the hopeless impelling thoughts, I still volunteered to keep her company. It was so humbling and noble to me. I felt young again, like a child. One morning, the sun seemed pitiless as we boarded Akamba bus back to Kisumu en route to Kosele. However, she wasn't in good shape and still needed some serious night vigil. She wanted somebody by her side, and we took a matatu to Kendu Bay—a rather sleepy automobile that caused all the discomfort. It was in a sorry state. The matatu was so cranky that even the band that played from the dusty radio sounded so weary. To us we were used to these other than walking. When we got to Kosele—thirty minutes later—she fanned herself with an old newspaper. That night, Amir and Razik brainstormed until the midnight; their mother wasn't surviving the diabetes—and ostensibly to try other avenues. Whispers spread across that Akumu's life wasn't that good, but she vowed to fight on. She couldn't give up, having gambled all this while. But Akumu's life continued to record bad gains. For three years, she sought for proper treatment.

At one time—on a rainy day of 24 May 2003—she was admitted at Gendia Mission hospital. Amir took her there in a taxi. She was in a really critical condition. The poor son was frightened and unnerved. He lost his bland smile. On 25 May, the doctor in charge bowed with a shy smile, cheerlesly, and broke the sad news of her death. Akumu passed on at the daybreak of that fateful day. Word went round. As a Muslim believer, Akumu's burial preparations were on top gear moments after her death.

She was laid to rest in Kosele.

Sara Nyaoke (aunt of Barack Obama Jr)

She was born in 1934 at Kanyadhiang Village in Karachuonyo to Onyango Hussein and Habiba Akumu. The firstborn in a family of three: Barak, Hawa, and Zeinab. Nyaoke spent most of the time babysitting Barak and Hawa before administering the same care to Omar and Zeituni. In this manner, she never got the opportunity to go to school. She spent most of her teen years at Kogelo Village.

And it's reported that she was the best friend of Onyango before he was taken ill and died. Most of Onyango's property was written in her name.

At seventeen, in 1949, she found her first husband in Kanyaluo Village, Karachuonyo, when she was sent there to visit Dorsila, Onyango's sister. She didn't stay at her aunt's for long before being lured off by a man for a hand in marriage. After a year, in 1950, she gave birth to a baby boy, who died days later.

The marriage went to the rocks after a short time, and she was forced out of it by the growing mistrust; she couldn't continue putting up with a cheating husband. First, she went to live with the mother, Akumu, in Kosele, but since this was no longer her real home, Onyango sent word that 'if she wanted to be alive, then she must report to him immediately.' She carried her belongings and went to Kogelo. Nyaoke stayed for a while in Kogelo, but the pressure was too much. She wanted to have her own independence, in her own way, to have a husband figure around her. Again, she went away and was married by another man in Kano, a muddy, hot, and unattractive land with little food—the population depending mainly on subsistence farming. During the dry season, the land was inhabitable, and cattle died in the open field due to hunger and lack of water. Onyango knew that his daughter couldn't live in such an environment; it was too harsh for human habitation, especially, in this case, she was his daughter. He even refused to take up the excuse that 'she shall adapt'. And he had refused the dowry. So six years in Kano with two children and no trace of dowry was a hard hurdle; in 1957, she joined Barack in Nairobi . . . she lived with her brother in a tiny tin-house at Ofafa Jericho. During this time, one of her children passed on and the other became seriously ill. This also marked the time when she started manning her father's small fragment plots at Huruma and Kariokor. The troubled times taught her one way of surviving to be an entrepreneur. In totality, Nyaoke had ten children—nine boys and a single girl, in her entire life.

Abubakar Otieno was the eldest of the boys. He has since passed on. Musa Ouma is the third born, although he was born when some of his siblings had passed on. He works with the Teachers' Service Commission as a head teacher in Homa Bay. The sturdy-looking man with a friendly voice shuttles between Homa Bay and Nairobi. His family is settled in Homa Bay Township. Musa loves his teaching profession and normally shuns politics; he believes in capacity building through imparting knowledge to Kenyans.

Rajab Ouko grew up in Huruma—the Eastland sprawling district of Nairobi. He schooled and married here. The jovial man with a sharp look is currently an employee of Kenya Forestry Service; his family lives in Eldoret Town, although he works in Nairobi after being transferred from Eldoret. Rajab is a regular traveler between the two cities, shuttling between the towns either on a work duty or while on holiday with the family. Rehema Awuor is the only surviving girl and the eldest in the family. The rest of the girls had since died. She lives and does business in the coastal city of Mombasa, Kenya. Rehema, unlike Musa, loves politics and talks fondly of her cousin, Barack Jr, the President. 'He is a good man, kind, and down to earth. I think, given a chance, he will turn around the economy of that country. I'm a businesswoman, and I know the steps to economic downturns. She is fond of one of her children called Saida.

Sara's low moment came in 2000 when one of her sons was shot dead at the Huruma Grounds. The armed officers knocked at the wee hours of the morning in their low-roofed shanty. They broke the iron door and dragged Idi out. While he was resisting arrest, he was shot and died at Kenyatta Hospital three hours later. In that particular arrest, George was also arrested. The young boys had fallen into crime. 'They were petty criminals, who would terrorize residents of Huruma and Mathare slums with machete and batons,' the police claimed. As Idi died at the referral Hospital, George was charged for robbery with violence and restlessness. A policeman said, 'His accomplice tried to flee and we laid ambush and, at the grounds, we shot him. He is recuperating at the hospital.' Little did he know that the man is dead! A witness said, 'The boys had been framed. That I know.' Although there is a gang masquerading as vigilante group calling themselves 'black mamba', George and Idi weren't part of it.

The death of Nyaoke

Hawa narrates:

5 July 2007

The doctor arrived at the ward. The Kenyatta National Hospital was teeming with sick people on wheel chairs and their relatives romping behind. Nyaoke had suffered a lot with unknown illness. The doctor attending to her had hands and build of a worker, without any hint of condescension; he wasn't sure of her survival. As I sat cross-legged on her bedside, I knew that her battle had lost vigor. I cried; she was the only one left in our family. And I started recounting the damages.

I felt that the world was restraining us from enjoying its fruits that it exerted some of its autocratic tendencies on each of us. Of course, on different measures—the death of my brother, my sister Atieno, and now Nyaoke battling cancer.

And I repeatedly ask, 'What of me? When will I join them?'

The doctor had advised me to look for a rather specialized treatment; maybe she could survive on life support system, while the diagnosis was underway. We had discussed this matter more closely. And everyone had a share of his or her opinion. But, of course, her very life dwindled; the disease was quickly eating her up.

On 6 July 2007, I woke up very early to catch a *matatu* from Huruma to town and then proceed to the hospital. Last night, I'd left her in a pretty jovial mood, and one of the nurses promised that 'she was now improving'. She had taken a cup of homemade porridge after days of poor appetite. I thought that the time to start improving had just begun. That night I assured Musa and Rehema that their mother was absolutely fine and that she would be with them again. Little did I know that she was pronounced dead a couple of hours later after I had left the facility! I was in a sorry state. Doctors' attempts to reach us were futile. I had to meet the rude shock myself. I found a different face at the bedside, a different patient. She wasn't Nyaoke.

I asked the guardian: Where is my sister?

I was overwhelmed with fear, and as I raced out, I remember her replying, 'Have no idea!' I wasn't sure exactly what she answered but something of the sort.

At the reception, I was directed to the hospital morgue. My sister, Nyaoke, had died.

Fifteen years later, after my brother's death and eighteen after my father's death, the shadow of death visited again; this time claiming the only surviving sibling.

I found myself fumbling in the streets of Nairobi to Huruma.

I went from one bus stop to the next, almost forgetting everything, through Tom Mboya Street back to Moi Avenue. I sat on one of the erected council seats at Kencom, completely blank and unaware of what was going on. I watched the sea of humanity going left and right. They were talking endlessly. And they stirred a cloud of dust that settled on my bare feet. I only realized that I didn't have footwear much later. I got courage and tumbled right to the *matatu*. I didn't even ask where it was heading to until I heard a tout shout 'Huruma hapa! Mbao mbao! Masaa!'

It was exactly nine thirty. We continued to receive heartfelt condolences from family and friends—the burial arrangement was underway. Relatives thronged her tiny house at the shanties of Huruma. At eleven forty five, the body was leaving for Kariokor Muslim Cemetery. This is where my sister's body was interred.

After the burial, we exchanged pleasantries, and we had time to laugh so that tears rolled down our cheeks. Each one of us brought a share of their experience with the departed. We assembled for an early supper. As I peered into the cooking pot, I realized that we've lost a good cook as well. My mother, Sara, Yusuf, Said, Malik, Auma, Amir, Razik, and many others, all approached the table and the meal was just good. Everyone agreed.

I remembered the young tout. He looked city-grown and kept shouting loudly in broken *Swahili*, what they called *Shen'g*—a slang language of English and *Swahili* mix. He wore a plus fours underpants, and he looked as if he'd spent his entire life in a bad state. The young teenager looked strong. However, his eyes were absolutely yellow or may be hit by highland malaria. And he sounded like a strangled man. I liked him because he behaved kindly to me.

Ezra Obama

'Call me "Obeid" anytime. I won't complain and I wouldn't ignore.' That's my name, and the name the President of the United States knows. However, this man Obeid is an Anglican with over a decade behind the pulpit. Meet Ezra Ogosa Obama aka Obeid. He's a jovial, bold, dark-complexioned five feet in height and one who has been in the shadow of Barack for most of his formative years—a fact he doesn't dispute. A bit spiritual, when Barack died, I knew we lost not only a hard worker but also a shrewd leader. He was our torchbearer. And when he died, the torch (the sole source of our light) also vanished. We felt cut out from the litten world and thrown into full darkness as if someone was turning off every light of our lives. However, a bigger and a better light has emerged through his son, the President. My many worries have since gone. I'm in another flipside of understanding that everything is possible.

I was born in Kendu Bay to my late father Blasto Adhiambo, son of Obama K'Opiyo and Mama Nyabolo. That was on 12 July 1950. I started schooling at Kanyadhiang Primary for my elementary at tender age; the teacher almost sent me back home the first day—he thought I was underage. But my father insisted saying that I'm just a tiny creature and nothing else, and that had nothing to do with my age. Of course, some of my colleagues were sent back home basically because they failed a simple test—'What's your name?'

Kanyadhiang Primary was a muddy school; classrooms were suffocating from mud and sucking wetland. We continued anyway.

When I passed the Common Entrance Examination, CEE, a new opportunity arose at Gendia Intermediate. I have to note that CEE served as a sieve that separated the 'chaff from the grains'. A number of the boys failed and joined fishing. Therefore, my achievement was remarkable. Barack had already come around and following our talk, all my eyes were now set on him.

In 1965, I sat the Kenya African Preliminary Education Examination and passed with 2As in mathematics and English and a credit in general paper. The same thing that happened at CEE repeated itself. And most boys once again were disappointed at the results. I didn't care much since my side was kind of safe and that sort of confidence lifted me to Nairobi in 1966 through an invitation. I lived with my elder brother, Rueben Abong'o, the flamboyant brother put up in the sprawling Maringo Estate in Eastlands. Barack was already settled back in Kenya after studies in Harvard. He invited me at his residence in the leafy suburb of Upper Woodley Estate, Adam's Arcade.

He advised me to take up a correspondence course at the New Nairobi Private School and GN School for A-Levels. And when I enrolled, daily commuting became so hard that I had to shift to his house full-time. The house was similarly full as well; there was the wife, Ruth, youthful Rita (Auma), Roy, Zeituni, and I; believe me or not, that was an already congested house, but no one realized or raised it the issue. To me he was more of a brother than a cousin but more remarkable was the fact that I was a son to him. Maybe I felt as a child under his roof. Or maybe the way he treated me that made the difference.

When Barack got an accident in 1971, we'd spoken a minute before. I was at my new work station at Coca Cola Bottling Co. in Industrial Area. An hour later, I was informed of his grisly accident and the white man who perished in the wreckage. I went to Kenyatta National Hospital. We talked briefly, and later, I rushed to the traffic police station to follow up the case. Here Barack stayed for months before being discharged. And the damage that surrounded his life was more of an accident than a preconceived matter. Even in his hospital bed, he still insisted I bring the children to his side. That aside, a year later when he had left the facility, I remember when he asked me to take Mark and David to the village to see the grandfather. These were some of the times he would be so busy at work, and no one would be there to take the boys to the rural. Of course, Ruth would remain in the city. I boarded the Lolwe bus, Mark and David romping behind me. Previously, at the bus station, passersby asked me where I was taking the white children—the children they called *wazungus*. I answered rudely, 'I'm taking them to their white father.' Some laughed, and others looked at me and said nothing.

I spent time with them in the village, in Kogelo and Kanyadhiang; they played with mud and roasted corn. I think they liked the setting even without their father around them. This is where they belonged. Their home and a place they called cradle of their forefathers.

During the return journey, we walked to the Oginga Odinga rural home to take the bus. The opposition leader received us so warmly and instructed his daughter, Akinyi, to sort us out. She took us to Muga, the General Manager of Lolwe buses—this was their business. Mr Muga would then take us to the driver en route to Nairobi with clear instruction to hand us over to Barack or whoever Barack would have sent to pick us up at the country bus. That's how caring this man was.

I became the employee of Coca Cola, a company that has modeled me to who I am at the moment. Barack always encouraged me saying, 'My brother, you know what's expected of you, so maintain that elusive integrity, honesty, and high-level transparency.' I credit him for informing me to start a degree. He got me application forms from a foreign college in London, where I took a diploma degree in public relations, and three years later, a diploma in sales and marketing. As I focus on the past, Barack was a pillar and a beacon, not only for us—the family—but to relatives and friends as well.

I remember him through his sons and his only daughter, Auma. I believe they hold a strand of his character that is manifested in each of them. I haven't forgotten all that he did for me—how he shaped me and how well he treated his children. He took us to exotic places for holidays and made us believe to appreciate good life and healthy living. We swum at North Coast, coast resorts in Mombasa, and visited Kilifi beaches. He booked us at Hilton and InterContinental Hotels for dinners.

In retrospect, I treated his family with love. I offered the young boys Roy, Said, and Abo jobs at Coca Cola whenever they were out on holidays so that they can save for their pocket money. I treated them well to the best of my ability and position.

I have been very close with this family as if Barack mandated me to. When Roy completed his accounting studies from the University of Nairobi and out of a job, I told him to apply for a job at an auditing firm, Delloitte. I learned of the vacancy through a long-time childhood friend at Woodley, Edward Ouko. His father was a doctor, Ouko Njenga, from Ugenya. Currently Edward works at African Development Bank. Roy convinced the panelists, and among the many applicants, he was employed at the accounting department, where he made a remarkable progress.

When Barack Jr came over to Kenya to learn about his African roots, I met him. They visited my house together with his aunties and siblings. We had plenty of drinks and foods. At the end of day-long partying, I took them to Huruma and Mathare on my company pickup. From the side mirror, I could see him smiling all through, from the back of the car, meaning he enjoyed the ride. He depicted a serious picture of a simple man to the point of being a mere ordinary personality.

And even when he clinched the Illinois seat, we flew to the United States to congratulate him. We booked at a hotel. I remember, I didn't spend there because I had gone to visit a long-time friend, who happened to be his father's friend, in Virginia, who felt he shouldn't be left behind at such a crucial moment. The following day, I was back and the senator arrived under heavy security. There was Michelle, Malia, and Sasha. We had breakfast that everyone enjoyed. I had a small talk with the senator, the wife, and the children. Also conspicuously present was Kalisha Page, his personal aide and special assistant. She was amazing.

I live a quiet life in Kenya, although I regularly visit abroad purely on business engagements. I have two homes: one in the city at Ongata Rongai and the other in the rural Migori County, where I practice farming. I keep dairy animals and chickens, and I do plant food crops. If things change, I may start cash-crop farming, which is a major income earner at the moment.

I'm married with three children. I love these children because they have made my life work toward the right direction. I schooled them, gave them the best education, and now they are reaping the benefits. They all schooled at All Saints Cathedral kindergarten, and then they moved to Catholic parochial School, almost at the same time.

Humphrey Ochieng', my firstborn and his brother, George Were (last born), both went to Nairobi School. Humphrey took Business Management Degree at Baraton University and once worked at East African Breweries Limited. Recently, he works at AccessKenya, an IT company (during this interview, he calls Humphrey to confirm). George Were is an Information Technology expert in Atlanta, Georgia. My only daughter, the source of my happiness, is Angela Auma. She schooled at Our Lady of Mercy. The jovial Angel is a practicing advocate, here in Nairobi.

That's my family—a happy family to be precise.

On top of parenting responsibilities, I offered to be a community organizer. This came when I retired from the soft drink company, CocaCola. I had risen to a corporate affairs manager after deputizing Joshua Okuthe for a while. That came in 2000. Currently, I serve as the fundraising chairperson of Kenya Freedom from Hunger—a nongovernmental organisation. I'm also the chair of Kenya Anglican Men Association, Kajiado Branch, Ongata Rongai Self-Help Group, and Obama Opiyo Foundation. These aren't the only caps that I hold. I have a huge responsibility for mankind. I can't mention all.

He quotes Barack's favorite tagline:

> 'Maybe it is better to have something perfunctorily done than none at all.'

Obeid drives around the town, where he is simply known as chairman, in an OPEL-made German gray metallic car registration KAE 991E. A happy man with a sense of humor is a friend to many. He says that this car serves him well. It takes me around and sometimes comfortably ferries my family to the village.

Zeinab Atieno

In striding the memory lane, donkeys in hard labour and bicycle taxis braving the baking sun, girls wearing wire ring in their punctured noses, and carts pulled by long striding donkeys, there was once this girl called Zeinab Atieno, a Muslim girl, with her long-lost love after she was married to pastor Enos' son Bahabu Odhiambo. The Muslim men had their beards and hair red with henna; the Christian men had their hair cut low. They spoke with some unfamiliar voice—voice she'd be happy to contend with; she busied herself into fixing or rather plugging in this background, heavily overcrowded with Christian material.

Zeinab was brought in from the previous relationship between Onyango and Akumu. Atieno lived with Akumu in Kanyadhiang after they left Kogelo. And later found another father Salmin Otieno. At eighteen, she was married to Bahabu. From a Muslim background to a Christian family was one aspect that really caused her a bitter confusion. But later, she adopted pretty well. She did not see any difference, after all. Pastor Enos called her Atieno because Zeinab is Islamic. A decade later, after the death of Bahabu (Atieno's husband), she also fell sick and died; Kanyaluo Village was masked in grief—young couples lived off their marriage, leaving three orphans at a tender age. They felt terribly alone.

An elderly said, 'She'd been buried here three days after her sudden death. They had barely enough life together. The lives of children left behind are a matter of dispute, like curse falling out of the sky. How will they live? Skid into the poverty lane? It's ridiculous! He picked his way strutting on top of a conglomerate of sand bugged terrain.' He mumbled something. 'In spite of the spite, Atieno faced the cruelty of life head-on, and she was doused into that cruelty.' As he clambered up an anthill, from the sunset rays, the old man is just too sure about the orphans' predicament, a darkening bloom that becomes his tomb. Their lives are uncertain. And all this uncertainty isn't ending soon.

Rita Auma Obama

My sister Auma was born in 1960 at Pumwani Maternity Hospital. A year after my father had gone to the United States. Her life started in Nairobi where we stayed with my mother, Kezia. Our life was not yet out of the wood yet. Our father was in America. Upon his return, we stayed in Rosslyn, and then Hurlingham before shifting to Woodley estate. Auma was well-mannered, neighborly; she wasn't that nervous creature, excitable, and restless, but determined and alert. She had a careful judgment, and my father liked her for this and for that. And she was consulted on this or that, on matters within the house and outside. Maybe she was a woman ready for an uphill struggle like she is in a hurry to fix a policy. My father believed her in conversations, and his comments about her oratory were beginning to get under her young skin at a tender age of five. I watched her in disbelief—in fascination. And 'she was the only child wondering about tomorrow'—that according to the old man. She became his domestic consultant. Auma joined me at Kilimani Primary School from Maryhill Girls' School. One thing I noted about her was her fierce independence and resolve. She couldn't let boys tease her; I know she would put them in a spin and kept the bully girls at an arm's length. Maybe her oratory skills and defense was her secret weapon. Of course, she was just as skinny as a needle. And so tiny, one could squeeze her between the fingers. We would walk to and from school along Kirichwa Road across the busy Ngong' Road through Adam's Arcade to our home in Woodley Estate. I guess my father wanted Auma and me to learn to live just like other school-going children, also from well-to-do families, but appreciate the basics of life.

The same applied in the evening; although the school bus was available, my father didn't trust our safety in that bus. The writing at the back 'We provide safety for your children' didn't make any meaning to him. So he made it a tradition to let us walk. To me that was the life I knew. I thought that I wasn't the son of a doctor of my father's caliber. Again I felt that he was overdoing it. I wanted Auma to learn to live just like other school-going children, also from well-to-do families.

We lived with my stepmother, something Auma didn't like. First, we had our own mother in the same city, and she found it ridiculous to live away from her without a concrete reason. Second, Ruth wanted space, I presumed, to nurture her children in her own way. She had tried but things didn't turn out like she had hoped. Every mother would love to live her private life. Our presence was like a hindrance, and I saw it when things heated up summed up in the phrase 'blood is thicker than water.' We had started out well, but things had changed. Ugly words would pass and accusations were labeled, especially on trail to put issues straight. I was cornered most of the time: Roy did this, Roy spoiled the toilet paper holder, and Roy went out with the bike. But Auma was sternly behind me—something my father described as a 'coup plot'. Sometimes my father's behavior became so unworkable, Auma would cool him down. When he announced gloatingly each week that life wouldn't be normal if a week passed without a finger, I called them dark-horse chances.

When she finished her primary schooling, she joined Kenya High School. She had 'blown up' the examination, and my father bragged about his daughter's achievement to his close friends.

'See, this girl has consumed the paper, whole.'

'I told you that this is not discouragement, like these other girls I see around with babies slung off their backs even before they finish their mandatory studies. I don't discourage parents—but my child has made me proud. See, she's a determined success story.'

Life in the new school had its own limitations—school fees, the bragging father who would come to visit empty-handed, as if he had the bragging rights.

In Kenyatta University, along Thika Road, I believed that sometime later, in a short while, Auma would be a beacon of hope. She took BA Education at the university for a few semesters and later found herself filling scholarship forms for a German Course. My sister learned German at Goethe Institute in Nairobi at the age of seventeen and that's where she came across the DAAD scholarships (a German Academic Exchange Service). In 1980, she went to Germany. At first, my father didn't approve of her ambition but that cold feet later waned off when he discovered that it was a worthy course. And that she was too determined not to grab the offer and learn the foreign language. She studied German at the University of Heidelberg from 1981 and graduated with a Magister Artium degree in 1987. She has been in West Germany for a while in the town of Heidelberg, Berlin, and Bayreuth. I believe she loves politics and held political sermons at SPD affiliated Friedrich Ebert Foundation, where she has been described as an intelligent and cosmopolitan individual. Auma has been an educationist; she got her doctorate at the University of Bayreuth. In her dissertation, she tackled the concept of labour in Germany and its reflections on the market. She has been a lecturer in university of Nairobi, at the Goethe Institute and at the Carl Duisberg Society. An ambitious Rita has been a street hustler as well, doing the odd jobs that, to her, are a source of inspiration and a pedal of her passion. She has worked as a supermarket attendant, in hospitals, and as an interpreter at fairs and exhibitions in both Kenya and Germany. The ups and downs had equally balanced her life. The xenophobic attacks almost dashed her hopes. Her low moments, she recalls, came when she spoke to the asylum seekers at a hostel in Lubeck.

And how about when she campaigned for the president at Iowa and New Hampshire? Or when she visited her brother at his office in the White House?

Obeid says that when Barack died, his daughter, Rita, was in Germany but came the following day or two days after. And I believe she's one person who was more shocked because the whole thing came as a surprise. She made arrangement to come to Kenya. It was the trying time for all of us. His death was unexpected, and by all means, we felt robbed of someone who would turn our lives inside out because he was truly a genuine man. And he thought of best! Best! Best! things.

Auma's book, *Das Leben kommit daswischen*, talks about her life and the experience she had and shared with the president of the United States of America. The book released in Germany was a culmination of a heart finally pouring out the truth and the desires of the particular soul. Auma speaks candidly and wonders how life can just be so amazing, with quick turn of events, miracles that come forth, and how we should appreciate people and live with love and tolerance.

Auma serves as East African Coordinator for the AID Organisation Care in Kenya. A published author (alongside Wilfried Lemke), my sister, in an interview with Beckmann, a German journalist, said, 'Somehow there are three souls in my heart—an African, a German, and an American.' Of course, that's her—my sister Rita.

Zeituni Onyango (Abon'go)

The role of Zeituni in this book is very significant. Her relationship with Barack opens the secrets that we did not know between the two. One Zeituni grew simultaneously as Barack's daughter and as a sister. With all the immense powers, in the presence of Zeituni, Barack just considered himself an apparatus. It was Zeituni who became his adviser on issues of family affairs. The bond that existed between the two was extraordinary. That kind of sister that he got was hard to find. His powers remained fixed and limited, maybe because he had other desires and concentration.

The little girl grew at the village, learning the basics of life. At some point, she schooled at Nyang'oma primary school. Upon completing her elementary studies, she joined Ng'iya Girls, but Barack called her to join him in the city after realizing that Ng'iya wasn't in her liking. There was the sucking wet earth, poor facilities, without the benefit of doubt she was absolutely stung. Zeituni came to Nairobi and enrolled at Ngara Girls—at the time a day school in the heart of the capital, Nairobi.

From the village foundation where she'd pottered around the compound, feeding chickens and having field day with other animals to the bustle of Nairobi—the rush, the traffic, and some sense of responsibility. She started juggling with computer programmes and secretarial studies—some of which accepted and some of which had snarled down. After all, she'd something to work on. Zeituni helped her brother draft papers; she'd revise again and again. It was her duty to make sure they made sense at all costs. That was worthwhile. Zeituni had accuracy in choice of words, and she wouldn't dwell on trivial matters. This made her a great friend. The affable lady grew up more as a binding force. She hung beside Rita and Roy Abon'go. To her, they were siblings. This is the time her strong faith in spiritual values was already evident. That is to say (that) her spiritual side of life was probably growing stronger than before.

At some point, Zeituni was amused when her brother would go down to the wine cellar in the town to purchase extraordinary amount of sweet red wine. The family had bundled it in a party. 'And we craved to celebrate at any cost, no matter the circumstance. He gave me the feeling of being entirely much a cipher.'

The source of Barack's strength could be heard from her own words. 'Barack was wise when it comes to policy formulation. Even if he made serious mistakes elsewhere, he always told me that life would be just very good. He called me from time to time to talk things over. I lived with his family, and I enjoyed the threshold of a sense of belonging.'

At the time, the country was going through uncertain period, although not so dangerous but in a position to threaten.

I saw friends stepping in and out of his life. They all regarded him as a true friend: those who were aging, their faces covered in moustache yellowed by the effect of black soot of tobacco, those with huge belly stomach, those with a shock of gray hair and still enjoying Scotch, those who loved golfing and were members of a local golf club, and those serving as ministers and only fond of his brains—that was Barack, my brother. And I saw former friends romping in to pay him a courtesy call, those who lived at the sprawling buildings of Jericho (built about forty years ago to cater for the low and middle class). They were fast aging, not because they were old, but because of poor lifestyle; however, they still afforded a radiant smile. They would just laugh and appear happy to those who do not know what they've been going through if there is such thing.

Oddly enough, my brother accepted everyone, whether poor, rich, educated, or illiterate. He welcomed strangers and that was my stock of worry. Maybe his chief error lay in insufficient scrutiny of friends; sometimes this landed him in trouble with the same friends who would find themselves locked in custody for causing unrest and calling on him for help—either for bail or fine ordered by the law court. Although he tried to take it as a responsibility, the action despaired his moods entirely. When he had determined to spend his quiet time in the library or somewhere else, he found himself arguing various cases. He'd say, 'If I don't reach out for them, they would rot behind those bars.'

His eating habit was also quite intriguing; during week days he'd take one meal, with a good deal of drink. And weekends were his time to settle for a three-course meal. That's when we would all settle for a conversation with a brother so much busy and always on traveling schedule in line of duty.

'Look, Barack taught me the Kabbalah. I learned few quotes from Quran. But I could read it only past three pages.' Quran formed part of his life, Islam being the religion of his father. He dealt with belief. 'That belief can be comforting only through your own making,' he said. He spoke with a voice that comments, that complains, that speculates, that provokes, that likes, that dislikes—that was his nature.' Here the delicate sister was reliable. Delicate in the sense that the two were more than siblings. They lived both during the tumultuous times and in successful days—in happy moments and the worse days—when they had no money of their own, and when Barack underwent both employment crisis and marriage failures.

'All these made me nervous. I had lost a few pounds in a month and was extremely devastated. Sadly, I fought back tears. Barack dared to live by the inner light of his ideas.' His pain was severe, above all, emotional torture akin to the lack of money. At this point, his views had lost their bite. Nor was he afraid to use them. There were obstacles. I read his comments and notes, and they weren't far from contours of failure.

My brother couldn't divulge the information to the 'enemies' or deemed enemies. He didn't stray from ethics and codes that made him feel that he lived in another mountain.

My take to various issues include when he pointed his trained ink to the Sessional Paper 10 that became a significant document of the government. He also trained himself to be kept waiting, especially by people he thought were just 'unpredictable lot'. Those days he did wait without complaining.

He took us (the family) to parties. Of course, that was the role of a vibrant, if not flamboyant, parent. We went to Mombasa Road Hotel for a family meeting and the entertainment galore. He drove past a wide, heavily guarded gate with plain black suit and manned by armed security apparatus. We passed through lush green pastures and high fences. We came to a halt at an expansive parking lot where hundreds of cars were parked. An immaculately arranged table stood there. And the welcoming party wore spotless white robes; doubtless they looked like some sort of army band ushering independence day. And their artifacts were antique, as if they lived thousands of years ago and were waiting reincarnation. It was one of the best joints in the country for a party and for the family gatherings. We sat with a mix of delicacies and a scotch or perhaps three bottles of scotch and vodka. Barack was always on record to offer a warm reception. Whenever he was free from work, he was good at that. A number of butlers, maybe five to seven, raced around serving canapés. There were traditional dancers bouncing around in kilts, under the surveillance of cameras and hovering security detail, holding wooden clubs and walkie-talkies against a highly raised six-foot fence as if waiting to quench a ritual terror.

Down the slope were horses, all resting below hundreds of towering bougainvillea trees. Besides there was an old man, 'a retiree' he said, who told us that he's fond of the place due to its serenity and outstanding ambience—Roy nodded, and when my father asked about his pastime, he was quick to tell of his reading of books, of all sorts of fiction books and African legendary sequels. In the early seventies, she was through with preliminary studies. Barack asked her to join a college 'in order to enhance her chances of securing a proper job and also to widen her scope.' She agreed.

At this point, Zeituni got married to Abel Mboya.

Also around that time the East African Breweries Limited was hiring qualified system analyst and that's how she secured a job at the alcohol firm.

2002

When violence broke in Kenya following stiffly contested general election, where a coalition of parties, under the banner of NARC, beat a long serving party, KANU, sporadic violence covered some parts of the country. At this particular time, National Rainbow Coalition (NARC) won the election with a landslide victory and some communities went out fighting. This violence caused furore in her life; indeed, it instilled fear into most peoples' life, including myself. Communities ganged against each other. There were a group of patent holders of violence and merchants of rumor-mongering and war. Also on the prowl were predatory and criminal gangs, masquerading on the streets. Youths spearheaded the heinous raid. And one would wonder what they stand to gain in war. The protests blotted her otherwise good patriotism; in actual terms, it exposed her politely buried trust within. In this manner, it pricked her conscience.

Like the rotten years of Suharto in Indonesia, Zeituni sought refuge in the USA as a political asylee in Boston. In South Boston, Massachusetts, months later, she applied, as an asylee, for public housing. This arrangement came to be just another violation of the policies of Department of Homeland Security (DHS). She was therefore treated as an illegal immigrant. This was the grim time she had a back surgery that has been with her for quiet sometime. Indeed, a relief at the time of trouble. Now a permanent resident in South Boston public housing project; deputy director of authority, William McGonagle, describes my aunt as a hard worker. 'She did a good job as a public health advocate on behalf of the Boston Housing Authority.'

My aunt believed that 'God knows that we're his children, and he can't eternally condemn his own'.

2004

I was ordered to leave the country. They said that 'I'd overstayed my visa and that I'd been on taxpayers' dollars while in an undocumented public assistance, although she was still living in a rundown public housing estate. Surprisingly, Obama, then a senator didn't know much of her immigration status; sources privy to him notes that he was equally surprised by the sudden turn of events.

2008

She had started fighting tooth and nail for her legitimate rights. I worked as a computer systems coordinator for Experience Corps, although on voluntary basis, and as an immigration lawyer. Following this case, McGonagle further said, 'We have no affirmative responsibility I am aware of to further check on their status after they are initially deemed to be eligible.'

Cases surrounded her life with various systems: Immigration and Customs Enforcement (ICE). This system required deportation approved at the level of ICE regional directors. This case caused a major media attention, and each day paparazzi knocked at her door in South Boston. 'Something that made me look so odd and uncomfortable.' At one point, I fled to Cleveland to live with friends. Look here, torture that forces you to quit your own house. See, they made a nightmare out of this! People complained strongly why I contributed to my nephew's 2008 presidential bid. Every sound-minded American contributed and voted for him! That was just the course and every American of goodwill found himself participating in his presidential bid. I have been called undocumented welfare queen and others calling him (the president) a Kenyan socialist; one who's turning a blind eye to immigration reforms.

17 May 2010

She was granted a waiver of deportation by the US government. She is now a legal resident. Immigration Judge Leonard I Shapiro granted her political asylum when her case was presented by lawyers Margaret Wong and Scott Bratton.

During the hearing:

> I entered the courtroom in a wheelchair, with a cane across my lap. I had been sick lately. I'd been suffering from Guillain Barre Syndrome, my doctors said, coupled with a massive back problem. I was nervous, but all I knew was the fact that I've always convinced myself that I've never violated any law, and whatever I was going through was the fact that I had a relative vying for the top seat and nothing else. They just wanted him to lose that very focus and get involved in their muddied stories.

I told the press as follows:

American dream became America's worst nightmare. I have been treated like public enemy. When I was interviewed by a leading media house here in Boston, I told Jonathan Elias, a reporter with WBZ-TV that I didn't mind. 'They can take that house. I can be on the streets with homeless people. They are also people you know. I didn't ask for that house after all. They gave it to me. Ask your system. I didn't create it or vote for it. Go and ask your system.' I said all these out of anger and annoyance.

Zeituni is a mother of four children—three boys and a girl—Feisal, Pascal, Shabir, and Rukia.

Posthumously remembered

Everyone in this family remembers my father in his own way. The president of the United States remembers our father in *Dreams*. This book sparsely connected him to our family here in Kenya. He remembers him in the name Barack Obama—a name, they share. He writes that our father may have contributed to the shaping of his life through dreams.

That might be correct. And something that gripped me most is the passion of his indifference. He writes within a solemn boundary—everything coming together and makes it seem effortless. That book made me feel and realize that a lot could be done. I believe and am convinced that our father did contribute to the shaping of his and all our lives.

I remember my father through his sons: Mark Okoth, who left Kenya to study in the United States at Stanford University. He studied physics and never forgot his skills behind his piano. Kudos brother! You made me proud. Through you, I see a better future. You went ahead to extinguish other flames in the circles of academics when you graduated with MBA at Brown University. Your amazing skills superseded my understanding. Maybe you continue keeping our flame lit because he loved excellence, you know. Your service to this mortal earth is seen in your works at WorldNexus and your love for kids in the streets of Shenzhen and your family and your wife Liu Xuenhua.

How about Abo, Bernard, or deceased David? I can't mention everything you did or how you contributed here, but the spirit of togetherness cement us together, especially Dave.

George, I see our father carrying you up on his shoulders. You struggled to get back to your loving mother. All these memories are still fresh in my mind. You grew to be a good brother from June 1982. And to date, you have done the best with what you had. Who can devote his life to the memory of our father? You, my brothers and sister have delivered to your surrounding with impressive and stellar results. I see you, I see our father, and my joy remains boundless—because nobody, the Jacobs', Firstbrooks', Remmicks' etc. can tell our story better than us.

Notes

1. 'Forty-four Americans have now taken the presidential oath. The words have been spoken during rising tides of prosperity and the still waters of peace. Yet, every so often the oath is taken amidst gathering clouds and raging storms . . .' An excerpt from President Barack Obama's inauguration speech.

2. '. . . The brilliant scholar, the generous friend, the upstanding leader—my father had been all those things . . .' Barack Obama, *Dreams from My Father: A Story of Race and Inheritance*, Three Rivers Press, New York.

3. 'And grant us forgiveness.
   Have mercy on us.
   Thou art our Protector . . .'
   The Holy Quran, Surat Al-Baqarah 2: 286.

   'Show us the straight way,
   The way of those on whom Thow has bestowed Thy Grace,
   Those whose (portion) Is not wrath . . .'
   The Holy Quran, Surat Ibrahim, 14: 40-41.

Chapters 1 and 2

4, 5. The birth, the life, and the journey of Veronica Akoko in a fictional book, *The River and the Source* by Margaret Ogolla, are highly similar to that of Sara Onyango. Born in the rural, with heavy traditional practices, Sara and Akoko's births bear a close resemblance. It is through these connections that forms the backbone of the Chapters 1 and 2. The leadership of the tribal council, the marriage rituals, the naming ceremony, and the traditional medicines are clearly brought out.

This chapter curves out the Luo tradition and custom, the practices, and their significance. The emergence of Christianity at *Aluor* (in the *River and the Source*) is the same at Gendia during the life of Sara: the struggle of the Western colonialist, building the railroad, introducing the cash crops into the depth of the savannah soils, and enhancing the spread of Christianity. In the thrilling book, *the River and the Source*, Akoko drummed up support from the district commissioner against confiscation decrees. As a widow, she fought to keep her properties and to train her family live a life of perseverance, determination, and resilience. In all mannerism, Akoko fought disappointment in death; Sara also found herself preparing inventories of all her difficulties: the death of her father Ogwel, accepting Omar in adoption, and introducing her into the Muslim family. The two women share a great deal in common. All these came at the backdrop of fight of identity among the people of AlegoKamser and the natives. Karachuonyo is likened to the land of great Kisuma District—the sitting office of *Diyo* (district officer) in the *River and the Source*. Kisumu (initially Kisuma) was buzzling with barter trade activities. Other publications synchronized include the works of Colonel Richard Meinertzhagen, *Kenya Diary 1902-06*, and Leakey LSB, *Mau Mau and the Kikuyu*.

Chapter 3

6, 7. Then the news of World War I, World War II, and the growing demand for soldiers: the formation of Kings Africa Rifles and the forceful recruitment of African soldiers, and the relaunch of a new administration.

The understanding of diseases and the search of Western medicine—the success in containing cerebral malaria, sleeping sickness, and jiggers. The Western science causing wonders here and there—at Gendia and Ng'iya. In Kisuma and the capital, Nairobi, the treatment brought from the rafters where no one could have reach to the empty shelves of Mission's Health Center.

8. In the Name of His Majesty King George the Sixth,
   This certificate is awarded to Gideon Magak of South Kavirondo,
   In recognition of the valuable services performed with devotion to duty.

8 June 1939

The certificate was offered to Kings African Rifles soldiers from Burma and Ceylon. This was given to Chief Gideon Magak of South Kavirondo. The deceased served with Onyango Hussein and later became Hawa Auma's father-in-law through an arranged marriage between the chief and Onyango Hussein. A similar certificate was given to Onyango but couldn't be traced.

9, 10. The National Archives sources reveal the protests that rocked the nation. Onyango was arrested and accused under Regulation 6 (1) of the Public Security Act with a minimum jail term of six months.

11. The construction of Ng'iya School complex and emergence of small schools. The contribution by Owen (Archdeacon), Albert Wright among others as described by William Mor and Dishon Ooko Oondo.

12. The invasion of *Mau Mau*, a sectarian violence that stocked a large casualty in a forest fight. Jomo Kenyatta, *Facing Mount Kenya*, East African Educational Publishers Ltd., 1938.

13. '. . . Or the stories of a wounded Hintsa. The King of the amaGcaleka of Xhosa was shot dead on command of Harry Smith in 1835 . . .' A story adopted from the *Times Magazine* that Oketch Ogwari believes frankly Albert narrated to the residents of Ng'iya and Nyang'oma Villages.

14. The plaque writings of Archdeacon W. E. Owen at Kisumu town Park where he was buried together with his wife, Lilian. The latter shaped the life of Barack at Maseno while the former archdeacon was behind the establishment of Ng'iya and Nyang'oma schools.

15. The Lord's Prayer—a compulsory memory verses that was recited by every student at Ng'iya. There was no alternative to this rule.

16, 17, 18. The history of Barak at Maseno. The information retrieved from the schools' records and archived material to keep tabs with his life in the mission school, and the description of Carey Francis a firebrand principal who shaped Maseno and later worked the same magic at Alliance School.

19. '*. . . On our way the white teacher stopped the lorries and eliminate two of the reserves . . .*' Jaramogi O. Odinga, *Not Yet Uhuru*, London, Heinemann.

20. '... *to the busy streets of Nairobi ...*, *the author* Andrew Morton narrates the state of racism in Nairobi's streets in his best selling book, *Moi, The Making of an African Statesman.*'

21. A decree of surrender distributed by Governor Sir Evelyn Baring and signed jointly with General Erskine as an order of amnesty urging the *Mau Mau* adherents and sympathizers to surrender.

22. '... camp to find nothing. This seems to have been the norm for the remote camps, like the one on Mageta Island, in Lake Victoria. There the batch of detainees arrived in shackles in the cargo hold of a boat ...' The camp that Onyango's friends were detained moments after they'd just departed. Caroline Elkins, *Britain's Gulag: Brutal End of Empire in Kenya*, Jonathan Cape, 2005, p. 143.

23. A letter drafted by Barak Obama to President Calhoun on advice from Mrs Roberts of Palo Alto, California, Barack Obama, *Dreams from My Father: A Story of Race and Inheritance.*

24. The details retrieved from Barak's Passport issued at Gill House.

25. Barak's souvenir records the University of Hawaii profile—what has changed slightly over time.

26. Tom Schachtman, *Airlift to America*, St Martin Press, and 2009. This is an excerpt of the Foreword by Harry Belafonte to the book *Airlift to America*. Harry was Barack's' mentor. They occasionally talked once in Kenya and a number of times in United States.

27. A record of eighty-one students airlifted to various universities in the United States by Tom Mboya Airlift programme in 1959 alone. Other airlifts came later in 1960s. This record is reproduced from the collections of the Manuscript Division, Library of Congress.

28. Philip Ochieng', '... *Of all my 50 high school classmates (1955-58), JC ("Jesus Christ") Kang'ethe—who hails from Meru—has been my closest friend, the one I know best. And it was not fortuitous. From Alliance, we flew together (in one of Tom Mboya's airlifts) to Chicago in 1959*_Sunday, 4 January 2009 Daily Nation Editorial Opinion.'

29. William Attwood, *The Reds and the Blacks*, The President warned: 'I want to see to it that the flow of these funds stopped.' p. 247.

30a. Odinge Odera, *My Journey with Jaramogi: A Memoir of a Close Confidant*. Odinge is a beneficiary of Tom Mboya Airlift. He worked with Barack and was one of his drinking pals and a family friend and a neighbor at Woodley.

30b, c. Philip Ochieng': 'From Home-Squared to the United States Senate. How Barack Obama Jr, was Lost and Found: The East African, Nation Media' and *Right Truth* by Robbie Hamilton.

31. Barak Obama, Dissertation: 'An econometric model of the staple theory of development.' The contribution that he later included in the Sessional Paper 10.

32. A report by the National Social Security Fund published in 2010.

BIBLIOGRAPHY

Decolonization and Independence in Kenya, 1940-93 edited by B. A. Ogot and W. R. Ochieng', p. 55.

A Biography of Yona Omollo, Kenya Biographies, Salim and King (eds.), Nairobi (1971), pp. 72-89.

William Attwood, *The Reds and the Blacks*. New York: Harper and Row, 1967, p. 247.

Mboya, *Challenges of Nationhood*, Andre Deutsch, 1970, pp. 73-104.

Tom Mboya, *Freedom and After*. London: Andre Deutsch, 1963.

Andrew Morton, *Moi, The Making of an African Statesman*, Michael Omara,1999.

Jaramogi O. Odinga, *Not Yet Uhuru*, London: Heinemann. East African Educational Publishers, 1967.

Barak Obama, *African Socialism for Kenyans East African Journal*, June (1965).

Duncan Ndegwa, *Walking in Kenyatta Struggles: My Story*, Kenya Leadership Institute, 2006.

Wangari Muta Maathai, *Unbowed: One Woman's Story*, Heinemann, 2004.

Jomo Kenyatta, *Facing Mount Kenya*, East African Educational Publishers Ltd., 1938.

Colonel Richard Meinertzhagen, *Kenya Diary 1902-1906*, Oliver and Boyd, 1957.

Barack Obama, *Dreams from My Father: A Story of Race and Inheritance*, Three Rivers Press, New York, 2004. Crown, 2007. Times Books, Random House, 1995

Auma Obama, Das Leben kommit immer dazwischen . . . 2010.

David Anderson, *Histories of the Hanged: Britain's Dirty War in Kenya and the End of the Empire*, Weidenfeld and Nicolson, 2005.

Caroline Elkins, *Britain's Gulag: Brutal End of Empire in Kenya*, Jonathan Cape, 2005.

E. S. Atieno Odhiambo and John Lonsdale, *Mau Mau and Nationhood*, James Currey Ltd., 2003.

Kenya National Commission on Human Rights, *An Evening with Tom Mboya: Speeches, Lectures and Remarks from Prominent Personalities*, KNCHR, 2006.

George Obama and Damien Lewis, *Homeland: An Extraordinary Story of Hope and Survival*, Simon and Schuster Publishing Group, 2010.

Odinge Odera, *My Journey with Jaramogi: A Memoir of a Close Confidant*, East Africa Education Publishers, 2009.

L. S. B. Leakey, *Mau Mau and the Kikuyu*. Methuen & Co. Ltd., 1952.

LIST OF PLATES (PICTURE GALLERY)

At a dinner party—East-West center, UH (Dad Hawaii)

At YMCA's Charles H. Atherton House
(Waikiki, Honolulu)-Dad Hawaii

Barack (Dad) a student at Harvard

Barack (Dad) at Ala Moana Park Rally- May1962(Hawaii)

Barack (Dad) in many faces 1

Barack (Dad) in many faces 2

Barack (Dad) working in the Kenya
Adults' Literary Program under Betty Mooney.

Barack Obama (Dad)—Barack Obama Sr.-Apr.29, 1959

Barack Obama (Dad)—Barack Obama Sr.-Apr.29, 1959 1

Dad-Hawaii

Dad

Dad

Dad-Hawaii

Dad-Hawaii

Barack Obama Sr.

Dad-Hawaii

First UH African Graduate Gives View On E-W Center

By JOHN GRIFFIN

The first African to graduate from the University of Hawaii leaves today with some parting advice for the East-West Center: Treat the visiting students more like adults, and don't herd them together in dormitories.

Barack H. Obama, a 26-year old straight-A student from Kenya, is heading for Harvard to work on his Ph.D. in economics.

He was not an East-West grantee, but did spend three years in Hawaii on an Afro-Asian Institute fellowship.

An off-campus resident himself (St. Louis Heights), Obama thinks it's a mistake to have the East-West students in dormitories.

"THEY MAY get to know the other students that way, but they won't get to know the community, the way people live here... Furthermore, the fact they will know this is a conscious policy, will make them resent having to socialize...

"They should concentrate on the training. That's what people come here for... Let the cultural things be a

OBAMA

by-product," Obama said.

THE THIN, English-accented African has pleasant memories of Hawaii, but mixed views on the Islands as an East-West meeting ground.

Various races get along better here than on the Mainland and in parts of Africa, he says. But he adds, Hawaii is not really a melting pot. Instead, he feels the various races still largely stick together in groups and coexist peacefully with other groups.

Although he personally had little trouble, Obama said, there is racial discrimination among the groups. It is, he said, "rather strange, even rather amusing, to see Caucasians discriminated against here."

"THERE IS, HOWEVER, one thing other nations can learn from Hawaii," Obama said. "Here in the government and elsewhere, all races work together toward the development of Hawaii.

"At home in Kenya, the Caucasians do not want to work as equals."

Obama, who has been away from Kenya for seven years, said he plans to go home after finishing at Harvard either to enter economic research, international trade or possibly politics.

Located primarily in the western provinces, Canada's ultimate natural gas reserves are estimated at about 300 trillion cubic feet.

Dad-Honolulu Article

During happy days at UH (Dad-Hawaii)

Malik, Mama Kezia, Rita Auma

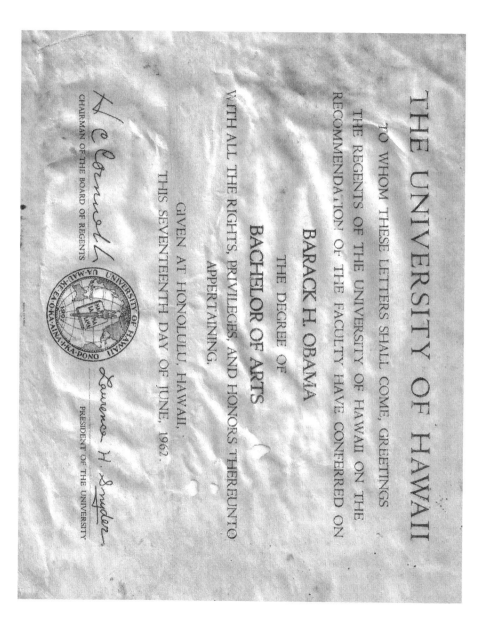

University of Hawaii—Degree Certificate(6-17-1962)

THE UNIVERSITY OF HAWAII

TO WHOM THESE LETTERS SHALL COME, GREETINGS

THE REGENTS OF THE UNIVERSITY OF HAWAII ON THE
RECOMMENDATION OF THE FACULTY HAVE CONFERRED ON

BARACK H. OBAMA

THE DEGREE OF

BACHELOR OF ARTS

WITH ALL THE RIGHTS, PRIVILEGES, AND HONORS THEREUNTO
APPERTAINING.

GIVEN AT HONOLULU, HAWAII,
THIS SEVENTEENTH DAY OF JUNE, 1962.

CHAIRMAN OF THE BOARD OF REGENTS

PRESIDENT OF THE UNIVERSITY

University of Hawaii—Degree Certificate(6-17-1962)photocopy

With Betty Mooney before Air lift (Dad,Mum(Mama Kezia),Malik)1959

Mboya and Sen. John F. Kennedy (Hyannisport, July 1960)

PICTURE_MACALDER-NYANZA MINES

The first students' airlift to the United States - Students Waving good-by to a crowd of over seven thousand at Nairobi Airport, September 7, 1959.

PICTURE-AIRLIFT STUDENTS

AN AERIAL VIEW OF NAIROBI CITY 1959

PICTURE-AN AERIAL VIEW OF THE CITY
OF NAIROBI IN 1959

PICTURE-FIRST DIESEL ENGINE LOCOMOTIVE

GOVERNMENT HOUSE, 1912

PICTURE-GOVERNMENT HOUSE, 1912

PICTURE-MACMILLAN LIBRARY

PICTURE-MAU MAU ARRESTED

PICTURE-NAIROBI RAILWAY STATION

PICTURE-TOM MBOYA CAMPAIGNS

WINTON CHURCHILLIS VISITS KENYA IN 1907

PICTURE-WINSTON CHURCHILL VISITS KENYA, 1907

Dad-Hawaii

Barack Obama(Dad)—Barack Obama Sr.

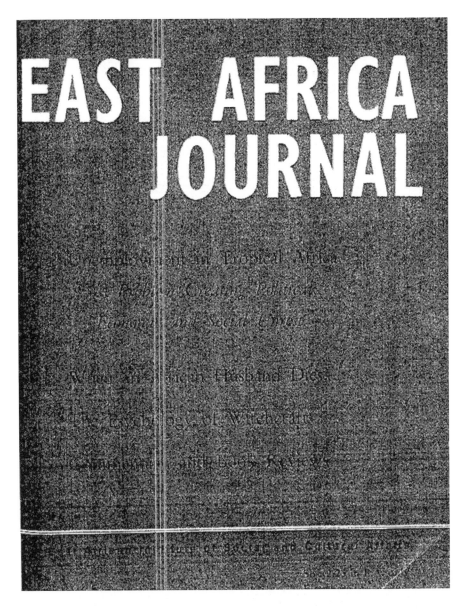

THE AUTHORS

Gus Edgren was formerly in the Research section of the Labour College, Kampala, Uganda. Mr. Edgren has put in print well dug out information for other researchers, and of course labour ministries in Central and Eastern Africa. His suggestions for solutions to the problems of unemployment and underemployment are worthy of note.

Gabriel H. M. Nyambu is a feature writer in the Kenya Ministry of Information, Broadcasting and Tourism. His piece introduces a different flavour to the readership of the Journal. He has tackled a field that is always around us which few have cared to plough.

Hilary Ojiambo is a consulting physician to the Kenyatta National and the Princess Elizabeth Hospitals in Nairobi. He is also honorary consulting physician to the Aga Khan Hospital in Nairobi. Dr. Ojiambo has cautiously attempted to answer the recent sensational question of whether or not witchcraft has a place in modern medicine, especially in Africa.

Barak H. Obama read his economics at Harvard University. He is currently in Nairobi working for his doctorate. His dissertation is on "An econometric model of the staple theory of development." His is one of the critiques picked among the many received in the Journal office of the Kenya's Sessional Paper No. 10, on African Socialism.

barack_sr_paper_12(1965—East Africa Journal)[1]_2

JULY, 1965

EAST AFRICA JOURNAL

Another Critique of Sessional Paper No. 10

Problems Facing Our Socialism

BY BARAK H. OBAMA

Since many of the African countries achieved their independence there has been much talk about African Socialism. Moreover, there has been no individual or country which has at any time defined this socialism nor has there been any common ground among the leaders as to what they meant when they talked of African Socialism. Where, then, could we look for the definition of this "ism"? If it is accepted that it is the leaders of a country who usually formulate and define ideologies, then the only source for this definition would be to get it from them either through their speeches, press reports or papers or through their actions. So far the statements made by such leaders as President Nkrumah, Nyerere, Toure etc., have not had much in common. Likewise, the actions of these leaders while diverting a little from the capitalistic system have not by any means been directed towards any particularly defined-ideology, be it scientific socialism — inter alia — communism.

As a first step, the Kenya Government must be congratulated for it has tried to clarify the situation in so far as it is possible to do so in the light of its planning needs. It not only specifies the objectives by which this country should be guided, but states the policies through which it hopes to fulfill these objectives. It also sets out targets, taking into account the priorities and shows ways by which to achieve these targets. The paper goes further to deal with matters of wide policy. The statement about non-alignment is for the first time explicitly expounded and one cannot help but be happy that those who wrote this paper realized the importance and the great urgency of this policy statement. The paper realizes that, as is true of any country, we must encourage international trade, foreign investments etc., since it is through these that we can hope to get the foreign exchange which we so desperately need for the purchases both of capital goods and consumer goods which we cannot produce locally, thereby enhancing development.

On population growth, the paper notes our high rate of growth and recognizes that this factor can be very detrimental to growth. The paper recognizes the detriments and adverse repercussions which nationalization can have on growth in this country. The policy of the government in this paper is to try to raise per capita incomes. This, it recognizes it can only do by getting high rates of growth and to achieve this high rate of growth there must be a high rate of capital accumulation. The government then tries to spell out means by which it intends to encourage accumulation and this is most important for development. It should be hoped that the government shall find the means by which it intends to achieve these objectives.

The title of the paper is given as "African Socialism and Its Applicability to Planning in Kenya". One would wonder whether the title is not misleading. Is it Kenya Socialism that we are talking about or African Socialism?

One would have been pleased to see African Socialism defined and how Kenya fits into this definition, and an indication of those characteristics in which Kenya is unique before one can think of the applicability of this definition to Kenya. The part which deals with the applicability can be excused in so far as the planning is taking place in Kenya, hence it has to be done within Kenya's peculiar and unique conditions. But this would mean that we have defined the larger context i.e. African Socialism and that our plans, while having points of variance, do not diverge so much from the defined context. Not only would we question the ideology as undefined, but we may find reason to question the pattern of the plans as to whether they follow the condition prevailing within the country and their practicability.

The applicability of planning within the embryo of African Socialism, while essentially an economic matter, cannot be divorced from the politico-socio-cultural context in which we find ourselves and as such we should not ignore these factors as seem to have occurred in the Sessional Paper No. 10. To avoid jumping the gun, however, I wish to follow step by step what has been included in the paper and analyze each point sequentially.

The first part of the paper deals with wide topics such as the objectives of societies. The paper states that there are universal desires of societies and these include political equality, social justice, human dignity and freedom of conscience, freedom from want, disease and exploitation, equal opportunities and, lastly, a high and growing per capita income and equitable distribution. While one may question the univerality and precedence of these ideals in all societies, let us assume that we take these as our ideals and objectives in Kenya and assume that as is said in the paper we want to satisfy these objectives within the context of African Socialism.

We have noted that African Socialism is undefined. We note also its independence from foreign ideologies, but this is not a positive description of an idea. It says that it abhors foreign ideology, but what foreign ideology is meant here? Does what occur in Ghana, Tanzania, Great Britain or the U.S.A. considered foreign? When looked at in this angle one immediately notices the first mistake viz., not defining African Socialism so as to embody a cross-section of Africa as the paper by its very title purports. It would have been more clear and logistic to define African Socialism and then state its independence. After all, how can one talk of the independence of something people do not know?

We then have a short description of African traditions and what these traditions imply within contemporary society; yet the interrelations which this bears to what follows is lost. This does not lead to any basic factors. As an example, the African tradition is fundamentally based on communal ownership of major means of production and sharing of the fruits of the labours, so expended in production, to the benefit of all; and yet the paper advocates land title deeds and private ownership of land — a major means of production. How do these two conflicting factors reconcile.

Paragraphs 13 and 14 attempt to define African Socialism. Yet even these paragraphs are incomplete as the very definition is lacking. In fact, one wonders how the statements made here differ from scientific socialism unless one takes the statement "society in turn will reward these efforts" to be different from "reward to each according to his needs." Certainly, the principle is the same. It is only in the manner the principle is fulfilled that may differ, but this is true in every case that applicability of ideologies have to be in accordance with prevailing circumstances.

If one says that the African society was classless as the paper says, what is there to stop it from being a class society as time goes on? Is what has been said in the paper, if implemented, enough to eschew this danger? It may be true that African traditions had no parallels in European Feudal society so that the problems arising there may not arise here, but can one be as blind as not to see that all through the colonial period this same class

It is interesting to note that the paper recognizes failures of both Marxian socialism and laissez-faire in solving these problems, yet recognition only leads to trying new means of doing things and it is a far cry to say that the blueprint put in the paper will enable us to solve them. It is basically passive rather than active as I shall come to show later.

The paper thus goes into foreign relations. It is a tautology to say that we want to be independent of other countries since every country has always wished this. It would have been more important to talk of how we intend to break our dependence on other countries politically and economically, since this is fait accompli. It may be true that this is still the case because of our lack of basic resources and skilled manpower, yet one can choose to develop by the bootstraps rather

distinction was transplanted here?

Can one deny that the African, while not pleased with the system, did not covet the high place given to the European and Asian? Can one deny the fact that we Africans have likewise started the same thing and that we have the haves and have-nots, which are poles apart, both in the living surroundings, social contacts, and language? How then can we talk of different causes to the same problems when we should be talking of how to correct them? Certainly it is solutions that we are interested in and one cannot say that solutions cannot be the same where causes are different. The question is how are we going is how are we going to remove the disparities in our country such as the concentration of economic power in Asian and European hands while not destroying what has already been achieved and at the same time assimilating these groups to build one country?

than become a pawn to some foreign powers such as Sekou Toure did. While the statement of the policy of non-alignment is good and encouraging, one would wish to see it put into practice.

Let us examine the operating characteristics of African Socialism as put down in the paper. Here the paper goes into use and control of resources. The first statement concerns conflict of opinion on attitude toward landownership. It is true that in most African societies the individual had sole right as to the use of land and proceeds from it. He did, however, own it only as a trustee to the clan, tribe or society. He could give it on loan to someone outside the tribe to use, but he had no right to sell it outside the tribe. In fact, most of our wars were fought because of land. How then can there be a conflict of opinion on communal ownership? The paper should have made this point quite clear. The paper on the other hand leaves the question there and only plunges into the use of resources. How can one talk of use, whether proper or improper, before one defines the owning unit and the rights thereof? It is true that proper uses of resources are of paramount importance if we are going to increase both productivity and per capita incomes, but we cannot deal with this unless and until we deal with ownership and within the African socialistic system.

The paper goes further to say that these traditions cannot be caried on indiscriminately in a modern, monetary economy. This curious, unless the paper means that what is produced communally is unsellable. The paper says that because of credit requirements there has to be land titles and registration. If this is the case, must these land titles and registrations be done on individual ownership? Does it mean that co-operatives cannot be registered or that what is owned in common cannot have title deeds? Is communal ownership of land incompatible with land consolidation? It is surprising that one of the best African traditions is not only being put aside in this paper but even the principle is not being recognized and enhanced. It is true that mismanagement can occur both in private as well as in public ownership, but we ought to look at the matter within the social context. Looked at this way, we can avoid economic power concentration and bring standardized use and control of resources through public ownership, let alone the equitable distribution of economic gains that would follow. One need not talk of state ownership of everything from a small garden to a big farm. One need only look at the problems now encountered in getting lands consolidated in some areas. Will this be easily done through individual action, through co-operatives or through government ownership? Realizing social stickiness and inflexibility and looking at the society's distrust of change, one would see that, if left to the individual, consolidation will take a long time to come. We have to look at priorities in terms of what is good for society and on this basis we may find it necessary to force people to do things they would not do otherwise.

Would it not seem, then, that the government could bring more rapid consolidation through clan co-operatives? Individual initiative is not usually the best method of bringing land reform. Since proper land use and control is very important if we are going to overcome the dual character of our economy and thereby increase productivity, the government should take a positive stand and, if need be, force people to consolidate through the easiest way, which, I think, would be through clan co-operatives rather than through individual initiative. If one were to suppose that the state is an instrument of society and if the society regards growth as well as the correction of the lopsided development which has characterized this country as important, then, the society, through the government, which is its instrument, should enforce means by which this growth and change can be brought about. This is not incompatible with the objectives enumerated in the first part of the paper. If the government should, however, feel that individual ownership is the best policy to take in order to bring development, then it should restrict the size of farms that can be owned by one individual throughout the country and this should apply to everybody from the President to the ordinary man.

On class problems, the paper states that since there was not such a thing in Africa, the problem is that of prevention. This is to ignore the truth of the matter. One wonders whether the authors of the paper have not noticed that a discernible class structure has emerged in Africa and particularly in Kenya. While we welcome the idea of prevention, we should also try to cure what has slipped in. The elimination of foreign economic and political domination is a good gesture towards this, so are plans to develop in order to prevent antagonistic classes. But we also need to eliminate power structures that have been built through excessive accumulation so that not only a few individuals shall control a vast magnitude of resources as is the case now. It is a case of cure and prevention and not prevention alone. The paper says that the principle of political equality eliminates the use of economic power as a political base. It is strange that the government can say this when, wherever we go, in America, in Africa, in Europe, the dollar, the proud and the mark have been used as political weapons despite professed ideologies. It is good to be optimistic, but so long as we maintain free enterprise one cannot deny that some will accumulate more than others, nor is it unlikely that in a country with low per capita incomes, to subject the poor into submitting to political ideologies and to persuade them to vote for those who offer them money, would not be difficult and has, in fact, been occurring.

We then turn to foreign investors. Here the paper outlines how foreign investors can take an active part in the development of the country and outlines areas of social responsibility in which they can take part. These are: making shares available for Africans, employing Africans on management levels "as soon as qualified people can be found and providing training facilities for Africans". Noble as these objectives are, one cannot fail to see that the government is not committed to any specific and active policy in guiding foreign investors i.e. foreign commercial firms to integrate themselves within the Kenya economy.

It is true that we do not have many people qualified to take up managerial positions in these enterprises nor those who could participate intelligently in policy-making functions. But this is not to say that there are none. At present, many highly qualified Africans are employed by commercial firms and are given very pompous titles. This is done only for publicity. If one were to go into the workings of these companies, however, one would find that they actually have no voice in the companies which give them these high titles. Key positions should be Africanized. They are given public relations work which is the only high position an African has held in commercial firms and this is understandable, or they are made directors in name but lack knowledge about the company's workings so that they are rubber stamps of what is decided. How can this go on with the government's knowledge without her taking a positive stand by seeing to it that real Africanization is taking place? Certainly foreign commercial firms are not going to push this enough unless the government takes a positive stand.

It is "strange" to note that some of the very big commercial firms deal in some products which are the lifeblood of this country but without the people of this country taking an active part in the formulation of policies thereof. If some of these firms were to stop functioning today the country would be at a standstill. Let the government take an active part in these spheres and see to it that the people are actively represented in them. It is true that there is lack of skilled manpower in the country, but I would rather that the few we have were properly used for the benefit of the country by giving them responsible positions in commercial firms as is being done in public bodies. The government should not only talk of training those who are not yet qualified but should also see to it that those who are qualified are given opportunities to do something for the country. It is strange to talk of lack of skilled manpower when the few who are available are not utilized fully.

The paper wishes to encourage domestic accumulation. This is a good gesture except for the underlying assumption which one only reads between the lines, that it is individual private enterprise and business that tends to encourage accumulation. True, in the paper there is a realization that taxation can be used as a means of forced saving, but it is given a secondary place in this respect. Certainly there is no limit to taxation if the benefits derived from public services by society measure up to the cost in taxation which they have to pay. It is a fallacy to say that there is this limit and it is a fallacy to rely mainly on individual free enterprise to get the savings. How are we going to rid ourselves of economic power concentration when we, in our blueprint, tend towards what we ourselves discredit? In paragraph 47 the paper states that the company form of business organization is a departure from the direct individual ownership typical of Marx's day. Yet one who has read Marx cannot fail to see that corporations are not only what Marx referred to as the advanced stage of capitalism but Marx even called it finance capitalism by which a few would control the finances of so many and through this have not only economic power but political power as well.

On the subject of application of African Socialism to planning in Kenya, the emphasis is put on economic growth. While recognizing the importance of growth, one can emphasize it to the detriment of other objectives.

We should not only put all our efforts on growth, but should cover a wider subjects which is development. We can have a high rate of growth economically and yet not develop both economically, politically and socially. A paper such as this one, produced by the government, which should be and is a blueprint of the country's policies, cannot confine itself to mundane and picayune factors when it ought to deal with development which includes growth. Surely this is the more encompassing subject which the paper should have dealt with fully.

I am glad this paper notes what we are short of and seeks ways to correct these shortages. Yet recognition of what we are short of is not the realization of why we are short of them nor how we can remedy these shortages. To say that per capita incomes are low is a thing that any man can see. Likewise, to say that we are short of domestic capital because of the low rate of saving is a tautology. The reasons are that the majority of the populace have such a low per capita income that it is almost impossible

foreign aid and assistance. Is not this the reason the government should tax the rich more so as to generate high tax surpluses?

Theoretically, there is nothing that can stop the government from taxing 100 per cent of income so long as the people get benefits from the government commensurate with their income which is taxed. Assuming that development and the achievement of a high per capita income is a benefit to society as a whole I do not see why the government cannot tax those who have more and syphon some of these revenues into savings which can be utilized in investment for future development, thereby reducing our reliance on foreign aid.

The paper notes lack of qualified and skilled manpower. Training must be expanded so that our already qualified manpower can gain the experience to participate fully in advancing development while the unqualified. Through some of the statistics given on paragraph 63 one can see what we have and what we lack in terms of skilled manpower and the period it takes to train it. It

for them to save. There is a small minority of people and worse still, on a racial basis, who have high incomes and who can afford to save, but no country can afford to rely on one group or a small segment of society to do all the saving. Nor is all of this saving being invested in this country. Some are sent abroad in the form of dividends and for many other reasons. What is more important is to find means by which we can redistribute our economic gains to the benefit of all and at the same time be able to channel some of these gains to future production. This is the government's obligation; it should have come out with a plan in the paper to achieve this. The government recognizes that each pound saved can generate three pounds in both

is, in fact, quite an achievement that the government has done so much within a short time. Yet one sometimes wonders why, despite these facts, the government sometimes refused some scholarships which are given to Kenya students, and is fussy in deciding those who can go abroad and those who should study in our East African universities. Are we looking at a gift horse in the mouth when we refuse scholarships?

It is important that we should give priorities in training to what we lack most, but this does not mean that we have to stop people from going to study abroad just because they are not going for what we want them to study, particularly when no one applies for what we want our people to study. It should be realized that one person who goes out to study leaves a chance in our universities for another person who would not otherwise have had the chance. It is the reason why we should not be so choosy in what we get in terms of scholarships. In fact, sooner or later we are going to wish we did not turn down some of the scholarships which we have been offered and that we had not been so choosy as to discredit those who have offered us those scholarships.

While it is true that Kenya does not suffer from foreign exchange shortages right now, we cannot say that we will not suffer from it in the near future. We should take measure to encourage more import substituting industries and have selective controls with high preference being given to capital goods purchased from abroad. A form of import licencing ought to be introduced which will only look at the goods imported in terms of their contribution to growth and development, unless they are things that we do not produce ourselves. In this way we will be able to make full use of foreign exchange which we can earn through our exports while at the same time satisfying the needs which we cannot satisfy locally.

Coming to critical issues and choices, it is surprising that no general mention is made of the dual characteristic of our economy. How can we afford to ignore the pockets of this economy which are underdeveloped without some positive statement about their development. In Kenya the colonial government only developed the so-called white areas. Thus we find that the central province, some parts of the Rift Valley and some parts of Kericho are developed, in farming, roads, water systems and the like when most of the former African reserve areas are eking a living on poor areas without even good road networks to serve them. How are these areas going to be monetized and bring development when we do not even have the infrastructure on which development depends unless the government takes a positive stand and does something to correct this lopsided way of development.

The government talks of dealing only with areas where the returns out of any development programme are ostensible. But surely the returns are low only because these areas are and were undeveloped in the beginning. Must we be so short-sighted as to look only into intermediate gains when these areas are rotting in poverty? In these areas we find a lot of disguised unemployment which, if we were to plan sensibly, could be utilized to the benefit of society. The government says that people who come into the cities in search of jobs should return to the land and farm it. This would have been more sensible if they had a land worth farming. I wonder whether the government really means that a family can live on an acre of undeveloped land. If these people come out in search of work, it is because they cannot make a living out of whatever land they have had. It is because these lands are undeveloped, it is because these lands are poor and it is because their marginal productivity is zero. In fact, their return to the land is only to stop them from contributing to increased output since those who remain on the land produce the same amount of product as when those who come out are also on the land. Isn't this the reason why the government should find projects either in the cities or in rural areas which could absorb them? It is a curious thing that the government does not recognize these facts in its policy paper.

There is a statement made on nationalization. True there are cases in which nationalization is bad, but there are, likewise, quite a few benefits to be derived from it. On this subject, I would like to refer the authors to Prof. Bronferbrenner's work on the "Appeals for confiscation in Economic Development"*. Nationalization should not be looked at only in terms of profitability alone, but also, or even more, on the benefit to society that such services render and on its importance in terms of public interest. If we were to look at these things purely on profitability, then the railways would not have been nationalized worldwide since it is the least profitable so that in all countries it is subsidized by government. There is also a statement that nationalization will apply to African enterprise. How can we talk of nationalizing African enterprise when

---

* Econ. Development and Cultural change — Vol. III, No. 3, April, 1955 pp. 201-18.

such enterprises do not exist. If we are going to nationalize, we are going to nationalize what exists and is worth nationalizing. But these are European and Asian enterprises.

One need not be a Kenyan to note that nearly al commercial enterprises from small shops in River Road to big shops in Government Road and that industries in the Industrial Areas of Nairobi are mostly owned by Asians and Europeans. One need not be a Kenyan to note that most hotels and entertainment places are owned by Asians and Europeans. One need not be a Kenyan to note that when one goes to a good restaurant he mostly finds Asians and Europeans, nor has he to be a Kenyan to see that the majority of cars running in Kenya are run by Asians and Europeans. How then can we say that we are going to be indiscriminate in rectifying these imbalances? We have to give the African his place in his own country and we have to give him this economic power if he is going to develop. The paper talks of fear of retarding growth if nationalization or purchases of these enterprises are made for Africans. But for whom do we want to grow? Is it the African who owns this country? If he does, then why should he not control the economic means of growth in this country? It is mainly in this country that one finds almost everything owned by the non-indigenous populace. The government must do something about this and soon. For these reasons, all paras, 80, 81, 82, 83 and 84 in this sessional paper are unfortunate in that they did not state the problem clearly and come out with possible solutions.

The paper touches on recent demographic trends in this country and says that the population is growing at the rate of 3 per cent per annum or more. True this is a high rate of population growth, but we have to look at it in terms of the population base and the area of Kenya. Surely we are not an overpopualted country. We have vast areas which are lying idle or sparsely populated or which could be inhabitable if irrigation and proper projects were to be under way. We cannot only absorb three times the population we have now but even more with proper planning. Further, we should not only look at the population as consumers of goods and services, but also as producers of these goods and services. If we realize this then we should not be worried about the rate of growth of population. All we need to think of is to plan properly and find projects, given priorities, which will absorb this populace. In this way we will not only be able to absorb the rising population growth, but also the overwhelming disguised unemployment.

On the question of priorities, there is nothing more demanding and important now than the consolidation and proper utilization of land in the former African areas. After consolidation, we should introduce modern farming methods. Consolidation will add relatively little to output unless productivity is increased and productivity can only be increased if the old methods and tools of production are abandoned. It is the more reason we need modern methods of production, and on this respect the government will have to play an active part, through the purchase and loaning of more small machinery and intensifying the training of people on how to use them in their lands and teaching them intensively ways of rotation of crops, grazing and prevention of erosion. Further there will be a need for more model farms run by the government as example. The government instead of worrying with the settlement schemes should have started with this in the beginning.

There is a statement in the paper about encouraging tourism. It is surprising that the government thinks only about lodges but not about making it cheap so as to include those who are not so rich. At the present time, the cost of living is too high for tourists. The hotels charge exhorbitant rates and there are no price controls so that only the very rich can afford to come to Kenya as tourists. How are we going to encourage tourism and on a wide basis if we make it too expensive for the middle-class people? The government ought to do something about this.

Despite my remarks, it is laudable that the government came out with the paper. But this is not to deny the fact that it could have been a better paper if the government were to look into priorities and see them clearly within their context so that their implementation could have had a basis on which to rely. Maybe it is better to have something perfunctorily done than none at all!

barack_sr_paper_12(1965 -East Africa Journal)[1]_10

Barack Obama—Letter from friend(1963)1

Barack Obama—Letter from friend(1963)2

Dad at a function

Dad at Conference

Dad at Conference-Government Business

Dad at Conference-Government Business

Dad at Conference-Government Business

Dad at Conference-Government Business

Dad at Conference-Government Business

Dad at Conference-Government Business

Dad at Conference-Government Business

Dad at Conference-Government Business

Dad at Conference-Government Business

Dad at Conference-Government Business

Dad at Conference-Government Business

David Opiyo-Mark Okoth

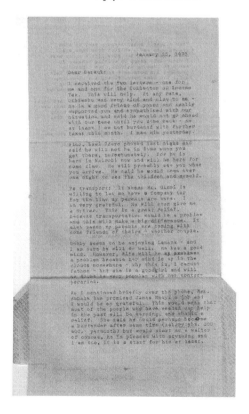

Letter - Step_mum Ruth to Dad (Jan 25, 1972) Pg 1

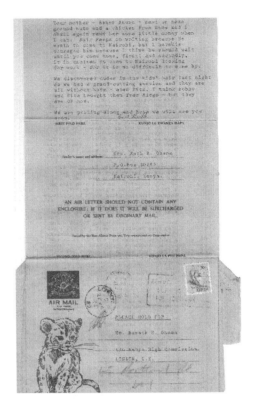

Letter - Step_mum Ruth to Dad (Jan 25, 1972) Pg 2

Years after graduating with Phi Beta Kappa, Phi Beta Phi from UH(Dad)

Auntie Hawa Auma & Grandma Habiba Njoga

Auntie Hawa Auma Onyango

Auntie Hawa Auma Onyango

Dad at Conference-Government Business

Dad at Conference-Government Business

Dad at Conference-Government Business

Dad at Conference-Government Business

Dad at Conference-Government Business

Dad at Conference-Government Business

Dad at Conference-Government Business

Dad at Conference-Government Business

Dad at Conference-Government Business

Dad at Conference-Government Business

Dad at Conference-Government Business

Dad at Conference-Government Business

Dad at work

Dad with coleagues-Treasury

Funeral procession-Death Grandma Habiba Njoga

Grandma Habiba Njoga

Grandma Habiba Njoga-beside Dad's coffin-Death Barack Obama Sr.(1982)

Malik Obama & Barack Obama Jr.

Malik Obama & Barack Obama Jr.

Mum(Mama Kezia)   Mum(Mama Kezia)

Oval Office-Malik and brother President Barack Obama

Plaque on Barack Hussein Obama's headstone-Grave

Plaque on Onyango Hussein Obama headstone-Grave

WhiteHouse-Malik with family,President Barack Obama&Mother(Mama Kezia)

Barack Obama—Barack Obama Sr.-British Passport (Apr.29, 1959)

Barack Obama—Barack Obama Sr.-British Passport (Apr.29, 1959) 1

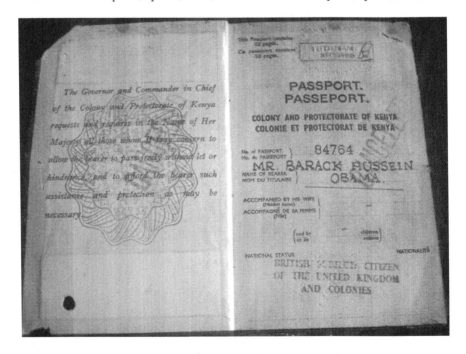

Barack Obama—Barack Obama Sr.-British Passport (Apr.29, 1959) 2

Barack Obama—Barack Obama Sr.-British Passport (Apr.29, 1959) 3

Barack Obama—Barack Obama Sr.-British Passport (Apr.29, 1959) 4

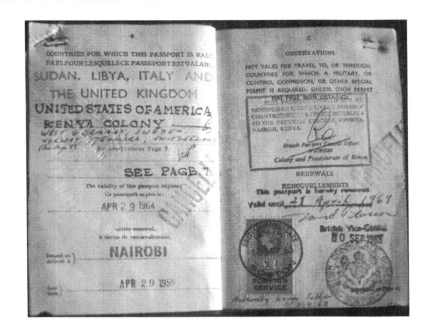

Barack Obama—Barack Obama Sr.-British Passport (Apr.29, 1959) 5

Barack Obama—Barack Obama Sr.-Kenya Passport (1964)

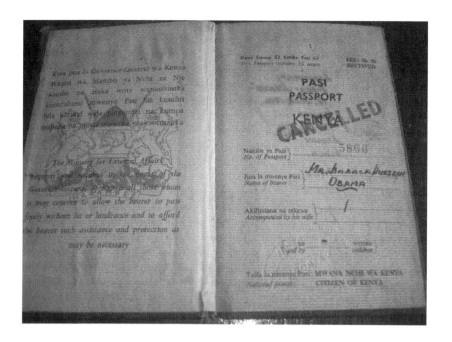

Barack Obama—Barack Obama Sr.-Kenya Passport (1964) 1,

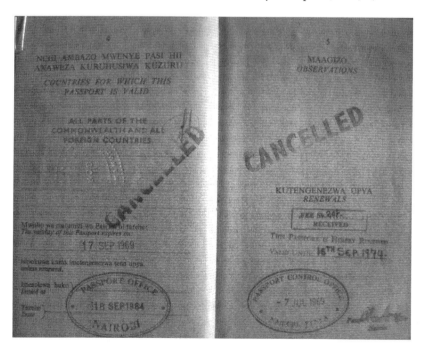

Barack Obama—Barack Obama Sr.-Kenya Passport (1964) 1

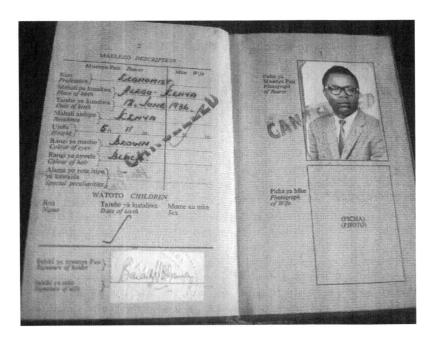

Barack Obama—Barack Obama Sr.-Kenya Passport (1964) 2

Barack Obama—Barack Obama Sr.-Kenya Passport (1964) 3

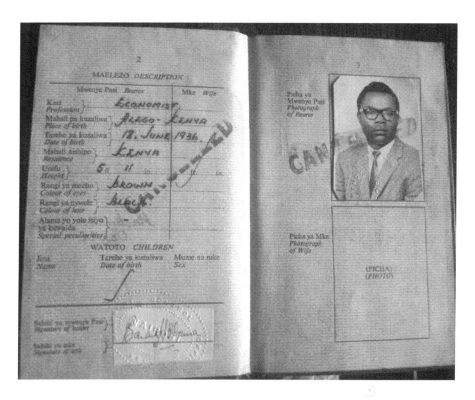

Barack Obama—Barack Obama Sr.-Kenya Passport (1964) 4

Barack Obama—Barack Obama Sr.-Personal Briefcase

Barack Obama—Barack Obama Sr.-Personal Briefcase 1

Barack Obama—Barack Obama Sr.-Personal Briefcase 2

Barack Obama—Barack Obama Sr.-Personal Briefcase 3

Dad 6-18-36 to 11-26-82   Dad & Grandma (Habiba Njoga)

Dad's graduation gown-Harvard

Dad's graduation gown-Harvard

Dad's shaving machine

Made in the USA
Lexington, KY
30 December 2013